Your Choice

A Basic Writing Guide with Readings

Your Choice

*A Basic Writing Guide
with Readings*

**KATE MANGELSDORF
EVELYN POSEY**
The University of Texas at El Paso

St. Martin's Press
New York

Sponsoring editor: Barbara Heinssen
Managing editor: Patricia Mansfield Phelan
Project editors: Jennifer Valentine, Nathan Saunders
Production supervisor: Dennis Para
Art director/Cover design: Lucy Krikorian
Text design: EriBen Graphics
Photo research: Susan Cottenden, Elissa Haney
Cover art: David Bishop

Library of Congress Catalog Card Number: 95-73184

Manufactured in the United States of America.

1 0 9 8 7
f e d c b

For information, write:
St. Martin's Press, Inc.
175 Fifth Avenue
New York, NY 10010

ISBN: 0-312-11153-3

Acknowledgments

Acknowledgments and copyrights are found at the back of the book on pages 532–535, which constitute an extension of the copyright page.

To the memory of
Charles James King

Contents

vii

CHAPTER 10: DEBATING THE LIMITS OF FREE EXPRESSION: Persuasive Writing   319

Computer Tips

Preface

For several years we have been responsible for choosing a developmental writing textbook for the freshman composition program at The University of Texas at El Paso. Selecting a text inevitably frustrated us as we searched for one that offered a rhetoric, a reader, and a handbook and that actively led students through each step of the writing process. Such an ideal text would empower students to choose their own topics and would enable them at the outset of the course to write whole essays rather than single paragraphs or sentences. It would illustrate many models of the writing process, would allow students to read and write about their own cultural contexts, and would help students use computer technology to enhance their writing. This book also would teach critical thinking skills and would engage students in collaborative activities. Above all, it would respect the wealth of knowledge and experience that students bring into their writing classroom.

During more than twenty years' combined experience in teaching developmental writing, we never found such a book, and so we decided to write *Your Choice: A Basic Writing Guide with Readings*. Every assignment in this book has proved successful in our classes. We believe our approach works because, rather than simply talking about how to write, it teaches students to write. It offers students comprehensive step-by-step instruction for writing expressive, informative, and persuasive essays. It showcases the writing process, presents a wide variety of engaging assignments, and maintains a respectful tone. It strengthens students' reading, thinking, and writing skills; validates their diverse and unique cultural experiences; and helps them use computers and the Internet for communication and learning. Most importantly, it builds students' confidence by encouraging them to think of themselves as writers with important ideas to communicate.

Organization of the Book

Your Choice is divided into three sections: Part I, "The Writing Process"; Part II, "Writing about Your World"; and Part III, a grammar handbook.

Part I: The Writing Process

This rhetorical section presents three introductory chapters that help students view writing as a purposeful, creative endeavor.

Chapter 1, "Composing Ourselves, Writing for Others," teaches students to analyze their writing situation in terms of audience, purpose, and context. Standard written English is introduced as a dialect necessary for success in school and the workplace, and the chapter is a springboard for two important aspects of the book: how students can bring their cultural context into their writing and how computer technology can enhance their learning and writing.

Chapter 2, "Keeping a Journal," shows students the advantages of keeping a personal journal, a dialogue journal, and a learning log and presents helpful models and step-by-step instructions for keeping each, whether in a notebook or on computer disk. Subsequent chapters prompt students to write in their journals, which increases writing fluency, encourages students to explore their reactions to their reading, and shows them ways to use writing to learn about the world and particular subject areas.

Chapter 3, "The Writing Process," presents easy-to-follow steps that students will use throughout this text and that can be modified to fit individual writers' preferences. By following one student through each stage of the writing process, students learn to gather ideas, draft, revise, edit, and publish—or share—their essays. They also begin a portfolio of the writing they do throughout the course.

Part II: Writing about Your World

Eight thematic chapters in Part II present a wide range of reading selections and topics for expressive, informative, and persuasive writing. Instructors can select the chapters that best fit their goals and students' interests. Each chapter includes the following elements and shows how one student carried out the assignment:

Writing Assignment

• A photograph and a quotation pertinent to the chapter's writing assignment introduce students to the chapter's theme.

Gathering Ideas

- Students read and respond to three essays by professional authors that present models for writing and that generate ideas for students to explore.
- Students gather ideas about the same three topics in the chapter's readings; they thus gain a rich source of materials for their own essays.

Drafting

- In preparation for drafting, students select one of the three topics about which they have gathered ideas, or they combine one or more of the topics.
- Before writing a discovery draft, students are shown how another student moved from gathering ideas to drafting.

Revising

- The "Revising" section of each chapter presents the core of the rhetorical instruction. Explanations are concise and are supported by numerous activities and models from both student and professional writers.
- Students use peer review to critique each other's drafts. A series of assignment-specific questions reinforce the chapter's instruction.
- Students revise their drafts, guided by instructions in the chapter and by their own classmates' suggestions. The chapter also presents a revised version of the student draft as a model.

Editing

- Students edit their drafts, referring to the handbook in Part III. During the editing process, they record errors (with corrections) in an Editing Log, so they can avoid them in later writing. Again, an edited version of the essay that students have read in draft and revised form guides them in the editing process.

Publishing

- Students publish, or share with their audience, their final essays. Depending on the chapter's theme, they might share their essay with friends or family, submit it to their school or local newspaper, or send it via e-mail to readers around the world.

Chapter Summary

- Each chapter concludes with a summary of its rhetorical instruction, providing a handy reference as the course progresses.

Writing Portfolio

· Chapter 12 shows students how to gather their best essays into a writing portfolio and also asks them to write a reflective cover letter about their progress as writers.

Part III: Handbook with Exercises

Parts I and II are supported by this concise handbook of grammar, usage, punctuation, spelling, and mechanics, which includes exercises. The emphasis is on identifying and correcting problems rather than on lengthy explanations of grammatical concepts and terms. Numerous activities provide practice in correcting common errors, and boxed material highlights grammatical instruction for ESL students.

Special Features

Choices in Writing Topics

Each of the eight thematic chapters in Part II helps students gather ideas about three potential topics for their essays. This broad range of topics allows students to choose the ones that interest them most, ensuring that they do their best work because they care about their topic.

Progression of Topics and Skills

Part II is progressive in three ways. First, the chapters' themes move from personal matters to the cultural and social issues that are often the subject of academic writing. Second, the chapters present rhetorical skills in a progression, moving from expressive to informative to persuasive writing; by the end of Part II, students are prepared to do rudimentary primary and secondary research. Third, in each chapter the progression of the writing process—gathering ideas, drafting, revising, editing, and publishing—strengthens students' writing through consistent practice.

Models of the Writing Process

Every chapter in Part II shows how one student writer carried out the assignment at every stage, resulting in three complete drafts. Students thus have an example on which to model their own writing for every assignment, and for every stage of the writing process.

Writing with a Computer

Throughout the text, a special icon in the margin calls attention to computer tips. These offer on-the-spot information about how to use word-processing technology in each stage of the writing process; how to use e-mail in collaborative writing; and how to use the Internet and the World Wide Web to facilitate research. We also seek to increase students' awareness of the benefits and hazards of computer technology. For example, one writing topic in Chapter 10 is about free expression on the Internet, and the student model in Chapter 11 is about identifying problems in a college computer lab.

Integrated Reading and Writing Instruction

Because good writers are also good readers, we provide instruction in reading as well as in writing. Chapter 1 shows students how to read as writers read—to discover ideas, learn rhetorical strategies, and expand their vocabulary. Students practice these skills throughout Part II. Each reading selection is followed by questions about content and rhetoric; students are also asked to define unfamiliar vocabulary through contextualized guessing or with the help of a dictionary; and when new rhetorical strategies are taught, examples are drawn from the chapter's readings.

Emphasis on Diversity

Students are invited at every opportunity to make connections between their own cultural experiences and their writing; Chapter 7 directly asks them to write about their cultures. Writing models, reading selections, and rhetorical examples throughout represent a diversity of cultural backgrounds, making students confident about adding their own voice to the classroom community.

Emphasis on Collaborative Activities

In sharing knowledge, we become better critics of our own and others' writing, and we discover how to work with others. Toward these ends, *Your Choice* offers over fifty collaborative activities. Throughout Part II, for example, students form peer groups to work on their drafts. Some collaborative activities can be carried out by e-mail and the Internet. These collaborative activities help make the classroom a community of writers.

The Writing Portfolio

Good writers know about themselves as writers. They know when and where they like to write, the kind of writing they prefer doing, and, most important, their strengths and weaknesses as writers. To build such self-knowledge, students are asked to do a Writing Progress Report at the end of every chapter in Part II. Then, in Chapter 12—the capstone chapter—we ask students to compile a portfolio of their best writing. Gathering their best work, creating a table of contents, and writing a reflective cover letter help students to see that they are writers worth reading.

Critical Thinking

Good critical thinking skills enable students to make effective decisions as writers, and so we emphasize critical thinking in each writing assignment, and we pose questions after each reading to stimulate reflection about the writer's content and rhetorical strategies. The critical thinking skills taught in each chapter gradually become more advanced, so that by the end of the book students can distinguish opinion from fact and can recognize logical fallacies—the skills that bring success in higher education as well as in life.

Primary and Secondary Research

As college students, developmental writers need to gather information from a variety of sources without being overwhelmed by an endless research process. To this end, we include easy-to-follow step-by-step instruction in how to conduct interviews and surveys; how to locate, evaluate, and cite sources; and how to summarize information. This instruction is presented in the context of specific writing assignments, making research a purposeful activity rather than an academic exercise.

Instructional Resources

The World Wide Web connects students to each other and to the world, making our classrooms global communities. It is for this reason that we have created a home page for this book at http://www.smpcollege.com/Your_Choice/ on the St. Martin's College Web site. Also available is an *Instructor's Resource Manual*, with information on the text's approach, sample syllabi, chapter-by-chapter teaching tips, and answers to the exercises.

Acknowledgments

Your Choice reflects years of collaboration with students, teachers, and editors, and we especially thank the many students at The University of Texas at El Paso. In particular, Jesus Ramirez, Sandra

Cordero, Armando Gutierrez, and Patricia Shahabi-Azad gave us suggestions in drafting this book and allowed us to include their writing. G. Douglas Meyers, our department chair, offered unqualified support when we needed it. Elizabeth Mangelsdorf contributed her excellent photographs to the project. Special thanks go to Lori Gravley-Novello, who helped select the readings and prepare the handbook; her dedication and skill are evident throughout.

We also thank the following reviewers for many suggestions that were incorporated into the text: Gail Bauer, St. Louis Community College; Paul Beran, McLennan Community College; Denise P. Bostic, Nicholls State University; Deborah L. Bradford, Roger Williams University; Hope E. Burwell, Kirkwood Community College; Martha French, Fairmount State College; Anne-Marie Hall, University of Arizona; Crystal L. Harris, Sinclair Community College; Lois Hassan, Henry Ford College; Paula Hillis, Idaho State University; Helen Hogan, Salt Lake Community College; Karen Houck, Bellevue Community College; Scott Kassner, Minneapolis Community College; Dr. Michael Kelly, Slippery Rock University; Jane Maher, Nassau Community College; Patricia J. McAlexander, The University of Georgia; Clyde Moneyhun, University of Arizona; Judith Olson-Fallon, Case Western Reserve University; George Otte, Baruch College of CUNY; Judy Shank, Valencia Community College; Ellen Shull, Palo Alto Community College; Marti Singer, Georgia State University; Marcia J. Songer, East Tennessee State University; Elaine Sundberg, Sonoma State University; William T. Sweet, Lane Community College; Victoria H. Taylor, New Mexico State University; Mark Wiley, California State University, Long Beach; and Gary Zacharias, Palomar College.

A great deal of our satisfaction with this book is a result of the work of a dedicated editor, Harriett Prentiss; her insights, perseverance, and encouragement are deeply appreciated.

At St. Martin's Press we thank Barbara Heinssen, whose commitment to our project was instrumental in making this book a reality. We also thank Elissa Haney and Natalie Hart for tending to countless details. Thanks, too, go to Rob Mejia, Michael Coons, Jennifer Valentine, Nathan Saunders, Susan Cottenden, and Lucy Krikorian.

Finally, Kate thanks her family for their patience, interest, and good humor. Her deepest gratitude goes to her husband, Robert Rowley, who supported the project in every possible way, and whose love and generosity kept her going. Evelyn thanks Michelle and Brian for their love and inspiration, and Bruce for reminding her that in addition to her work there are love, laughter, and wildflowers.

Kate Mangelsdorf
Evelyn Posey

Your Choice

*A Basic Writing Guide
with Readings*

I
The Writing Process

Why write when it's easier to pick up the telephone and speak to someone in person? Well, writing is still an important way to communicate—on campus, in the workplace, and for personal enjoyment. Moreover, with the growing popularity of computers, many people find themselves writing more often than ever before. As a result, they value good writing skills.

Part I will show you why and how—and even where—writers write. You'll understand why it's important to know your purpose and audience before you begin writing. You'll learn how to keep a journal. Perhaps most important, you'll discover your own writing process. You'll also begin to collect your best writing in a portfolio.

*We are all apprentices in a craft where
no one ever becomes a master.*
—ERNEST HEMINGWAY

1

Composing Ourselves, Writing for Others

In this chapter you will

- examine different purposes for writing.
- understand how to analyze your audience.
- learn the importance of standard written English.
- explore the composing process.
- see the importance of a writer's space and routine.
- learn how to read to improve your writing.
- study how computers make writing easier.

What comes into your mind when you think of a writer? You might remember a writer you studied in school, such as William Shakespeare, Langston Hughes, or Emily Dickinson. Or you might think of the stereotypes we have of writers. One stereotype is of a newspaper writer who pounds out a late-breaking story on a computer minutes before deadline. Another common stereotype of a writer is someone who wears a beret, lives in a cold attic, composes brilliant poems on scraps of paper, and dies before receiving any recognition. Or maybe you picture a writer you like to read, such as Maya Angelou, Stephen King, or Dave Barry. Our favorite writers can inspire us, teach us, entertain us, scare us, and make us cry.

But writers are more common than you might at first imagine. A consumer who writes a letter to the electric company is a writer. So is a student who completes a report for a course, a child who writes her name for the first time, a father who records the birth of his baby in a journal, and an engineer who writes a proposal to build a bridge. A lover who sends a valentine is a writer, and so is an angry voter who writes a letter to the city council. A writer is anyone who uses written language to communicate a fact, an opinion, or a feeling.

In our world of word processors, fax machines, and electronic mail, more of us are required to write. The title of this chapter, "Composing Ourselves, Writing for Others," refers to the people we write for—ourselves and others. *Composing ourselves* means that we write to create and express ourselves. Just as a writer of music uses various sounds to compose and play a piece of music, we use words to discover and communicate our identities. Our words reveal what we think, believe, and feel. *Writing for others* means that we also write to affect the way others think, believe, and feel. Thus, composing ourselves and writing for others are closely connected aspects of writing. We all need to communicate our ideas and feelings to the world. At the same time, we're the first readers of our words when we discover and explore our thoughts.

A Writer's Purpose

Whenever you write, whether for yourself or others, you have a *purpose*. Most writing—including the kind you'll do in this textbook—is primarily expressive, informative, or persuasive.

Expressive Writing

In *expressive writing*, writers communicate their thoughts, feelings, and personal history. When you keep a diary, write a letter to a friend, or tell about something that happened to you, you're writing expressively.

In the following example of expressive writing, student Scott Weckerly describes the morning he was to leave home for college.

> The impact of saying good-bye and actually leaving did not hit me until the day of my departure. Its strength woke me an hour before my alarm clock would, as for the last time Missy, my golden retriever, greeted me with a big, sloppy lick. I hated it when she did that, but that day I welcomed her with open arms. I petted her with long, slow strokes, and her sad eyes gazed into mine. Her coat felt more silky than usual. Of course, I did not notice any of these qualities until that day, which made me all the more sad about leaving her.

The sample paragraph is expressive because it describes Weckerly's thoughts and feelings at an important time in his life. When he tells us that the reality of his departure didn't sink in until that morning, we understand what he was thinking. By describing his reactions to his dog, we know he was sad about leaving home. In re-creating an important incident in his life, Weckerly's writing is expressive.

Informative Writing

We write not only to express ourselves, but to convey information as well. *Informative writing* explains: it tells how something works or how to do something, what something looks like, how two things are alike or different, the cause of an event or its outcome. Informative writing typically uses facts, examples, or statistics. Most writing we encounter is informative. Nutritional labels on food containers are informative, as are directions on how to set up a computer or administer CPR. Textbooks, incuding the one you're reading now, are also in this category. Most sections of the newspaper are informative.

The following example of informative writing is from the *Wall Street Journal*.

> The music business has never sounded so good. Driven by soaring compact disk sales and a new generation of hot artists, industry revenues rose 20% to more than $12 billion in 1994, the largest single year-to-year gain since 1920, when the Recording Industry Association of America began keeping such statistics.
>
> JEFFREY TRACHTENBERG, "NEW ARTISTS AND OLDER BUYERS INSPIRE A
> RECORD YEAR IN MUSIC"

This piece of writing is informative because it explains that the music business is thriving.

Persuasive Writing

Persuasive writing differs from expressive and informative writing because it attempts to change a reader's opinion or convince a reader to take a particular action. Newspaper editorials and advertisements are two types of persuasive writing. The *Times Picayune* wants you to support the school bond issue and Ben and Jerry's wants you to buy their brand of ice cream. Some of the world's most memorable writing is persuasive, such as these words from President John Kennedy's 1961 Inaugural Address: "Ask not what your country can do for you; ask what you can do for your country."

Martin Luther King's famous "I Have a Dream" speech is another example of persuasive writing. His purpose was to motivate civil rights workers to continue striving for racial equality. Here's an excerpt:

> Go back to Mississippi, go back to Alabama, go back to South Carolina, go back to Georgia, go back to Louisiana, go back to the slums and ghettos of our northern cities, knowing that somehow this situation can and will be changed. Let us not wallow in the valley of despair.

As with many persuasive pieces, King's audience is urged to believe something—in this case, that the battle for civil rights will be won. At the same time, the audience is told to do something: King wants the marchers to return home to continue the fight.

A Primary Purpose

While most writing is *primarily* expressive, informative, or persuasive, rarely is a piece of writing entirely one or the other. Much of the time, all three types occur in a single piece.

The following essay, "Whose Lungs Are They, Anyway?" by Janet Singleton, has expressive, informative, and persuasive sections. As you read the essay, think about Singleton's primary purpose.

JANET SINGLETON

Whose Lungs Are They, Anyway?

I grew up in a toxic cloud. Every adult close to me—my mother, father, grandmother—smoked. Yet even at 5, I knew I'd never do it. To me, cigarettes snuffed out a face's innocence, drawing the features into one big squint, transforming people into unadorable, fuming dragons.   *1*

The movement to make smokers keep their smoke to themselves makes precious sense to me. No one should suffer for others' vices. Proposals for high taxes and dragon-fanged restrictions, however, seem geared toward *forcing* people to quit.   *2*

Whose lungs are they, anyway? I can't believe 50 million American smokers are helpless zombies animated by the tobacco industry.   *3*

The new allegations that cigarette companies secretly pumped up nicotine levels to further hook smokers only make me shrug. I guess I never expect anything from a pig but an oink.   *4*

Who among us hasn't been thoroughly warned? I remember the   *5*
high-gloss gym-wall posters and the siren of public service commer-
cials admonishing my generation about smoking. But a job well
done is becoming a job overdone as politicians and activists try to
snuff out one of the last safe things to hate.

My grandmother smoked like a forest fire but lived to be 82.   *6*
Without cigarettes, she might have lived longer. Maybe not. You
never know.

I *do* know my non-smoking, seldom-drinking, seat belt-wearing   *7*
ways will not change the fact that life is temporary. And as long as
life remains a burden as well as a gift, people will seek comfort for
the scary parts. For some, that means a pack a day; for me, it means
a dessert a day. OK—two for the rough times.

One rough fact is that while blacks don't smoke at a higher rate   *8*
than whites, we tend to use stronger cigarettes and die dispropor-
tionately of tobacco-related illnesses. But that doesn't make smoking
a racial oppressor. The least of my worries about being black is that a
pack of Kools will force itself on me.

Critics say ad campaigns inspire underage smoking. Nearly one-   *9*
fifth of teens smoke. But so many kids are undernurtured and un-
dereducated, it's a wonder they're not sucking on dynamite. To im-
ply that a cartoon camel should haul the blame for misdirected teens
is sillier than the ads themselves.

In the symphony of anti-smoking objections, there is a disturb-   *10*
ing melody of denial of personal responsibility and the reality of
death. It's not that I don't see smoke as a serious environmental
threat. For the first 17 years of my life, my invisible playmates were
the carcinogens that snaked from the tips of others' cigarettes. I now
live and work in a smokeless atmosphere and can't fathom people
who insist on lighting up around children.

Little kids don't have a choice. The rest of us do. Many things in   *11*
life are unfair, but this isn't one of them. Black, white, male, female—we all stand warned. We need to make our own decisions
about the risks we'll take, and we must be prepared for the consequences.

What will the consequences be? You never know.   *12*

Identifying the Primary Purpose in Writing. Answer these
questions about Singleton's essay.

ACTIVITY

1

1. Where does Singleton use expressive writing in her essay?

_____

_____

_____

_____

2. Where does Singleton use informative writing? _____

_____

_____

_____

3. Give examples of persuasive writing from the essay. _____

_____

_____

_____

4. What is Singleton's primary purpose in this essay? _____

_____

_____

_____

5. Do you agree or disagree with Singleton's main point? Explain your position.

_____

_____

_____

_____

ACTIVITY
2

Identifying Purpose. Identify the following paragraphs as either primarily expressive, informative, or persuasive.

1. From the Comtrad Industries Catalog:
    We are so confident that the 900 MHz cordless phone is the best

phone on the market that we challenge you to compare it to any other. For a limited time, you can buy the 900 MHz phone at the factory-direct introductory price of $399. Try it for 30 days. If you don't agree that this phone gives you incredible clarity and convenience, return it for a full refund.

Purpose: _____

2.   From *Frommer's Australia* by Elizabeth Hansen:
      Is Paul Hogan in *Crocodile Dundee* a typical Aussie? Some Australians might like you to think so, but facts show that less than 15% of the population lives in rural areas. Instead, the average Australian lives in one of eight capital cities and has never seen native fauna anywhere but in a zoo or wildlife park.

Purpose: _____

3.   From *Silent Spring* by Rachel Carson:
      The thin layer of soil that forms a patchy covering over the continents controls our own existence and that of every other animal of the land. Without soil, land plants as we know them could not grow, and without plants no animals could survive.

Purpose: _____

4.   From the American Association of Retired Persons bulletin:
      We must create a more positive and accurate image of aging and help people recognize that people are living longer, more productive lives. As a nation, we must let go of our obsession with the number of years in life and focus instead on the life in those years.

Purpose: _____

5.   From *One Writer's Beginnings* by Eudora Welty:
      Of course it's easy to see why they both overprotected me, why my father, before I could wear a new pair of shoes for the first time, made me wait while he took out his thin silver pocket knife and with the point of the blade scored the polished soles all over, carefully, in a diamond pattern, to prevent me from sliding on the polished floor when I ran.

Purpose: _____

Discovering Purposes for Writing. Bring to class three pieces of writing composed by you or someone else. For example, you might bring a letter you wrote to a friend or relative, an article from your campus newspaper, the recording notes to a CD, a flyer from an election campaign, or your favorite recipe. Identify each piece of writing as primarily expressive, informative, or persuasive.

Form a group with several classmates and exchange your pieces of writing. How well do you and your classmates agree on the primary purpose of each piece?   ❑

A Writer's Audience

Whether your purpose is to express yourself or to inform or persuade others, your audience affects what you write. A writer's *audience* consists of those who will read the writing—ourselves, family members, friends, classmates, instructors, colleagues at work, or political leaders. The list could go on and on.

Writing to an audience is not the same as speaking to an audience. There are some advantages to writing. Have you ever said something you wished you could take back? This is less likely to happen when you write because you can revise your words before your audience sees them. If you're shy, you might prefer to communicate through writing rather than face-to-face.

Writing is also different from speaking because your audience isn't actually in front of you. When you speak, your audience can smile, frown, or ask you questions. When you write, however, you must envision, or picture in your mind, how your readers will respond to your words. To envision your audience, ask yourself these questions:

- **Who are my readers?** Sometimes your reader is someone very specific, such as your sociology professor who will read your term paper or fellow students who will see the flyer you intend to post about an upcoming event at the student union. At other times, your readers will be the general educated public, such as subscribers to the local newspaper who read your letter to the editor.

- **What do my readers know about my topic?** Your readers' knowledge of the topic is important because you don't want to bore them by telling them what they already know. Instead, you want to tell them something new—where they might go for spring break, how they can fix their VCR, whom they should vote for in the next election.

- **What do my readers need to know about my topic?** Answering this question can help you decide how much information you need to give your readers. For instance, if you're explaining how to change a tire, will your readers know what a tire jack is? Or must you describe it and tell how to use it?

- **How do my readers feel about my topic?** If your readers know nothing about your topic or might even find it dull, you'll want to find a way to get their interest. Or your readers may be opposed to your message. If you're writing a letter asking your supervisor for a raise, don't assume that he or she will automatically agree with you. Instead, try to anticipate your supervisor's reasons for not giving you a raise and take them into account when you make your case.

Analyzing Your Audience. Imagine that you're writing to a close friend or family member asking for a loan to buy a car. Analyze your audience using these questions.

ACTIVITY
4

1. What does my reader already know about my financial situation?

   _____

   _____

   _____

2. What does my reader know about why I need a car? _____

   _____

   _____

   _____

3. What does my reader *not* know that he or she needs to know?

   _____

   _____

   _____

4. How will my reader feel about my request? _____

   _____

   _____

   _____

Now, imagine that you're writing to a loan officer at a bank asking for a loan to buy a car, and answer these same four questions.

1. What does my reader already know about my financial situation?

    _____

    _____

    _____

2. What does my reader know about why I need a car? _____

    _____

    _____

    _____

3. What does my reader *not* know that he or she needs to know?

    _____

    _____

    _____

4. How will my reader feel about my request? _____

    _____

    _____

    _____

Answer one more question:

5. How and why do your answers differ when your reader changes?

    _____

    _____

    _____

Getting to Know Your Readers. Sometimes your readers will be your classmates, so you'll want to get to know them. To start, use these questions to interview a classmate about his or her first name. Then trade places so your classmate can interview you.

GROUP ACTIVITY 5

- Who gave you your name, and why?
- Do you know the history, origin, or definition of your name? What is it?
- Do you have any nicknames? What are they?
- How do you feel about your name?
- If you could change your name, what would you change it to? Why?

After you and your classmate interview each other, write nonstop for five minutes about your classmate's name. Introduce your classmate to the rest of the class by reading what you have written. Your classmate should then introduce you to the class in the same way. ❑

Standard Written English

You may identify yourself as an English-speaking person, but actually you speak a dialect of English. A *dialect* is a variety of a language, and every language has many dialects. Dialects are characterized by pronunciation, word choice, and sentence structure. People speak different dialects based on where they live and what their ethnic backgrounds are.

Here are some examples of dialects. The first is from *The Quilters: Women and Domestic Art*. It shows Rosie Fischer talking in 1974 about her life on a farm in Rowlett, Texas. The second is from *Sadie Shapiro's Knitting Book* by Robert Kimmel Smith, a novel about a Jewish widow from Queens named Sadie Shapiro. The third is from Dorothy Z. Seymour's essay, "Black Children, Black Speech."

1. Well, anyway, I was dreaming on havin' all kinds of pretty things in my home after I married. Well, I found out right quick that livin' out on a farm, what with all the chores that had to be done, a person didn't have a whole lot of time for makin' pretty things.

2. "Listen, darling," Sadie said patiently, "we all have our ways and that's it. . . . I lived with my son Stuart and his wife for three years after my Reuben died, he should find eternal peace. And what happened? My daughter-in-law and I drove each other crazy. I'm a neat person, I think you can tell that, but she. . . . Well, I wouldn't

exactly call her a slob, but the best housekeeper in the world she isn't. Not that I want to talk badly about her, mind you. But by me you don't wash a floor with a mop. That's not what I call clean."

3. "C'mon, man, les git goin'!" called the boy to his companion. "Dat bell ringin'. It say, 'Git in rat now!'" He dashed into the school yard.

"Aw, f'get you," replied the other. "Whe' Richuh? Whe' da muvvuh? He be goin' to schoo'."

"He in de' now, man!" was the answer as they went through the door.

Northern, southern, and midwestern dialects have developed from the languages spoken by European immigrants. The structure of African American spoken English is similar to several west African languages. In the Southwest and California, dialects such as Chicano English have developed as a result of Mexican immigration.

All of these dialects are different from *standard English*, which is taught in American schools and used in business, government, and the media. The written version of standard English is *standard written English*, or *SWE* for short.

The following examples show the differences between standard written English and three dialects.

AFRICAN AMERICAN SPOKEN ENGLISH

He always be walkin' dere.

SWE

He always walks there.

CHICANO ENGLISH

They put his broken arm a cast.

SWE

They put a cast on his broken arm.

CREOLE ENGLISH

In Main Street have plenty shop.

SWE

Main Street has plenty of shops.

Because standard written English is used by educated people in many professional settings, it's often considered the appropriate language to use in school and business. However, no language is better than another; languages are just different. Standard written English is a tool that will help you advance in college and in your workplace. It doesn't replace the other regional or ethnic dialects you might speak; it just adds to them.

Thinking about Standard Written English. Working in a group of several students, discuss the following questions. Ask one member of the group to summarize your discussion for the rest of the class.

1. Why are you learning standard written English?
2. What is your attitude toward SWE and your experience with it?
3. In your opinion, is too much or too little value placed on SWE? Why? ❏

A Writer's Composing Process

It's easy to think of writing as simply putting words on paper. In actuality, however, when we write we use a particular *writing process* or method of writing. Generally, here is the writing process that many writers follow:

- Gathering ideas to write about

- Drafting to explore ideas

- Revising one of these drafts

- Editing the draft for SWE

- Publishing, or sharing, the final draft with the audience

Whether you pass through every stage of this process depends partly on your audience and purpose. If you're jotting down a grocery list for your spouse, for instance, you might write "salad dressing," knowing that he or she will understand that you mean creamy low-fat ranch dressing because that's the kind both of you like. You don't worry about spelling or neatness, nor do you write a draft of your list and then revise it. Your purpose is to convey simple information to someone who will easily understand it.

But imagine yourself writing a letter to your city council because you think there should be a stoplight at a busy intersection near your house. You gather ideas by talking to the city traffic manager about how many cars use that intersection each day and how many accidents occurred there in the past year. You also interview neighbors whose children must cross the intersection on their way to and from school. Next, you write a draft of your letter and read it to a friend, who suggests how it can be improved. Then you rewrite the letter, perhaps several times, taking out unnecessary details and more forcefully restating your point in your conclusion. Finally, you edit the letter for correct grammar, spelling, and punctuation. This writing process might take several days, but in the end you have a well-written letter that might end up saving lives.

Your writing process—how you go about writing—changes each time you write. Sometimes you can simply write down what you're thinking, and that is sufficient. Other times you need to gather ideas, write and revise several drafts, and edit your final draft to eliminate errors. In this textbook you'll learn about this longer writing process because it applies to most college writing assignments. You'll also learn different strategies for each stage of the writing process—gathering ideas, drafting, revising, editing, and publishing.

ACTIVITY

7

Comparing Your Writing Process. One way to become a better writer is to exchange ideas about how people write. Compare your answers to the following questions with your classmates' answers. What can you learn from your classmates' writing processes?

1. In the writing I have done in the past, did I gather ideas, draft, revise, edit, and share my work? If not, what was my process?

_____

_____

_____

2. What would I like to change about my writing process?

_____

_____

_____

❏

A Writer's Space and Routine

As a student, you probably prefer to occupy the same seat in your classes, even though you have the freedom to sit elsewhere. This seat has become your territory, and you're unsettled if you find another person sitting there. When you write, you probably also prefer being in your own territory—a space where you write best. Do you prefer a study room in the library or a chair at the kitchen table? Although you may find yourself jotting down ideas while on the bus or eating lunch, it's best to write in a setting that is conducive to concentration, where others in your life know you shouldn't be interrupted.

Developing routines can also make you a better writer. Do you prefer to write early in the morning or late at night? Do you prefer to work on a computer or to write in longhand? Do you need to read over your class notes before you get started? Do you like to take frequent breaks, or do you prefer to write nonstop until you complete a draft? The more you write, the more you'll find out which routines work best for you.

Thinking about Your Ideal Place and Time to Write. Respond to the following questions. If you need more room, use a separate piece of paper. When you're through, share your responses with your classmates. Then compile a list of different writing spaces and routines.

ACTIVITY
8

1. Where and when do I currently write? _____

_____

_____

_____

2. What do I use to write—pen, paper, computer? _____

_____

_____

_____

3. When I am in my writing space, what do I see in front of and on both sides of me? What do I hear, smell, feel, and taste?

_____

_____

_____

4. What do I like about my writing space and routine? How could I improve one or both?

_____

_____

_____

_____

5. What is my ideal place to write? What is my ideal writing routine?

_____

_____

_____

❑

Reading to Improve Writing

Many of us read a newspaper to keep up with what's going on around us, and it's always fun to read a book and then compare it with the movie version of the same story. Some people read during their commute to and from work to make the ride pass more quickly. At times reading occupies a particularly special place in our lives. Nancy Mairs, a writer whose physical disability prevents her from traveling, uses reading to explore exotic sites, as she describes in her essay "On Having Adventures."

> With Peter Matthiessen I have trekked across the Himalayas to the Crystal Mountain. One blistering July I moved with John McPhee to Eagle, Alaska, above the Arctic. David Bain has hiked me along a hundred and ten miles of Philippine coast, and Edward Abbey has paddled me down the Colorado River. I've ridden on the back of Robert Pirsig's motorcycle, climbed ninety-five feet to George Dyson's tree house, grown coffee in Kenya with Isak Dinesen. With wonder I contemplate the actions of these rugged and courageous figures.

The advantages of reading multiply when you read the way that writers read—to learn how to improve their writing. When you examine a piece of writing to learn how the author communicates a certain idea, you're like an athlete who watches a game to observe the moves of the players. Examining the writing strategies of a particular author helps you use these strategies in your own writing. If you read like a writer, you can learn ways to organize, develop, and express your ideas in your own writing.

Suppose you can't decide how to begin an informative paper on whales for your biology course. Around the same time, you read an article on hallucinogenic drugs in *Outside* magazine called "One Toad over the Line," written by Kevin Krajick. Here is its beginning:

> It's big, it looks like a cowpie with eyes, and many people believe it can bring them face to face with God. It's the Colorado River toad, a

once obscure amphibian whose fame has spread in recent years thanks to the venom secreted by its skin. When dried and smoked, the venom releases bufotenine, a substance that one California drug agent calls "the most potent, instantaneously acting hallucinogen we know."

From this paragraph you learn two strategies for beginning an essay. First, a startling comparison ("a cowpie with eyes") can get your audience's attention. Second, it's a good idea to state the topic of an essay (in this case, the hallucinogen bufotenine) at the beginning so your audience will understand right away what your piece is about.

Reading can also improve your vocabulary. Suppose that one of your favorite authors is the suspense novelist Mary Higgins Clark. Here's an excerpt from Clark's *While My Pretty One Sleeps*, a book about a fashion designer named Neeve:

To Neeve's dismay, as she crossed Thirty-seventh Street she came face to face with Gordon Steuber. Meticulously dressed in a tan cashmere jacket over a brown-and-beige Scottish pullover, dark-brown slacks and Gucci loafers, with his blaze of curly brown hair, slender, even-featured face, powerful shoulders and narrow waist, Gordon Steuber could easily have had a successful career as a model. Instead, in his early forties, he was a shrewd businessman with an uncanny knack of hiring unknown young designers and exploiting them until they could afford to leave him.

The word *meticulously* might be unknown to you, but from the context of this passage you can guess that it means "carefully" or "precisely." From this passage you can also guess that *uncanny* means "unusual or remarkable," and that *exploit* means "to use." Verify your guesses by looking up unfamiliar words in a dictionary.

Sharing Favorite Books. Make a list of your favorite books or magazines. You might want to list them in different categories. For example, you could classify books as science fiction, romance, or horror, and magazines as music, fashion, or sports. As a class, compile a list of recommended readings.

GROUP
ACTIVITY
9

Collecting New Words. Read an article that interests you in your campus or local newspaper. Circle any words that are unfamiliar to you. Based on your understanding of the article, guess the meaning of each unfamiliar word. Then test your accuracy by looking the words up in a dictionary.

ACTIVITY
10

Keep a list of new words and their meanings so you can refer to them when you read and write. Try to add at least five words a week to your list. ❑

Using a Computer to Write

A computer can help you in all stages of the writing process. You can use a computer to:

- gather ideas for a topic.
- investigate a topic through electronic databases.
- draft your writing.
- revise your writing.
- edit your writing.
- publish, or share, your writing with readers.

Throughout this textbook, you'll find numerous Computer Tips, which tell you how to use the computer during each stage of the writing process.

ACTIVITY

11

Using Computers. Read this excerpt from *Computing Unbound* by David Patterson, Denise Kiser, and Neil Smith. Then use the questions that follow to compare your experience using computers with the experiences of your classmates.

Computers are simple. There is nothing magical in the way they work or what they do. They *should* be easy to use: they are tools built by humans for other humans, to remove tedium from existing chores, and to enable you to undertake creative work that would be impractical without the speed and accuracy of a computer. If computers are not simple, then we have failed as tool builders.   *1*

Writing is an example of an everyday task that computers can simplify. Writing well is an art, difficult to teach or to learn, but best developed by constant practice. Ten or fifteen years ago no one would have suggested that computers could help people write more effectively, but today writing is the predominant use of personal computers, and most professional writers use them. When people could write only with quill and ink, the physical act of writing was slow and making corrections was painful. The invention of the typewriter in the 19th century made it possible to put words on paper much more quickly; electric typewriters and "self-correcting" typewriters simplified the process still further, but editing each successive draft of a composition still required completely retyping the whole manuscript.   *2*

With a computer it is possible to edit a composition quickly and easily on the computer screen, and then print it when you have a draft you're pleased with. You can save a copy of your doc-   *3*

Writing Assignment

Your first writing assignment is to "compose yourself" as a writer by relating what you have learned in this chapter to your own life. You could describe your writing process and the types of writing you prefer to do. You might discuss where you like to write and your attitude toward writing. Have you used a computer to write? If not, would you like to? Your audience for this assignment will be your instructor and classmates.

Before you start writing, you might want to get your ideas flowing by writing nonstop in response to some of the following questions. Then use your best ideas to "compose yourself" as a writer.

- Up until now, what have I written that I really liked? What have I written that I didn't like? Why?

- What are my strengths and weaknesses as a writer?

- How do my classmates' writing experiences compare with mine?

- How have the books I've read improved my writing?

- What three words best describe me as a writer?

ument on a magnetic disk so that you can continue to edit your work later—perhaps after your instructor or editor has made suggestions—and print your revised version at the push of a button. By taking the tedium out of producing drafts of a composition, the computer simplifies what writing teachers have always suggested is one of the keys to writing well: revise, revise, and revise again.

Questions

1. Do you agree with the authors' claim that computers are simple to use? Why or why not?

_____

_____

_____

2. In what ways have you used a computer in the past? _____

    _____

    _____

    _____

    _____

3. What are the advantages of using a computer to write versus writing
    in longhand or on a typewriter? What are the drawbacks?

    _____

    _____

    _____

❏

Chapter Summary

- You can have three purposes for writing:
    —Expressive writing communicates thoughts, feelings, or personal history.
    —Informative writing conveys information.
    —Persuasive writing seeks to change the reader's opinion or to convince the reader to take a particular action.
- Most writing is a combination of the expressive, informative, and persuasive types, but one purpose is usually primary.
- Your audience, or readers, affect what you write. Identify your readers and take into account what they know about your topic, what they don't know about your topic, and how they feel toward your topic.
- A dialect is a variety of a language. Every language has many dialects.
- Standard written English (SWE) is taught in American schools and used in business, government, and the media. It is important to learn SWE for writing in college and in the workplace.
- Most writers follow a writing process that consists of gathering ideas to write about, drafting to explore ideas, revising, editing, and publishing (or sharing the final draft with readers).

- You should find your best place to write and develop an effective routine for writing.
- Through reading you can learn writing strategies and improve your vocabulary.
- Using a computer may make writing easier.

The blank page gives the right to dream.
—GASTON BACHELARD

2

Keeping a Journal

In this chapter you will

- discover why writers keep journals.
- learn how to keep a journal.
- practice keeping three types of journals.
- learn tips for keeping your journal on a computer.

Imagine that you want to become a great musician or athlete. How would you go about it? First, knowing that it would take hard work and a long time, you would have to be motivated to achieve your goal. Then you would seek out a teacher or coach to work with you. Finally, you would do what great musicians and athletes do—practice: musicians rehearse and athletes work out. The same is true if you want to be a writer. But, you say, "I don't want to become a great writer, just a better one. I don't want to be Shakespeare; I just want to write well enough to get better grades on my term papers or a promotion at work." The path is still the same, whether you're aiming for the major leagues, the minors, or a spot on your neighborhood sandlot team: you'll need to make a commitment, study, and practice.

You may ask, "Aren't some people just born musicians, athletes, or writers?" Yes and no. Some people may have more natural skill in an area, but that doesn't mean the rest of us can't become better if we set our minds to it. Even people with natural talent must be willing to learn and practice to realize their potential.

Why Writers Keep Journals

Let's think more about practice: Would a musician wait until the night before a concert to practice? Would a basketball player wait until the day before the big game to practice slam dunks? Of course not. The same is true with writing. If you want to write well, you must start practicing *now*. As a writer, your equivalent to the musician's instrument or the athlete's equipment is a *journal*, a notebook for jotting down your ideas, opinions, feelings, and memories. The more time you spend writing in your journal, the more practice you'll get as a writer.

Use your journal to try out ideas, to experiment with different ways of writing, and to write without the pressure of being evaluated. Journal writing can help you find topics for writing. It can also help you clarify and organize your ideas. But most important, writing in a journal helps you become an active thinker, rather than being a passive reader or listener. This, in turn, will help you write better papers in college and get that promotion at work.

Roy Hoffman, in "On Keeping a Journal," describes the value he places on his college journals.

ROY HOFFMAN

From *On Keeping a Journal*

Wherever I go I carry a small notebook in my coat or back   *1*
pocket for thoughts, observations and impressions. As a writer I use this notebook as an artist would a sketch pad, for stories and essays, and as a sporadic journal of my comings and goings. When I first

started keeping notebooks, though, I was not yet a professional writer. I was still in college.

I made my first notebook entries in the summer of 1972, just after my freshman year, in what was actually a travel log. A buddy and I were setting out to trek from our Alabama hometown to the distant tundra of Alaska. With unbounded enthusiasm I began: "Wild, crazy ecstasy wants to wrench my head from my body." The log, written in a university composition book, goes on to chronicle our adventures in the land where the sun never sets, the bars never close and the prepipeline employment prospects were so bleak we ended up taking jobs as night janitors.

When I returned to college that fall I had a small revelation: the world around me of libraries, quadrangles, Frisbees and professors was as rich with material for my journals and notebooks as galumphing moose and garrulous fishermen.

These college notebooks, which built to a pitch my senior year, are gold mines to me now. Classrooms, girlfriends, cups of coffee and lines of poetry—from mine to John Keats's—float by like clouds. As I lie beneath these clouds again, they take on familiar and distinctive shapes. . . .

I believe that every college student should attempt to keep some form of notebook, journal or diary. A notebook is a secret garden in which to dance, sing, muse, wander, perform handstands, even cry. In the privacy of this little book, you can make faces, curse, turn somersaults and ask yourself if you're *really* in love. A notebook or journal is one of the few places you can call just your own. . . .

By keeping notebooks, you improve your writing ability, increasing your capacity to communicate both with yourself and others. By keeping notebooks, you discover patterns in yourself, whether lazy ones that need to be broken or healthy ones that can use some nurturing. By keeping notebooks, you heighten some moments and give substance to others: even a journey to the washateria offers potential for some offbeat journal observations. And by keeping notebooks while still in college, you chart a terrain that, for many, is more dynamically charged with ideas and discussions than the practical, workaday world just beyond. Notebooks, I believe, not only help us remember this dynamic charge, but also help us sustain it.

Not long ago, while traveling with a friend in Yorktown, Va., I passed by a time capsule buried in the ground in 1976, intended to be dug up in 2076. Keeping notebooks and journals is rather like burying time capsules into one's own life. There's no telling what old rock song, love note, philosophical complaint or rosy Saturday morning you'll unearth when you dig up these personal time capsules. You'll be able to piece together a remarkable picture of where you've come from, and may well get some important glimmers about where you're going.

ACTIVITY

1

Reading to Improve Writing. Discuss the following questions about "On Keeping a Journal" with your classmates.

1. What does Hoffman mean when he refers to a journal as "a secret garden"?

   _____

   _____

   _____

2. What kinds of events and activities does Hoffman write about in his journal?

   _____

   _____

   _____

3. Which college activities or events would you like to write about in a journal?

   _____

   _____

   _____

4. Why does Hoffman refer to his journal as a "time capsule" of his life?

   _____

   _____

   _____

5. How might your journal serve as a time capsule?_____

_____

_____

_____   ❏

How to Keep a Journal

To begin keeping a journal, purchase a notebook that is comfortable for you to write in. Many students prefer standard 8 1/2-by-11-inch paper, whether in a spiral, bound, or loose-leaf notebook. The notebook should have at least one hundred pages so you can write in it daily.

There are three types of journals that you may choose to keep: a personal journal, a dialogue journal, and a learning log. Once you decide which type works best for you, set aside some time each day to write in your journal.

Personal Journals

A *personal journal* is a collection of your thoughts and feelings. You write simply to express yourself. You need not be concerned about grammar, spelling, or punctuation, and you need not write in complete sentences. Just as the musician practices scales and the sprinter runs laps to loosen up, you develop fluency and the ability to express yourself smoothly and easily by writing in a personal journal. In addition to written entries, you may include lists, pictures, drawings, newspaper clippings—anything that gives you ideas for future writing.

Because you do not share a personal journal, you can, as Hoffman says, "put your true thoughts on paper" without worrying about others' reactions to your writing. You can relax and write in your own style, using language that is natural to you.

Here are some sample entries from student writer Alyssa's personal journal:

April 4

Here I am on a cloudy day headed to my house. My mom is driving at thirty-five miles per hour. She has always been a

COMPUTER TIP

KEEPING YOUR JOURNAL ON COMPUTER

If you have access to a computer, you may prefer to keep your personal journal on disk. Set up a file called "journal," and then set aside some time each day to add entries to it, just as you would to a notebook. Enter text as quickly as you can, concentrating on your ideas and resisting the urge to backspace, delete, or correct your writing. You can always go back and move an entry to a new file or revise and edit later on, if you decide to use it as part of a paper.

cautious driver. Every other car seems to be passing us. Some of the drivers turn, maybe wondering why my mother is driving so slow. Now we're passing the old factory. Sometimes it looks nice, especially at night. But today it looks really ugly. All the smoke is more noticeable because it is cloudy, too. I get sick just thinking about how many chemicals we breathe every day.

As I look around, I notice that this town is desperately in need of some trees. All I can see are poles, billboards, and dirt.

April 5

I called to see if I can get my old job back again. It's not exciting, but the pay's good and the people are nice. Maybe there'll be more part-timers around my age now. I hope I hear soon because otherwise I've got to get to work on finding something else.

April 6

Went to see *Interview with the Vampire* last night. UNBELIEVABLE! I'm going to read the rest of the vampire books.

April 7

I like this poem by Pat Mora.

"Clever Twist"
The best revenge
is pouring the tears
into a tall, black hat
waving a sharp No. 2 pencil
slowly over the blue echoes
then gently, gently
pulling out
a bloomin' poem.

April 8

Heard from APCO. Got my summer job. Wow! That takes a load off of my mind. I wasn't looking forward to applying for jobs again.

Starting a Personal Journal. With your notebook in hand, you're ready to begin your personal journal. Try keeping one for several days. Write about what you observe around you and how you feel about it. Clip articles, cartoons, and photographs that interest you, and write about why you find them interesting. Try writing on some of the following questions, which will help you loosen up. Choose the questions that appeal to you and on which you can write freely.

 ACTIVITY
2

- What are two things I would rather be doing right now?

- Am I well organized? How often must I search for something that I have misplaced?

- If I could change anything about the way I have been raised, what would it be?

- If I could take a one-month trip anywhere in the world (and money were not a consideration), where would I go and what would I do?

- What do I most strive for in life: accomplishment, security, love, power, excitement, knowledge, or something else?

- Is there something I have dreamed of doing for a long time? Why haven't I done it?

- Do I have long-term goals? What is one such goal, and how do I plan to reach it?

- What is the greatest accomplishment of my life?

- What is my most treasured memory?

- Would I be willing to eat a bowl of live crickets for $50,000? Why or why not? ❑

Dialogue Journals

The *dialogue journal* is a written conversation—or dialogue—between you and another person. As in a personal journal, your primary concern in a dialogue journal is expressing your thoughts. Unlike a personal journal, however, what you write in a dialogue journal will be read by someone else. Therefore, you should record your thoughts and ideas more completely so that your reader will understand them. You need not be overly concerned with grammar, spelling, and punctuation, but you should take more care than in a personal journal to ensure your reader's easy reading of your dialogue journal. You may focus on one topic or change topics each time you exchange journals. You may also exchange your dialogue journal with one or more friends or classmates.

One advantage of a dialogue journal is that it helps you clarify your understanding of an idea or issue by explaining it to someone else. Another advantage comes from sharing your dialogue journal with someone who can respond to what you have written. Your reader can help you determine how clearly you communicate your thoughts to someone else. You may even ask specific questions of your reader.

In the following sample entry from a student's dialogue journal, Kirk writes about a school issue that concerns him. Because he is primarily concerned with getting his thoughts down on paper, Kirk makes some errors in punctuation and grammar.

> One incident that really upset me this past week was the fact that on tests people are always cheating. It makes me mad that people expect others to always do their work for them. This might have been okay in high school but this is college and that means everyone has to make it on their own.
>
> We don't go to college expecting to "just pass." Well maybe some people do and those who do feel that way have no business in college.
>
> However what do my friends say. "Oh what a small classroom. Great for cheating. Come sit by me and let me see your paper, okay." What kind of people are they. They are wasting their parents money because it is obvious they don't plan to study or have a career.

Here's how Kirk's student reader, Michelle, responded to his journal entry:

> Kirk, rather than thinking so much about other people's cheating, concentrate on your own goals. In the long run, the cheaters will be the ones who lose out for not doing their own work. Just don't let them cheat off of you. Concentrate on not cheating yourself—be honest to your own work, your own future.

COMPUTER TIP

KEEPING AN INTERACTIVE JOURNAL ON COMPUTER

If you have access to electronic mail (e-mail), you may wish to keep an interactive journal whereby you and your reader send messages back and forth via the electronic computer network. If you have access to the Internet— a network of computers that connects you to other computers around the world—you can even begin a dialogue journal with someone in another city, state, or country.

And here's what Kirk's writing instructor had to say after reading the same journal entry:

> *Kirk, I can see that you have strong feelings about cheating. You may want to explore this topic further by writing a personal letter to a friend who cheats, expressing how you feel about this behavior, or a persuasive letter to the editor of the campus newspaper. Why do you suppose students cheat? Why do you say that cheating might have been okay in high school? Is cheating acceptable some times, but not at other times?*

Starting a Dialogue Journal. You begin a dialogue journal just as you would a personal journal, with one exception: because a dialogue is a conversation, you must first find someone to read and respond to it. Ask a classmate to exchange journals with you for a few days.

ACTIVITY
3

Write on anything of interest to you. If you need help getting started, try writing on a few of the following questions.

- What do I value most in a relationship?
- Do I judge others by higher or lower standards than I use to judge myself?
- When did I last yell at someone? Why? Did I later regret it?
- Do I find it hard to say "no" to family and friends? Why or why not?
- Who is the most important person in my life? Why?
- Are there people whose lives I envy enough to want to trade places with them? Who are they?
- Have I ever disliked someone? If so, why and for how long?
- What do I most regret *not* having told someone? Why haven't I told that person yet?
- What is my best advice for getting along with others?
- How important is family life to me? Do I think of family as including only those people related to me by birth? Or do I include close friends and neighbors as well? ❑

Learning Logs

A *learning log* is a journal that focuses on your response to course content. In it you summarize, synthesize, or react to a class lecture, discussion, or assigned reading. You may restate the objectives of each class or try to pinpoint what confuses you about a particular

COMPUTER TIP

KEEPING A LEARNING LOG ON COMPUTER

You can keep a learning log on computer by using a word-processing program that permits you to set up columns. In one column, enter your class notes into your file, reorganizing and improving them as needed. Then add your comments and questions about the notes in a second column. When it is time to review your notes, you'll probably want to make a printout of your file.

topic. By keeping a learning log, you'll not only improve your understanding of the subject; you'll also improve your attitude toward the course in general. As you ask questions and voice your concerns in your log, you'll become an active learner, which will give you more to contribute in class discussions. You'll also find yourself making connections between new ideas and previous knowledge.

Get into the habit of placing the letter *T* in the margin, next to learning log entries that you think might make good essay topics for that course. What makes a good topic? A good topic is one that you're interested in and that others might also want to learn about. Consider, too, how much you already know about the topic and whether you can find additional information about it.

Student writer Tom's learning log entry is about his first-year college composition class. By writing about his own writing, Tom gains insight into how to become a better writer.

> I am glad to hear that I am not expected to write excellently from the beginning. I now understand that everyone can improve their writing.
>
> I like the idea that we will be sharing our work with our classmates. I always thought that in college we would not have an opportunity to share.
>
> Today we learned about freewriting, which means to write off the top of your head as fast as you can. We did freewriting in my English class. I liked it because it lets ideas flow out freely without worrying about grammar or punctuation. I'm glad we will be freewriting this semester.
>
> The essays we have to do seem hard. I already feel the pressure of my first paper. Maybe freewriting will help me.

Tom keeps his learning log in a traditional full-page format. Some students, however, prefer to integrate their logs with their class notes in a double-column format. To do this, simply divide each page down the middle, with one column labeled "Notes" and the other "Thoughts." In the "Notes" column, record key concepts, important details, and examples from class lectures and outside reading. In the "Thoughts" column, reflect on what you're learning: What does it mean to you? How do you feel about it? How will you use this information in the future? You may also summarize, keep a list of new vocabulary words, and jot down notes on upcoming assignments.

Keeping a two-column learning log helps you integrate what you're studying in college into the fabric of your own thinking and past experiences. Personal examples help you understand the course material and how it relates to your life. Whichever type of learning log you choose to keep, getting into the habit of responding to your class notes will help you recall information when you need it for a class discussion or exam.

Here's an entry from the two-column learning log that student writer Tammy kept for her psychology class.

Notes	*Thoughts*
Memory — *Where information is held.* *3 types* * sensory* * short-term* * long-term* *sensory — all info. that* * enters the senses* *short-term — where all* * conscious thought takes* * place* *long-term — representation* * of all that is known*	*I never realized there were* *three kinds of memory. I'm* *not surprised that we forget* *so much sensory info. —* *there's so much of it. Short-* *term memory is what I am* *thinking now, drawing on* *what is happening around* *me. I think of long-term* *memory kind of like a book in* *the library. If I want to* *retrieve it, I hope that it is* *there.*

Starting a Learning Log. Try keeping a full-page or two-column learning log for several days. To get started, select a course you're currently enrolled in, and during class take notes as you always do. After class, reflect in your log on what you learned in class, how you feel about it, and how you'll use this information in the future. ❑

ACTIVITY
4

Keeping a Journal on Computer

Many college students keep their journals on computer. They may keep their personal journals on computer for only themselves to read, or send messages to other students using e-mail, or post their messages on an Internet bulletin board or on a listserv.

Student writer C. J. posted this message about a childhood pastime on a listserv for discussing campus life called CAMPCLIM.

Other than riding motorcycles, my favorite childhood pastime was to take my sister's Barbies, take a smaller size glass of water, turn Barbie upside down in the water, freeze the water, then take the "Barbiesickle" out of the freezer, wait about 4–5 minutes for the ice to melt just around the edges and pull. If you use just the right motion you can pull off Barbie's body and leave the head frozen in the ice. Usually you can get this really funny-looking face with the long blond hair standing straight up. To preserve this creation, I'd often leave it in the freezer to show it off later. These Barbiesickles drove my sister, Rebecca, crazy!

Reading to Improve Writing. Discuss the following questions about C. J.'s e-mail message with your classmates.

1. What do you think the college students were discussing on CAMP-CLIM that prompted C. J. to post this message?

_____

_____

_____

2. What childhood pastimes could you write about in your journal?

_____

_____

_____

3. What are the advantages of keeping a journal on computer? What are the disadvantages?

_____

_____

_____

4. Does your college have access to e-mail and listservs on the Internet? How can you go about accessing these services on your campus?

_____

_____

_____

Writing Assignment

You have practiced writing three types of journals: a personal journal, a dialogue journal, and a learning log. To help you decide which one you want to continue to keep this semester, answer the following questions.

- How will keeping a journal be worthwhile to me as a student?
- How do journals differ from regular class notes?
- If I keep a dialogue journal, who will I ask to read and respond to it?
- How will journal writing give me practice as a writer?
- For which course would I keep a learning log?
- How will keeping a journal help me discover topics for future papers?

After you choose the type of journal you prefer, keep writing in it, adding entries daily.

Chapter Summary

- You may keep a journal to jot down ideas, opinions, feelings, and insights. By keeping a journal you can practice writing and gather topics for future writing assignments.
- You may keep a journal in a notebook or on a computer, adding entries regularly.
- Three types of journals are the personal journal, the dialogue journal, and the learning log.
  - —The personal journal is for the writer's eyes only and contains personal thoughts and feelings.
  - —The dialogue journal is shared with someone who reads and responds to it.
  - —The learning log is kept for a particular course and contains class notes and reactions to those notes, sometimes in a two-column format.
- You may use campus e-mail or the Internet as a source of journal writing.

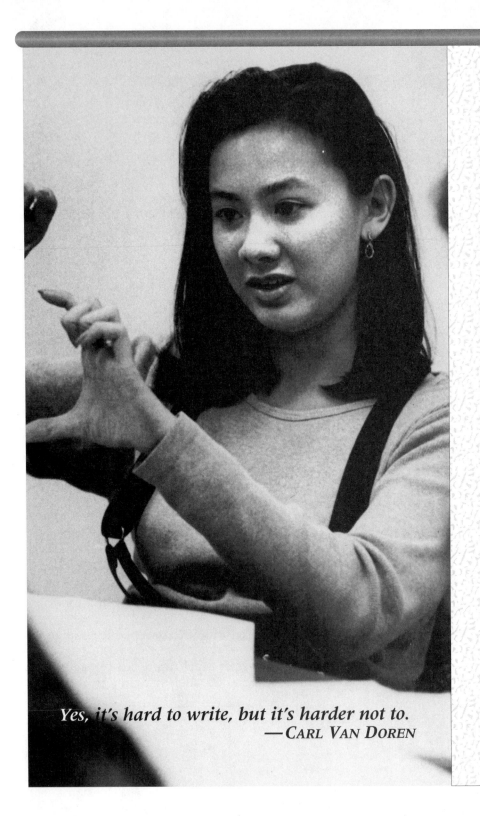

Yes, it's hard to write, but it's harder not to.
—CARL VAN DOREN

3

The Writing Process

In this chapter you will

- learn about the stages of the writing process.
- discover your own writing process.
- follow one student through the writing process.
- learn how a computer can—and cannot—help you write.

Imagine that your history instructor gives you this assignment:

Write an essay describing how a war or other armed conflict changed your outlook on life.

What is your reaction to this assignment? Just the thought of it may cause you to tense up. How do you organize a paper like this, much less find the right words to communicate what you have to say?

Student writer Jeff, writing in his personal journal, expressed his apprehension about the assignment:

This essay really worries me. I don't even know where to begin. I haven't been in a war—thank goodness—but Uncle George was in Vietnam. Maybe I could write about him. But I'm such a terrible writer. I dread this assignment. Before coming to college, I never, never, I mean never had a writing assignment like this.

The Writing Process

In Chapter One, you learned the stages of the writing process:

- gathering ideas
- drafting
- revising
- editing
- publishing

In Chapter Two, you learned that writers become more skilled through commitment, study, and practice and that they often practice by keeping a journal. But how do they transform their commitment and practice into a polished piece of writing to be shared with readers and turned in for a grade? What do they do first, next, and last?

Polished writing is best completed over a period of time. Let's look at each stage of the writing process in more detail.

Gathering Ideas

The first stage, gathering ideas, includes all that you do before you actually begin to write a draft. You must first select a subject and narrow it to a manageable topic. In the history assignment, for instance, you're given the subject—war—and a fairly narrowed

---

Writing Assignment

Do you share any of Jeff's fears? Most students approach writing assignments with some degree of anxiety. Take a few minutes to reflect on your fears by writing in your journal. Then consider what you might do to overcome those fears.

Write a short essay for your instructor and fellow classmates in which you describe the steps you plan to take to overcome your anxiety about writing. Recall, from Chapter Two, that to become a skilled writer, you need motivation, instruction, and practice. You may want to organize your essay around these ideas.

---

topic—how war changed your outlook on life—but you must narrow the topic further. Specifically, *which* war affected you and *how?*

Purpose. In Chapter One, you learned that most writing is primarily expressive, informative, or persuasive. Since the history assignment specifies that you're to describe how a war has affected you, your job is to share your own thoughts, feelings, and personal history. Therefore, your purpose is primarily expressive.

Audience. As you begin to think about the assignment, you also want to keep your reader in mind. After all, you're writing this essay to communicate something of interest, so you want to be sure the reader gets your message. The more you know about your reader, the easier it will be for you to write.

Use the questions you learned in Chapter One to analyze your audience for the history assignment.

- Who is my reader?
- What does my reader know about my topic?
- What does my reader need to know about my topic?
- How does my reader feel about my topic?

Methods. Once you know your subject, purpose, and audience, you must narrow your subject to a topic that you can cover in an essay-length piece of writing. You'll probably focus on one incident or experience. You could use any of the following ways to help you select a topic and gather ideas about it.

Journal writing. If you're keeping a learning log for your class, read over your notes. Do they contain information that pertains to your topic? For example, if you're writing about how a war has affected you, look for notes that may give you ideas for your essay. If you're keeping a personal or dialogue journal, use it as a place to begin writing about your topic.

Brainstorming. When you brainstorm, you list all of the thoughts that come into your head on a topic. You don't consider whether your ideas are good or bad; you just write them down. For the history assignment, you could brainstorm a list of the people you know who have been in a war. Then you could brainstorm again on the one person who interests you the most. You might then brainstorm a third time on how that person changed your outlook on life in some way.

Brainstorming is also useful for gathering ideas while you are writing a paper. In addition, it can be done in a group. Name a topic and then ask each group member to call out ideas on it. Write these ideas down. Asking others to brainstorm with you greatly increases the number of ideas you have to choose from for your essay.

Here is student writer Glynda's brainstormed list on her brother's experience in the Persian Gulf War.

Bruno to Saudi Arabia
Marines — repaired runways
also built tents
wrote lots of letters
Saddam Hussein declared war Jan. '91
lots of tears — my mom, me, Karen
Ozzie there, too, but Air Force
Air Force a lot safer
never want to go through that again

Freewriting. Freewriting helps you develop fluency as a writer. Freewriting is writing without pausing for a specific time limit or until reaching a certain page limit. You don't stop, go back, or correct freewriting. You can focus on one topic or go on to new ones as they pop into your mind.

This is Brian's freewriting about his grandfather's participation in World War II.

My grandfather Ratcliff was in World War Two, stationed in Britain and France. He was in the infantry, I think. Or at least I know he carried a gun and killed German soldiers. I don't know how long he was there or exactly what he did during the war. I guess I don't know much more than that he was in World War Two! What do I already know about World War Two? I think it was from 1941 to 1945 with countries fighting against Germany, and later Japan. Americans were involved because we considered Hitler a threat to world peace. This war has affected my life because my grandfather talks about it all of the time!

Clustering. Clustering is similar to brainstorming, but instead of listing your ideas, you draw a cluster of those ideas. It can thus help you organize your ideas as well as generate ideas. To begin clustering, you write your subject in the center of a blank page and draw a circle around it. Then, as ideas about the topic come to mind, you write them down, put circles around them, and draw lines from them to the center circle. As you think of additional details, you circle and join them to their main ideas.

In the diagram shown in Figure 3-1, notice how student writer Jerome used clustering to gather ideas about the Vietnam War.

Questioning. The six questions that journalists use to gather details about the news can also help you discover ideas about your topic.

- Who?
- What?
- When?
- Where?
- Why?
- How?

Reading. The more you read about your topic, the more information you'll have for your paper. Reread your textbook, lecture notes, or learning log. Then go to the library to do further research on your topic.

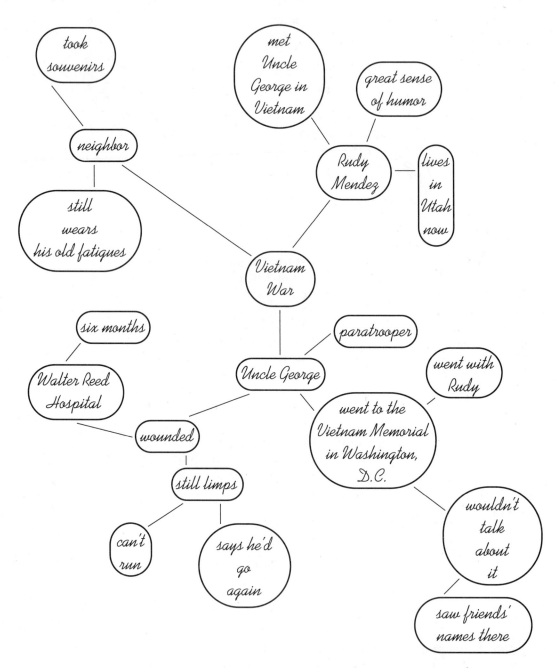

Figure 3-1. Clustering

Interviewing. Interviewing someone who knows about your topic is an excellent way to gather additional information and interesting details for your paper. Also, by using quotations from the interview you can enliven your writing.

The first step is finding someone to interview. For the history assignment, you might interview a family member or friend who participated in a war to determine how that person's experience has affected you.

Once you identify someone to interview, follow these suggestions for conducting a successful interview.

- Set a time to meet.
- Prepare questions to ask. You might begin with the journalists' *who, what, when, where, why,* and *how* questions. Avoid *yes-no* questions.
- Design questions that will keep the person talking about the topic. Write these down.
- Listen carefully and take notes during the interview. (Or, you may wish to tape-record the interview with the person's permission.)
- Go over your notes with the person to fill in any gaps in your understanding.
- Thank the person for agreeing to be interviewed.

Soon after the interview, look over your notes and record your reactions to what you learned. Try to connect what you learned from the interview with what you already know about the topic.

Relating Aloud. Relating aloud simply means talking about your topic with others. Tell friends or classmates about what you plan to write and get their feedback. Do you need more details? Do they ask questions that indicate you need to supply background information? Talking through what you plan to write is also a good way to realize that you have more to say than you think.

Reflecting. After you have tried some of the other ways of gathering ideas, reflect on your topic for a few hours or days, letting your ideas percolate before you begin to write.

Having narrowed your subject to a manageable topic that interests you and that you think will interest your reader, and having gathered ideas to begin writing, you are now ready to begin drafting.

Drafting

In this stage of the writing process, you'll write a discovery draft. It is a draft for getting your ideas down on paper without too much concern about sentence structure, word choice, grammar, spelling, or punctuation. Drafting styles vary widely. Some writers draft quickly

---

COMPUTER TIP
INVISIBLE WRITING

Try freewriting and brainstorming with your word-processing program. To resist the urge to evaluate or delete your writing, concentrate instead on your thoughts by using *invisible writing.* To do so, simply turn down the brightness on your monitor so that you can't see what you're writing. This forces you to stay in touch with your thoughts rather than worry about what you have already written.

and spend considerable time revising; others draft more slowly and write fewer drafts. You may write out your discovery draft by hand, type it, or use a word processor.

Thesis Statement. As you begin your discovery draft, you want to think about your *thesis statement,* the sentence or sentences that reveal to your reader the main point of the essay.

A good thesis statement:

• announces the topic or general subject of your essay.

• explains why the topic is important to you.

Let's look at some examples of good thesis statements.

> By examining how my uncle's death in Vietnam affected my family, I have come to understand the tragedy of war in a very personal way.

> My grandmother's stories of rationing during World War II make me realize how we take everyday things for granted.

> When I get depressed about something in my life, remembering the courage of the Salvadoran family next door helps me keep things in perspective.

These thesis statements are effective because they do two things: they announce the topic and they tell why it is significant. Compare the following effective and ineffective thesis statements:

POOR

We always have big birthday parties in my family.

STRONG

Our family's big birthday celebrations show how much we appreciate each person's uniqueness.

POOR

Playing a team sport is fun.

STRONG

Playing a team sport teaches you to cooperate with others, a skill you need throughout life.

In the first example, we learn the topic but not why it's important. In the second example, we learn the topic and part of its importance, but we need to know more. Put yourself in the reader's place: Which essay would you rather read, one that says a team sport is fun (you probably already know that) or one that reveals how it prepares you for life?

From a writer's point of view, an effective thesis statement gives you a lot more to say than an ineffective one. If you have trouble gathering ideas for your essay, look again at your thesis statement.

Maybe it doesn't explain the significance of your topic effectively or at all.

Where should your thesis statement appear in your essay? Usually the thesis is given at the beginning. Knowing the main idea from the start gives your reader a road map for reading the whole essay.

Evaluating Thesis Statements. Identify the following thesis statements as poor or strong. Then rewrite the thesis statements that need improvement. (Keep in mind that a good thesis states both the topic and its significance.)

ACTIVITY

1

1. My friends and I like to watch the soaps at lunch. _____

   _____

   _____

   _____

2. A successful marriage requires patience, good communication, and a sense of humor.

   _____

   _____

   _____

3. Registering for classes is always the worst day of the year for me.

   _____

   _____

   _____

4. Studying a foreign language should be a requirement in high school.

   _____

   _____

   _____

5. If you have time on your hands, do community volunteer work.

_____

_____

_____

COMPUTER TIP

**DRAFTING ON
A COMPUTER**

Use your word-
processing program to
develop your draft. Try to
write the entire draft in
one computer sitting,
using the ideas you have
already gathered and
saved to disk. If you
reach a place where you
need additional
information, write
yourself a note in
boldface, such as "add
information here," to
remind you to find that
additional material later
on.

6. One of my life goals is to go to the Winter Olympics. _____

_____

_____

_____

❏

As you draft using your thesis statement as a guide, keep in mind that you are free to change your main idea. After all, your discovery draft is for exploring your ideas. The most important thing is to write.

Revising

When you revise, you improve your discovery draft. You want your reader to understand what you have to say and to be interested in reading your paper. At this stage you look at the contents of your draft and at how your ideas are organized. While you write only one discovery draft, you may revise it many times. The more you revise, the better your essay will be.

Ask yourself these questions as you revise:

COMPUTER TIP

USING CUT-AND-PASTE

Use the cut-and-paste
or block-and-move
function of your word-
processing program to
move sentences or
whole blocks of text
when you revise. You can
print out different
versions of the essay
and then compare them
to see which one is the
most effective. You might
also ask a friend or
classmate to evaluate
the different versions.

• Have I followed all instructions for this assignment?

• Do I begin the essay in a way that encourages my reader to continue reading?

• Is my thesis statement effective?

• Do I include enough main ideas to support my thesis statement?

• Do I support each main idea with details?

• Do I end the essay in a way that makes it clear to my audience that this is the end?

You may wonder how you'll know the answers to these questions. One way is to set your paper aside for a day or two, reread it, and then rewrite it as you see fit. But a better way is to enlist the help of others. Ask a friend or classmate to read your paper and suggest ways it could be improved.

Editing

When you edit, you check your revised draft for errors in grammar, spelling, and punctuation. Since you have already devoted a great deal of time and effort to communicating your ideas, you don't want to spoil the paper with distracting errors. The more your readers must pay attention to errors in your writing, the less attention they'll pay to what you have to say.

Here are some tips for effective editing:

- Use a dictionary to check your spelling.

- Use a handbook, such as the one in Part III of this textbook, to check on questions about grammar, spelling, and punctuation.

- Ask another student to read your essay for errors in grammar, spelling, and punctuation that you might have missed.

As you edit, keep an editing log. In a section of your journal, record the errors you discover as you edit.

- Date your entry and give the title of your essay.
- Copy the sentence with the error.
- Identify the type of error.
- Rewrite the sentence, correcting the error.

Here, for example, is an entry from student writer Glynda's editing log:

9/20/96 — "Never Again, I Hope"

• INCORRECT:	My mom carried Bruno's first letter with her. Reading it over and over again.
ERROR:	Sentence fragment
CORRECT:	My mom carried Bruno's first letter around with her, reading it over and over again.

Publishing

In the final stage of the writing process, you share your revised and edited essay with your audience. This may involve submitting the paper to your instructor for a grade. But if you're proud of what you have written, you may wish to share it with others as well.

At times you may share your writing in a more public way. For example, you may submit it to your local or campus newspaper for possible publication. Many magazines are also interested in publishing essays and articles submitted by their readers.

COMPUTER TIP
USING SPELL-CHECK AND STYLE-CHECK

Use the spell-check and style-check features of your word-processing program to help you edit. Spell-check can spot "typos" (typographical errors) and some words that you misspell. Style-check calls attention to possible errors in grammar and punctuation. Record the errors you find in an editing log file on your disk.

ACTIVITY   **Reviewing the Writing Process.** Review an essay assignment that
2   you recently completed by answering these questions in your jour-
         nal.

- What was the subject of my essay?
- How did I narrow it to a manageable topic?
- What was the purpose, and who was the audience?
- What was my thesis statement?
- How did I gather ideas for this assignment?
- How did I revise the paper so that it communicated my ideas more clearly?
- What errors did I discover when I edited?   ❑

Discovering Your Own Writing Process

To discover your own writing process, experiment with the various ways of gathering ideas, drafting, revising, and editing. The
methods that work best for you will lead you to a discovery of your
preferred writing process.

You'll probably find that your writing process does not exactly
follow the stages in the order outlined in this chapter, but that you
prefer to move back and forth among the various stages. For example, while revising your essay you may discover a need for more information. To get that information, you need to return to the gathering ideas stage. You may discover, too, that you prefer to stay in the
revision stage for quite a while, producing perhaps three or four revised drafts. Figure 3-2 below illustrates the recursive nature of the
writing process.

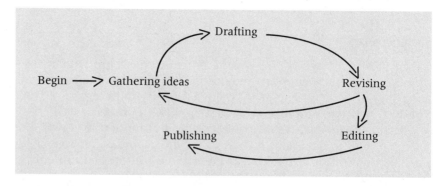

Figure 3-2. The Recursive Nature of the Writing Process

Freewriting about the Writing Process. Do some freewriting about the writing process in your journal. Use these questions to focus your freewriting.

ACTIVITY
3

- Which methods of gathering ideas have I used most successfully?
- Which other methods of gathering ideas am I willing to try?
- How do I draft best?
- How do I prefer to revise and edit?
- In what ways have I shared my writing with others in the past? ❑

One Student's Writing Process

On the following pages you'll follow Patricia Thomas, a student writer, as she writes her essay for the history assignment given at the beginning of this chapter. As you see Patricia work through the writing process, think about your own writing process and how it is similar and different. Recall the assignment:

Write an essay describing how a war or other armed conflict changed your outlook on life.

Patricia's Ideas

In her journal, Patricia explains how she decided on a topic and started to gather ideas for her paper:

Oct. 8

We read about the Iranian war in class. I was especially interested because I lived in Iran in 1979 when the Shah of Iran was overthrown.

Since I was only eight at the time, I asked my mom to tell me the story of the fall of the Shah in order to get a clearer picture of what had happened. While interviewing my mom, I took notes on what she said.

Next, while the ideas were still fresh in my memory, I sat down to do a cluster diagram.

Patricia's Drafting

Using her memory of the war, the notes she took while interviewing her mother, and her cluster diagram (Figure 3-3), Patricia wrote the following discovery draft. (Note that the example includes the types of errors that typically appear in a first draft.)

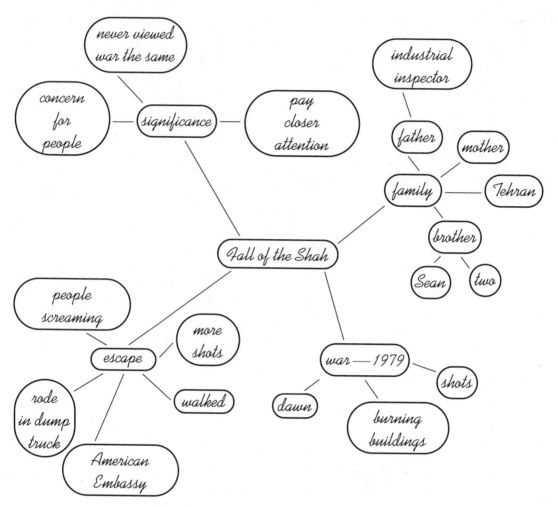

Figure 3-3. Patricia's Cluster Diagram

Death to the King

Being in Iran at the outbreak of the Iranian war made me aware of how war affects innocent people's lives. My father had accepted a position as an industrial inspector in a small town near Tehran. There were rumors of a revolt against the government, but no one really thought it would happen. One morning at dawn, we were awakened by the sounds of gunshots and people screaming in the streets. My father's first reaction was to protect me and my brother. "We must get to Tehran. We will be safe at the embassy". We decided to walk to the main road and wait for a ride. The driver of an old dump truck gave us one. We could hear shots being fired nearby. We had to skirt roads blocked with burning tires. When we reached Tehran, the roads were impassable. We had to continue on foot. After a while, we reached the gate of the American Embassy. Until then, I didn't realize the danger we were in. I will never forget the faces on the people.

After completing her discovery draft, Patricia thought further about her audience—her history instructor. What did she know about him that would help her improve her draft? She knew that he wasn't from Iran, but since he taught history he probably knew the details of the fall of the Shah, so she wouldn't have to provide much background. Because he liked history, she assumed he would be an interested reader if she told the story of what happened to her in an interesting, suspenseful way. She realized, too, that she would need details that would help him to understand the events as they happened.

Patricia describes her thoughts in her journal:

Oct. 10

I knew that my topic was how the fall of the Shah of Iran changed my outlook on war. Even though my purpose was expressive, I organized my draft in such a way that I built some suspense. What was happening to me and my family? How did it turn out? I wanted my instructor to keep reading to find out.

I started with this thesis statement: "Being in Iran at the outbreak of the Iranian war made me aware of how war affects innocent people's lives." Having a thesis statement helped guide the rest of my draft.

I decided that revision was going to have to wait for another day, though. I did this on purpose because I knew that I wasn't going to be able to break down my draft or come up with clear details at this point. I needed time to think about it.

Patricia's Revising

In her journal, Patricia describes revising her essay:

Oct. 12

I began to revise my essay by breaking down my draft into paragraphs. I then took each paragraph and added details where they were needed. The body was pretty easy to do, but I found the introduction and conclusion more diffi-

cult. I could not come up with a good introduction or conclusion no matter how hard I tried. Nevertheless, I had my first revised draft completed.

I then read that draft to three other students in my class. They showed me how to improve my introduction and conclusion and where to add details. The sentence that reads, "For the first time I did not enjoy the beautiful vineyards on the side of the road, nor the orchards, nor the shepherds taking their flocks to graze on the green hills," is an example of the vivid description that I added.

Here is Patricia's revised draft. (Because Patricia focused on getting down her ideas, you may spot editing errors she must still correct.)

Death to the King

Introduction added

Every day we hear about one country invading another, guerrilla warfare, and civil war. Often, we simply change the channel to watch a more interesting program. I did this, too, until the day I experienced war firsthand. Being in Iran at the outbreak of the Iranian war made me aware of how war affects innocent people's lives. *1*

Detail added

My father had accepted a position as an industrial inspector in a small town north of Tehran, Iran. We lived on the outskirts, in a two-story house, with my mother and two-year-old brother, Sean. One morning at dawn, we were awakened by the sounds of gunshots and people screeming. As we looked through the upstairs windows, we saw smoke in every direction. We could see orange and yellow flames on the horizon several buildings were already on fire. *2*

Description added

Dialogue added

My fathers first reaction was to protect his family. "We've got to get to the American Embassy in Tehran", he said breathlessly. Because our car was in the shop, we decided to walk to the main road and wait for a ride. Fortunately, a dilapedated bus from Tabriz stopped and picked us up. *3*

Description added

The people around us were talking excitedly about the uprising. For the first time I did not enjoy the beautiful vineyards on the side of the road, nor the orchards, nor the shepherds taking their flocks to graze on the green hills.

It took us four hours to reach the outskirts of Tehran, and the bus dri-ver would not risk driving further. We had no choice but to get off the bus even though we could hear shots being fired nearby and see clouds of dark smoke covering the town. We spotted an old dump truck parked on the side of the road. My father convinced the driver to take us as close to the embassy as possible. As we drove down the streets, the dump truck felt like a war tank. We had to skirt roads blocked with burning tires, forcing us to drive on the sidewalks. My father told me to lie down to avoid stray bullets, but I couldnt. I had to know what was happening. There were al-ready blood-covered bodies lying on the pavement. Mothers were crying for their children. Shots were being fired everywhere, and the air smelled of gunpowder and smoke.

By now, the roads were almost impassable. We had to leave the truck and continue our journey on foot. After a few minutes, we reached the gate to the embassy. Just then we heard screams. I looked back and saw several boys and girls being pursued by a tank. They had been caught chanting "Lib-erty to the oppressed", and "God is great".

A few hours later, the streets were empty. Until it all passed, I didn't re-alize the danger we were in. Now, when I watch a television news report about an armed conflict somewhere in the world, I am not so quick to change the channel. I often think back to my firsthand experience with war and am reminded that there may be innocent people in serious danger.

4   **Detail added**

Detail added

Description added

5   **Detail added**

Dialogue added

6   **Conclusion added**

Patricia's Editing

Patricia describes editing her essay in her journal:

Oct. 13

I used my word processor to check for misspelled words. I checked to see if I had used any fragments or run-on sen-tences. I also asked a friend to read the essay in case I'd missed any misspelled words and punctuation errors. My friend pointed out to me that commas and periods go inside quotation marks, so I fixed these. I then added these errors to my editing log to remind me of the correct way to handle them next time..

Here is Patricia's edited essay. (The underlining indicates where she corrected errors during the editing stage.)

Death to the King

Every day we hear about one country invading another, guerrilla warfare, and civil war. Often, we simply change the channel to watch a more interesting program. I did this, too, until the day I experienced war firsthand. Being in Iran at the outbreak of the Iranian war made me aware of how war affects innocent people's lives.   *1*

My father had accepted a position as an industrial inspector in a small town north of Tehran, Iran. We lived on the outskirts, in a two-story house, with my mother and two-year-old brother, Sean. One morning at dawn, we were awakened by the sounds of gunshots and people <u>screaming</u>. As we looked through the upstairs windows, we saw smoke in every direction. <u>We could see orange and yellow flames on the horizon. Several buildings were already on fire.</u>   *2*

My <u>father's</u> first reaction was to protect his family. "We've got to get to the American Embassy in <u>Tehran,</u>" he said breathlessly. Because our car was in the shop, we decided to walk to the main road and wait for a ride. Fortunately, a <u>dilapidated</u> bus from Tabriz stopped and picked us up. The people around us were talking excitedly about the uprising. For the first time, I did not enjoy the beautiful vineyards on the side of the road, nor the orchards, nor the shepherds taking their flocks to graze on the green hills.   *3*

It took us four hours to reach the outskirts of Tehran, and the bus driver would not risk driving further. We had no choice but to get off the bus even though we could hear shots being fired nearby and see clouds of dark smoke covering the town. We spotted an old dump truck parked on the side of the road. My father convinced the driver to take us as close to the embassy as possible. As we drove down the streets, the dump truck felt like a war tank. We had to skirt roads blocked with burning tires, forcing us to drive on the sidewalks. My father told me to lie down to avoid stray bullets, but I <u>couldn't.</u> I had to know what was happening. There were already blood-covered bodies lying on the pavement. Mothers were crying for their children. Shots were being fired everywhere, and the air smelled of gunpowder and smoke.   *4*

By now, the roads were almost impassable. We had to leave the truck ⁵
and continue our journey on foot. After a few minutes, we reached the gate
by the embassy. Just then we heard screams. I looked back and saw several
boys and girls being pursued by a tank. They had been caught chanting "Lib-
erty to the <u>oppressed</u>," and "God is <u>great</u>."

A few hours later, the streets were empty. Until it all passed, I didn't re- ⁶
alize the danger we were in. Now, when I watch a television news report
about an armed conflict somewhere in the world, I am not so quick to turn
the channel. I often think back to my firsthand experience with war and am
reminded that there may be innocent people in serious danger.

Here is Patricia's editing log:

10/13/96—"Death to the King"

- INCORRECT: screeming (2)
  ERROR: misspelled word
  CORRECT: screaming

- INCORRECT: We could see orange and yellow flames on the horizon several buildings were already on fire. (2)
  ERROR: run-on sentence
  CORRECT: We could see orange and yellow flames on the horizon. Several buildings were already on fire.

- INCORRECT: my fathers first reaction (3)
  ERROR: possessive without an apostrophe
  CORRECT: my father's first reaction

- INCORRECT: "We've got to get to the American Embassy in Tehran", he said breathlessly. (3)
  ERROR: quotation mark misplaced
  CORRECT: "We've got to get to the American Embassy in Tehran," he said breathlessly.

- INCORRECT: dilapedated (3)
  ERROR: misspelled word
  CORRECT: dilapidated

- INCORRECT: couldnt (4)
  ERROR: contraction without an apostrophe
  CORRECT: couldn't

- INCORRECT: They had been caught chanting "Liberty to the oppressed", and "God is great". (5)
  ERROR: quotation marks misplaced
  CORRECT: They had been caught chanting "Liberty to the oppressed," and "God is great."

Publishing

Writing in her journal, Patricia sums up her feelings about the assignment.

Oct. 25

When I turned in my essay, I thought I would get a B, but when the paper was returned it was an A-. Following the writing process resulted in a well-written paper. The A- gave me confidence in my writing, too. The instructor also asked me to read my paper to the class. Was I ever thrilled! My mother was so proud of me, too. I will continue to use the writing process because it has proven to be effective.

GROUP
ACTIVITY
4

Improving Patricia's Essay. Discuss the following questions with your classmates.

• What changes did Patricia make from the discovery draft to the revised draft that most improved it?

• What else could Patricia do to improve her essay?   ❑

The Computer and the Writing Process

Most people report that they enjoy writing more when they use a computer instead of a pen or typewriter. We know that the computer motivates writers to revise more, too. The little blinking cursor seems to invite writers to keep writing and the ease of revision encourages them to improve their writing. They are usually pleased with the printed format—no more erasures or white-out. Indeed, the computer can be an extremely useful tool.

Of course, you can use a word processor to delete, cut-and-paste, and check grammar, spelling, and punctuation. But you should be aware of the types of mistakes that the spell-check and grammar-check functions *cannot* catch. One student writing a research paper, for example, listed her sources on a "Works Sighted" rather than a "Works Cited" page. The computer didn't catch this error because both words were spelled correctly.

Your best writing tool, then, is between your ears, not at your fingertips. The computer has no ideas, no imagination, no feelings. You bring these qualities to your writing, and it is your job as a writer to express and organize your ideas clearly. So, use your computer, but use it wisely. Use the Computer Tips in this book, but remember that your most powerful writing tool is brainpower.

Using a Computer to Improve Writing. Discuss the following questions with your classmates or freewrite on them in your journal.

ACTIVITY
5

- In what ways does using a computer motivate you as a writer?
- How can using a computer improve your writing?
- In what ways should you *not* depend on a computer? ❑

Your Writing Portfolio

Musicians and athletes demonstrate their developing skills through performance. Artists do so by displaying or collecting their finished works. This collection of works is called a *portfolio*. Professional writers also keep writing portfolios. Writers who hope to land a job writing for an advertising agency, for instance, submit portfolios of their writing.

You can start your own writing portfolio by gathering examples of your previous writing in a folder. Reflect on your writing process by adding a process report to your portfolio; that is, add a short list of your writing strengths, weaknesses, and plans for improvement.

Writing Process Report

Date:

Strengths:

Weaknesses:

Plans for improvement:

Once you complete your process report, freewrite in your journal on what you now know about your writing process and what you still hope to learn.

Chapter Summary

- There are five stages in the writing process:
  —gathering ideas
  —drafting
  —revising
  —editing
  —publishing
- The writing process is recursive; that is, you often need to go back and forth among the stages.
- The techniques for gathering ideas include:

  —journal writing   —reading
  —brainstorming   —interviewing
  —freewriting   —relating aloud
  —clustering   —reflecting
  —questioning

- As you prepare to write, consider your purpose and audience.
- When you draft, focus on getting your ideas down on paper. Use an effective thesis statement as a guide.
- When you revise, aim to improve your writing and to communicate your ideas effectively and clearly.
- Skilled writers usually revise a draft several times.
- You edit your writing to eliminate distracting errors in grammar, spelling, and punctuation, which if left uncorrected may prevent your reader from focusing on your message
- You publish your finished work by sharing it with others.
- A computer can make the writing process easier, but it is not a substitute for brainpower or careful editing.

II
Writing about Your World

Expressive Writing

Informative Writing

Persuasive Writing

Portfolios

Writing provides you with a permanent record of your thoughts and ideas, your feelings and decisions. Writing also allows you to communicate with others and to share what you know in ways that entertain, inform, and persuade.

In Part II, you will learn how to improve your writing in many ways. You'll experiment with different methods for gathering ideas and practice writing discovery drafts. You'll learn revision techniques for developing and organizing your ideas. You'll develop skill in editing and perhaps use a computer to help you write. You'll also have many opportunities to write about topics that interest you and to share those interests with others. Finally, you'll compile a writing portfolio of your best work.

Good families are fortresses with many windows and doors to the outer world.
— JANE HOWARD

4

Family Connections

In this chapter you will

- write about a family photograph, story, or ritual.

- brainstorm, freewrite, and cluster to gather ideas about your topic.

- use detailed observations, sensory description, and dialogue to enliven your writing.

- learn how to organize a descriptive essay.

- learn how to organize a narrative essay.

Different cultures tend to define the concept of family in different ways. In America in the 1950s, for example, family was usually limited to the nuclear family—that is, parents and children. We saw the nuclear family in such television shows as *Leave It to Beaver* and *Father Knows Best*. Today family is defined in many different ways: as single parents and their children, as stepparents and stepchildren, as grandparents raising grandchildren. Even close friends are sometimes considered family. In Israel many people live on a kibbutz, a kind of communal farm where work and child-rearing are done together. Though not related by blood, the people of a kibbutz function as an extended family. The Navajos in the southwestern United States have extended families, or clans, which consist of ancestors, grandparents, and cousins in addition to parents and children.

But who we include as part of our family isn't as important as the significance that our family has in our lives. Don Juan, the philosopher in Carlos Castaneda's *Journey to Ixtlan*, said of his family: "I had a terribly strong attachment to my personal history. My family roots were deep. I honestly felt that without them my life had no continuity or purpose." Like Castaneda, many of us feel grounded in our families no matter how we define the concept.

ACTIVITY
1

Analyzing Your Purpose and Audience. Before you begin gathering ideas about your topic, think about your purpose and audience. For this chapter's assignment, you'll explore an aspect of your family. Your audience includes your classmates and instructor. Your responses to the following questions will help you decide how to approach your topic.

1. Does this assignment call for expressive, informative, or persuasive writing?

   _____

2. What is your reader's average age? _____

3. How many are female? _____ male? _____

4. What parts of the country or world are they from? _____

   _____

   _____

Writing Assignment

This chapter offers you three opportunities to explore the significance of family in your life: by describing a family photograph, by telling a family story, and by narrating a family ritual. You, your class, or your instructor may decide to do this assignment in one of several ways:

- You may gather ideas on one, two, *or* three topics.
- Then, you may write a discovery draft on one, two, *or* three of these topics.
- You may choose one discovery draft to develop into a polished essay.
- Or, you may combine your discovery draft ideas into a new topic for your essay.

After completing your essay, share it with your instructor, classmates, and (if you wish) family members.

5. What, if anything, do you know about their families? How many are married? How many have children? How many live on their own or live with family members (such as parents)?

_____

_____

_____

Given your responses to the preceding questions, ask yourself these questions:

6. What do my readers know about my topic? _____

_____

_____

_____

7. What information do I *not* have to give them? _____

_____

_____

_____

8. What do my readers need to know about my topic? _____

_____

_____

_____

9. How do my readers feel about my topic? Will they find it interesting, or will I have to work to get their attention?

_____

_____

_____

❏

Gathering Ideas

In Chapter Three, you learned about the various strategies for gathering ideas about a writing topic. For this chapter's assignment, you'll use brainstorming, freewriting, and clustering to prepare yourself for writing a discovery draft.

Family Photographs

Photographs can convey powerful emotions and meanings. Think of the photo of John F. Kennedy, Jr. saluting his father's funeral procession. It captures the mood of the nation at that time. Family photographs can be just as powerful, illustrating truths of family life that we might not otherwise know.

Nancy Friday, in her autobiography *My Mother/My Self*, describes a family photograph this way:

> I have a photo of the three of us when I was twelve: my mother, my sister Susie, and I on a big chintz sofa, each with a separate cushion, leaning away from one another with big spaces in between. I

grew up fired with a sense of family spirit, which I loved and needed, with aunts and uncles and cousins under the omnipotent umbrella of my grandfather. "All for one and one for all," he would say at summer reunions, and no one took it more seriously than I. I would have gone to war for any one of them, and believed they would do the same for me. But within our own little nucleus, the three of us didn't touch much.

Nancy Friday's photograph shows not just her mother, her sister, and herself, but also the emotional distance between them. Most photographs are much more than pictures of people and objects. They represent significant events, objects, and relationships.

The following reading about a family is from *Having Our Say* by Sadie Delany and Bessie Delany, who were 103 and 101 years old, respectively, when the book was written in 1993.

SADIE DELANY AND BESSIE DELANY

Saint Aug's

Our Mama was always a bit embarrassed that her parents were   *1*
not—could not have been—legally married. She was determined that she was going to have a legal marriage someday, or not get married at all! Virginia was a much more conservative state about these things than North Carolina, and that may have figured into her decision to go to college at Saint Aug's, in Raleigh, and leave Virginia behind.

She got her pick of beaus at Saint Aug's, and it didn't matter to   *2*
her in the least that her favorite was a lot darker than she was. Some colored women who were as light as Mama would not have gotten involved with a dark-skinned man, but Mama didn't care. She said he was the cream of the crop, a man of the highest quality. Oh, Mama was a smart woman. It takes a smart woman to fall in love with a good man.

Our Papa felt the same way about her, but he was told at gradua-   *3*
tion time by his advisers that he should not marry, at least not yet. Now that he was educated, they hoped to see him devote himself to the ministry before starting a family. But Papa ignored this advice. He never looked for a fight, but he always managed to do what he wanted, in such a pleasant way that folks could not get mad at him. He took the train home to Fernandina Beach, Florida, after graduation and told his parents he had met the woman he wanted to marry. They presented him with an illustrated Bible in which he wrote: "Given to Henry Beard Delany by his parents upon graduating from college." Then, he took the train back to Raleigh and he and Miss Logan were married at the chapel at Saint Aug's on the sixth of October 1886.

Lemuel Thackara Delany, their firstborn, arrived the next year,   *4*
on September 12, 1887. He was named after the white Episcopal

priest who helped Papa go to college. Every two years after Lemuel's birth, there was a new baby: Sadie in 1889, Bessie in 1891, Julia Emery in 1893, Henry Jr. (Harry) in 1895, Lucius in 1897, William Manross in 1899, Hubert Thomas in 1901, Laura Edith in 1903, and Samuel Ray in 1906. Laura is the only one besides us that is still living. She is our baby sister and lives in California. All of our brothers and our sister Julia have gone on to Glory.

Every child was named for somebody. Sadie (Sarah Louise) was named for her two grandmas. And Bessie (Annie Elizabeth) was named for Dr. Anna J. Cooper.* Our parents counted Dr. Cooper as a close family friend, and she was known to them as Annie. They met when Dr. Cooper was a teacher at Saint Augustine's School.

*Dr. Anna J. Cooper (1858–1964) was an educator and early advocate of higher education for black women. She was a graduate of St. Augustine's School and Oberlin College, and received a doctorate from the University of Paris in 1925. She received national recognition for her work as principal of M Street High School, for years the only academic high school for Negroes in Washington, D.C.

When Saint Aug's was founded after the Civil War, it was both a   6
seminary and a school for teachers. A family by the name of Smedes
founded Saint Aug's as a school for Negroes and another Episcopal
school for whites, Saint Mary's, on the other side of town. Mama remembered one of the Smedes brothers. She said he used to ride up
to the school on his horse, and he would get down and take off his
hat and bow to the ground at the feet of the students at Saint Aug's
with his hat almost touching the ground. Mama said it was a strange
sight, a white man bowing to these colored students!

Many fine, young colored people graduated from Saint Aug's   7
and went on to share what they had learned with countless others.
Growing up in this atmosphere, among three hundred or so college
students, reading and writing and thinking was as natural for us as
sleeping and eating. We had a blessed childhood, which was unusual in those days for colored children. It was the rare child that
got such schooling!

But since we were girls, our every move was chaperoned. All lit-   8
tle girls and young women were chaperoned in those days. That's
because things hadn't improved much since slavery days as far as
the right of colored women and girls to be unmolested. If something
bad had been done to us, and our Papa had complained, they'd have
hung *him*. That's the way it was.

Our family lived right on the campus. We were not allowed to go   9
off the campus without an escort. Matter of fact, we were not allowed
to go to certain places *on* the campus without someone to go with us.
If it wasn't our Mama or Papa, the escort was one of the teachers at
Saint Aug's or very often Papa's Cousin Laura from Florida. Papa called
Cousin Laura, "Cousin Lot." As children, we shortened that to "Culot."

Poor Culot was a seamstress who had had a miserable job in   10
Florida, working for some white lady. The white lady made a lot of
money, and Culot got next to nothing and did all the work. You
know, one of those deals. So, Culot had joined up with a convent in
Baltimore, but left when she found out that the way those sisters
raised money was to beg in the streets. She couldn't stand it. So our
Papa got her a job teaching sewing at Saint Aug's, where she stayed
until she was a very old woman, when she went back to Fernandina
to die. She never worked for white folks again.

Culot took her job as our escort very, very seriously. She looked   11
after us like an old watchdog, and Lord help anyone who came near
us. We used to work in the fields that belonged to the school and
chop cotton to make a little money for ourselves, and Culot would
be sitting under a tree, with one eye on her sewing and the other
eye on us—at the same time, yes, sir!

The farm on the campus of Saint Aug's provided food for the   12
staff and students, and it also gave the poorest students a way to pay
their tuition and expenses because they could work in the fields and

get paid a small amount. Every free chance we got, we worked in those fields to get a little money. Sometimes, they couldn't pay us, because they ran out of money at the school.

Of the two of us, Bessie was the champion cotton-picker. Sadie *13* could pick one hundred pounds of cotton in a day as a teenager, which was a most respectable amount, but Bessie could pick two hundred pounds, which was more than most men. It didn't take brute strength to pick cotton. Women were generally faster pickers than men, especially if they were wiry and agile like Bessie.

Culot was a maiden lady with no children of her own, and she *14* liked to spoil us sometimes, so she would take us on the trolley car to Johnson's drugstore for a limeade, or bring back some candy when she went downtown by herself. Funny thing about Culot is that she never could make a decision. She would tell us, now clean out my dresser drawer and throw most of it out while I am downtown, but *don't ever tell me what you threw away.* And we'd do it. She just couldn't stand to throw anything away herself. A lot of former slaves were like that—they'd never owned anything, so they hung on to all kinds of junk they didn't know what to do with.

Of course, there were many people still alive then who had *15* been slaves—including our Papa. Most of these former slaves were down on their luck. Papa used to say that they didn't know how to live free, especially the ones that had been treated badly. Our parents thought it was their responsibility to treat these former slaves with courtesy and kindness, and with the dignity those folks had been denied by others.

ACTIVITY

2

Reading to Improve Writing. Discuss the following questions about "Saint Aug's" with your classmates.

1. What do you learn in the reading about the Delany family and the society in which they lived?

2. How do the authors use description to depict Mama, Papa, and Culot?

_____

_____

3. Study the photograph of the Delany family on page 68. It was taken at the turn of this century. What does the photograph tell you about the family? How is the family arranged in the photo? What can you tell about the family members from the expressions on their faces? From the house in the background? From the fact that the family dog is included?

_____

_____

_____

_____

_____

Collecting New Words. Try to determine the meanings of the following words from the way they're used in "Saint Aug's." Then verify their meanings by checking a dictionary.

ACTIVITY
3

conservative (1) _____

beaus (2) _____

seminary (6) _____

chaperoned (8) _____

Brainstorming about a Family Photograph. Select one family photograph. It could be a photograph of you and members of your family, one that was taken before you were born, or one that includes a friend who is considered a member of your family. Or, if you cannot find a family photograph, choose a special object in your home that reveals something meaningful about your family, such as a diploma, a quilt, or a wedding dress. Then gather ideas about the family photograph or special object by brainstorming in your journal.

ACTIVITY
4

❏

Here's an example of how one student, Allen, brainstormed a list of ideas about a photograph of his grandfather.

carved stone statue

wrinkles

long nose

wisdom

shadowy eyes

wavy, grey hair

open mouth

funny eyebrows

old

sideburns

To gather more ideas about the photograph, Allen spent about fifteen minutes freewriting in his journal on the topic. (Because Allen concentrated only on getting his ideas down on paper, his freewriting contains some spelling and grammatical errors.)

The picture is an old yellow black and white photo of a man. Their he stands with his coat and tie, leaning to the right. His facial expression is unlike anyone else. His head is perfectly angled to the right. His head is square with his chin flat and firm, like a carved stone statue. His mouth is slightly opened, with one wrinkle at each end of the mouth. His nose is rather long. The eyebrows are thick and short, but not bushy, like something funny out of a comic strip. The forehead is more noticeable than anything else, its both long and wide. Judging from his forehead alone, he seems to be a man of great knowledge. His hair is both wavy and gray, on the sides and top of his head. Judging from the look in his eyes, his bold face and combed hair, He seems to be a man of great importance in this world, or certainly in my life. Yet I have never met this great man, for he died long before I was born. My grandfather really haunts me. And as I look upon this picture I feel a great pride in him and in myself.

ACTIVITY
5

Freewriting about a Family Photograph. Freewrite in your journal about your family photograph or special object. Then read your freewriting aloud to several classmates, asking them to identify what they find most interesting about the photograph or object as well as what they want to know more about. Finally, do some more freewriting, but this time focus it on an idea raised by your classmates. ❏

Put your material about a family photograph or object aside for now. You want to explore ideas about another aspect of families—family stories. This is another possible topic for your essay.

Family Stories

What family stories were you told as a child? Did you hear stories about how your parents, grandparents, and great-grandparents met and married? About your father's journey across the country or your mother's first job? Why do you think you were told stories about your family?

Amy Tan writes about family stories in her book *The Joy Luck Club*. In the excerpt that follows, "Double Face," Lindo Jong tells her daughter the story of how she became engaged.

AMY TAN

Double Face

So that is how I met An-mei Hsu. Yes, Yes, Auntie An-mei, now   *1*
so old-fashioned. An-mei and I still laugh over those bad fortunes and how they later became quite useful in helping me catch a husband.

"Eh, Lindo," An-mei said to me one day at our workplace.   *2*
"Come to my church this Sunday. My husband has a friend who is looking for a good Chinese wife. He is not a citizen, but I'm sure he knows how to make one." So that is how I first heard about Tin Jong, your father. It was not like my first marriage, where everything was arranged. I had a choice. I could choose to marry your father, or I could choose not to marry him and go back to China.

I knew something was not right when I saw him: He was Can-   *3*
tonese! How could An-mei think I could marry such a person? But she just said: "We are not in China anymore. You don't have to marry the village boy. Here everybody is now from the same village even if they come from different parts of China." See how changed Auntie An-mei is from those old days.

So we were shy at first, your father and I, neither of us able to   *4*
speak to each other in our Chinese dialects. We went to English class

together, speaking to each other in those new words and sometimes taking out a piece of paper to write a Chinese character to show what we meant. At least we had that, a piece of paper to hold us together. But it's hard to tell someone's marriage intentions when you can't say things aloud. All those little signs—the teasing, the bossy, scolding words—that's how you know if it is serious. But we could talk only in the manner of our English teacher. I see cat. I see rat. I see hat.

But I saw soon enough how much your father liked me. He would pretend he was in a Chinese play to show me what he meant. He ran back and forth, jumped up and down, pulling his fingers through his hair, so I knew—*mangjile!*—what a busy, exciting place this Pacific Telephone was, this place where he worked. You didn't know this about your father—that he could be such a good actor? You didn't know your father had so much hair? 5

Oh, I found out later his job was not the way he described it. It was not so good. Even today, now that I can speak Cantonese to your father, I always ask him why he doesn't find a better situation. But he acts as if we were in those old days, when he couldn't understand anything I said. 6

Sometimes I wonder why I wanted to catch a marriage with your father. I think An-mei put the thought in my mind. She said, "In the movies, boys and girls are always passing notes in class. That's how they fall into trouble. You need to start trouble to get this man to realize his intentions. Otherwise, you will be an old lady before it comes to his mind." 7

That evening An-mei and I went to work and searched through strips of fortune cookie papers, trying to find the right instructions to give to your father. An-mei read them aloud, putting aside ones that might work: "Diamonds are a girl's best friend. Don't ever settle for a pal." "If such thoughts are in your head, it's time to be wed." "Confucius say a woman is worth a thousand words. Tell your wife she's used up her total." 8

We laughed over those. But I knew the right one when I read it. It said: "A house is not home when a spouse is not at home." I did not laugh. I wrapped up this saying in a pancake, bending the cookie with all my heart. 9

After school the next afternoon, I put my hand in my purse and then made a look, as if a mouse had bitten my hand. "What's this?" I cried. Then I pulled out the cookie and handed it to your father. "Eh! So many cookies, just to see them makes me sick. You take this cookie." 10

I knew even then he had a nature that did not waste anything. He opened the cookie and he crunched it in his mouth, and then read the piece of paper. 11

"What does it say?" I asked. I tried to act as if it did not matter. And when he still did not speak, I said, "Translate, please." 12

We were walking in Portsmouth Square and already the fog had   *13*
blown in and I was very cold in my thin coat. So I hoped your father
would hurry and ask me to marry him. But instead, he kept his serious look and said, "I don't know this word 'spouse.' Tonight I will
look in my dictionary. Then I can tell you the meaning tomorrow."

The next day he asked me in English, "Lindo, can you spouse me?"   *14*
And I laughed at him and said he used that word incorrectly. So he
came back and made a Confucius joke, that if the words were wrong,
then his intentions must also be wrong. We scolded and joked with each
other all day long like this, and that is how we decided to get married.

Reading to Improve Writing. Discuss the following questions
about "Double Face" with your classmates.

ACTIVITY
6

1. What three words best describe the relationship between Lindo and
    her future husband?

    _____

2. Why does Lindo tell this story to her daughter? _____

    _____

    _____

    _____

3. How does the writer's use of dialogue add interest to the story?

    _____

    _____

    _____

Collecting New Words. Try to determine the meanings of the following words from the way they're used in "Double Face." Then verify their meanings by checking a dictionary.

ACTIVITY
7

dialect (4)   _____

character (4)   _____

intentions (4) _____

scolding (4) _____

situation (6) _____

spouse (9) _____

ACTIVITY
8

 Brainstorming about Family Stories. In your journal, brainstorm about some of the family stories you were told as a child. Or, if you can't remember any family stories, try brainstorming stories about your life that you would want to tell your own children. In either case, structure your ideas in a chart. Set up the chart in three columns, identifying each story, who told you the story, and why you think you were told the story. If you are telling a story about your own life, identify the story, who you would tell it to, and why you would tell it. Here's an example of a brainstorming chart:

Story	Who Told It	Why It Was Told
My father stealing money from his brother	My father	Don't steal.
My aunt running away from home	My mother	Don't marry too young.
My parents' wedding	My grandmother Anna	Being nervous is okay.
My great-grandparents' life before they came to the United States	My grandmother Grace	Remember my heritage.

❑

For one student, Brian, listening to family stories is one of his favorite childhood memories. After brainstorming a chart of family stories, Brian decided to write about a story his grandmother used to tell. To explore his ideas, he did some freewriting. Here's the first part:

> *My grandparents used to tell me stories in order to continue the family traditions. This would happen when I spent a weekend with them, because we lived about three hundred miles away. Both grandparents told their stories in Navajo. I can't speak my own language very well, but I understand it. After dinner we would sit in the living room which was cozy warm from the burning fireplace. My grandma would put her hand around me and tell me about her girlhood. Some of her favorite stories were about weaving.*
>
> *Among the Navajos, it was the girls and women who kept the sheep and made the looms and did the weaving. The looms were very wide, and working on them was a skill that took a long time to learn. The weaving was very dense, so the blankets were warm and rain-proof. All the patterns and colors meant something.*

Freewriting about a Family Story. Just as Brian did, freewrite in your journal about a family story that you want to share with others. Also tell why the story is important to you. For instance, the story told by Brian's grandmother helps Brian remember his heritage.

ACTIVITY
9

Read your freewriting aloud to several classmates, asking them what they find most interesting and what they want to know more about. Jot down their responses so you can refer to them when you write your draft. ❑

Now, put away your writing about a family story so you can gather ideas about another aspect of your family.

Family Rituals

Like family photographs and family stories, family rituals teach us about our families. Rituals are ceremonies and activities performed in the same way over and over again. Graduation from school is a ritual, with its special dress (cap and gown), music ("Pomp and Circumstance"), and treasured piece of paper (diploma). The presidential inauguration is also a ritual, with its swearing-in ceremony, inaugural address, and parade to the White House.

Families have rituals, too. Often these rituals involve meals, such as birthday celebrations, family picnics, and Sunday suppers.

In "Papa's Ritual," educator Leo Buscaglia writes about his father's dinnertime ritual.

Leo Buscaglia

Papa's Ritual

Papa had natural wisdom. He wasn't educated in the formal sense. When he was growing up at the turn of the century in a very small village in rural northern Italy, education was for the rich. Papa was the son of a dirt-poor farmer. He used to tell us that he never remembered a single day of his life when he wasn't working. The concept of doing nothing was never a part of his life. In fact, he couldn't fathom it. How could one do nothing? 1

He was taken from school when he was in the fifth grade, over the protestations of his teacher and the village priest, both of whom saw him as a young person with great potential for formal learning. Papa went to work in a factory in a nearby village, the very same village where, years later, he met Mama. 2

For Papa, the world became his school. He was interested in everything. He read all the books, magazines, and newspapers he could lay his hands on. He loved to gather with people and listen to the town elders and learn about "the world beyond" this tiny, insular region that was home to generations of Buscaglias before him. Papa's great respect for learning and his sense of wonder about the outside world were carried across the sea with him and later passed on to his family. He was determined that none of his children would be denied an education if he could help it. 3

Papa believed that the greatest sin of which we were capable was to go to bed at night as ignorant as we had been when we awakened that day. This credo was repeated so often that none of us could fail to be affected by it. "There is so much to learn," he'd remind us. "Though we're born stupid, only the stupid remain that way." To ensure that none of his children ever fell into the trap of complacency, he insisted that we learn at least one new thing each day. He felt that there could be no fact too insignificant, that each bit of learning made us more of a person and insured us against boredom and stagnation. 4

So Papa devised a ritual. Since dinnertime was family time and everyone came to dinner unless they were dying of malaria, it seemed the perfect forum for sharing what new things we had learned that day. Of course, as children we thought this was perfectly crazy. There was no doubt, when we compared such paternal concerns with other children's fathers, Papa was weird. 5

It would never have occurred to us to deny Papa a request. So 6 when my brother and sisters and I congregated in the bathroom to clean up for dinner, the inevitable question was, "What did *you* learn today?" If the answer was "Nothing," we didn't dare sit at the table without first finding a fact in our much-used encyclopedia. "The population of Nepal is . . . ," etc.

Now, thoroughly clean and armed with our fact for the day, we were ready for dinner. I can still see the table piled high with mountains of food. So large were the mounds of pasta that as a boy I was often unable to see my sister sitting across from me. (The pungent aromas were such that, over a half century later, even in memory they cause me to salivate.)   7

Dinner was a noisy time of clattering dishes and endless activity. It was also a time to review the activities of the day. Our animated conversations were always conducted in Piedmontese dialect since Mama didn't speak English. The events we recounted, no matter how insignificant, were never taken lightly. Mama and Papa always listened carefully and were ready with some comment, often profound and analytical, always right to the point.   8

"That was the smart thing to do." "*Stupido,* how could you be so dumb?" "*Così sia,* you deserved it." "*E allora,* no one is perfect." "*Testa dura* ('hardhead'), you should have known better. Didn't we teach you anything?" "Oh, that's nice." One dialogue ended and immediately another began. Silent moments were rare at our table.   9

Then came the grand finale to every meal, the moment we dreaded most—the time to share the day's new learning. The mental imprint of those sessions still runs before me like a familiar film clip, vital and vivid.   10

Papa, at the head of the table, would push his chair back slightly, a gesture that signified the end of the eating and suggested that there would be a new activity. He would pour a small glass of red wine, light up a thin, potent Italian cigar, inhale deeply, exhale, then take stock of his family.   11

For some reason this always had a slightly unsettling effect on us as we stared back at Papa, waiting for him to say something. Every so often he would explain why he did this. He told us that if he didn't take time to look at us, we would soon be grown and he would have missed us. So he'd stare at us, one after the other.   12

Finally, his attention would settle upon one of us. "*Felice,*" he would say to me, "tell me what you learned today."   13

"I learned that the population of Nepal is . . ."   14

Silence.   15

It always amazed me, and reinforced my belief that Papa was a little crazy, that nothing I ever said was considered too trivial for him. First, he'd think about what was said as if the salvation of the world depended upon it.   16

"The population of Nepal. Hmmm. Well."   17

He would then look down the table at Mama, who would be rit- *18*
ualistically fixing her favorite fruit in a bit of leftover wine. "Mama,
did you know that?"

Mama's responses were always astonishing and seemed to *19*
lighten the otherwise reverential atmosphere. "Nepal," she'd say.
"Nepal? Not only don't I know the population of Nepal, I don't
know where in God's world it is!" Of course, this was only playing
into Papa's hands.

"*Felice*," he'd say. "Get the atlas so we can show Mama where *20*
Nepal is." And the search began. The whole family went on a search
for Nepal. This same experience was repeated until each family
member had a turn. No dinner at our house ever ended without our
having been enlightened by at least a half dozen such facts.

As children, we thought very little about these educational won- *21*
ders and even less about how we were being enriched. We couldn't
have cared less. We were too impatient to have dinner end so we could
join our less-educated friends in a rip-roaring game of kick the can.

In retrospect, after years of studying how people learn, I realize *22*
what a dynamic educational technique Papa was offering us, rein-
forcing the value of continual learning. Without being aware of it,
our family was growing together, sharing experiences, and partici-
pating in one another's education. Papa was, without knowing it,
giving us an education in the most real sense.

By looking at us, listening to us, hearing us, respecting our opin- *23*
ions, affirming our value, giving us a sense of dignity, he was un-
questionably our most influential teacher.

I decided upon a career in teaching fairly early in my college *24*
years. During my training, I studied with some of the most
renowned educators in the country. When I finally emerged from
academia, having been generously endowed with theory and jargon
and technique, I discovered, to my great amusement, that the professional educators were imparting what Papa had known all along.
He knew there was no greater wonder than the human capacity to
learn, that no particle of knowledge was too insignificant not to
have the power to change us for the better. "How long we live is
limited," Papa said, "but how much we learn is not. What we learn
is what we are. No one should miss out on an education."

Papa was a successful educator. His technique worked and has *25*
served me well all my life. Now, when I get home, often exhausted
after a long working day's adventure, before my head hits the pillow
I hear Papa's voice resound clearly in my room. "*Felice*," he asks,
"what did you learn today?"

On some days I can't recall even one new thing I have learned. *26*
I'm surprised at how often this is the case (since most of us move in
a world of the familiar and are too preoccupied to be bothered or

challenged by the unfamiliar). I get myself out of bed and scan the bookshelves to find something new. Then, with that accomplished, Papa and I can rest soundly, assured that a day has not been wasted. After all, one never can tell when knowing the population of Nepal may prove to be a very useful bit of information.

Reading to Improve Writing. Discuss the following questions about "Papa's Ritual" with your classmates.

ACTIVITY
10

1. Why does Papa value learning? _____

   _____

   _____

2. What does the author learn about education as a result of his family's dinnertime ritual?

   _____

   _____

3. How does the author use description and dialogue to convey his message?

   _____

   _____

   _____

Collecting New Words. Try to determine the meanings of the following words from the way they're used in "Papa's Ritual." Then verify their meanings by checking a dictionary.

ACTIVITY
11

fathom (1)   _____

protestations (2) _____

credo (4)   _____

complacency (4) _____

stagnation (4)   _____

pungent (7)   _____

imprint (10)   _____

potent (11)   _____

dynamic (22)   _____

jargon (24)   _____

ACTIVITY
12   **Clustering about a Family Ritual.** Try clustering some ideas about your family's rituals. Write the topic—family rituals—in the middle of a blank page in your journal. Circle the topic, and begin adding ideas that branch out from it. One student, Caroline, produced the cluster shown in Figure 4-1 on page 83.

If you can't think of a ritual in your family, make a cluster about a ritual that you would like your family to follow.   ❑

After Caroline completed her cluster of ideas, she decided to do some freewriting about her family's birthday dinner ritual. Here is her freewriting. (It contains some errors because she concentrated on getting down her ideas.) Notice, in the last two sentences, how Caroline explains the importance of the ritual to her family.

I always work hard to make my children's birthdays special. The gifts aren't that special, but the celebration is. My mother is always in charge of baking the cake the day before. She bakes the kind of cake that the birthday child wants. Louise always wants a yellow cake with coconut frosting, for some reason. Anyway, I always make a big dinner, whatever the birthday child wants. So it's never very nutricious. Then we turn out the lights and the boys light the candles (some day they'll burn the house down) and I carry in the cake and everyone sings while my husband takes pictures.

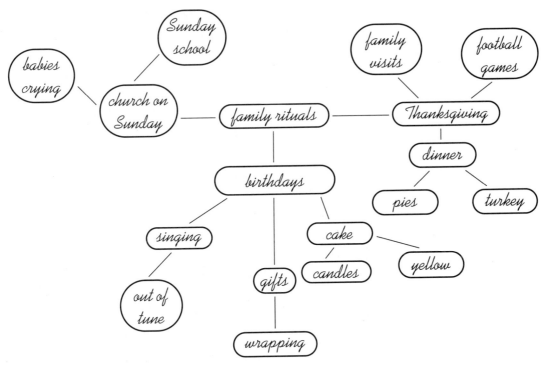

Figure 4-1. Caroline's Cluster Diagram

*I'm proud of the way we make a big deal about birth-
days. It makes the children feel special, even if they might
not receive very fancy gifts. It's how our family shows love.*

Freewriting about a Family Ritual. Look over your cluster of
ideas about family rituals. Choose one ritual that you'd like others to
know about. Then freewrite about that family ritual in your journal.
Include as many thoughts and details about the ritual as you can.

ACTIVITY
13

Read your freewriting aloud to your classmates. Compare and
contrast your family's ritual with those of your classmates' families.
Discuss what the rituals mean to each family. ❑

Drafting

You've now gathered ideas on three aspects of your family—a
family photograph or special object, a family story, and a family rit-

ual. You thus have a rich source of material for writing, but you need to decide how to proceed. Here are some of your options:

- You may select one of the three topics for your discovery draft.

- You may write drafts on two or three of the topics to see which one you prefer to continue working on.

- You may combine related topics in your discovery draft. For example, you might describe a family photograph that depicts a family ritual.

To prepare for writing your discovery draft, look over the material you have gathered thus far and highlight the ideas you want to use in your draft. Write a preliminary thesis statement, keeping in mind that you may revise it as you continue to write. If you find that you don't have enough ideas to start drafting, repeat the strategies you used for gathering ideas or use others that you learned in Chapter Three. You might also reread the three essays on family in this chapter to see how other writers approach the topic. Keep your audience and purpose in mind, but remember that your main goal at the drafting stage is to get your ideas down on paper. You'll have time later on to revise and edit your discovery draft.

When you begin to write, remind yourself that you're still discovering your ideas, not producing a finished essay. Therefore, don't worry yet about *how* you express your ideas. Concentrate instead on *what* you want to communicate to your audience.

As you write this draft, you might find that your thoughts take you in an unexpected direction. Follow the path that seems most interesting to you. When you write a discovery draft, you aim to explore possibilities rather than follow a map that's already been drawn.

Here's an example of a discovery draft written by a student, Alicia Gomez. After reading the draft, discuss with your classmates what Alicia might do to revise it. (Note that the example includes the types of errors that typically appear in a first draft.)

Breaking Away

Picture this, my entire family is gathered at my grandmother's house.   *1*
The women are in the kitchen preparing salsa, beans, and tortillas, while the men stand around the grill cooking the meat and talking about sports. When the food is ready, the men eat first, and the women wait on them before they sit down to eat with the children. Afterwards, the men go to one side of the patio and the women to the other.

It's quite unfair how after the women prepare the meal on special occa-   *2*
sions the men sit down first to devour the food without a sign of gratitude. While they eat the women are waiting hand and foot, tending to the men's every need. The women feel that it is their role as a wife and mother to serve

their families before themselves. It has always been part of the Mexican culture that women tend to others before they tend to their own welfare.

I once asked my grandmother why the men ate first, and she said that   *3*
the men have bigger appetites than the women. This also meant that the women and children received what was left over. I started to feel contempt toward the men and especially the women because they don't have the courage to stand up for themselves or to change.

Many women of Mexican culture have low self esteem because they   *4*
never had as children what they have here in America and that is opportunity. The opportunity to become successful individuals. For instance, when I decided to become a doctor my grandmother said I'd never succeed. I don't want those words to rule my life. I must change the attitudes and the old ways of my family, but we can't because it's a ritual that the women serve the men. Even though we can't change the ritual, it's a good idea for the younger generation to bring new ways to the family.

Revising

When you revise a discovery draft, you focus not only on *what* you want to communicate to your audience, but also on *how* you communicate it. In this stage, then, you concentrate on such tasks as adding detailed observations, sensory description, and dialogue to enliven your writing.

As you learned in Chapter Three, writers often move back and forth among the stages of the writing process. Thus, it's possible that as you revise you might need to return to the gathering ideas stage. After you've gathered enough ideas, you can go back to revising.

> **COMPUTER TIP**
> **NUMBER YOUR DRAFTS**
> Since you'll probably revise your draft several times, number each draft so you'll know which one is the latest version.

Adding Supporting Details

When you wrote your discovery draft, you probably did as Alicia did—simply told the story as you remembered it. Now, as you revise, you want to add details to make your piece interesting and memorable. The key is to go beyond describing experiences in general ways ("We had a great time; that day really changed me") to describing them in enough detail that your readers relive those moments with you.

Writers use supporting details in their writing to:

• increase interest.

• help the reader understand their thoughts.

• support their main ideas.

There are several types of supporting details that you may consider using in your essay:

- *Detailed observations* provide specific details about what happened and why.

- *Sensory description* creates images by describing how something looks, sounds, smells, tastes, or feels.

- *Dialogue* reports the exact words that people say to each other.

Notice how one writer, Benjamin Alíre Saenz, improves the following paragraph from his short story "Ceballeros" by adding supporting details in the revised version:

ORIGINAL

He was getting good grades in everything except chemistry. And the teacher hated him. His brother wrote to him and told him to calm down, told him everything would be all right.

REVISED

He was getting good grades in everything except chemistry. If he didn't pass, he'd have to go to summer school because it was a required course. All those good grades, and it had come down to this. He was a borderline student in that class and he knew it, but there wasn't any time. There wasn't any time.

And the teacher hated him. He could feel the teacher's hatred, the blue-eyed wrestling coach who favored athletes and nice-looking girls.

His brother wrote to him and told him to calm down, told him everything would be all right. "Just graduate and go to college. Do whatever it takes, just don't join the army."

Detailed observation added

Sensory description added

Dialogue added

Detailed Observations. To add detailed observations, start with a general statement and add details to make it more specific. Use the journalists' questions given in Chapter Three.

- *Who* is involved?

- *What* happens?

- *When* and *where* does it happen?

- *Why* does it happen?

- *How* does it happen?

Here's an example of a general statement to which detailed observations have been added.

ORIGINAL

My cousin's wedding was really beautiful.

REVISED

My cousin Veronica's wedding took place in the flower garden of Haven Park on a sunny June day. Veronica and Samuel took their vows surrounded by red, pink, and yellow roses. In addition to the three bridesmaids and the best man, my four-year-old son, Jason, was the ring bearer. I've never seen Jason smile so much. Other family members were both smiling and crying. My aunt Liz had tears streaming down her face as she watched Veronica and Sam enter the garden arm-in-arm. Even my uncle Albert, usually so stern, had tears in his eyes.

Sensory Description. To add sensory description, focus on the five senses of sight, sound, taste, touch, and smell. You might have already used the sense of sight in your draft to describe what something looks like. But how many of the other senses did you use?

One way to go about adding sensory description is to make a chart of the five senses. For example, suppose you're revising an essay about your family's annual picnic. This is how you described the picnic in your draft:

> We always spread the tablecloths on the grass and eat until we're stuffed. My favorites are the fried chicken, watermelon, and ice cream. We're so busy eating we don't even notice the mosquitos.

Because the picnic is the centerpiece of your essay, you realize that you need to describe it more vividly. To help you do this, you list the five senses and brainstorm these ideas:

Sight
red-and-white tablecloth
bright blue sky
grandfather's lined face

Sound
chattering birds
children noisily eating

Taste
sweet, crunchy watermelon
cold ice cream
tangy lemonade

Touch
prickly grass
greasy chicken
sweat on my face

Smell
barbecued chicken
insect repellent

Finally, here's your revised paragraph with the sensory details added:

> I can feel the prickly grass under the red-and-white tablecloth, and my face is wet with sweat from the sun. But I don't care because I'm happy to be with my family at our annual picnic. I fondly examine my grandfather's lined face and wise eyes as he proudly observes his large family. The children noisily eat sweet, crunchy watermelon, their faces red with juice that their parents try to wipe off. The aroma of barbecued chicken blends with the pungent insect repellent. Overhead, a flock of birds chatters in the bright blue sky.

Dialogue. Just as detailed observations and sensory description can enliven your writing, so can dialogue, which consists of the actual words that people say. Direct dialogue is indicated by quotation marks. Use dialogue when you want to highlight an important scene or portray a certain person.

You may recall Amy Tan's use of dialogue in "Double Face" earlier in this chapter. We overhear a conversation between Lindo and her future husband that makes us feel as if we are part of the story as it unfolds. Similarly, we feel like an accomplice to Lindo's trick as we read this paragraph:

> After school the next afternoon, I put my hand in my purse and then made a look, as if a mouse had bitten my hand. "What's this?" I cried. Then I pulled out the cookie and handed it to your father. "Eh! So many cookies, just to see them makes me sick. You take this cookie."

Dialogue is used effectively by Leo Buscaglia in "Papa's Ritual" as well. In fact, Papa's question—"*Felice*, what did you learn today?"— is probably the single most important line in the story. The writer tells us of its importance throughout his life.

Refer to pages 509 and 517–518 of the Handbook for guidelines on how to punctuate dialogue.

ACTIVITY
14

Adding Supporting Details. Add detailed observations, sensory description, and dialogue to make the following paragraphs more interesting and to convey the ideas within them more clearly.

1. The first time I babysat for my brother's children was a disaster. One of them kept throwing things around. The other one wouldn't stop crying. I was relieved when my brother and his wife returned home.

_____

_____

_____

_____

_____

_____

_____

_____

_____

2. I was so happy when the Little League team I coach won the city tournament. The final play was very suspenseful. The score was tied. The parents were probably more nervous than the players. But no one could have been happier than the kids when they won.

_____

_____

_____

_____

_____

_____

3. One of my favorite pastimes is backpacking in the mountains. I love the fresh air and the scenery. At night my friends and I lie awake and look up at the stars. One night we even saw a shooting star.

_____

_____

_____

_____

_____

_____

_____

❏

Organizing Descriptive Writing

You must organize your ideas. If you don't, your readers won't be able to follow what you're saying, they'll become frustrated, and they'll stop reading. There are two primary patterns of organization for descriptive writing: directional order and order of importance.

Directional Order. When you use *directional order*, you describe the direction of something, such as left to right, down to up, or near to far. For example, suppose you want to describe a photograph of your brother taken while he was in the Air Force. To organize your description, you might use top-to-bottom directional order, as in this example:

> This is my brother Antonio in his Air Force uniform. His face is clean-shaven, and his haircut is regulation-style. He's smiling his big lopsided smile. He has an athletic build, like a bodybuilder's. He wears his uniform proudly. It is perfectly pressed, and every brass button is perfectly shined. The crease in his pants is as sharp as a blade. His shoes are like black mirrors.

Order of Importance. Another way to organize a description is by *order of importance*. Here you arrange the details of your description from the least important to the most important or vice versa. Notice how the details about Antonio might be arranged using order of importance:

> My brother Antonio wears his Air Force uniform proudly. It is always perfectly pressed and every brass button perfectly shined. His shoes are like black mirrors, and the crease in his pants is as sharp as a blade. He has an athletic build, like that of a bodybuilder, and he's clean-shaven. His haircut is regulation-style. He's smiling his big lopsided smile.

Organizing Narrative Writing

A narrative, which tells a story, may be organized in one of two ways: in chronological order or by using the flashback technique.

Chronological Order. If you're writing about a family story or ritual, you can use *chronological order*, in which you relate the events in the order in which they actually happened. Imagine that you want to narrate a story about your family's ritual of taking a family photograph at the start of every new year. Here's how you might organize a paragraph using chronological order:

> On picture-taking day, we all rush around trying to get ourselves to look as good as possible for the camera. In the bathroom, my mother puts makeup on my stepfather's nose to hide the redness caused by a cold. I hear my stepsister tell them she refuses to be in the picture because her hair is too puffy. My brother rushes into the kitchen to clean up the grape juice he spilled on his shirt, while I look through the cupboards in the utility room for shoelaces. Finally, we're ready to make our trip to the photographer's studio.

Flashback. An alternative way to organize a narrative about a family story or ritual is to use a *flashback:* you begin the story in the middle, flash back to the beginning, and then resume telling the story in the middle again. You often see this technique used in movies, such as when the picture becomes fuzzy and a scene from an earlier time appears. The flashback technique is useful when you want to contrast then and now or highlight a key scene. Here's how the paragraph about the picture-taking ritual might be organized using the flashback technique:

> In the photograph, my family appears calm and relaxed. Our hair is perfectly combed, and our clothes are neatly pressed. The expressions on our faces seem calm and happy. But as I stare at the photograph, I recall the chaos that preceded the snap of the camera. My stepfather had such a terrible cold that my mother had to put makeup on his nose to cover the redness. My stepsister didn't want to be in the picture because her hair was too puffy. My brother had spilled grape juice on his shirt, and I had broken my shoelace. To make matters worse, we had a flat tire going to the studio. But when I look at this photograph, I know it was all worthwhile.

Organizing Your Essay. Which pattern of organization—directional, order of importance, chronological, or flashback—is best for your essay? If you're not sure, experiment with the four patterns. Which pattern most helps you organize and communicate your ideas? ❑

ACTIVITY
15

Alicia's Revised Draft

Before you read Alicia's revised draft, reread her discovery draft (on pp. 84–85). Notice, in particular, how the focus of Alicia's essay changes in the revision. Rather than simply describing her family's ritual, she now focuses on the meaning of the ritual and how it could sabotage her dreams. (You will notice some errors in the revised draft; they will be corrected when Alicia edits her essay later on.)

Breaking Away

Detailed observations added to make the introduction more interesting

Thesis is made clearer

Sensory description added

Chronological order is used throughout

Detailed observations and sensory description added

Dialogue added

Detailed observations added

1   Its a summertime ritual for my entire family to gather at my grandmother's house on Sundays for a barbecue. We eat spicy food, play loud music, laugh a lot, and exchange family news and gossip. Up until now, this ritual has made me feel closer to my family. After one barbecue, however, I felt totally seperate from them. I realized that to fulfill my dream of becoming a doctor I'd have to break out of the old-fashioned sex roles they believe in.

2   Grandmother's small house was as crowded and hot as a standing-room-only nightclub. Smoke filled the air, and swarms of flies searched for leftovers discarded by children. As usual, my family was following traditional male and female roles. The women, speaking Spanish at the rate of twenty words a second, were in the kitchen preparing the salsa, beans, and tortillas. While the men, with beers in their hands, stood around the grill cooking the meat and talking about sports.

3   I was excited because I'd just decided to become a doctor. I wanted my grandmother to be the first to know. I squeezed by my aunts, uncles, and cousins to make my way into the kitchen. Finally I had a chance to talk to my seventy-year-old grandmother alone. Who was cheerful as usual. She was cutting up black olives to put in the potato salad. She doesn't look her age. Maybe because she dies her hair or because she keeps up with all her grandchildren. But she's still old-fashioned and suffers from low self-esteem. She excepted her role as a Mexican woman to put her family first. In Mexico she never had the oppurtunities for school or career. After my grandfather's death, it was very difficult as a widow and a single mother of seven to give her children a better life.

4   Addressing my grandmother in Spanish, I said, "Grandma, I've decided I'm going to college to become a doctor."

5   She paused a few seconds, looked directly into my eyes and said, "Women should not become doctors."

6   I froze at those horrible words. I went out on the patio so she wouldn't see my tears. The men standing at the grill suddenly declared the meat was ready and sat down at the table. While the women hurriedly served them. My mother asked me to help serve the children.

7   I asked, "Mom, why is it that the men always eat first?"

She replied, "Because they have bigger appetites." Then she and the   *8*   **Dialogue added**
other women took care of the children while the men ate and talked, doing
absolutely nothing to help.

Its unfair how the women wait on the men and tend to their every need.   *9*
Mexican women can't fulfill their individual dreams because they don't believe they can be anything but wife and mother. The women in my family must
realize that I want to be more than a wife and mother. I don't want to be
caught in their trap.

Analyzing Alicia's Revised Draft. Use the following questions to
discuss with your classmates how Alicia improved her draft.

ACTIVITY
16

1. Is the purpose of Alicia's draft clear? What is that purpose?

_____

_____

_____

2. What is Alicia's thesis statement? Is it effective? Could it be im-
    proved?

_____

_____

_____

3. Is Alicia's revised draft better organized than her first draft? Explain.

_____

_____

_____

4. How effectively does Alicia use detailed observations, sensory de-
    scription, and dialogue?

_____

_____

5. How could Alicia's revised draft benefit from further revision?

Using Peer Review. Form a group with two or three other students and exchange copies of your drafts. Read your draft aloud while your classmates follow along. Take notes on your classmates' responses to the following questions about your draft.

1. Have I followed all of the instructions for this assignment?

2. How interesting is my introduction? Do you want to continue reading the paper? Why or why not?

3. What is my thesis statement? Do I need to make the thesis clearer?

4. Where in the essay could I add detailed observations, sensory description, and dialogue for interest and to help convey my message?

_____

_____

_____

5. Which pattern of organization do I use? Could my organization be improved?

_____

_____

_____

6. What parts of my essay, if any, don't support my thesis and could be omitted? Are there any sentences or words that seem unnecessary?

_____

_____

_____

7. Where in the essay did my writing confuse you? How can I clarify my thoughts?

_____

_____

_____

8. How clear is the purpose of my draft? How well have I met the needs of my audience?

_____

_____

_____

_____

9. How effective is my ending? Do I end in such a way that you know it's the end?

_____

_____

_____

Use the peer review notes from this activity to help you revise your draft.

ACTIVITY
18

Revising Your Draft. Taking your classmates' suggestions for revision into consideration, revise your draft. In particular, focus on adding detailed observations, sensory description, and dialogue. Use the pattern of organization that best communicates your ideas. You might also decide to omit unnecessary material or to rearrange parts of your essay more effectively. ❏

Editing

At this point you have worked hard to communicate your thoughts about some aspect of your family, and your essay is almost ready to be shared with your audience. But first you must edit it for correctness. Editing is important; as noted in Chapter Three, the more your readers must pay attention to errors in your writing, the less attention they can pay to what you have to say.

Alicia's Edited Essay

As you probably noticed, Alicia's revised draft contained errors in grammar, spelling, and punctuation. Alicia corrected these errors in her edited draft. Her corrections are underlined here. Her editing log follows her essay.

Breaking Away

It's a summertime ritual for my entire family to gather at my grand-   *1*
mother's house on Sundays for a barbecue. We eat spicy food, play loud music, laugh a lot, and exchange family news and gossip. Up until now, this ritual has made me feel closer to my family. After one barbecue, however, I felt
totally separate from them. I realized that to fulfill my dream of becoming a
doctor I'd have to break out of the old-fashioned sex roles they believe in.

Grandmother's small house was as crowded and hot as a standing-room-   *2*
only nightclub. Smoke filled the air, and swarms of flies searched for leftovers discarded by children. As usual, my family was following traditional
male and female roles. The women, speaking Spanish at the rate of twenty
words a second, were in the kitchen preparing the salsa, beans, and tortillas. The men, with beers in their hands, stood around the grill cooking the
meat and talking about sports.

I was excited because I'd just decided to become a doctor. I wanted my   *3*
grandmother to be the first to know. I squeezed by my aunts, uncles, and
cousins to make my way into the kitchen. Finally I had a chance to talk to my
seventy-year-old grandmother alone. Cheerful as usual, she was cutting up
black olives to put in the potato salad. She doesn't look her age, maybe because she dyes her hair or because she keeps up with all her grandchildren.
But she's still old-fashioned and suffers from low self-esteem. She accepted
her role as a Mexican woman to put her family first. In Mexico she never had
the opportunities for school or career. After my grandfather's death, it was
very difficult as a wife and a single mother of seven to give her children a
better life.

Addressing my grandmother in Spanish, I said, "Grandma, I've decided   *4*
I'm going to college to become a doctor."

She paused a few seconds, looked directly into my eyes and said,   *5*
"Women should not become doctors."

I froze at those horrible words. I went out on the patio so she wouldn't   *6*
see my tears. The men standing at the grill suddenly declared the meat was
ready and sat down at the table while the women hurriedly served them. My
mother asked me to help serve the children.

I asked, "Mom, why is it that the men always eat first?"   *7*

She replied, "Because they have bigger appetites." Then she and the   *8*
other women took care of the children while the men ate and talked, doing
absolutely nothing to help.

It's unfair how the women wait on the men and tend to their every need.   *9*
Mexican women can't fulfill their individual dreams because they don't believe they can be anything but wife and mother. The women in my family must
realize that I want to be more than a wife and mother. I don't want to be
caught in their trap.

Alicia's Editing Log

- INCORRECT: Its (1)
  - ERROR: contraction without an apostrophe
  - CORRECT: It's

- INCORRECT: seperate (1)
  - ERROR: misspelled word
  - CORRECT: separate

- INCORRECT: While the men, with beers in their hands, stood around the grill cooking the meat and talking about sports. (2)
  - ERROR: sentence fragment
  - CORRECT: The men, with beers in their hands, stood around the grill cooking the meat and talking about sports.

- INCORRECT: dies (3)
  - ERROR: misspelled word
  - CORRECT: dyes

- INCORRECT: Who was cheerful as usual (3)
  - ERROR: sentence fragment
  - CORRECT: Cheerful as usual, she was cutting up black olives to put in the potato salad.

- INCORRECT: Maybe because she dies her hair or because she keeps up with all her grandchildren. (3)
  - ERROR: sentence fragment
  - CORRECT: She doesn't look her age, maybe because she dyes her hair or because she keeps up with all her grandchildren.

- INCORRECT: excepted (3)
  - ERROR: wrong word
  - CORRECT: accepted

- INCORRECT: oppurtunities (3)
  - ERROR: misspelled word
  - CORRECT: opportunities

- INCORRECT: While the women hurriedly served them. (6)

ERROR:	sentence fragment
CORRECT:	The men standing at the grill suddenly declared the meat was ready and sat down at the table while the women hurriedly served them.

• INCORRECT:	Its (9)
ERROR:	contraction without an apostrophe
CORRECT:	It's

Editing Your Essay. Edit your revised draft to eliminate errors in grammar, spelling, and punctuation. To edit your draft, read it word-for-word. Do *not* read for content or organization. If you know you often make a particular kind of error, such as the sentence fragment, read the essay one time for only that error. Also ask a friend or classmate to help you spot errors you might have overlooked. Finally, use a dictionary and the Handbook in Part III of this book to help you correct the errors you find. ❑

ACTIVITY
19

Publishing

After you edit your essay, you're ready to share it with your audience—your instructor and classmates. You may also want to share it with one or more members of your family, perhaps even mailing a copy to a family member who lives in another state or country. Maybe your essay will inspire other family members to write about some other aspect of your family.

Most importantly, you should be proud of your finished work. It expresses your thoughts and feelings about a topic that you believe is important.

Your Writing Portfolio

As you learned in Chapter Three, your writing portfolio consists of your best writing as well as your reflections on your writing. To help you reflect on the writing you did in this chapter, answer the following questions:

1. In writing your essay on family, which stages of the writing process (gathering ideas, drafting, revising, editing, and publishing) did you find most easy to do? Which were most difficult? Why?
2. What about your essay are you most proud of?

3. If you had more time, what parts of your essay would you continue to revise? Why?

Using your answers to these questions, update the writing process report you began in Chapter Three.

Writing Process Report

Date:

Strengths:

Weaknesses:

Plans for improvement:

Once you complete this report, freewrite in your journal about what you learned about your writing process in this chapter and what you still hope to learn.

Chapter Summary

- You may gather ideas for an essay by brainstorming, freewriting, and clustering.
- When you draft an essay, you concentrate on *what* you want to say, *not* on how to say it.
- When you revise a draft, you focus on both *what* you want to say *and* how to say it.
- Detailed observations, sensory description, and dialogue can enliven

your writing, provide support for your main ideas, and aid your readers' understanding.

- You can organize descriptive writing by using the directional order or the order-of-importance pattern.

- You can organize narrative writing by using chronological order or a flashback.

- Your final essay can be shared with family members, as well as with your classmates and instructor.

Change alone is unchanging.
　　　　—HERACLITUS

5

The Ways We Change

In this chapter you will

- write about a significant person, event, or period of time in your life.

- gather ideas by questioning and relating aloud.

- learn to write effective topic sentences.

- learn to write unified paragraphs.

- add interest to your writing by using examples, comparison-contrast, and cause and effect.

- add to your writing portfolio.

We all have memories of the important people and events in our lives. Some of these memories are happy: a special grandfather or coach, a first kiss or date, the night following high school graduation. Others are less pleasant: a serious illness, an accident, or the death of a family member or friend.

While the memories may be pleasant or unpleasant, the people and events changed who we are and how we now see ourselves. To a great extent, then, we are defined by the important people and events in our lives. By exploring them in writing, we can come to a deeper understanding of who we are and what is meaningful to us. Just as important, writing about our personal history also allows us to share it with others so that they, too, can know us better.

ACTIVITY

1

Analyzing Your Purpose and Audience. Before you begin gathering ideas about your topic, think about your purpose and audience. For this chapter's assignment, you'll share your thoughts and feelings about a significant person, event, or period of time in your life. Your audience will include your instructor, your classmates, and other students on campus. Your responses to the following questions will help you decide how to approach your topic.

1. Does this assignment call for expressive, informative, or persuasive writing?

    _____

2. What is your reader's average age? _____

3. How many are female? _____ male? _____

4. What parts of the country or world are they from? _____

    _____

    _____

    _____

5. How many have had experiences similar to your own?_____

    _____

Writing Assignment

This chapter offers you the opportunity to consider the significant people and events in your life and how they have shaped who you are. You, your class, or your instructor may decide to do this assignment in one of several ways:

- You may gather ideas on one, two, *or* three topics.
- You may write a discovery draft on one, two, *or* three of these topics.
- You may choose one discovery draft to develop into a polished essay.
- Or, you may combine your discovery draft ideas into a new topic for your essay.

After completing your essay, share it with your instructor, classmates, and possibly with readers of a campus magazine that accepts submissions from students.

Given your responses to the preceding questions, ask yourself these questions:

6. What do my readers know (and *not* know) about my topic?

_____

_____

_____

_____

7. What information do I need to provide? _____

_____

_____

_____

_____

8. Will my readers be interested in my topic? If not, how can I get their attention?

_____

_____

_____

❏

Gathering Ideas

To gather ideas for your paper, you may use brainstorming, freewriting, or clustering, as you did in Chapter Four. Or, you may try two new methods: questioning and relating aloud.

A Significant Person

Think about the significant people in your life. Who would you name? You might name your parents, for example, or a mate, a teacher, or a friend. You might even name an acquaintance or a stranger you met once, but who nevertheless gave you a new perspective at a critical time in your life. Whoever you choose, the significant person should be someone who has helped you understand who you are and who you strive to be.

Dawn Sanders, in "Beth," tells us about an elementary school classmate who changed the way Sanders treats other people.

DAWN SANDERS

Beth

I used to see her walking alone in the crowded hallways. Some-   *1*
times a group of girls would follow behind whispering and giggling after her. Occasionally, boys would tease. Our eyes met once, but her gaze fell quickly to the floor, as if in shame. If she only knew that it was I, not she, who should have felt ashamed.

Beth did not graduate with my grade-school class, but we had   *2*
been classmates through seventh grade. As I look back, I realize that those were the best years of my childhood, unburdened with cares and responsibilities. But even carefree, innocent children can be cruel.

From the very beginning, Beth was different, an outsider. Her   *3*
physical appearance set her apart. Stringy blond hair framed her

homely face and accentuated her long pointy nose. She had a bad
overbite, probably caused by her incessant thumb-sucking. On her
bony shoulders hung an old, faded sweater, out of shape from too
many washings, and hopelessly out of style. With her sallow com-
plexion, she looked malnourished. We all thought she was dense.
The ideas that were easy for us to understand seemed out of her
reach. She remained at the bottom of the class, never seeming to
benefit from the teacher's help.

4   We excluded Beth from our games. If we did let her join, it was
so we could gang up and laugh at her. The boys all called her names,
pulling her hair and stealing her food at lunch. At first, Beth fought
back, but after a time she seemed to lose spirit. She became quiet
and withdrawn.

5   I remember one incident in particular. It was in the fifth grade.
The class bully, Fred Washek, was also the teacher's son. Fred did
whatever he wanted to do, which was normally something cruel.
During Fred's reign of terror, Beth was his main target. He taunted
and tormented her.

6   One day, while Mrs. Washek was running an errand, Fred put a
tack on Beth's chair. I don't know if she noticed it, but she hesitated
to sit down. Fred commanded her to sit and threatened to knock her
down if she disobeyed. Beth refused. Fred pushed her hard into the
chair. Immediately, she jumped up, wincing in pain. Fred angrily
pushed her down again and held her there. The class had been en-
joying Fred's prank but became increasingly uneasy. Still, no one
dared come to Beth's defense for fear of Fred's vengeance. Finally,
the teacher returned and Fred calmly went back to his seat. In the
meantime, Beth began to whimper. Mrs. Washek ignored her as
usual, but as Beth's sobs became louder, she scolded her for being a
cry baby and disturbing the class.

7   That incident made me realize how terribly we all had been
treating Beth. When the others teased her, I no longer joined in. But
I did nothing to stop them. Nor did I become her friend. The term
was nearly over by then and Beth's grades were so poor that she
was held back. She was probably happy to get away from us. I think
I was a little relieved to get away from her.

8   Her being held back turned out to be the best thing for her. The
class she moved into was more accepting. I saw her now and then
over the next five years and saw her make friends and gain confidence. Her grades improved. She joined the varsity volleyball team
and became assistant librarian. She got a part-time job and was able
to get some stylish clothes.

9   I came more and more to admire Beth. She cast off the label of
loser that our class had given her and made something of herself. In
fact, she always had been special; we just never noticed. We saw
only the shell, not the person within.

ACTIVITY
2

Reading to Improve Writing. Discuss the following questions about "Beth" with your classmates.

1. How does Sanders describe Beth? _____

   _____

   _____

   _____

2. Why do the students make fun of Beth? _____

   _____

   _____

   _____

3. Why is Beth a significant person in Sanders's life? _____

   _____

   _____

   _____

4. What do you want to know about Beth that the writer doesn't reveal?

   _____

   _____

   _____

5. What details does Sanders use to show how Beth influenced her life?

   _____

   _____

   _____

Collecting New Words. Try to determine the meanings of the following words from the way they're used in "Beth." Then verify their meanings by checking a dictionary.

unburdened (2) _____

accentuated (3) _____

incessant (3) _____

sallow (3) _____

taunted (5) _____

tormented (5) _____

Questioning to Gather Ideas about a Person. Think of a person who is (or has been) important to you. Write the person's name at the top of a blank page in your journal. Then use the questioning technique to gather ideas about that person. Begin with the journalist's *who, what, when, where, why,* and *how* questions. Continue with questions of your own, perhaps even combining questioning with brainstorming or freewriting. For example, try brainstorming whatever comes to mind in response to the following questions.*

1. How would you describe this person to someone who has never met him or her?

   _____

   _____

   _____

2. How would you describe some of the places you have visited with this person?

   _____

   _____

   _____

*From *A Writing Project* by Harvey Daniels and Steven Zemelman.

3. What special objects do you associate with this person? Why?

_____

_____

_____

4. What song, book, or movie do you associate with this person? Why?

_____

_____

_____

5. What holidays or other special occasions are memorable because of this person? Why?

_____

_____

_____

6. How do you feel when you think of this person? Describe these feelings.

_____

_____

_____

COMPUTER TIP

GENERATING QUESTIONS

To gather ideas through questioning, you might consider using a software program that provides sets of questions intended to generate writing. Or, you can create your own questions. Begin by creating a file with the seven questions you used in Activity 4 to gather ideas about a significant person.

7. Why do you think this person is significant to you? _____

_____

_____

_____ ❑

Here's how one student writer, J. Ramirez, responded to the first four questions of the preceding activity.

My father

1. 5 feet, 6 inches tall
   green eyes
   brown hair
   full head of hair
   in good shape
   kind
   understanding
   always tries to be helpful
   soft-spoken, but firm!
   doesn't talk much, but when he does everyone listens!

2. We've been so many places together that it's hard to
       name only a few:
   baseball games
   church
   the mall
   auto parts store
   Disneyland
   grandparent's house
   Uncle Jim's
   fishing
   I could go on and on!

3. anything about baseball
   his Cardinals' baseball cap
   fishing gear
   lawn mower
   '56 Chevy
   TV remote control
   favorite chair
   newspaper
   coffee mug

4. *Field of Dreams*—*My dad loves baseball so much that if he had a cornfield he'd turn it into a baseball field, too.*

ACTIVITY
5

Clustering Ideas about a Person. Return to the material you generated in Activity 4. Evaluate your responses to questions 2 and 5 about the times you shared with your special person. Choose the one event that most fully reveals why this person is significant to you. Then do some clustering to gather ideas about the event and person.   ❏

You now have some ideas for a discovery draft about a significant person in your life. Set this material aside for a time. You want to turn to gathering ideas on a different topic—an event that changed your life.

A Memorable Event

COMPUTER TIP
CLUSTERING ON A COMPUTER
You can use your computer to cluster. Instead of circling your ideas, use the bold feature to highlight them.

Along with the important people in your life are important events that changed you in some way. Whether you worked to make these events happen—such as achieving a goal or overcoming a personal problem—or saw them change your life unexpectedly—such as winning a scholarship or needing surgery—such events have influenced who you are. As you consider the many memorable events in your life, choose one that has helped define who you are today.

Beverly Dipo, in "No Rainbows, No Roses," describes how caring for a dying patient was a significant event in her life.

BEVERLY P. DIPO

No Rainbows, No Roses

I have never seen Mrs. Trane before, but I know by the report I received from the previous shift that tonight she will die. Making my rounds, I go from room to room, checking other patients first and saving Mrs. Trane for last, not to avoid her, but because she will require the most time to care for. Everyone else seems to be all right for the time being; they have had their medications, backrubs, and are easily settled for the night.

At the door to 309, I pause, adjusting my eyes to the darkness. The only light in the room is coming from an infusion pump, which is flashing its red beacon as if in warning, and the dim hall light that barely confirms the room's furnishings and the shapeless form on the bed. As I stand there, the smell hits my nostrils, and I close my

1

2

eyes as I remember the stench of rot and decay from past experience. In my mouth I taste the bitter bile churning in the pit of my stomach. I swallow uneasily and cross the room in the dark, reaching for the light switch above the sink, and as it silently illuminates the scene, I return to the bed to observe the patient with a detached, medical routineness.

Mrs. Trane lies motionless: the head seems unusually large on a *3* skeleton frame, and except for a few fine wisps of gray hair around the ears, is bald from the chemotherapy that had offered brief hope; the skin is dark yellow and sags loosely around exaggerated long bones that not even a gown and bedding can disguise; the right arm lies straight out at the side, taped cruelly to a board to secure the IV fluid its access; the left arm is across the sunken chest, which rises and falls in the uneven waves of Cheyne-Stokes respirations; a catheter hanging on the side of the bed is draining thick brown urine from the bladder, the source of the deathly smell.

I reach for the long, thin fingers that are lying on the chest. *4* They are ice cold, and I quickly move to the wrist and feel for the weak, thready pulse. Mrs. Trane's eyes flutter open as her head turns toward me slightly. As she tries to form a word on her dry, parched lips, I bend close to her and scarcely hear as she whispers, "Water." Taking a glass of water from the bedside table, I put my finger over the end of the straw and allow a few droplets of the cool moisture to slide into her mouth. She makes no attempt to swallow; there is just not enough strength. "More," the raspy voice says, and we repeat the procedure. This time she does manage to swallow and weakly says, "Thank you." I touch her gently in response. She is too weak for conversation, so without asking, I go about providing for her needs, explaining to her in hushed tones each move I make. Picking her up in my arms like a child, I turn her on her side. She is so very small and light. Carefully, I rub lotion into the yellow skin, which rolls freely over the bones, feeling perfectly the outline of each vertebrae in the back and the round smoothness of the ileac crest. Placing a pillow between her legs, I notice that these too are ice cold, and not until I run my hand up over her knees do I feel any of the life-giving warmth of blood coursing through fragile veins. I find myself in awe of the life force which continues despite such a state of decomposition.

When I am finished, I pull a chair up beside the bed to face her *5* and, taking her free hand between mine, again notice the long, thin fingers. Graceful. There is no jewelry; it would have fallen off long ago. I wonder briefly if she has any family, and then I see that there are neither bouquets of flowers, nor pretty plants on the shelves, no brightly crayon-colored posters of rainbows, nor boastful self-portraits from grandchildren on the walls. There is no hint in the room anywhere that this is a person who is loved. As though she has been reading my mind, Mrs. Trane answers my thoughts and quietly tells me, "I sent . . . my family . . . home . . . tonight . . . didn't want . . . them . . . to see. . . ." She cannot go on, but knowingly, I have understood what it is she has done. I lower my eyes, not knowing what to say, so I say nothing. Again she seems to sense my unease, "You . . . stay. . . ." Time seems to have come to a standstill. In the total silence, I noticeably feel my own heartbeat quicken and hear my breathing as it begins to match hers, stride for uneven stride. Our eyes meet and somehow, together, we become aware that this is a special moment between us, a moment when two human beings are so close we feel as if our souls touch. Her long fingers curl easily around my hand and I nod my head slowly, smiling. Wordlessly, through yellowed eyes, I receive my thank you and her eyes slowly close.

Some unknown amount of time passes before her eyes open again, only this time there is no response in them, just a blank stare. Without warning, her breathing stops, and within a few moments, the faint pulse is also gone. One single tear flows from her left eye, across the cheekbone and down onto the pillow. I begin to cry quietly. There is a tug of emotion within me for this stranger who so quickly came into and went from my life. Her suffering is done, yet so is the life. Slowly, still holding her hand, I become aware that I do not mind this emotional tug of war, that in fact, it was a privilege she has allowed me, and I would do it again, gladly. Mrs. Trane spared her family an episode that perhaps they were not equipped to handle and instead shared it with me, knowing somehow that I would handle it and, indeed, needed it to grow, both privately and professionally. She had not wanted to have her family see her die, yet she did not want to die alone. No one should die alone, and I am glad I was there for her. *6*

Two days later, I read Mrs. Trane's obituary in the paper. She had been a widow for five years, was the mother of seven, grandmother of eighteen, an active member of her church, a leader of volunteer organizations in her community, college-educated in music, a concert pianist, and a piano teacher for over thirty years. *7*

Yes, they were long and graceful fingers. *8*

ACTIVITY
6

Reading to Improve Writing. Discuss the following questions about "No Rainbows, No Roses" with your classmates.

1. How does Dipo describe Mrs. Trane so that we know she is dying?

_____

_____

_____

_____

2. How does the writer's use of dialogue carry the action forward?

_____

_____

_____

3. What does the title of the essay mean? _____

_____

_____

_____

4. Why does the writer say "it was a privilege" to be with Mrs. Trane during her final moments?

_____

_____

_____

Collecting New Words. Try to determine the meanings of the following words from the way they're used in "No Rainbows, No Roses." Then verify their meanings by checking a dictionary.

ACTIVITY

7

infusion (2)   _____

beacon (2)   _____

bile (2)   _____

respirations (3) _____

catheter (3)   _____

thready (4)   _____

parched (4) _____

coursing (4) _____

boastful (5) _____

ACTIVITY
8
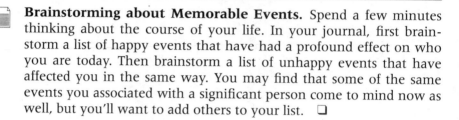
Brainstorming about Memorable Events. Spend a few minutes thinking about the course of your life. In your journal, first brainstorm a list of happy events that have had a profound effect on who you are today. Then brainstorm a list of unhappy events that have affected you in the same way. You may find that some of the same events you associated with a significant person come to mind now as well, but you'll want to add others to your list. ❑

One student writer, Karla, brainstormed the following list of significant events:

Happy events:
the day I got my driver's license
the day I graduated from high school
when I fell in love for the first time
when I got my own apartment near campus

Unhappy events:
when I lost my close friend
when I got a speeding ticket
when my mom almost died
when Greg dumped me last year
my history class this semester

Karla then worked with a peer response group to see which event her classmates found most interesting and wanted to know more about. Possibly because the class had just read "No Rainbows, No Roses," the group seemed most interested in the time Karla's mother almost died. Karla then related that event aloud as one of her classmates took notes. This is Karla's story:

It all began on my first day in fifth grade. After I arrived home, I wanted to go shopping for school supplies. My mom didn't really want to take me, but I just had to get some things. My sister, Norma, and I jumped in the back seat of the car while my mom and older sister, Ana, got in front. Ana was going to drive since my mom has heart trouble and can't drive. It was then that we spotted another one of my sisters, Mary, driving my Dad's truck. There was only one place she could be going—to her boyfriend's house. My mom had forbidden Mary to see him because he was separated but not divorced. "Do you want me to follow her?" Ana asked. My mother said yes. I was thinking why does this always happen to me!

At last the truck stopped and Mary went to the front door of the house. Her boyfriend came out and hugged her. My mother was hysterical! "How could she? What does she think she's doing?" Then she leaped out of the car and ran toward the house, yelling at Mary, "Get in the car!" Mary yelled back, "I will not! I hate the way you treat me, the way you follow me, the way you are! I hate you." Then the moment I dreaded came. My mom sank to the ground. She began to gasp for breath. I remember the panicky look in my mother's eyes, the look of fear in Mary's eyes, and the blank look on Ana's face.

Mary's boyfriend called 911 and Mom was taken to the hospital. I prayed hard for my mom, and we all cried a lot. After a while, things turned out all right. She had had a heart attack, but she was going to live. While my mom was in the hospital, my sister Mary moved out. When mom came home, she talked to me more than she ever used to. We began to share our lives more, the way a mother and daughter should.

Karla's story prompted many questions from her peer response group. For example, one student asked, "Did your mom and sister make up?" Karla responded:

Yes, they had a long talk and they're trying to work out their differences.

Other group members asked, "Can you remember anything else that was said?" and "How did you feel during all of this?"

I remember Norma screaming and crying, "You killed Momma." Mary didn't say anything. She just stood with her boyfriend. She seemed frozen with fear. Ana was kneeling next to Mom saying, "It's going to be all right." I was really scared. I knew what was coming. My heart sank. I thought my mother was going to die.

Finally, someone asked Karla why this event was significant to her.

It made me realize how much I loved my mother. It also led to a better relationship between me and my mom.

Relating the event aloud and reading over the group member's notes helped Karla focus on the details and significance of the event. She now had useful description and dialogue to add to her piece. Relating aloud and answering the group's questions also helped Karla zero-in on her main idea: none of her family's difficulties were as sig-

COMPUTER TIP

NETWORKED DISCUSSION

If you have access to a networked computer lab, you can discuss your topic on-line with other students in your class, on your campus, or even at different colleges. Use a program that allows everyone on the network to read and post messages. Post your topic and explain why you chose to write about it. What questions do others on the network have about the topic? Their questions can help you add supporting details to your essay.

nificant as the possibility of losing her mother. This would become her thesis statement.

GROUP
ACTIVITY
9
Relating Aloud. Working with a peer response group, relate your significant event aloud. The event may be a happy or sad one that has markedly affected who you are. Ask someone to take notes on your story, or use a tape recorder. When you finish relating aloud, respond to the group's questions about your topic. Then read over the notes (or listen to the tape) to gather additional ideas. ❑

Set your material on a memorable event aside for a time. You now want to turn to gathering ideas on a different topic—an important period in your life.

An Important Period in Your Life

Unlike an event, which occurs at a specific time or on a particular day (such as Karla's mother's heart attack), a period in your life includes events that take place over a longer stretch of time. For example, it could be a time when your life came together or fell apart, the year you lived in New York, your first year of marriage, or the months you spent in rehabilitation after a car accident.

Malcolm X, in "Prison Studies," describes the period in his life when he came to love reading. He also describes the effect that reading had on his life.

MALCOLM X

Prison Studies

Many who today hear me somewhere in person, or on television, or those who read something I've said, will think I went to school far beyond the eighth grade. This impression is due entirely to my prison studies.   *1*

It had really begun back in the Charlestown Prison, when Bimbi first made me feel envy of his stock of knowledge. Bimbi had always taken charge of any conversation he was in, and I had tried to emulate him. But every book I picked up had few sentences which didn't contain anywhere from one to nearly all of the words that might as well have been in Chinese. When I just skipped those words, of course, I really ended up with little idea of what the book said. So I had come to the Norfolk Prison Colony still going through only book-reading motions. Pretty soon, I would have quit even these motions, unless I had received the motivation that I did.   *2*

I saw that the best thing I could do was get hold of a dictionary—to study, to learn some words. I was lucky enough to reason also that I should try to improve my penmanship. It was sad. I couldn't even write in a straight line. It was both ideas together that moved me to request a dictionary along with some tablets and pencils from the Norfolk Prison Colony school.   3

I spent two days just riffling uncertainly though the dictionary's pages. I'd never realized so many words existed! I didn't know which words I needed to learn. Finally, to start some kind of action, I began copying.   4

In my slow, painstaking, ragged handwriting, I copied into my tablet everything printed on that first page, down to the punctuation marks.   5

I believe it took me a day. Then, aloud, I read back, to myself, everything I'd written on the tablet. Over and over, aloud, to myself, I read my own handwriting.   6

I woke up the next morning, thinking about those words—immensely proud to realize that not only had I written so much at one time, but I'd written words that I never knew were in the world. Moreover, with a little effort, I also could remember what many of these words meant. I reviewed the words whose meanings I didn't remember. Funny thing, from the dictionary first page right now, that "aardvark" springs to my mind. The dictionary had a picture of it, a long-tailed, long-eared, burrowing African mammal, which lives off termites caught by sticking out its tongue as an anteater does for ants.   7

I was so fascinated that I went on—I copied the dictionary's next page. And the same experience came when I studied that. With every succeeding page, I also learned of people and places and events from history. Actually the dictionary is like a miniature encyclopedia. Finally the dictionary's A section had filled a whole tablet—and I went on into the B's. That was the way I started copying what eventually became the entire dictionary. It went a lot faster after so much practice helped me to pick up handwriting speed. Between what I wrote in my tablet, and writing letters, during the rest of my time in prison I would guess I wrote a million words.   8

I suppose it was inevitable that as my word-base broadened, I could for the first time pick up a book and read and now begin to understand what the book was saying. Anyone who has read a great deal can imagine the new world that opened. Let me tell you something: from then until I left that prison, in every free moment I had, if I was not reading in the library, I was reading on my bunk. You couldn't have gotten me out of books with a wedge. Between Mr. Muhammad's teachings, my correspondence, my visitors—usually Ella and Reginald—and my reading of books, months passed without my even thinking about being imprisoned. In fact, up to then, I never had been so truly free in my life. . . .   9

As you can imagine, especially in a prison where there was *10* heavy emphasis on rehabilitation, an inmate was smiled upon if he demonstrated an unusually intense interest in books. There was a sizable number of well-read inmates, especially the popular debaters. Some were said by many to be practically walking encyclopedias. They were almost celebrities. No university would ask any student to devour literature as I did when this new world opened to me, of being able to read and *understand.*

I read more in my room than in the library itself. An inmate *11* who was known to read a lot could check out more than the permitted maximum number of books. I preferred reading in the total isolation of my own room.

When I had progressed to really serious reading, every night at *12* about ten P.M. I would be outraged with the "lights out." It always seemed to catch me right in the middle of something engrossing.

Fortunately, right outside my door was a corridor light that cast *13* a glow into my room. The glow was enough to read by, once my eyes adjusted to it. So when "lights out" came, I would sit on the floor where I could continue reading in that glow.

At one-hour intervals the night guards paced past every room. *14* Each time I heard the approaching footsteps, I jumped into bed and feigned sleep. And as soon as the guard passed, I got back out of bed onto the floor area of that light-glow, where I would read for another fifty-eight minutes—until the guard approached again. That went on until three or four every morning. Three or four hours of sleep a night was enough for me. Often in the years in the streets I had slept less than that.

I have often reflected upon the new vistas that reading opened to *15* me. I knew right there in prison that reading had changed forever the course of my life. As I see it today, the ability to read awoke inside me some long dormant craving to be mentally alive. I certainly wasn't seeking any degree, the way a college confers a status symbol upon its students. My homemade education gave me, with every additional book that I read, a little bit more sensitivity to the deafness, dumbness, and blindness that was afflicting the black race in America. Not long ago, an English writer telephoned me from London, asking questions. One was, "What's your alma mater?" I told him, "Books." You will never catch me with a free fifteen minutes in which I'm not studying something I feel might be able to help the black man. . . .

Every time I catch a plane, I have with me a book that I want to *16* read—and that's a lot of books these days. If I weren't out here every day battling the white man, I could spend the rest of my life reading, just satisfying my curiosity—because you can hardly mention anything I'm not curious about. I don't think anybody ever got more out of going to prison than I did. In fact, prison enabled me to study far more intensively than I would have if my life had gone differently and I had attended some college. I imagine that one of the biggest troubles with colleges is there are too many distractions, too much panty-raiding, fraternities, and boola-boola and all of that. Where else but in prison could I have attacked my ignorance by being able to study intensely sometimes as much as fifteen hours a day?

ACTIVITY
10

Reading to Improve Writing. Discuss the following questions about "Prison Studies" with your classmates.

1. In what ways is the period of time spent reading significant in Malcolm's life?

_____

_____

_____

2. How do you think this period in Malcolm's life affected him after his release from prison?

_____

_____

_____

3. Which details about Malcolm's prison life do you find especially interesting? Why?

_____

_____

_____

4. The writer says in paragraph 9, "I never had been so truly free in my life." What does he mean?

_____

_____

_____

ACTIVITY
11

Collecting New Words. Try to determine the meanings of the following words from the way they're used in "Prison Studies." Then verify their meanings by checking a dictionary.

emulate (2)   _____

penmanship (3)   _____

riffling (4)   _____

painstaking (5)   _____

inevitable (9)   _____

devour (10)   _____

engrossing (12)   _____

intervals (14)   _____

feigned (14)   _____

vistas (15)   _____

dormant (15)   _____

ACTIVITY
12

Gathering Ideas about an Important Period in Your Life. So far in this chapter, you have used various methods for gathering ideas on a topic—questioning, brainstorming, clustering, relating aloud, and perhaps freewriting. Choose the one or two methods that work best for you and use them to gather ideas in your journal about an important period in your life. ❑

Drafting

You have now gathered ideas on three topics—a significant person, a memorable event, and an important period in your life, each of which changed you in some meaningful way. You are ready to begin drafting. Here are some of your options:

• You may select one of the three topics for your discovery draft.

• You may write drafts on two or three of the topics to see which one you prefer to continue working on.

- You may combine related topics in your discovery draft. For example, you might connect your significant person with a significant event or period of time in your life.

Before you begin drafting, write a preliminary thesis statement that names your topic and states its significance. Keep your audience and purpose in mind, but remember that your main goal at the drafting stage is to get your ideas down on paper. You'll have time later on to revise and edit your discovery draft.

Student writer J. Ramirez, whose brainstorming you saw earlier in the chapter, wrote the following discovery draft about a significant person in his life. Notice that although J. decided to write about his father, he narrowed his topic to going to baseball games with his father. A more specific topic allowed J. to provide supporting details and thereby develop his ideas more fully in this short essay. (Note that J.'s discovery draft includes the types of errors that typically appear in a first draft.)

Baseball Memories

There is more to baseball than a game. It is the sport through which my   *1*
father taught me valuable lessons. I love this sport because of my father.

My father is the reason I love baseball. He cares for his family, always   *2*
putting them above everything else. He works hard at his job to ensure that
we have all of the necessities of life. He loves to rent videos for us to watch,
too. Ever since I was two years old my father has taken me to baseball
games.

On one ocassion, a player struck out two times and threw his bat out on   *3*
the baseball field. My father told me that the next time, he would strike out
again. I didn't believe him when the player was at bat again, I was ready to
disprove my dad. But he was right. I asked him how he knew that the batter
was going to strike out. He told me that it is very hard to get things accomplished though anger or frustration because anger gets in the way of performance.

He also showed me the importance of not giving up. During one ball   *4*
game, a player struck out three times. As he stepped up to the plate for the
fourth time, the crowd was booing and cursing him. I asked my dad, "Why
are all of these people being rude to this player?" He said that he was not
doing too well. He was having a bad night, but that did not make him a bad
player.

But of all of the times I went with my father to the ball games, this one   *5* stands out. It was a warm afternoon when my father asked me to go with him. When we got there, it was very cold and the wind was blowing. My father had to put his arms around my bare legs to protect me.

My memories of my father at the ball park will always be special to me.   6
He used baseball games to teach me about life.

Revising

When revising your discovery draft, focus on how to communicate your message more effectively to your reader. Consider what your reader needs to know in order to understand the significance of that special person, event, or period of time in your life. Also consider the importance of writing effective topic sentences, creating unified paragraphs, and developing your ideas through examples, comparison-contrast, and cause and effect.

Writing Topic Sentences

When it comes to paragraphs, the phrase "one thing at a time" is useful to remember. The "one thing" that you explain in a paragraph is stated in a *topic sentence*. To write an effective topic sentence for each paragraph in your essay, follow these guidelines:

- Break up your thesis statement into several specific supporting ideas.
- Write a complete thought for each of these specific ideas.

A topic sentence functions like a mini-thesis for each paragraph. Here are some examples of thesis statements and the topic sentences that might follow from them:

THESIS STATEMENT

My friend, James, is the most significant person in my life because he taught me how to keep life's little discouragements in perspective.

TOPIC SENTENCES

Once, when my car wasn't running and I had no money to fix it, James and I bicycled out to see a field of poppies.

Another time, when I'd gotten a low grade on a paper, James took me to visit his grandmother in the nursing home.

Once when we were playing golf and I was losing again, James suddenly yelled, "Hey, is that Elvis over there on that hill?" while kicking my ball closer to the hole.

These are good topic sentences because they support the thesis statement with examples of how James taught the writer to overcome discouragement.

Here is another set of topic sentences that supports the thesis statement:

THESIS STATEMENT

The day I witnessed a car accident in front of my house convinced me never to drink and drive.

TOPIC SENTENCES

The van was wrapped around a pole, with smoke rising from the engine and glass scattered all around.

I immediately ran to help the injured driver and passengers.

It was obvious from the stench of alcohol and the beer bottles littering the van's floor that the driver and passengers had been drinking.

It was very upsetting to see an accident that could have been prevented.

These topic sentences are effective because they support the thesis statement with observational details. They also explain the cause and effect of the accident.

Consider one more set of examples:

THESIS STATEMENT

Before I moved to the United States, I lived in Japan. The two countries and cultures are very different in many ways.

TOPIC SENTENCES

Housing is much more spacious in the United States than it is in Japan. Even small apartments in this country are large by Japanese standards.

Americans are very informal, and even strangers use first names, whereas people in Japan are very reserved and formal.

People in the United States emphasize individuality, whereas people in Japan emphasize conformity to a group.

Writing Topic Sentences. Write three topic sentences for each of the following thesis statements.

ACTIVITY
13

1. My computer programming instructor changed my life by convincing me to stay in school.

    a. _____

    b. _____

    c. _____

2. Living with your parents when you're an adult has its disadvan-
    tages, but so does living on your own.

    a. _____

    b. _____

    c. _____

3. The years I held a full-time job while working toward my college de-
    gree were the most significant years of my life because of the per-
    sonal management skills I was forced to learn.

    a. _____

    b. _____

    c. _____

4. Today's communications technology—from cellular telephones to
    fax machines—makes life more stressful, not more efficient.

    a. _____

    b. _____

    c. _____

5. No two people could be more different than Matt and Jerry, but
    they are my two closest friends.

    a. _____

    b. _____

    c. _____

    ❏

Should your topic sentence appear at the beginning, middle, or
end of the paragraph? A topic sentence can fall anywhere in the
paragraph. Most often, however, it comes first. Just as placing the
thesis statement at the beginning of an essay helps guide the reader through the paper, putting the topic sentence at the beginning
of the paragraph helps guide the reader through the paragraph.
Or, to put it another way, giving the main idea at the beginning is

like giving the reader a hook on which to hang the details that follow.

Notice in the following paragraph from the Sanders reading that the topic sentence (*italicized*) comes first and the rest of the paragraph tells us how Beth was different.

> *From the very beginning, Beth was different, an outsider.* Her physical appearance set her apart. Stringy blond hair framed her homely face and accentuated her long pointy nose. She had a bad overbite, probably caused by her incessant thumb-sucking. On her bony shoulders hung an old, faded sweater, out of shape from too many washings, and hopelessly out of style. With her sallow complexion, she looked malnourished. We all thought she was dense. The ideas that were easy for us to understand seemed out of her reach. She remained at the bottom of the class, never seeming to benefit from the teacher's help.
>
> DAWN SANDERS, "BETH"

Sometimes, however, you may need to provide background information or explain the connection between two paragraphs before the topic sentence can be presented. In either case, the topic sentence may fall in the middle of the paragraph. In the following paragraph, the topic sentence (*italicized*) is given after the first sentence, which explains the connection between this paragraph and the previous one.

> I don't mean that some people are born clearheaded and are therefore natural writers, whereas others are naturally fuzzy and will never write well. *Thinking clearly is a conscious act that writers must force upon themselves, as if they were working on any other project that requires logic: adding up a laundry list or doing an algebra problem.* Good writing doesn't come naturally, though most people obviously think it does. Professional writers are constantly being bearded by strangers who say that they'd like to "try a little writing sometime"—meaning when they retire from their real profession, which is difficult, like insurance or real estate. Or they say, "I could write a book about that." I doubt it.
>
> WILLIAM ZINSSER, "SIMPLICITY"

Occasionally placing a topic sentence at the end of a paragraph can dramatize the main idea. In the following example, the topic sentence (*italicized*) appears at the end. By giving several specific examples before stating the general fact, the writer emphasizes the main point of the paragraph.

> Most black Americans are *not* poor. Most black teenagers are *not* crack addicts. Most black mothers are *not* on welfare. Indeed, in sheer numbers, more *white* Americans are poor and on welfare than are black. *Yet one never would deduce that by watching television or reading American newspapers and magazines.*
>
> PATRICIA RAYBORN, "A CASE OF 'SEVERE BIAS,'" *NEWSWEEK*, 2 OCTOBER 1989

ACTIVITY
14

Writing Your Own Topic Sentences. In your journal, write several topic sentences for your revised draft. First break up your thesis statement into several specific .ideas. Then write a complete thought—a topic sentence—for each of these ideas. Remember that you may change these topic sentences if your ideas change in the process of revising.   ❑

Creating Paragraph Unity

Once you have an effective topic sentence, you need to make sure that all other sentences within the paragraph relate to the topic sentence. This is called *paragraph unity*. Paragraphs that lack unity contain irrelevant sentences that distract and confuse readers. In the following paragraph from "Beth," several irrelevant statements have been added (in *italics*); notice how these irrelevancies detract from the topic sentence.

> We excluded Beth from our games. *I wish I were still a kid and could play some of those games; they were really fun.* If we did let her join, it was so we could gang up and laugh at her. The boys all called her names, pulling her hair and stealing her food at lunch. *This was in the days before there were individual canned servings of pudding and fruit, and all we ever got were apples and bananas or a little box of raisins.* At first, Beth fought back, but after a time she seemed to lose spirit. She became quiet and withdrawn.

During the drafting stage, you may include irrelevant statements as you focus on getting your thoughts down on paper. When you revise, however, you need to eliminate irrelevant statements in order to achieve paragraph unity. Reread your paragraphs and topic sentences, and delete any statements that are off the topic.

COMPUTER TIP

PEER REVIEW ON A COMPUTER

Use boldface to highlight the thesis statement and topic sentences in your draft. Then ask a student to read your draft on the computer screen. Are the thesis statement and topic sentences effective? Use your reader's comments to revise as needed.

ACTIVITY
15
Identifying Irrelevant Statements. Identify and delete the irrelevant sentences that have been added to the following paragraphs from readings in this chapter. Then check your work against the original paragraphs on the pages indicated.

1. From "No Rainbows, No Roses" (p. 112):

> I have never seen Mrs. Trane before, but I know by the report I received from the previous shift that tonight she will die. The shift nurse who is on before me has terrible handwriting. Making my rounds, I go from room to room, checking other patients first and saving Mrs. Trane for last, not to avoid her, but because she will re-

quire the most time to care for. Everyone else seems to be all right for the time being; they have had their medications, backrubs, and are easily settled for the night. Nursing is rewarding work, but there are times I wish someone would give me a backrub.

2. From "Prison Studies" (p. 118):

It had really begun back in the Charlestown Prison, when Bimbi first made me feel envy of his stock of knowledge. Bimbi had always taken charge of any conversation he was in, and I had tried to emulate him. But every book I picked up had few sentences which didn't contain anywhere from one to nearly all of the words that might as well have been in Chinese. I have since been to China, a fascinating country. When I just skipped those words, of course, I really ended up with little idea of what the book said. So I had come to the Norfolk Prison Colony still going through only book-reading motions. Norfolk is a large prison, and old. I'll always remember one guard who reminded me of my older brother. Pretty soon, I would have quit even these motions, unless I had received the motivation that I did.

Improving Paragraph Unity. Place a checkmark next to the sentences that do not relate to this topic sentence: *I had defied a direct order, but I didn't expect my dad to do anything about it.*

____ My dad looked like he was trying to recover from a gunshot wound.

____ Gun control is a topic I would like to write about some day.

____ His eyes fluttered and his mouth gaped. "You're saying no to me?" was all he could say.

____ "Yea, I'm saying no to you."

____ I felt like a newborn colt, prancing around, kicking, testing my limits.

____ Riding horses is one of my favorite hobbies.

____ "Well, pack your bags and leave," he shouted.

____ Uh-oh, I hadn't expected that.

____ My Samsonite bag is stored on the top shelf of my closet.

____ "Okay, I will." ❑

Developing Your Ideas

In Chapter Four, you used detailed observations, sensory description, and dialogue to develop your ideas and add interest to your writing. You may use one or more of these techniques for this chapter's writing assignment as well. But you will also develop your ideas and support your topic sentences through examples, comparison-contrast, and cause and effect. These techniques serve several important functions in an essay:

• They increase the reader's interest in your topic.
• They help the reader understand your main ideas.
• They help to persuade the reader to accept your point of view.

Examples. In writing, *examples* are used to clarify, explain, and support ideas. Suppose, for instance, you want to clarify the distinction between the *make* and the *model* of a car. You could do so by giving examples of the makes of cars—Ford, Chevrolet, and Toyota—as well as of the models—for Ford, the Escort, Taurus, and Mustang.

In addition to clarification, writers use examples (sometimes called *illustration*) to convince their readers to accept their point of view. In the following paragraph, the writer gives examples of what Nola likes to try on while shopping.

> Nola is efficient and matter-of-fact about shopping, though she acts solely upon instinct. Mrs. Dietrich likes to watch her at a short distance—holding items of clothing up to herself in the three-way mirrors, modeling things she thinks especially promising. A twill blazer with rounded shoulders and blouson jacket, a funky zippered jumpsuit in white sailcloth, a pair of straight-leg Evan-Picone pants, a green leather vest: Mrs. Dietrich watches her covertly.
>
> JOYCE CAROL OATES, *SHOPPING*

Comparison-Contrast. When you *compare*, you identify the similarities between two or more things; when you *contrast*, you identify the differences between things. Sometimes the focus is on one or the other, but at other times both similarities and differences are included.

Writers use *comparison-contrast* to clarify relationships. How are people, places, or ideas alike? How are they different? For example, in "Beth," Dawn Sanders dedicates most of her essay to describing Beth and how her classmates mistreated her. But toward the end of the piece the writer contrasts Beth's new class with her old one to make a point: that eventually Beth came to be accepted by her peers.

> Her being held back turned out to be the best thing for her. The class she moved into was more accepting. I saw her now and then over the next five years and saw her make friends and gain confidence. Her grades improved. She joined the varsity volleyball team and became assistant librarian. She got a part-time job and was able to get some stylish clothes.
>
> DAWN SANDERS, "BETH"

Cause and Effect. When you use *cause and effect*, you explain why something happened (the cause) and the result of it (the effect). Writers use cause and effect to show a necessary or logical connection between two things. It is not enough to say that two things happened at the same time. For example, if a freeze ruins the orange crop, and orange prices go up, that's cause and effect. If there also happens to be a full moon on the night of the freeze, that's a coincidence. It is the freeze, not the full moon, that ruins the crop.

In the following example from "Prison Studies," Malcolm X first describes how he learned to read and then explains the effect that reading had on him. He shows a clear and logical connection between the cause—reading—and the effect—a new view of life.

> I have often reflected upon the new vistas that reading opened to me. I knew right there in prison that reading had changed forever the course of my life. As I see it today, the ability to read awoke inside me some long dormant craving to be mentally alive. I certainly wasn't seeking any degree, the way a college confers a status symbol upon its students. My homemade education gave me, with every additional book that I read, a little bit more sensitivity to the deafness, dumbness, and blindness that was afflicting the black race in America. . . .
>
> MALCOLM X, "PRISON STUDIES"

Developing Ideas. Following are several topic sentences. For each one, first decide whether you will use examples, comparison-contrast, or cause and effect as the primary method of development. Then use that method to develop the topic sentence into a brief paragraph.

ACTIVITY

17

1. My mother has the cleanest kitchen.

    Primary method of development: _____

    _____

    _____

    _____

    _____

    _____

    _____

    _____

    _____

2. The most important rule of parenting, however, is setting rules and sticking to them.

    Primary method of development: _____

    _____

    _____

    _____

    _____

    _____

    _____

_____

_____

3. Both my boss and my mate are total introverts.

    Primary method of development: _____

    _____

    _____

    _____

    _____

    _____

    _____

    _____

    _____

    _____

    _____

                                                          ❏

J.'s Revised Draft

Before you read J.'s revised draft, reread his discovery draft
(pp. 123–124). Notice, in particular, how he has improved his topic
sentences, developed his ideas, and focused on eliminating irrelevant
sentences to achieve paragraph unity in the revision. (You will also
notice some errors in the revised draft; these will be corrected when
J. edits his essay later on.)

Baseball Memories

To some baseball is just a sport where someone tries to reach base be-   *1*
fore getting thrown out. To others it is "America's pastime," a baseball sta-
dium filled with people cheering, eating hot-roasted peanuts, and, when the   **Examples added**

seventh inning approaches, singing "Take Me Out to the Ball Game." To me, though, baseball will always be more than just a game. My father used baseball to teach me valuable lessons about life. I also love baseball because of the memories it holds of times I spent with my father.

From the time I was two years old, my father took me to baseball games. On one ocassion, when we were at a game, a player struck out two times and threw his bat out on the baseball field. My father told me that the next time, the player would strike out again. I didn't believe him when the player was at bat again, I was ready to disprove my dad. But he was right. I asked him how he knew the batter would strike out again. He told me that it is very hard to get things accomplished though anger or frustration; anger gets in the way of performance. He added that I should not throw things when I get mad because this could hurt someone else or myself. Instead, he suggested that I take the time to think things over before I do something that I will regret later on.

Example added of a lesson learned

Cause and effect added

He also used baseball to show me the importance of not giving up. During one ball game, a player struck out three times. As he stepped up to the plate for the fourth time, the crowd booed and cursed him. I asked my dad, "Why are all of these people being rude to this player?" He replied, "He is one of the best players the team has, he is not doing too well. There are days when we are not ourselves we are humans and make mistakes. Just because he struck out three times does not make him a bad person. You should learn from his experience -- life is made of strikeouts, but it doesn't matter how many strikeouts you have, what matters is that you get another chance to hit the ball. If you are confident, you will succeed, but if you are not confident and do not believe in yourself, you will fail."

Example added of another lesson learned

Dialogue added

Comparison added

But of all of the times I went with my father to the ball games, one stands out. It was a warm afternoon when my father asked me to go with him. When we got there, it began to get very cold and the wind was blowing. I remember that I was just wearing shorts my legs were freezing. I told my father that I was cold, but that I didn't want to leave. He then suggested that we move to another place where the wind didn't blow as hard. But when we moved to the new place, it was still cold, so my father sat in back of me and asked me to bend my knees toward my chest and lean back. Then he put his warm hands on my legs, like a duck protecting his duckling from bad weather or a predater that might hurt him. Not only did I feel warmed by my father, but I felt protected as well.

Example added of another lesson learned

Sensory description added

Comparison added

2

3

4

My memories of my father at the ball park will always be special to me.   5
He used baseball to teach me the importance of controlling my temper and
of not throwing or hitting things when I become upset. He also used baseball
to teach me to work toward goals without giving up. Like a batter facing that
next pitch, he taught me to face life head on.

Cause and effect added

Comparison added

Analyzing J.'s Revised Draft. Use the following questions to analyze how J. has improved his draft through revision.

ACTIVITY
18

1. Is J.'s introduction interesting? Why or why not? _____

    _____

    _____

    _____

2. What is J.'s thesis statement? Is it effective, or could it be im-
    proved?

    _____

    _____

    _____

3. Does J. use topic sentences effectively? Identify his topic sentences
    and tell how he develops the idea in each one.

    _____

    _____

    _____

4. Look back at paragraph 2 of J.'s draft (p. 123), which he omitted in
    his revision. Why do you think he decided to omit that paragraph?
    Was it a good decision?

    _____

    _____

_____

_____

5. Does J. convince you—his audience—that his father is the most
    significant person in his life? Explain.

_____

_____

_____

6. What other revisions could J. make to improve his draft?

_____

_____

_____

GROUP
ACTIVITY
19

Using Peer Review. Form a group with two or three other students
and exchange copies of your drafts. Read your draft aloud while
your classmates follow along. Take notes on your classmates' responses to the following questions about your draft.

1. Have I followed all of the instructions for this assignment?

_____

_____

_____

2. How interesting is my introduction? Does it make you want to con-
    tinue reading my paper? Why or why not?

_____

_____

_____

3. What is my thesis statement? Do I need to make the thesis clearer?

_____

_____

_____

4. Where in the draft could I better develop my ideas by using examples, comparison-contrast, and cause and effect?

_____

_____

_____

5. Is each paragraph in my draft unified? Or do some paragraphs contain irrelevant sentences or words that need to be omitted?

_____

_____

_____

6. What paragraphs in my draft, if any, do not support my thesis and could be omitted?

_____

_____

_____

7. Where in my draft did my writing confuse you? How can I clarify my thoughts?

_____

_____

_____

8. How clear is the purpose of my draft? How well have I met the needs of my audience?

_____

_____

_____

_____

9. How effective is my ending? Do I end in such a way that you know it's the end?

_____

_____

_____

_____

ACTIVITY
20

Revising Your Draft. Taking your classmates' suggestions for revision into consideration, revise your draft on a signficant person, event, or period in your life. Pay particular attention to improving your topic sentences, paragraph unity, and development of ideas through examples, comparison-contrast, and cause and effect. ❑

Editing

Now that you've revised your draft, you're ready to edit it for correctness. Remember, the more your readers pay attention to the errors, the less attention they pay to what you have to say.

J.'s Edited Essay

You probably noticed that J.'s revised draft contained misspelled words, run-on sentences, and comma splices. J. corrected these errors in his edited essay. His corrections are underlined here. His editing log follows his essay.

Baseball Memories

To some baseball is just a sport where someone tries to reach base before getting thrown out. To others it is "America's pastime," a baseball stadium filled with people cheering, eating hot-roasted peanuts, and, when the seventh inning approaches, singing "Take Me Out to the Ball Game." To me, though, baseball will always be more than just a game. My father used baseball to teach me valuable lessons about life. I also love baseball because of the memories it holds of times I spent with my father.

From the time I was two years old, my father took me to baseball games. On one occasion, when we were at a game, a player struck out two times and threw his bat out on the baseball field. My father told me that the next time, the player would strike out again. I didn't believe him. When the player was at bat again, I was ready to disprove my dad. But he was right. I asked him how he knew the batter would strike out again. He told me that it is very hard to get things accomplished through anger or frustration; anger gets in the way of performance. He added that I should not throw things when I get mad because this could hurt someone else or myself. Instead, he suggested that I take the time to think things over before I do something that I will regret later on.

He also used baseball to show me the importance of not giving up. During one ball game, a player struck out three times. As he stepped up to the plate for the fourth time, the crowd booed and cursed him. I asked my dad, "Why are all of these people being rude to this player?" He replied, "He is one of the best players the team has, but he is not doing too well. There are days when we are not ourselves; we are humans and make mistakes. Just because he struck out three times does not make him a bad person. You should learn from his experience -- life is made of strikeouts, but it doesn't matter how many strikeouts you have. What matters is that you get another chance to hit the ball. If you are confident, you will succeed, but if you are not confident and do not believe in yourself, you will fail."

But of all of the times I went with my father to the ball games, one stands out. It was a warm afternoon when my father asked me to go with him. When we got there, it began to get very cold and the wind was blowing. I remember that I was just wearing shorts, so my legs were freezing. I told my father that I was cold, but that I didn't want to leave. He then suggested that we move to another place where the wind didn't blow as hard. But when we moved to the new place, it was still cold, so my father sat in back of me and asked me to bend my knees toward my chest and lean back. Then he put his warm hands on my legs, like a duck protecting his duckling from bad weather or a <u>predator</u> that might hurt him. Not only did I feel warmed by my father, but I felt protected as well.

My memories of my father at the ball park will always be special to me. He used baseball to teach me the importance of controlling my temper and of not throwing or hitting things when I become upset. He also used baseball to teach me to work toward goals without giving up. Like a batter facing that next pitch, he taught me to face life head on.
5

J.'s Editing Log

- INCORRECT: ocassion (2)
  - ERROR: misspelled word
  - CORRECT: occasion

- INCORRECT: I didn't believe him when the player was at bat again, I was ready to disprove my dad. (2)
  - ERROR: run-on sentence
  - CORRECT: I didn't believe him. When the player was at bat again, I was ready to disprove my dad.

- INCORRECT: though (2)
  - ERROR: wrong word
  - CORRECT: through

- INCORRECT: He replied, "He is one of the best players the team has, he is not doing too well." (3)
  - ERROR: comma splice
  - CORRECT: He replied, "He is one of the best players the team has, but he is not doing too well."

- INCORRECT: There are days when we are not ourselves we are humans and make mistakes. (3)
  - ERROR: run-on sentence
  - CORRECT: There are days when we are not ourselves; we are humans and make mistakes.

- INCORRECT: You should learn from his experience—life is made of strike-outs, but it doesn't matter how many strikeouts you have, what matters is that you get another chance to hit the ball. (3)
  - ERROR: comma splice
  - CORRECT: You should learn from his experience—life is made of strike-

outs, but it doesn't matter how many strikeouts you have. What matters is that you get another chance to hit the ball.

- INCORRECT: I remember that I was just wearing shorts my legs were freezing. (4)
- ERROR: run-on sentence
- CORRECT: I remember that I was just wearing shorts, so my legs were freezing.

- INCORRECT: predater (4)
- ERROR: misspelled word
- CORRECT: predator

Editing Your Essay. To edit, read your essay carefully, word-for-word, looking for errors in grammar, spelling, and punctuation. Also use a dictionary and the handbook in Part III of this book to help you correct the errors you find. Finally, record those errors in your editing log. ❏

ACTIVITY
21

Publishing

Share your final essay with your instructor, friends, and classmates. Ask your reviewers to comment on the improvements you made after their review of your discovery draft. Don't be surprised if someone says, "I can't believe this is the same essay. It's so much better!"

You might also consider submitting your essay to the campus magazine for possible publication.

Your Writing Portfolio

If you are pleased with the essay you wrote in this chapter, add it to your writing portfolio. To help you continue to improve as a writer, answer the following questions about this assignment.

1. Did you enjoy writing an expressive piece, one in which you shared your thoughts and feelings?
2. Which method of gathering ideas worked best for you?
3. Which details most improved your essay?
4. If you had more time, what parts of your essay would you want to improve before sharing it with readers? Why?

Using your answers to these questions, update your writing process report.

Writing Process Report

Date:

Strengths:

Weaknesses:

Plans for improvement:

Once you complete this report, freewrite in your journal on what you learned about your writing process in this chapter and what you still hope to learn.

Chapter Summary

- Choose a topic, analyze your audience and purpose, and write a preliminary thesis statement.
- Gather ideas on your topic by brainstorming, freewriting, and clustering, as well as by questioning and relating aloud.
- Remember the phrase "one thing at a time" when you write paragraphs. The "one thing" you explain in each paragraph is stated in the topic sentence.
- Write effective topic sentences by breaking down your thesis statement into several specific supporting ideas; then write a complete thought for each specific idea.
- Maintain paragraph unity by sticking to the topic introduced in your topic sentence.

- Develop your ideas by using examples, comparison-contrast, and cause and effect.
- Revise your writing to ensure that you present your ideas clearly, and edit your writing for correctness.
- Publish your essay by sharing it with your instructor and classmates or by submitting it to the campus magazine for possible publication.

Satisfaction lies in the effort, not in the attainment. Full effort is full victory.
—MAHATMA GANDHI

6

Pastimes and Interests

In this chapter you will

- write about music, sports and recreation, or some other interest.
- gather ideas by questioning and interviewing.
- support and clarify your ideas by using definition, classification, process analysis, facts, and expert testimony.
- compose an effective introduction.
- write a powerful conclusion.
- create a lively title.
- add to your writing portfolio.

People define themselves in many ways: through the kind of work they do, where they live, their choice of friends, how they dress, even the car they drive. People also define themselves in part by the ways they spend their free time.

Suppose your best friend calls and says, "Let's do something really fun this weekend." What activity would you suggest to your friend? Would it be rock climbing, skydiving, or some other daring sport? Or would you opt for a visit to an art museum or a walk in the woods? What would your choice say about you as a person? Whether your interests include knitting sweaters or hiking a back trail, they reveal what is meaningful to you.

ACTIVITY

1

Analyzing Your Purpose and Audience. Before you begin gathering ideas about your topic, think about purpose and audience. For this chapter's assignment, you will tell others about one of your special interests. Your audience will include your classmates and instructor, as well as the readers of your campus or local newspaper. Your responses to the following questions will help you decide how to approach your topic.

1. Does this assignment call for expressive, informative, or persuasive writing?

   _____

2. Who are the readers of your campus or local newspaper? What is the ethnic composition of the community?

   _____

   _____

   _____

3. Is the community located in an urban, suburban, or rural area?

   _____

4. Is it a low, average, or high income community? _____

   _____

   _____

Writing Assignment

This chapter offers you the opportunity to share one of your interests with others. By writing about an interest, your readers will come to know you better, and you will come to understand yourself better by looking at the choices you make. In addition, you will provide your readers with valuable information that may lead them to discover a new interest of their own.

You or your instructor may decide to do this assignment in one of several ways:

- You may gather ideas on one, two, *or* three topics.
- You may write a discovery draft on one, two, *or* three of these topics.
- You may choose one discovery draft to develop into a polished essay.
- Or, you may combine your discovery draft ideas into a new topic for your essay.

After completing your essay, share it with your instructor and classmates. You might also submit it to your campus or local newspaper for possible publication.

5. What cultural, recreational, and other activities are available in the community?

_____

_____

_____

Given your responses to the preceding questions, ask yourself these questions:

6. What do my readers already know about my topic? _____

_____

_____

_____

7. What do they need to know to better understand my topic?

    _____

    _____

    _____

8. How do my readers feel about my topic? Will they find it interesting, or will I have to work to get their attention?

    _____

    _____

    _____

    ❑

Gathering Ideas

For this chapter's assignment, you may gather ideas by using one or more of the methods you learned in the preceding chapters: brainstorming, freewriting, clustering, questioning, and relating aloud. You may also try two new methods—the "twenty questions" technique and interviewing.

Keep in mind that music, sports and recreation, and other interests are general subject areas that are too broad for an essay. Before you gather ideas, then, you need to narrow your topic to a manageable one. For example, although rock music is too broad a topic for an essay, the concert you attended last summer would work. Similarly, golf is too broad, but how to improve your chip shot could be handled in an essay; hiking is too broad, but hiking safety would be manageable.

Music

Long before most of us began to write, we probably enjoyed listening to music. Some of us even play a musical instrument. Our musical likes and dislikes often reveal certain qualities about us.

For this chapter's first discovery draft, you'll write about some aspect of music. Think about your musical likes. Do you prefer rock, rap, jazz, or reggae? What about classical music? What do you think your taste in music reveals about you?

Ethan Smith, in "Travelin' Band," describes the band Sebadoh's recent tour.

ETHAN SMITH

Travelin' Band

"Touring's the greatest job you could have," says Lou Barlow, 1
28, founder and leader of the folk-rock act Sebadoh. "Not only do
you get to wear the same clothes all the time, but you work for just
six weeks and then you're off." There are also the four- to eight-
hour daily commutes in a packed van; nights that end at 5 a.m., often in some of your divier hotels; and 24–7 contact with your
coworkers. Not everyone would quit his or her day job to be the
biggest indie-rock phenomenon in the land.

In figures, Sebadoh's success translates to a sixth album, *Bakesale,* 2
with a No. 1 debut on the college music charts last August, and over
50,000 copies sold (massive by indie standards). Critics love the
Northampton, Mass., trio for their combination of insightful lyrics
and catchy but slightly jarring melodies. Major labels have courted
them persistently for years, but the band refuses to budge from its
small label, Sub Pop. Fans worship them for this refusal to go main-
stream—the ultimate barometer of integrity among indie fans.

But integrity demands sacrifice. Unlike platinum acts, with their 3
armies of support staffers, the members of Sebadoh must often serve
as their own drivers, roadies, accountants, managers, and technicians.
In fact, the band's "crew" consists of old friend Mike Flood, along as
much for comic relief as brawn or technical expertise, and Menko,
their combination soundman/road manager. Transportation is equally
low-key: Where a major label might provide a small fleet of buses,
tractor-trailers, and planes, Sub Pop's given the band just two vehi-
cles: "The Town Car they loaned us for free," says Barlow, "and this
van is being rented half by them, half out of future royalties."

A typical day begins with a $6 breakfast at a place like Charlotte, 4
N.C.'s Waffle House, whose jukebox is legendary among touring
bands for its repertoire of trademark songs. "Every Waffle House, all
over the South, has these same 15 songs about waffles and cooks
and waitresses," says bassist Jason Loewenstein, 23. When your
days are spent driving monotonous interstates, entertainment is definitely a limited concept.

On this third afternoon of its six-week tour, Sebadoh is heading 5
toward a gig at Atlanta's Masquerade. After a four-hour drive, it
takes 15 minutes to load the equipment and boxes of Sebadoh T-
shirts (sold at the shows by Flood) into the cavernous, three-floor
venue, which holds more than 2,000 people. The band's backstage
catering selection focuses on peanut butter (crackers, cups, etc.); the
windowless dressing room is sparsely furnished and so cold the band
members keep their coats on.

Tonight's show is costing fans $10—and sometimes a little extra: 6

"When [Sebadoh] are on tour I'll miss school for a week to go see them every night," says one teenage boy. "It's my downfall. I like [them] too much." Security is pretty lax at smaller clubs, so the more aggressive fans can get backstage without much hassle. "Usually if they're pushy enough to get backstage, they're pretty colorful people," says Loewenstein. Barlow, the object of most of the hardcore adulation, is more guarded: "I got mobbed out there [in the audience]," the distraught-looking singer says after a spin through the club. "People were circling me, acting like I was important." Still, when a kid named Marc shows up and reminds Barlow of a series of letters they exchanged, the guitarist hangs out with him for several hours.

At the end of the night (4 a.m.), Menko receives a $5,000 wad of cash—a better-than-average take, of which the band will see approximately $4,000 after expenses. Sebadoh packs up, and all head to the Atlanta hotel listed on the booking agent's itinerary. In a twist that reveals the precarious nature of any indie band's success, the Highland Inn turns out to be a creepy former welfare hotel on a dreary street. Before heading inside, drummer Bob Fay, 32, turns and points at their van: "This may be the last time we see it." And so it goes.   7

ACTIVITY

2

Reading to Improve Writing. Discuss the following questions about "Travelin' Band" with your classmates.

1. What type of music does Sebadoh play? _____

_____

_____

_____

2. Why does Sebadoh refuse to sign with a major recording company?

_____

_____

_____

3. How does Sebadoh minimize the expenses of touring? _____

_____

_____

4. What are the pros and cons of Sebadoh's professional lifestyle?

5. What details does the author use to develop each topic sentence?

Collecting New Words. Try to determine the meanings of the following words from the way they're used in "Travelin' Band." Then verify their meanings by checking a dictionary. (If you are not familiar with the term *indie-rock* and it isn't in your dictionary, ask a salesperson at a local music store.)

ACTIVITY
3

indie-rock (1) _____

phenomenon (1) _____

barometer (2) _____

repertoire (4) _____

monotonous (4) _____

venue (5) _____

sparsely (5) _____

adulation (6) _____

itinerary (7) _____

ACTIVITY
4

Using the Twenty Questions Method to Gather Ideas about Music. Think about a favorite musician, band, or type of music that you would like to write about. Gather ideas for your discovery draft using the twenty questions that follow. (These questions can be applied to just about any topic.) In your journal, first identify your topic. Then write your responses to the twenty questions.

Twenty Questions (from *Twenty Questions for the Writer* by Jacqueline Berke)

x = your topic

1. What does *x* mean?
2. How can *x* be described?
3. What are the parts of *x*?
4. How is *x* made or done?
5. How should *x* be made or done?
6. What is the essential function of *x*?
7. What are the causes of *x*?
8. What are the consequences of *x*?
9. What are the types of x?
10. How does *x* compare to *y*?
11. What is the present status of *x*?
12. How can *x* be interpreted?
13. What are the facts about *x*?
14. How did *x* happen or come about?
15. What kind of person or thing is *x*?
16. What is my personal response to *x*?
17. What is my memory of *x*?
18. What is the value of *x*?
19. How can *x* be summarized?
20. What case can be made for or against *x*? ❑

COMPUTER TIP

SAVING TWENTY QUESTIONS ON A COMPUTER

Consider saving the twenty questions in Activity 4 on a computer disk so you can retrieve them with ease for future assignments.

Here's how one student writer, Luchia, using classical music as her topic, answered the first four questions. Notice that by the fourth question, she realized she needed to narrow her topic.

1. Classical music is the music of Bach, Tchaikovsky, Beethoven, and Mozart. It takes you to another time and place.

2. People tend to think of classical music as stuffy and formal. But sometimes it is loud and dramatic, while at other times it is very soft and romantic. Some classical music sounds like church music, and some sounds like the folk songs and peasant dances on which it is based. There are almost as many kinds of classical music as there are kinds of popular music.

3. Classical music is written in movements. Each movement is a part. Some of these movements have been used in movies, such as Fantasia and Amadeus.

4. The movie Amadeus is about Mozart's life (his whole name was Wolfgang Amadeus Mozart). I'll rent the movie to learn more about my favorite classical composer. Maybe I'll write my essay on my interest in Mozart's music.

Freewriting about Music. Look at your answers to the twenty questions in Activity 4. Choose the one aspect of your topic that most appeals to you. Then freewrite about your narrowed topic in your journal. ❏

ACTIVITY
5

Put your material about music aside for now. You want to think about another interest and topic for writing, one related to sports and recreation.

Sports and Recreation

When we think of sports, competitive activities such as softball, baseball, football, tennis, and golf come to mind. Recreation includes activities we do for pleasure and exercise, such as hiking, fishing, and river rafting. Both sports and recreational activities require physical stamina and skill.

Do you play a sport? What is your favorite spectator sport? Your favorite recreation? What is it that you most enjoy about the sport or recreation? What qualities do you admire in your favorite sports figure or in the people who participate in your favorite recreation? Which of these qualities would you like to develop in yourself? What do you think your favorite sport or recreation reveals about you?

Mark Mardon, in "City Kids Go Wild," writes about the importance of a recreational program.

MARK MARDON

City Kids Go Wild

Each year some 7,500 kids from housing projects and poor   *1*
neighborhoods in cities across the United States get a taste of the
great outdoors by taking part in the Sierra Club's Inner City Outings
program. For many participants, getting away to the wilds for a
weekend of camping, hiking, boating, or skiing is more than a
lark—it's a desperately needed respite from the dehumanizing effects of poverty, pollution, and hopelessness.

Now in its 23rd year of operation, ICO is one of the Sierra Club's   *2*
longest-running and most successful community-outreach programs. Its dedicated corps of volunteer leaders works year-round to
get disadvantaged young people of diverse ethnic and cultural backgrounds out of their concrete-and-asphalt environs and into the natural world.

Many kids come to the outings program from schools, neighbor-   *3*
hood and church youth groups, rehabilitation centers, and recreation
clubs. They live in such far-flung cities as Atlanta, Ft. Lauderdale,
Chicago, and Seattle. So far ICO groups have been established in 42
municipalities nationwide. All participants learn outdoor skills appropriate to their region. The outings might take place in areas just beyond city limits, or a full day's journey away, but under the tutelage
of qualified ICO leaders (many of whom got their training through
ICO involvement) the youngsters strap on backpacks, hike or bike,
canoe and fish, pitch tents, and prepare meals. Some go on service
trips to help build and maintain trails, clean up debris on beaches and
along streams, and repair meadows; others work on projects such as
building bat shelters, studying pond ecology, or helping to rehabili-
tate injured wildlife. Most of the equipment they use—tents, skis,
bikes, stoves, shovels, canoes, sleeping bags, and the like—is donated
by ICO supporters and leaders.

Such activities are a world apart from most ICO kids' daily lives.   *4*
Few of the 7- to 17-year-olds who join have ever set foot in the
wilderness, much less spent the night there. One recent group from
New Orleans—which to some extent typifies all ICO groups—included a 10-year-old girl whose home had no running water and no
electricity, who had never known her father, and whose mother was
addicted to crack cocaine; a 12-year-old boy whose father had repeatedly courted death by overdosing on heroin; several youths
from a tough neighborhood where shootings and drug dealing are
commonplace; a teenage boy who was HIV positive; and other kids
who had seen one or both of their parents stricken with AIDS.

"You'd never think they come from the background they do,"   *5*
says Kate Mytron, founder and coordinator of the New Orleans ICO

group. "They're so normal, so hungry for knowledge. They go on one canoe trip and learn the names of snakes and birds, and on the next trip they're delighted to remember them."

Perhaps the most important thing the young people get out of ICO, adds Mytron, "is a little personal power over their own lives, an opportunity to make choices—not to mention some of the things most people take for granted, like breakfast, lunch, and dinner." 6

Reading to Improve Writing. Discuss the following questions about "City Kids Go Wild" with your classmates.

ACTIVITY
6

1. What types of recreation does the Sierra Club's Inner City Outings (ICO) program provide?

    _____

    _____

    _____

2. How does the ICO program benefit the participants? _____

    _____

    _____

    _____

3. According to the author, why have some of the participants never before set foot in the wilderness?

    _____

    _____

    _____

4. What details does Mardon use to inform his audience about the ICO program?

    _____

    _____

    _____

5. How does the writer organize these details? What is the effect?

    _____

    _____

    _____

6. What similar recreational programs could you write about?

    _____

    _____

    _____

ACTIVITY
7

Collecting New Words. Try to determine the meanings of the following words from the way they're used in "City Kids Go Wild." Then verify their meanings by checking a dictionary.

lark (1)   _____

respite (1)   _____

dehumanizing (1)   _____

environs (2)   _____

municipalities (3) _____

tutelage (3)   _____

ecology (3)   _____

courted (4)   _____

ACTIVITY
8

Interviewing Someone about a Sport or Recreation. If after using some of the other methods of gathering ideas you discover a need for additional information on your topic, consider interviewing an expert in the field. Use the following guidelines to plan and conduct your interview. (See Chapter Three for more on interviewing.)

1. Set a time to meet.
2. Prepare your questions in advance. Focus on the journalist's *who, what, when, where, why,* and *how* questions. Avoid *yes-no* questions.
3. Design other questions that will keep the expert focused on your topic.
4. Listen carefully and take notes during the interview.
5. Review your notes with the expert and fill in any gaps in your understanding.
6. Thank the expert for agreeing to be interviewed. ❏

One student writer, Arnold Allen, found that he didn't know enough about his favorite recreation—karate—to write an essay on the topic. He decided to interview an expert on the subject—his karate instructor on campus. This is what Arnold learned from the interview:

- *Who?* Anyone who wants to learn self-defense can learn karate. People as young as five or six have studied it.
- *What?* Karate is a martial art that means "the way of the empty hand." It was developed in the seventeenth century in Okinawa during its occupation by the Japanese forces.
- *Where and when?* Many fitness centers, YMCAs, and colleges offer day and evening karate classes. There are also privately owned karate schools.
- *Why?* Karate is the most popular form of self-defense that people study because it combines both skill and stamina.
- *How?* Karate is best learned from a skilled teacher, one step at a time. Progress is marked by the color of the belt or sash that the student wears. A black belt indicates the top rank of master.

Put your material on a favorite sport or recreation aside for now. You want to explore ideas on yet another possible topic for your essay—other interests.

Other Interests

Do you collect stamps, coins, or baseball cards? Do you like to try new recipes and prepare special meals for your family and friends? Perhaps you regularly spend time reading or working on your car or volunteering at a neighborhood outreach center. What are some of your interests, and what do they reveal about you as a person?

Many people have discovered a new interest in computers. They spend hours chatting with other users on Internet newsgroups or playing computer games. The essay "Gone Fishin'" describes a computer game that enables users to combine their interests in fishing and computers.

COMPUTER TIP

GATHERING IDEAS FROM INTERNET NEWSGROUPS

If you have access to the Internet, locate a newsgroup (sometimes called a *bulletin board* or a *listserv*) on a topic related to sports or recreation. You can post messages to other users with the same interests and discuss your topic with people all over the world. Newsgroup discussions can also help you become a more fluent writer. Contact your campus computer center for a list of the newsgroups it makes available to students.

FAMILY PC

Gone Fishin'

Avid anglers know that to catch a keeper, you have to outsmart   *1*
the fish. And in Gone Fishin' . . . all of your fishing wits and abilities are put to the test.

This game simulates fresh- and warm-water fishing in the Bay   *2*
of Quinte on the shore of Lake Ontario. It's detailed enough to sat-
isfy serious anglers (fish for muskie, walleye, pike, and smallmouth
bass) yet flexible enough to provide entertainment for novices of all
ages.

To find where the fish are jumping, start by checking the best   *3*
spots on the bay; they're clearly marked on the map. Then note conditions. All aspects of the fishing ecosystem are accurately modeled,
including weather and water temperature—conditions that can
greatly affect fish behavior. On windy days, for example, the lake's
surface is stirred up, decreasing the amount of light entering the water. This entices the walleye to come out of the depths and feed in
the shallows.

When you're in a bind, consult the Fishin' Buddy on the tool   *4*
bar located along the top of the screen. He'll give you advice on how
to choose the right tackle and bait.

Casting is an essential skill for anyone interested in more   *5*
than just a view of the bay. Center your mouse on the Cast on-
screen button; then hold down the left mouse button. As you
pull your mouse back toward you, the rod will also pull back.
Sweep the mouse forward, release the button, and let your lure
fly.

If you're not having much luck, try a different lure or live   *6*
bait; the leopard frog is a delicacy for feisty largemouth bass. If
you're in deep water on hot, windless days, select lures that dive
down quickly, such as the deep diver. Make sure your speed stays
within the green zone of the lure-speed gauge; this zone gives the
lure the most attractive wiggle, to attract even the most stubborn
fish.

You'll know you've hooked one when there is a sudden increase   *7*
in tension on the line or when your line starts going out even as
you're reeling it in. Don't panic. Just tighten the drag on the reel by
pressing the + button on the Cast and Reel control. Make the drag
tight enough to reel in your fish, but not too tight, or you'll lose
everything—hook, line, and lunker.

Play your cards right and you'll be locked in a 10-minute battle   *8*
that, if you're victorious, will reward you with a beautiful 10-pound
walleye.

Reading to Improve Writing. Discuss the following questions about "Gone Fishin'" with your classmates.

1. What details does the author use to inform his or her audience about the computer game?

   _____

   _____

   _____

2. How does the writer organize these details? At what point in the essay does he or she begin to describe how to use the game? What is the effect of this organization?

   _____

   _____

   _____

3. According to the author, why would someone want to "fish" on a computer?

   _____

   _____

   _____

4. What do the writer's interests in fishing and computer games tell you about him or her as a person?

   _____

   _____

   _____

5. What similar interests could you write about?

   _____

   _____

_____

_____

ACTIVITY
10

Collecting New Words. Try to determine the meanings of the following words from the way they're used in "Gone Fishin'." Then verify their meanings by checking a dictionary.

anglers (1)   _____

simulates (2)   _____

ecosystem (3)   _____

casting (5)   _____

lure (5)   _____

feisty (6)   _____

lunker (7)   _____

GROUP
ACTIVITY
11

Gathering Ideas on Your Interests. In your journal, brainstorm a list of your interests. Then, working with a peer response group, discuss each student's list and identify the one interest that the group considers most promising as a topic for an essay. Next, use the twenty questions listed in Activity 4 to gather ideas about your topic. Finally, if necessary, gather additional details by freewriting or by interviewing someone knowledgeable about your special interest. ❏

Drafting

You've now gathered ideas on three possible topics for your essay: music, a sport or recreation, and a special interest. You're ready to begin drafting, but you must decide how to proceed. Here are some of your options:

• You may select one of the three topics for your discovery draft.

• You may write drafts on two or three of the topics to see which one you prefer to continue working on.

• You may combine related topics in your discovery draft. For example, you might describe how a special song is played at some sporting events.

Your topic should, above all, be one that interests you and motivates you to write. You should also know enough about the topic to write an interesting and informative essay about it. Or, you should be prepared to interview experts who can provide you with the information you need. Also think about your purpose and audience—your classmates, your instructor, and the readers of your campus or local newspaper. Will your topic appeal to your readers?

In addition, remember to narrow your topic if it is too broad to cover in an essay. Then write a preliminary thesis statement that announces the topic and explains its significance to you. If, as you draft, you find that you don't have enough information to support your thesis, return to the gathering ideas stage to collect more information. Finally, remember that your main goal at the drafting stage is to get your ideas down on paper. You'll have time later on to revise and edit your discovery draft.

Here's the discovery draft that student writer Arnold Allen wrote on karate.

COMPUTER TIP

SAVING JOURNALISTS' QUESTIONS ON A COMPUTER

Create a file of *who, what, when, where, why,* and *how* questions about your special interest. Then use the questions to do some freewriting or to conduct an interview. Here are some sample questions to get you started.

• *Who* would be interested in my topic/special interest?
• *Who* has information on it?
• *What* does it entail and cost?
• *When* do people participate in it?
• *Where* do they participate in it?
• *Why* do they participate in it?
• *How* do people participate in it?

Karate

Karate can be used for fitness and self-defense. The average person   *1*
needs some form of defense that does not require a weapon. This martial
art was developed in the seventeenth century in Okinawa when the island
was invaded by Japan.

Karate offers students a great degree of self-discipline, self-confidence,   *2*
and peace of mind. It can help you prepare physically, mentally, and even
help you in your everyday life.

Julie Avalon, senior education major, studies karate to keep fit and to   *3*
feel good about herself. Andrew Henderson, another student, also feels that
karate has made a difference in his life.

Where can you learn karate? There are many karate schools, and the   *4*
YMCA offers karate lessons.

Revising

As you revise your discovery draft, focus on making your ideas clear to your audience—your instructor, your classmates, and the readers of your campus or local newspaper. Also consider what your audience needs to know to understand your topic. At this stage, then, you should concentrate on such tasks as developing your ideas through various methods, writing an effective introduction and conclusion, and creating a lively title for your essay.

Developing Your Ideas

Developing ideas in a draft can involve using definition, classification, process analysis, facts, and expert testimony, depending on your topic, purpose, and audience. For example, to explain an unfamiliar topic to readers, you would need to define new vocabulary and classify your topic in terms of how it fits within the bigger picture. For a topic that requires you to explain how something works or how to do something, you would use process analysis. Finally, you would collect facts and expert testimony to support the validity of your ideas and your thesis statement. Let's look at how each of these techniques can help you develop the ideas in your draft.

Definition. Writers use *definition* to explain and clarify. Thus, when you define something, you tell your reader what it means. A good definition has two parts: first the term being defined is placed in a general category, and then an explanation of how it fits within that category—by way of its distinguishing features—follows. For example, to define the topic *skydiving*, you might first define it generally as a risky sport, and then go on to explain what distinguishes skydiving from other risky sports, such as rock climbing and hang gliding.

Notice how definition is used in the following paragraph from the Mardon reading. The writer generally defines the Sierra Club's Inner City Outings (ICO) program first, and then goes on to describe its activities. He thus categorizes the topic generally as a type of community-outreach program before pointing out its distinguishing feature: that it takes disadvantaged young people out of the city and into the "natural world" for a time.

> Now in its 23rd year of operation, ICO is one of the Sierra Club's longest-running and most successful community-outreach programs. Its dedicated corps of volunteer leaders works year-round to get disadvantaged young people of diverse ethnic and cultural backgrounds out of their concrete-and-asphalt environs and into the natural world.
>
> MARK MARDON, "CITY KIDS GO WILD"

Classification. Writers use *classification* to organize their ideas and thereby to aid their readers' understanding of those ideas. When you classify, then, you categorize something into types on some particular basis. For example, you might classify cars on the basis of their size (sports car, compact, midsize, and full size) or on the basis of whether they're American-made or foreign-made (Ford, Chevrolet, and GMC versus Volkswagen, Toyota, and Volvo). You might also classify cars on the basis of their resale value, safety record, popularity as judged by sales, or some other basis you deem important.

In the following paragraph about the camera collection of Cheng Jianguo, a student from China, the writer classifies cameras first by type and then by name.

> Cheng mainly collects China-made cameras. The brands of Chenguang, Tiantan, Changhong, Huashan, Changle, Yuejin, Haiou and others vividly show the development of China's camera industry. In addition, he has also gathered many different types of foreign cameras, some produced early in this century. They include the Leica and Roland from Germany, Minolta and Fuji models from Japan, and Kodak and Browning cameras from the United States as well as models from the former Soviet Union and Czechoslovakia.
>
> "CAMERA COLLECTOR CHENG JIANGUO"

Process Analysis. Writers use a technique called *process analysis* to explain how something works or how to do something—in other words, to explain the process involved. Cookbooks and repair manuals come to mind when we think of process writing, but bookstore shelves are filled with all sorts of other "how to" books explaining processes—from how to work a computer to how to arrange your closet.

In an essay about your favorite hiking trail, for instance, you might explain the process of preparing to hike the trail and locating the trailhead, as Laurence Parent does in the following paragraphs about hiking to Wheeler Peak in New Mexico.

> Be sure to get a very early start on this hike. To minimize problems with storms, you ideally want to be on the summit before noon. Snow flurries are possible even in mid-summer. Be sure to take rain gear and extra warm clothing. Lightning and hypothermia are real threats on Wheeler Peak and the exposed summit ridge. . . .
>
> At just short of one mile you will pass marked Trail 63, the Long Canyon Trail to Gold Hill, coming in from the left. Ignore it and continue climbing up the northeast valley. Just past the trail junction, the trail hits an old road. Turn left onto the road and follow it the rest of the way up the valley.
>
> LAURENCE PARENT, *THE HIKER'S GUIDE TO NEW MEXICO*

Facts. Unlike opinions or guesses, *facts* are statements that can be objectively verified as true. For example, the statement "Golden retrievers are beautiful," represents the opinion of the writer. In contrast, the statement "A golden retriever is a breed of dog," is a fact that can be verified in an encyclopedia or other reliable source.

You use facts in writing to provide support for your ideas and thereby to convince your readers that you know your topic well. Facts may include names, dates, numbers, statistics, and other data relevant to your topic or idea. Notice in the following paragraph that facts are used to support the idea that Asian Americans are a diverse group.

> Asian Americans are an especially diverse group, comprised of Chinese, Filipino, Japanese, Vietnamese, Cambodians, Hmong, and other groups. The largest Asian-American groups are Chinese Americans (24 percent), Filipino Americans (20 percent), and Japanese Americans (12 percent). Other groups, such as Vietnamese, Cambodians, Laotians, and Hmong, are more recent arrivals, first coming to this country in the 1970s as refugees from the upheavals resulting from the Vietnam War. In the 1980s, Koreans and Filipinos began immigrating in larger numbers. The majority of Asian Americans live in the West.
>
> BRYAN STRONG AND CHRISTINE DEVAULT,
> *THE MARRIAGE AND FAMILY EXPERIENCE*

Expert Testimony. Statements made by knowledgeable people are considered *expert testimony*. Having experts confirm what you say makes your writing more convincing. For example, citing the Surgeon General's warning that cigarette smoking greatly increases your risk of lung cancer is more convincing than offering the statement alone or citing someone with no medical background or authority to advise American citizens on health matters.

In the following paragraph, the author uses expert testimony to convince his readers that lead vocalist Edward Kowalczyk and his band Live are headed for national success.

> After only two albums, the four farm boys from York, Pa., are being groomed for the big leagues. "We look for artists that we think can go to the next level," says MTV's senior vice president of music and programming, Andy Schoun, who helps pick bands for *Unplugged*. "In the case of Live, they've got what it takes."
>
> JEFF GORDINIER, "LIVE THROUGH THIS"

ACTIVITY
12

Recognizing How Ideas Are Developed. Reread the essays "Travelin' Band," "City Kids Go Wild," and "Gone Fishin'" that appear earlier in the chapter. In the margin, identify where the writers use definition, classification, process analysis, facts, and expert testimony to develop their ideas. Compare your work with that of your classmates and discuss the similarities and differences you discover.

Developing Ideas within Paragraphs. Working with a peer response group, exchange discovery drafts with members of the group for evaluation. Use the following questions to evaluate group members' drafts, focusing on the development of ideas within paragraphs. Then save the group's feedback on your draft for reference during revision.

1. What, if anything, is unclear or confusing in the draft?
2. Are terms defined well? Does each definition have the two required parts?
3. Is classification used where it's needed to organize ideas and assist readers' understanding?
4. Is process analysis used to explain how something works or how to do something?
5. Are facts or statistics included? Do they support or verify the writer's ideas?
6. Have the writer's ideas been made more convincing through expert testimony?   ❑

Writing an Effective Introduction

Readers expect to find not only well-developed ideas in an essay; they also expect an effective introduction and a forceful conclusion. Let's look first at introductions and how to make them effective.

The *introduction* to an essay serves two major purposes: it gets your readers' attention and it announces your thesis statement. By using the opening sentences of your essay to hook your readers' interest, you convince them that your essay is worth reading. By presenting your thesis statement in the introduction, you give your readers a road map of sorts for reading your essay. (Although a thesis statement may sometimes appear elsewhere in an essay, it usually works best in the introduction. See Chapter Three for more information.)

How do you go about writing an introduction that gets your readers' attention *and* presents your thesis? One way is to hook your readers' interest while also leading up to the thesis, which is placed at the end of the first paragraph. You may do this by using one of the following techniques for introducing a topic in an interesting and effective way.

1. definition
2. classification
3. facts
4. expert testimony
5. examples
6. questions

7. anecdote
8. description

Definition. This type of introduction works well when you need to define an unfamiliar topic for your readers. In the following introductory paragraph, the writer uses *definition* to ensure her readers' understanding of her topic and thesis statement. Notice also that she defines *clambake* by first placing it in the general category of cookouts and then describing some of its distinguishing features. Her thesis statement (italicized here) follows the definition and appears last in the paragraph.

> The clambake is a huge cookout held on the beach, usually in the summertime. Friends get together and gather rocks and firewood and prepare mounds of soft-shell clams and milky sweet corn-on-the-cob for the pit. The bake stretches through the cool evening as the smoky aroma of seaweed and seafood blend with the salty air. *Attending a clambake, one of New England's most cherished traditions, can be a festive affair.*

Classification. You may use *classification* in an introduction when categorizing by types is needed to help narrow your topic and focus your readers' attention on the one type discussed in your essay. For example, in the following introduction, the writer classifies various types of musicians before focusing attention on the essay's topic: the two types of musicians who play percussion instruments, "drummers" and "percussionists." The writer's thesis statement (italicized here) comes last in the introduction.

> Quick—what do you call a person who plays a trumpet? A trumpeter, of course. A person who plays the flute is referred to as a flutist, or flautist, if you prefer. Someone who plays a piano is usually known as a pianist, unless of course he plays the player piano, in which case he is known as a player piano player rather than a player piano pianist. Got the hang of this yet? Okay, then, what do you call someone who plays that set of instruments belonging to the percussion family? Why, you call him a percussionist, don't you? Wrong! It's not quite as easy as all that. *There are two types of musicians who play percussion instruments, "drummers" and "percussionists," and they are as different as the Sex Pistols and the New York Philharmonic.*
>
> KAREN KRAMER, "THE LITTLE DRUMMER BOYS"

Facts. Introducing a topic with *facts*—statements that can be verified as true—has two important effects on readers. It signals them that you know your topic well, and it encourages them to read further to see what you have to say. This technique is used effectively in the following introduction, where the writer begins with several facts about the topic—the Citation X airplane—that lead into the thesis statement (italicized here).

When Cessna announced development of the Citation X in 1990, the company promised a maximum speed of Mach .90, which is 90 percent of the speed of sound. With more than 550 test-flying hours on three airplanes, it looks like Cessna engineers were being conservative. *Maximum speed on the Citation X will probably be Mach .92, making the airplane the fastest business jet and the quickest subsonic civilian jet of any type.*

Mac J. McClellan, "Citation X"

Expert Testimony. Beginning an essay with *expert testimony*—statements made by knowledgeable people in the field—is an effective way to convince your readers that you know your topic well *and* that someone in authority agrees with you. In the introduction that follows, notice that the writer quotes an *Esquire* food columnist to convince her readers that anyone can make gourmet pizza. The expert testimony thereby reinforces the thesis statement, which is given at the end (in italics).

So you want to learn how to make a gourmet pizza topped with pepperoni, olives, green peppers, and capers. According to John Mariani, *Esquire* food columnist, you are in good company. He says, "Nothing, absolutely nothing, comes close to pizza as a true international favorite." *By following easy step-by-step instructions, you, too, can become a gourmet pizza chef, dazzling your college friends with trendy New York-style pizza.*

Examples. Using *examples* in an introduction helps readers focus on and understand the topic. This technique is used in the following introduction to an essay about Juliette Low, the founder of the Girl Scouts. The writer uses examples of Low's eccentricity and stubborn nature to lead us into the essay's thesis: that these aspects of Low's character played a crucial role in her motivation to establish the Girl Scouts.

She drove on the right side of the road in England and on the left in America, studied palm reading and wore real vegetables on her hats. Some people excused her unconventional attitudes about women as being those of an eccentric. *But fortunately for women, Juliette Gordon Low, the founder of the Girl Scouts, prided herself on her eccentricity and her stubbornness (which often got her into trouble) and used these qualities to show Victorian women that their lives could be whatever they dared to make them.*

Nancy Lyon, "Juliette Low:
The Eccentric Who Founded the Girl Scouts"

Questions. Posing one or more *questions* at the start of an essay can arouse readers' curiosity about your topic and encourage them to read on for the answers. A series of questions is used in this way in the following introduction to an essay about Brad Peavy, a student athlete with a disability. The questions arouse our interest in the topic, which is stated in the thesis statement at the end.

> What person with a handicap would return to play golf only two months after having his lower right leg amputated? What person with a handicap would win the city golf tournament six months after such an amputation? Brad Peavy of the Columbus, Ohio, police department is that person. *Brad hates the word* handicapped *and has set out to prove that it doesn't apply to him.*

Anecdote. Beginning with an *anecdote* or brief story can help draw readers into your essay. In the following introduction, the writer uses an anecdote to dramatize the topic of his essay: his interest in writing for pleasure.

> A man quietly resting on a log reached down and picked up a stick and began writing in the sand. He moved the stick slowly, carefully drawing his letters. He looked at what he had written and smiled. Seeing him smile, other people came over to see what he had done. They looked at the words and nodded and smiled, too. *He realized, then, that writing was a powerful way to communicate; he began to look for more permanent ways to record his thoughts.*

Description. An introduction that contains sensory *description* sets the scene and draws readers into your essay. This introduction to an essay about a neighborhood softball team provides numerous descriptive details about the players:

> John's Lawn Rangers are a gutsy, grimy group of guys. Yes, they mow overgrown lawns, trim bushy hedges, and spread fertilizer on your neighbor's lawn, but when they show up at the ball field on Saturday, they are wearing their starched white uniforms, black cleated shoes, and fire-engine red baseball caps. John's Lawn Rangers are ready for their favorite pastime, softball. *Our local sandlot team is the team to beat this season.*

ACTIVITY
14

Revising Your Introduction. Reread the introductory paragraph of your essay. Then rate your introduction on a scale of 1 to 4, as indicated in the list that follows.

1—effective (forceful, attention-getting hook; clearly stated thesis statement)

2—adequate (satisfactory hook; clearly stated thesis statement)

3—so-so (uninteresting hook; vague thesis statement)

4—ineffective (no hook and/or no thesis statement)

Discuss your rating with your classmates. Then revise the introduction to your essay using one of the techniques discussed in this chapter. Also look at your thesis statement to see how you can make it more effective. It should announce your topic clearly and reveal the significance of your topic. ❑

Writing a Powerful Conclusion

Unlike elementary school reading and writing where "The End" marks the conclusion of a story, the ending of a college essay requires the writer to create a natural sense of closure.

The *conclusion* serves two major functions in an essay: it makes clear that you've made the point you set out to make at the start of the essay, and it draws the essay to a satisfactory close. Thus, in the conclusion you do not introduce new material or end abruptly; instead, you wrap up what you have already said. Writers use various techniques to create effective conclusions. These techniques include:

1. restating the thesis.
2. making a recommendation.
3. using an effective quotation.
4. asking a question.
5. including a call for action.
6. providing a summary.

Restate the Thesis. By *restating the thesis* in your conclusion, you remind readers of its significance and thereby give emphasis to your main point or idea. For example, look back at the introduction to an article about making New York-style pizza on page 167. Then notice, in the following conclusion to that article, how the writer restates her thesis. After giving the step-by-step instructions in the body of her essay, she wants to remind readers of her purpose in the conclusion; that is, that anyone can become a gourmet pizza chef.

> By following these easy step-by-step instructions, you, too, can become a gourmet pizza chef. Invite your friends over for a pizza party this weekend. Impress them with your knowledge of how to make a pizza crust and how to select just the right olive oil and mozzarella cheese. You might even convince them to try the anchovies.

Make a Recommendation. By making a *recommendation* in the conclusion, you leave readers with a bit of useful advice about your topic. Because you have special knowledge of the topic, you can inform others about how to put the information you have provided to good use. In the following conclusion to an essay about windsurfing, for instance, the writer recommends a certain sailboard.

> All things considered, the Robert's 9'4" is a well-rounded race-board at a competitive price. It'll work well with race sails from 5.5 to

7.5, and its particular strength is the way it handles outrageously rough water in upwind-downwind courses. Anyone in the 160- to 185-pound range looking for excellent all-around course-slalom and light-wind slalom performance would have to buy a hand-built board to do better.

"EQUIPMENT" FROM *WINDSURFING* MAGAZINE

Use an Effective Quotation. With an *effective quotation* you can conclude an essay in an interesting, attention-getting way that emphasizes your main point. In the essay you read earlier in the chapter, Mark Mardon concludes with a powerful quotation to emphasize the importance of his topic—the Sierra Club's Inner City Outings (ICO) program.

> Perhaps the most important thing the young people get out of ICO, adds Mytron, "is a little personal power over their own lives, an opportunity to make choices—not to mention some of the things most people take for granted, like breakfast, lunch, and dinner."

MARK MARDON, "CITY KIDS GO WILD"

Ask a Question. By posing a meaningful *question* in the conclusion, you increase your readers' interest in the topic and leave them pondering its importance. In his essay in the *Utne Reader* about the American tendency to turn sports figures into heroes, Matthew Goodman concludes by asking his readers a thought-provoking question.

> Thanks to the years of hard work and uncompromising work that athletes have invested in themselves, sports is often able to provide us a glimpse of that "supreme beauty" that Bertrand Russell wrote of as characteristic of mathematics: "sublimely pure, and capable of a stern perfection such as only the greatest art can show." Can't we just leave it at that?

MATTHEW GOODMAN, "WHERE HAVE YOU GONE, JOE DIMAGGIO?"

Include a Call for Action. A *call for action* helps personalize your essay by asking readers to do something or to continue thinking about the topic after they read the essay. In the following example from an article about the popularity of collecting baseball cards, the writer concludes with a call for action by asking readers to consider joining a baseball card club.

> After collecting baseball cards for several years, our greatest desire is to start a baseball card club in Los Angeles. If you would be interested in joining such a club, write to the above address with a note, "Count me in!"

Provide a Summary. For a lengthy and complex essay, a *summary* can pull ideas together and reinforce main points in the conclusion.

The author of the essay on the New England clambake quoted earlier, for example, summarizes her important points about the clambake in her conclusion.

> A clambake may remind you of Boston and Paul Revere's ride, but to ensure a successful meal, remember these important points: start early, dig a pit that is at least 2 feet deep, feed the charcoal fire with hardwood, and use seaweed-soaked canvas. While your clams are cooking, get out the iced-tea and beer and enjoy playing volleyball or strolling along the beach while taking part in this cherished New England tradition.

Revising Your Conclusion. Reread the concluding paragraph of your essay. Then rate the conclusion on a scale of 1 to 4, as indicated in the list that follows.

ACTIVITY
15

1—powerful (memorable closure; main points reinforced)
2—adequate (interesting closure; main points reinforced)
3—so-so (uninteresting closure; main points reinforced)
4—ineffective (no sense of closure; main points are not reinforced)

Discuss your rating with your classmates. Revise the conclusion to your essay using one of the techniques discussed in this chapter. Try to leave your readers with a lasting impression about your topic and its significance. ❏

Writing a Lively Title

You have something else to do at this point: write a title for your essay. A good title helps focus your readers' attention even before they begin reading the essay.

At the very least your title must reflect your topic. A *lively* title, however, catches readers' attention by using language that is both specific and imaginative. Look at the difference between the following mediocre titles and the livelier revisions. The mediocre titles simply state the general topic or subject area, whereas the livelier ones are more specific and imaginative.

MEDIOCRE: The Sierra Club's Program for Kids
LIVELIER: City Kids Go Wild

The livelier title uses a play on words—children can both *be wild* and go hiking *in the wild*.

MEDIOCRE: Karate
LIVELIER: Karate: For Fitness and Self-Defense

The revised title describes the particular focus of the essay. The author knows that fitness and self-defense are popular topics that may encourage readers' interest in his essay.

MEDIOCRE: Sports Legend Joe DiMaggio

LIVELIER: Where Have You Gone, Joe DiMaggio?

The livelier version poses a question to engage readers' curiosity about the topic.

MEDIOCRE: Rock Music

LIVELIER: Rock and Rap Have Never Been Better

The livelier title narrows the focus of the essay and uses a popular expression to catch readers' attention.

MEDIOCRE: Sebadoh

LIVELIER: Travelin' Band

The revision uses a popular phrase from a song lyric to engage readers' interest in the topic.

ACTIVITY

16

Writing a Lively Title. Imagine that you're writing an essay on each of the following topics. Revise the titles to make them livelier. Share the revised titles with your classmates, explaining how you made them livelier.

1. The Best Rock Group

    _____

2. Stamp Collecting

    _____

3. Yoga

    _____

4. How to Make Pizza

    _____

5. My Favorite Sport

    _____

Adding a Lively Title. Look at the title of your essay. How can it be made more lively? Revise the title so that it captures your readers' attention and makes them want to read your essay. ❏

ACTIVITY
17

Arnold's Revised Draft

Before you read Arnold's revised draft, reread his discovery draft (p.161). Notice, in the revision, that Arnold includes additional details about his topic. He gathered these details by using the twenty questions technique and interviewing his karate instructor and other karate students. Notice, too, his revised introduction and conclusion, as well as his use of definition, classification, process analysis, facts, and expert testimony to develop his ideas. (The errors in Arnold's revised draft will be corrected later on when he edits his essay.)

Karate: For Fitness and Self-Defense

Do you want to learn a martial arts skill that can keep you fit as well as help you fight off an attacker? Karate is just that: it is a martial art used for fitness and self-defense.

1 Introduction poses a question and provides a definition
Thesis statement

According to the latest figures from the Criminal Justice Department. Crime in the United States has increased over 50 percent in the last twenty years. These crimes include forcible rape, aggravated assault, and murder. The average person needed some form of defense that does not require a weapon.

2 Facts added

Classification added

Karate was developed in the seventeenth century in Okinawa during its occupation by the Japanese forces. The Japanese forbade the Okinawans to carry weapons. Left unarmed, they developed karate, which relies on the power of the hands and feet. The term itself means "the way of the empty hand."

3 Facts added

Definition added

Karate is physically demanding, and its practice gives the student mobility, flexability, speed, stamina, and endurance. These can be more important than strength, especially when confronted by an overwhelming, large attacker. As a pastime, karate offers students the opportunity to develop self-discipline, self-confidence, and peace of mind. It can help you prepare physically and mentally, and even help you in your everyday life.

4 Process analysis added

What kind of people learn karate? Larry Yarrell, a well-known karate instructor, has been studying and practicing karate for twenty-four years. He has been an instructor for the last ten years.

5 Facts added

Expert testimony added

"People should study karate because it gives them fundamental stabil-   6
ity," Yarrell says. "It will also help them to focus on their careers and personal lives." It is obvious from talking to Yarrell that once a person earns a
black belt in karate, he can do anything.

Expert testimony added

Julie Avalon, a senior education major, studies karate to keep fit and to   7
feel good about herself. "I also want to change the stereotype that karate is
only for men. Hopefully, I can get my two-and-a-half-year-old interested, too."

Expert testimony added

Jerry Holmes, another student, also observes that karate has made a   8
difference in his life. "I first started taking lessons to learn how to 'kick butt.'
However, now that I've earned my brown belt, I find that I have more self-control and confidence."

Facts added

Where can you learn karate. There are many karate schools, and the   9
YMCA offers karate lessons. On campus, Yarrell teaches both a beginners
and an intermediate class each semester. To sign up for one of these
classes, simply call Intramurals and add your name to the list. Yarrell will
then call and interview you to determine your skill level. You will be notified of
your assigned class several weeks before it begins.

Conclusion uses an effective quotation to sum up the writer's main point

As a student in Yarrell's class assert, "I have walked away from fights   10
because I now know that just by staring into a person's eyes, I can get my
message across." You, too, can develop this skill and confidence by learning
the "way of the empty hand."

GROUP
ACTIVITY
18

Analyzing Arnold's Revised Draft. Look again at Arnold's revised draft. Then use the following questions to discuss with your
classmates how Arnold improved his draft.

1. Does Arnold both capture his readers' attention and make his thesis
    clear in the introduction? What is his thesis statement?

    _____

    _____

    _____

2. How does Arnold develop and support his main ideas?

    _____

    _____

_____

_____

3. Is Arnold's conclusion powerful? Why or why not? _____

_____

_____

_____

4. Is his title effective? Why or why not? _____

_____

_____

_____

5. How could Arnold's revised draft benefit from further revision?

_____

_____

_____

_____

Using Peer Review. Form a group with two or three other students and exchange copies of your drafts. Read your draft aloud while your classmates follow along. Take notes on your classmates' responses to the following questions about your draft.

GROUP
ACTIVITY
19

1. Have I followed all of the instructions for this assignment?

_____

_____

_____

2. How interesting is my introduction? Do you want to continue reading my paper? Why or why not?

    _____

    _____

    _____

3. What is my thesis statement? Do I need to make the thesis clearer?

    _____

    _____

    _____

4. Where in the essay could I improve the development of ideas by using definition, classification, process analysis, facts, or expert testimony?

    _____

    _____

    _____

5. Are my paragraphs unified, or do any of them contain irrelevant information or ideas?

    _____

    _____

    _____

6. What parts of my essay, if any, don't support my thesis and could be omitted?

    _____

    _____

    _____

7. Where in the essay did my writing confuse you? How can I clarify my thoughts?

_____

_____

_____

_____

8. How effective is my conclusion? Do I end in such a way that my reader knows it's the end?

_____

_____

_____

9. How clear is the purpose of my essay? How well have I met the needs of my audience?

_____

_____

_____

_____

Revising Your Draft. Taking your classmates' suggestions for revision into consideration, revise your essay about a favorite pastime or interest. In particular, focus on improving the development of your ideas and revising your introduction and conclusion using the techniques discussed in this chapter. Also create a lively title for your essay. ❑

ACTIVITY
20

Editing

Once you're satisfied with the content of your revised draft, you're ready to edit it to eliminate errors, which distract readers from the content and message of an essay.

Arnold's Edited Essay

You probably noticed that Arnold's revised draft contained errors in grammar, spelling, and punctuation. Arnold eliminated these errors in his edited essay. His corrections are underlined here. His editing log follows the essay.

Karate: For Fitness and Self-Defense

Do you want to learn a martial arts skill that can keep you fit as well as help you fight off an attacker? Karate is just that: it is a martial art used for fitness and self-defense. [1]

According to the latest figures from the Criminal Justice Department, crime in the United States has increased over 50 percent in the last twenty years. These crimes include forcible rape, aggravated assault, and murder. The average person needs some form of defense that does not require a weapon. [2]

Karate was developed in the seventeenth century in Okinawa during its occupation by the Japanese forces. The Japanese forbade the Okinawans to carry weapons. Left unarmed, they developed karate, which relies on the power of the hands and feet. The term itself means "the way of the empty hand." [3]

Karate is physically demanding, and its practice gives the student mobility, flexibility, speed, stamina, and endurance. These can be more important than strength, especially when confronted by an overwhelming, large attacker. As a pastime, karate offers students the opportunity to develop self-discipline, self-confidence, and peace of mind. It can help you prepare physically and mentally, and even help you in your everyday life. [4]

What kind of people learn karate? Larry Yarrell, a well-known karate instructor, has been studying and practicing karate for twenty-four years. He has been an instructor for the last ten years. [5]

"People should study karate because it gives them fundamental stability," Yarrell says. "It will also help them to focus on their careers and personal lives." It is obvious from talking to Yarrell that once people earn a black belt in karate, they can do anything. [6]

Julie Avalon, a senior education major, studies karate to keep fit and to feel good about herself. "I also want to change the stereotype that karate is only for men. Hopefully, I can get my two-and-a-half-year-old interested, too." [7]

Jerry Holmes, another student, also observes that karate has made a difference in his life. "I first started taking lessons to learn how to 'kick butt.' [8]

However, now that I've earned my brown belt, I find that I have more self-control and confidence."

Where can you learn <u>karate</u>? There are many karate schools, and the YMCA also offers karate lessons. On campus, Yarrell teaches both a beginners and an intermediate class each semester. To sign up for one of these classes, simply call Intramurals and add your name to the list. Yarrell will then call and interview you to determine your skill level. You will be notified of your assigned class several weeks before it begins. *9*

As a student in Yarrell's class <u>asserts</u>, "I have walked away from fights because I now know that just by staring into a person's eyes, I can get my message across." You, too, can develop this skill and confidence by learning the "way of the empty hand." *10*

Arnold's Editing Log

• INCORRECT:	According to the latest figures from the Criminal Justice Department. Crime in the United States has increased over 50 percent in the last twenty years. (2)
ERROR:	sentence fragment
CORRECT:	According to the latest figures from the Criminal Justice Department, crime in the United States has increased over 50 percent in the last twenty years.
• INCORRECT:	The average person needed some form of defense that does not require a weapon. (2)
ERROR:	shift in verb tense
CORRECT:	The average person needs some form of defense that does not require a weapon.
• INCORRECT:	flexability (4)
ERROR:	misspelled word
CORRECT:	flexibility
• INCORRECT:	It is obvious from talking with Yarrell that once a person earns a black belt in karate, he can do anything. (6)
ERROR:	sexist language
CORRECT:	It is obvious from talking with Yarrell that once people earn a black belt in karate, they can do anything.
• INCORRECT:	Where can you learn karate. (9)
ERROR:	incorrect end punctuation
CORRECT:	Where can you learn karate?
• INCORRECT:	As a student in Yarrell's class assert, "I have walked away from fights because I now know that just by staring into a person's eyes, I can get my message across." (10)
ERROR:	incorrect subject–verb agreement
CORRECT:	As a student in Yarrell's class asserts, "I have walked away from fights because I now know that just by staring into a person's eyes, I can get my message across."

ACTIVITY
21

Editing Your Essay. To edit your draft, read it word-for-word, looking for errors in grammar, spelling, and punctuation. If you know that you often make a particular type of error, read the essay one time for only that error. Also ask a classmate or friend to help you spot errors you might have overlooked. Then use a dictionary and the Handbook in Part III of this book to help you correct the errors you find. Finally, record those errors in your editing log. ❑

Publishing

When you put as much effort into an essay as you have for this one, you want others to read and learn from it. Share your essay with your instructor and classmates. In addition, you may want to submit it to your campus or local newspaper for possible publication.

Your Writing Portfolio

You may now add your essay to your writing portfolio, which consists of your best writing as well as your reflections on your writing. To help you reflect on the writing you did in this chapter, answer the following questions:

1. How did you decide which discovery draft to develop into an essay?
2. Did your audience affect your topic choice? Why or why not?
3. Which paragraphs in your essay do you consider the most effective? The least effective? Why?
4. Which details best support your main point? Why?
5. How did you revise your introduction and conclusion? Are you satisfied with the results? Explain.
6. Are you pleased with the title of your essay? Why or why not?

Using your answers to these questions, update the writing process report you began in Chapter Three.

Writing Process Report

Date:

Strengths:

Weaknesses:

Plans for improvement:

Once you complete this report, freewrite in your journal about what you learned about your writing process in this chapter and what you still hope to learn.

Chapter Summary

- Gather supporting details for an informative essay by questioning and interviewing.
- Develop your ideas through definition, classification, process analysis, facts, and expert testimony.
- Write a good introduction, one that catches your readers' attention and leads into your thesis statement.
- Write an effective introduction by using one of several techniques: definition, classification, facts, expert testimony, examples, questions, an anecdote, or description.
- Announce your topic and its significance in the thesis statement, usually given at the end of the introduction.
- Write a good conclusion, one that provides a sense of closure to the essay.
- End your essay effectively by restating the thesis statement, making a recommendation, using a powerful quotation, asking a question, calling for action, or providing a summary.
- Create a lively title, one that catches your readers' attention through specific and imaginative language.

Culture is simply how one lives.
—LEROI JONES

7

Understanding Cultures

In this chapter you will

- write about a cultural symbol, ritual, or hero.

- gather ideas by questioning, clustering, freewriting, and brainstorming.

- learn how to organize the ideas in your paragraphs.

- learn how to make the ideas in your paragraphs flow together.

- add to your writing portfolio.

Have you ever traveled to another country? Were you surprised at what you saw and heard? Did people drive on the left or right side of the road? Were prices higher or lower than in this country? Were you introduced to new foods or styles of dress? Although initially unsettling at times, such encounters enable us to learn not only about other cultures, but also about our own. The term *culture* refers to the customs, beliefs, values, objects, and language shared by members of a particular group.

Many people grow up as part of a single culture—Chinese, American, or French, for instance. But more and more people are recognizing themselves as *multicultural*, or as having roots in more than one culture. Sometimes this is indicated when people say, for example, that they are Vietnamese American, African American, or Mexican American. What they mean is that they uphold the beliefs and customs of their original culture as well as their new culture. Because the United States evolved from a variety of cultures—Native American, European, African, Latin American, Asian—all of its people are, to some degree, multicultural.

Culture can refer not only to ethnic heritage, but also to the beliefs and customs of a particular group. The "hippy" culture of the 1960s believed in social and personal rebellion, had a distinctive lifestyle, and represented itself with the peace symbol. Businesses typically have their own "corporate cultures." One corporate culture, for example, may encourage teamwork, whereas another may value competition. Computer devotees have their own culture as well, including a set of customs and on-line language.

What cultures do you belong to? Consider your ethnic heritage, age group, school, workplace, and pastimes. In what ways have these cultures contributed to the kind of person you are? What have you learned from the different cultures you belong to?

ACTIVITY

1

Analyzing Your Purpose and Audience. Before you begin gathering ideas about your topic, think about your purpose and audience. For this chapter's assignment, you'll explore a symbol, ritual, or hero that is important in your culture. Since some of your readers come from a different culture, it's important that you understand what they already know about your topic and what their attitude is toward it. Your responses to the following questions will help you decide how to approach your topic.

1. Does this assignment call for expressive, informative, or persuasive writing?

    _____

2. What is your readers' average age? _____

Writing Assignment

In this chapter you'll write about a cultural symbol, ritual, or hero. You or your instructor may decide to do this assignment in one of several ways:

- You may gather ideas on one, two, *or* three topics.
- You may write a discovery draft on one, two, *or* three of these topics.
- You may choose one discovery draft to develop into a polished essay.
- You may combine your discovery draft ideas into a new topic for your essay.

After completing your essay, share it with your instructor, classmates, and students who come from cultures other than your own. You might also want to send your essay via e-mail to a college friend in another part of the country or world.

3. How many are female? _____ male? _____

4. What parts of the country or world are they from?

_____

_____

_____

Given your responses to the preceding questions, ask yourself these questions:

5. What do my readers already know about my topic? If I asked them to list five words about my topic, which five might they list?

_____

_____

_____

---

6. What do my readers need to know about my topic? Which terms and concepts do I need to define? Which objects or events do I need to describe in detail?

_____

_____

_____

_____

_____

7. How do my readers feel about my topic? Will they find it interesting, or will I have to work to get their attention?

_____

_____

_____

_____

_____

❏

Gathering Ideas

In previous chapters, you gathered ideas by brainstorming, freewriting, clustering, interviewing, questioning, and relating aloud. In this chapter, you'll combine some of these methods to gather ideas about a cultural symbol, ritual, and hero.

Cultural Symbols

A *symbol* is something that stands for or represents something else. For example, the American flag symbolizes the United States. It also stands for freedom and democracy. A skull symbolizes death, while a red rose stands for love. Cultural symbols tell us about a culture's values and lifestyle, what the people of the culture consider good or bad.

In the following reading, "Feather," Gerald Hausman writes about the symbolic importance of the feather in Native American life.

GERALD HAUSMAN

From *Feather*

For decorations of war, worship, and as an expression of flight, the feather is the universal Native American symbol. In Arctic regions, the Indian sought water birds. On the North Pacific coast, they captured or killed ravens and flickers. In California, the tribes hunted woodpeckers, meadowlarks, crested quail, mallard ducks, blue jays, blackbirds, and orioles. Around the southwestern pueblos, hunters went after eagles, hawks, turkeys, and parrots. Using the feathers and skins and even bodies of birds, the tribes made clothes, masks, hats, blankets, and robes.

Parkas in the Arctic were made of water-bird skins sewn together, the feathers acting as insulation and waterproofing. Tribes to the south used the skins of young waterfowl, while still downy, and sewed them into robes. Eastern tribes cut bird skins into strips and wove them into blankets in the same way that western tribes used rabbit skins.

Captain John Smith and other early European settlers observed that the Indians of the East fashioned turkey robes: feathers tied in knots to form a network out of which beautiful patterned cloaks were wrought.

Fans and other accessories of dress were made of wings or feathers by the Iroquois. The western Eskimo sewed little sprays of down into the seams of garments. California tribes decorated their basketry with feathers; quills of small birds were incorporated into basketry in much the same way as porcupine quills. Of course, one of the most common uses of the feather was in arrow making. For giving directness in flight, arrow feathers were split so that halves could be glued to the shaft of the arrow in twos and threes.

An unusual use of bird scalps was practiced by certain California tribes, who used them as money, being both a standard of value and a medium of exchange.

The down feathers of birds have a special value to Native Americans. Light and airy, fluffy and snowy, these feathers can be seen as a bridge between the spirit world and Mother Earth, or simply as messenger and prayer feathers. *Pahos*, as they are called among the Hopi, are used to mark sacred sites and to summon the deities as well as to ask their blessing.

The symbolism of the feather is a compression, so to speak, of   7
the bird. Humankind, seeing that birds can fly, has always been de-
sirous of flight. The mythology of angels, airborne deities residing in
heaven or heavens, is common to the collective human tribe. The
wish to fly, understood on its primary level, is merely the desire to
have something one does not or cannot have. On a deeper philosophical level, however, flight is the dreamlike movement of the unconscious, the freedom of will, the connection between the spiritual
and the material. In flight, man releases his earthbound nature and
is reborn in spirit. . . .

ACTIVITY   **Reading to Improve Writing.** Discuss the following questions
2   about "Feather" with your classmates.

1. What are some ways that Native Americans used feathers?

    _____

    _____

    _____

    _____

    _____

2. Why did down feathers have special value? _____

    _____

    _____

    _____

    _____

3. Why has the feather become "the universal Native American sym-
    bol" (1)?

    _____

    _____

_____

_____

_____

4. Explain the author's meaning in this sentence: "In flight, man releases his earthbound nature and is reborn in spirit" (7).

_____

_____

_____

5. How does Hausman use description to support his points about the feather in Native American culture?

_____

_____

_____

_____

_____

Collecting New Words. Try to determine the meanings of the following words from the way they're used in "Feather." Then verify their meanings by checking a dictionary.

ACTIVITY
3

insulation (2) _____

wrought (3) _____

incorporated (4) _____

medium (5) _____

summon (6) _____

deities (6) _____

compression (7) _____

unconscious (7) _____

GROUP
ACTIVITY
4

Collecting Contemporary Symbols. People tend to think of symbols as including only important and permanent representations, such as the flag of the United States. But symbols can be quite ordinary and represent any number of things, as this activity shows.

Imagine that you and your classmates are collecting objects of the 1990s to put into a time capsule that will be opened a hundred years from now. What objects would you choose to symbolize contemporary American culture? Here are some examples.

Superbowl T-shirt	episode of *Court TV*
Barney toy	bottle of polluted water
Internet directory	*Pulp Fiction* video
nose ring	the U.S. budget
Calvin Klein ad	twinkie
pair of baggy jeans	Ice-T CD
"Official English" button	"AIDS Awareness" banner

What would you omit from this list? What would you add to it?

ACTIVITY
5

Questioning and Freewriting about a Cultural Symbol. Select an object that you think symbolizes contemporary American culture or some other culture. Then, writing in your journal, respond to the following questions about the object.

1. When was the last time you encountered or used the object?
2. Describe the object to someone who has not seen it before.
3. What ideas, events, or other objects do you associate with the object?
4. How does the object symbolize the culture's lifestyle or beliefs?

Keeping your responses to these questions in mind, freewrite about the object and the culture it symbolizes. ❏

Here's how one student, Clara, answered some of the questions in Activity 5 and freewrote about the object she chose—an artificial Christmas tree.

1. My mother and I used this artificial Christmas tree last Christmas after we moved out of our big house and into a small apartment.

2. The tree is about two feet tall, with pointed silver leaves. Little red balls hang from each branch.

3. The tree reminds me of Christmas, but not the kind of Christmas I had as a little girl, when we had a big, natural tree that smelled up the living room.

4. To me this tree symbolizes how artificial and commercial Christmas can be in our culture.

I wish people would think more about the spirit of the Christmas season than about gifts. But that's not the way it happens. To me this artificial tree symbolizes the commercialism of Christmas. It doesn't look or smell like a real tree. It's just something to put gifts under. I know that having a real tree is impractical because our apartment is so small. But it almost seems that having no tree at all would be better than having one that looks so artificial.

Put your material about a cultural symbol aside for now. You want to gather ideas about another aspect of culture and another possible topic for your essay—cultural rituals.

Cultural Rituals

A *ritual* is an event or activity repeatedly performed in the same way, usually to celebrate an important occasion and bring people closer together. In Chapter Four, you may have written about a family ritual. In this chapter, however, you want to focus on a *cultural ritual,* one that extends beyond your family and reflects the values of a culture.

Thanksgiving and the Fourth of July are cultural rituals unique to the United States. Other American cultural rituals have been adapted from other parts of the world and changed to suit American lifestyles and values. In Europe, the figure of St. Nicholas represents religious values, while in America St. Nicholas has become Santa Claus, a figure associated with the giving of gifts. New cultural rituals develop all the time. Kwanzaa, for instance, is an African American ritual that takes place during the final week of the year. In this ritual, African Americans remember their African heritage by celebrating the customs and beliefs of several African tribes.

One of America's oldest cultural rituals is the Thanksgiving holiday, when people celebrate their heritage and give thanks. In the following essay, "Our Thanksgiving Tradition," William C. Brisick describes how the Thanksgiving ritual began.

WILLIAM C. BRISICK

Our Thanksgiving Tradition

Thanksgiving is the quintessential American holiday, the oldest, *1* the most tradition-bound of our holidays. Oh, sure, there's the Fourth of July, that red-white-and-blue day when we Americans celebrate the sloughing off of our colonial servitude, the commitment to our freedom, our independence. The backyard barbecues are busy every Fourth, no doubt about that, and there's always a good deal of frolicking outdoors.

Thanksgiving, by contrast, is usually cast on a cold, wind-swept, *2* perhaps snow-swept, day—it's an indoor holiday. Yet its muted warmth—from the fire of the hearth rather than from the sun— casts its own spell, reminding us of how it was that America got started in the first place. It tells of immigrants in a new land, grateful for a bountiful harvest after long and difficult days; it speaks of settler and native breaking bread together in a time of peace and understanding; and finally, pointing up a more universal quality, it conjures images of friends and relatives setting aside some moments to come together, to reconnect with each other, to enjoy the pleasures of good food and drink.

For those of us who have experienced more than a few Thanksgivings, the warm glow of holidays past suffuses—perhaps befogs— *3* our memory. We're absolutely sure about the presence of turkey, reasonably sure of who was there to eat it, but a bit uncertain about most everything else.

For the first Thanksgiving in 1621 we have only a few recorded *4* facts from two sources: a letter written by Edward Winslow, one of the participants, to a friend in England, and Governor William Bradford's famous document, *Of Plimouth Plantation*. We know that fifty-two Pilgrims, survivors of the Mayflower voyage and the first winter/spring/summer, celebrated with ninety Indians, date unknown but sometime between September 21 and November 9. Only four of the Pilgrim wives were in attendance, the others having succumbed to the rigors of life in the New World.

The Pilgrims, heirs to the English tradition of marking the end of *5* the harvest, were doing just that, but they were also setting aside a time to give thanks to God for blessings received. The feast lasted three days, not one, and they ate cod and sea bass, cornmeal, wild fowl, and deer brought by the Indians, pumpkins (boiled, not in pies), and cranberries (pudding rather than sauce because sugar was scarce). The wild fowl probably consisted of ducks, geese, swans, and the staple of today's Thanksgiving table, turkey.

Until well into the 19th century Thanksgiving was a regional   6
holiday, focused in the Northeast. There the states celebrated it during the fall but on varying dates; the governors, by proclamation, decided when it would take place. In each case it marked the boundary between the season of harvest with its arduous work schedule, and the onset of winter, a time of enforced leisure. People looked forward to it, prepared weeks in advance, and when the day finally arrived celebrated not only with the traditional dinner but with long walks or rides in the countryside, with indoor games and storytelling. Many New Englanders made it the occasion for weddings.

Sara Josepha Hale, editor of the journal *Godey's Lady's Book*, as   7
early as 1846 began to campaign to make Thanksgiving a national holiday. Her letters to various presidents didn't bear fruit until Abraham Lincoln decreed in 1863 that the fourth Thursday in November would be set aside as a national holiday. That proclamation had only limited effect since the Civil War was still raging. In its aftermath the Southern states spent quite a few years adjusting to the celebration of what they considered a Yankee holiday.

But was it a Yankee holiday? There are some who believe that   8
the first Thanksgiving actually occurred on Southern shores. The event took place December 4, 1619, on the banks of the St. James River shortly after the first landing of the English there. In affirmation, contemporary Virginians celebrate the gala Virginia First Thanksgiving Festival at the Berkeley Plantation on the first Sunday in November each year.

Not to be outdone, the Southwest has staked a claim of its own   9
for a 16th-century Thanksgiving—April 1598, to be exact. A few weeks earlier a Spanish expedition under Don Juan de Oñate had ventured forth from Chihuahua in what is now Mexico, and after an arduous journey crossed the Rio Grande near present-day El Paso, Texas. Four hundred hardy souls they were, men and women; they netted fish from the river, shot ducks and geese, gave thanks and feasted—"a repast the like of which we had never enjoyed before," one participant wrote.

Historical one-upmanship aside, the act of getting together with   10
family and friends for camaraderie and fellowship, a celebratory meal and an offering of thanks has been a tradition through the centuries. No doubt our cave-dwelling ancestors took the opportunity to relax and rejoice after a successful hunt. Happy to say, we've embellished the cuisine since then.

But whether or not our holiday fare reaches the highest stan-   11 dards of culinary art, the essence of what we do on the fourth Thursday of November remains remarkably similar to what our forebears did on Thanksgivings past. They, like us, looked upon all sorts of weather outside, but managed, like us, to create a peculiar, very special warmth inside.

ACTIVITY
6

Reading to Improve Writing. Discuss the following questions about "Our Thanksgiving Tradition" with your classmates.

1. What did you learn about Thanksgiving from reading Brisick's essay?

2. Why do Americans continue to celebrate Thanksgiving?

3. When do *you* think the first Thanksgiving took place? _____

4. Explain the first sentence from the essay: "Thanksgiving is the quintessential American holiday, the oldest, the most tradition-bound of our holidays."

_____

_____

_____

_____

_____

5. How effective are the title, introduction, and conclusion?

_____

_____

_____

_____

_____

Collecting New Words. Try to determine the meanings of the following words from the way they're used in "Our Thanksgiving Tradition." Then verify their meanings by checking a dictionary.

ACTIVITY
7

quintessential (1) _____

sloughing (1) _____

muted (2) _____

conjures (2) _____

suffuses (3) _____

arduous (6) _____

aftermath (7) _____

hardy (9) _____

embellished (10)   _____

cuisine (10)   _____

ACTIVITY
8   **Clustering and Questioning about a Cultural Ritual.** In your journal, do some clustering about the cultural rituals you are familiar with. Then choose one of those cultural rituals to write about. Use these questions to help you decide which ritual you know a lot about and are most interested in:

1. When does this ritual take place?
2. What happens during the ritual?
3. Who participates in the ritual?
4. What special clothes, food, music, or dance accompany the ritual?
5. Why is the ritual important to the participants? ❑

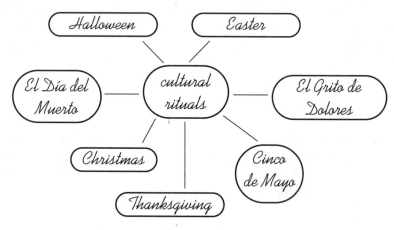

Figure 7-1. Sandra's Cluster Diagram

COMPUTER TIP

MAKING A CHART

Use the format options of your word-processing program to make a chart of the questions about a cultural ritual and your responses to them. If your ideas encompass more than one cultural ritual, the chart can also help you compare and contrast your responses.

Figure 7-1 is a quick cluster of cultural rituals completed by one student, Sandra Cordero. From the rituals in her cluster, Sandra decided to answer the questions in Activity 8 about "El Grito de Dolores":

1. This ritual takes place in Mexico on the evening of September 15 and the morning of September 16.

2. During this ritual, the people reenact the time when Miguel Hidalgo told his people in Dolores to fight for freedom from Spain.

3. The governor of each city participates by pretending to be Hidalgo. Then the people of the city attend a parade.

4. Fireworks are set off on September 15; the next day a parade is held and some people dress in traditional costumes.

5. This ritual is important because the Mexican people celebrate their freedom from Spain.

Put your writing about a cultural ritual aside for now. You want to explore one more possible topic—cultural heroes—for your essay.

Cultural Heroes

We all have personal heroes—family members, friends, teachers, or coaches—whom we admire because of their courage, dedication, or hard work and who serve as role models. *Cultural heroes*, people who inspire an entire culture, also serve as role models. Unlike personal heroes, however, cultural heroes are known by many people within the culture. Some cultural heroes come from the contemporary culture, while others are a part of our cultural heritage. Martin Luther King, Jr., Abraham Lincoln, and Eleanor Roosevelt are some examples of cultural heroes.

Many Americans consider Oprah Winfrey a contemporary cultural hero because of the way she triumphed over personal hardships and has encouraged others to do the same. In the following reading, John Culhane describes one of Winfrey's most precious values: telling the truth.

JOHN CULHANE

From *Oprah Winfrey: How Truth Changed Her Life*

In January 1984 a phenomenon hit the airwaves. Chicago's WLS-TV needed someone to take over its floundering morning program, which ranked third in local competition for the 9 A.M. slot. So it brought in a little-known news anchor from Baltimore. Her name was Oprah Winfrey.

Earthy, articulate and spontaneous, Oprah seemed to have a knack for connecting emotionally with her guests, her studio audience and her viewers. In a single season, she brought the show to the No. 1 spot in its time period. In 1985 the program was retitled *The Oprah Winfrey Show*, and in 1986 it was syndicated nationally. Oprah won an Emmy for the 1986–87 year, and her approximately

20 million loyal viewers have made her program television's most popular daytime show.

But hers is not the typical celebrity success story, by any means. Oprah actually calls her program "a kind of ministry." And there is something more, something intensely personal and powerful in the advice she often gives nervous guests before air time. "Just tell the truth," she says quietly, gazing directly into their eyes. "It'll save you every time." *3*

It is a lesson Oprah learned against great odds. Significantly, this 35-year-old woman noted for the unflinching honesty of her interviews learned the value of truth only after she tried—and failed— to lie her way to happiness. *4*

As Oprah explains: She was born January 29, 1954, in Kosciusko, Miss., to an unmarried 18-year-old farm girl. Vernon Winfrey, a soldier at Fort Rucker, didn't even know until much later that Vernita Lee had become pregnant with his child. *5*

The infant was named after Orpah, the sister-in-law of Ruth in the Bible. (The midwife misspelled the name "Oprah" on the birth certificate.) Shortly after, Vernita Lee left Oprah in the care of the child's grandmother and headed for Milwaukee, where unskilled black women could find jobs as maids. *6*

On the farm where she was reared, little Oprah began her broadcasting career declaiming to the pigs in the barnyard. At three, she was reciting in church. By the time her grandmother enrolled her in kindergarten, Oprah could already read and write well enough to send a note to her teacher: "Dear Miss New. I do not think I belong here." Agreeing, Miss New advanced her to the first grade, where envious classmates soon nicknamed her The Preacher. *7*

"From the time I was eight years old," says Oprah, "I was a champion speaker. I spoke for every women's group, banquet, church function—I did the circuit. Anybody needed anybody to speak anything, they'd call me." Oprah begins to recite, in the commanding voice she's had since childhood, from the famous old poem "Invictus" by William Ernest Henley: *8*

> *Out of the night that covers me,*
> *Black as the Pit from pole to pole,*
> *I thank whatever gods may be,*
> *For my unconquerable soul.*

Oprah grins. "Very impressive, especially when you're eight." *9*

Between ages six and nine, Oprah lived part-time with her mother in Milwaukee, part-time with her father in Nashville. But then she moved in full-time with her mother. Perhaps her precociousness was one reason the relationship was difficult. In Oprah's words, "My mama really wasn't prepared to take on this child— me." *10*

Oprah's childhood innocence came to a traumatic end when, at   *11*
nine, she was raped by a teen-age cousin. "Three people abused me
from the time I was nine until I was 14," she says. The horror of this
sexual abuse would come out years later on one of Oprah's famous
talk shows, but at the time she kept it secret, and it fed an enormous
sense of shame and insecurity.

When Oprah was 13 she decided new, octagon-shaped glasses   *12*
would make her beautiful and popular. Her mother refused, telling
Oprah they couldn't afford such an extravagance. The next day, after her mother had gone to work, Oprah smashed her old glasses on
the floor. She pulled down the curtains, knocked over a table and
threw things around the room. Then she called the police.

"I decided to be unconscious when they came in and to have   *13*
amnesia."

At the hospital, the doctor brought her mother to her bed, but   *14*
Oprah pretended not to recognize her. "All we know is that someone broke into the apartment, hit her over the head and broke her
glasses," explained the doctor.

"Broke her *glasses*?" asked Vernita Lee. "Do you mind if I'm   *15*
alone with the child for a few minutes?"

The mother glared at her daughter and counted to three. As   *16*
Oprah tells it: "She got to two, and I knew she was going to kill me.
And so I said, 'It's coming back to me now . . . you're my mother!'
She dragged me from the bed and we went home. Yes, I got the oc-
tagons."

But Oprah wasn't any happier. She ran away from home, only   *17*
to be brought back.

She tells these stories on herself with her usual candor and hu-   *18*
mor, but it seems clear that the teen-age Oprah was using theatrical
lies to win acceptance and love, just as she had won admiration in
the past through her dramatic speaking roles.

Finally, Vernita Lee had had enough. "And that's how I ended   *19*
up with my father."

Vernon Winfrey had married and grown into a responsible   *20*
member of the community, a barber and pillar of the Baptist church.
He and his wife, Zelma, were unsettled by the heavily made-up
teen-ager with the tight skirt and belligerent expression. "You will
not live in this house unless you abide by my rules," he told her.
Those rules, and, more important, Vernon Winfrey's air of confidence and certainty, would change Oprah's life.

His first rule was that she had to be home by 11 P.M. Another   *21*
was that she read a book a week and submit a written report on it.
When she came home with C's on her report card, he told her: "If
you were a child who could only get C's, then that is all I would expect of you. But you are not. So in this house, C's are not acceptable."

Oprah found herself getting home by ten minutes *before* eleven. 22
And she became an honor student and president of the student
council. But the most significant turn-around was her newfound
honesty.

"I never told another lie. I wouldn't dream of making up a story 23
to my Dad. Let me tell you, there is something about people who
believe in discipline—they exude a kind of assurance and realism."

Five feet, seven inches tall, about 135 pounds, with the same 24
dramatic eyes and magnetic presence we see today, Oprah entered a
Nashville beauty pageant in high school. She figured she would be
asked what she planned to do with her life, and calculated the best
answer would be: "I want to be a fourth-grade schoolteacher."

But on the morning of the interview, she happened to watch the 25
Today show, then featuring Barbara Walters. And when the judges
asked her about her life's ambitions, she found herself stating firmly:
"I believe in truth, and I want to perpetuate truth. So I want to be a
journalist."

She won the contest and was offered a part-time news position 26
at a local radio station. In an oratorial contest, sponsored by the
Elks, she won a four-year scholarship that she used to attend Tennessee State University in Nashville.

Once she was in college, the management of the CBS affiliate in 27
Nashville offered her a job on television.

In 1976, the year she should have graduated, Oprah still had to 28
make curfew—which her father had now extended to midnight.
Later that year, she moved to Baltimore to join WJZ-TV; "her primary motive," according to her official biography, "was to escape
her father's curfew." And in Baltimore, destiny—in the form of a
Chicago TV station searching for a talk-show host—found her.

The topics on her nationally syndicated show have ranged from 29
overcoming weight problems (a longtime concern for Oprah, who
recently shed more than 60 pounds) to racism. For her most famous
show, in February 1987, she went to an all-white county in Georgia
and asked an audience composed entirely of white residents some
simple questions: "Why has Forsyth County not allowed black people to live here in 75 years? What is it you're afraid black people are
going to do?" Though there were some dissenters, Oprah found
many in her audience who believed in co-existence with blacks. The
show made newspaper stories across America.

Through her show, Oprah won a substantial victory over herself. 30
Her lawyer had advised her against ever disclosing that she had been
sexually abused as a child, arguing that many people still blame the
victims of abuse. He didn't want his client to suffer from that stigma.
Oprah agreed. Nevertheless, during a program in which victims of
sexual abuse spoke of their experiences, Oprah suddenly decided to

tell her story. She put her arms around another victim and wept
with her. It was an honest, moving moment. . . .

Now there was just one more old fence to mend. Every time she   *31*
visited, her father warned her that she would not amount to anything without a college degree. Oprah had left Tennessee State without a diploma: she had finished all her course work, but not her senior project.

Through a friend, Oprah made discreet inquiries: Would Ten-   *32*
nessee State University waive the senior-project requirement if
Oprah did independent work or study? TSU would not.

Oprah had to re-enroll and then put together a project to fulfill   *33*
her requirement in the media course. So she did it. TSU informed
her that she would receive her diploma at the 1987 commencement
ceremonies and invited her to address the graduating class.

Vernon Winfrey was in the audience that packed Howard C.   *34*
Gentry complex on TSU's North Nashville campus. "Even though
I've done a few things in life, every time I've come home, my father
has said, 'You need that degree,'" she told the crowd. "So this is a
special day for my dad." With that, she announced she was estab-
lishing scholarships at the school in his name.

She was her father's daughter, too, in the advice she gave to fel-   *35*
low graduates: "Don't complain about what you don't have. Use
what you've got. To do less than your best is a sin. Every single one
of us has the power for greatness, because greatness is determined
by service—to yourself and to others."

She was Oprah the graduating senior, and she was also Oprah   *36*
the famous and wealthy entertainer. But she was still the Oprah
they used to call The Preacher, who had herself learned the most
valuable lesson of all: *Just tell the truth. It will save you every time.*

Reading to Improve Writing. Discuss the following questions
about "Oprah Winfrey: How Truth Changed Her Life" with your
classmates.

ACTIVITY
9

1. What did you learn about Oprah Winfrey from this reading that you
    didn't already know?

    _____

    _____

    _____

_____

_____

2. Of the events that are described by Culhane which one do you think had the most effect on Winfrey? Why?

_____

_____

_____

_____

_____

3. Why is telling the truth so important to Winfrey? _____

_____

_____

_____

_____

4. Do you admire Winfrey? Why or why not? _____

_____

_____

_____

_____

5. How does Culhane keep his audience interested in his topic?

_____

_____

_____

_____

_____

Collecting New Words. Try to determine the meanings of the following words from the way they're used in "Oprah Winfrey: How Truth Changed Her Life." Then verify their meanings by checking a dictionary.

ACTIVITY
10

floundering (1)   _____

earthy (2)   _____

articulate (2)   _____

unflinching (4)   _____

precociousness (10)   _____

octagon (12)   _____

candor (18)   _____

belligerent (20)   _____

abide (20)   _____

dissenters (29)   _____

Gathering Ideas about a Cultural Hero. With your classmates, brainstorm a list of cultural heroes. Consider musicians, athletes, public officials, actors, entrepreneurs, celebrities, and ordinary citizens who are widely known because of their extraordinary talent, dedication, or achievements.

GROUP
ACTIVITY
11

Then select one of the heroes to freewrite about in your journal. Use these questions as a guide:

1. What facts do you know about this person (age, accomplishments, and so on)?
2. Which five words best describe this person?
3. What do you most admire about this person?

Finally, talk about this person with one of your classmates. Explain why you believe this person is a cultural hero. How does your classmate feel about this person? What more does your classmate want to know about this person?   ❑

Here's how one student, Mark, gathered ideas about the reggae musician Bob Marley by freewriting in his journal.

Bob Marley was a great musician. He wrote songs that celebrated Jamaican music. His songs popularized Jamaican music for the rest of the world. He also celebrated his Jamaican heritage by reminding people of the beauty and strength of Jamaican culture. He died tragically at age thirty-six, but his spirit lives on in his music.

Drafting

You have now gathered ideas on three aspects of culture—cultural symbols, rituals, and heroes. You thus have a rich source of material for writing, but you need to decide how to proceed. Here are some of your options:

• You may select one of the three topics for your discovery draft.

• You may write drafts on two or three of the topics to see which one you prefer to continue working on.

• You may combine related topics in your discovery draft. For instance, you might describe a cultural symbol that is part of a cultural ritual.

The topic you choose should be one that interests you and that you are already fairly well informed about. Although you may need to collect such basic information as dates and names for your discovery draft, most of the information should come from your own knowledge and experience.

Before you begin drafting, write a preliminary thesis statement that announces your topic and states its importance—both to you and the culture, in this case. As you draft, you may decide to revise your thesis as new ideas emerge. Keep your audience and purpose in mind, but remember that your main goal at the drafting stage is to get your ideas down on paper. You'll have time later on to revise and edit your discovery draft.

Here's the discovery draft written by Sandra Cordero about a cultural ritual. After reading the draft, discuss with your classmates what Sandra might do to revise it. (Note that the example includes the types of errors that typically appear in a discovery draft.)

El Grito de Dolores

I am proud to be part of the Mexican culture. The Mexican culture honors events important to its history. To celebrate Mexicos independence, Mexicans have "El Grito de Dolores." "El Grito de Dolores" tells about what happened the day when the fight for our independence was over. Every Mexican participates in this event because it's the way we thank our heroes and ancestors for giving us freedom.   *1*

Our celebration begins the night of the 15th of September. The main event is celebrated in Mexico's capital, which is "El Distrito Federal." The holiday is celebrated everywhere in Mexico. Even the most little towns have their own celebration. People get together in the Main Plaza to celebrate the fiesta.   *2*

Exactly at midnight the governor of each city goes on top of the municipal building. "Viva Don Miguel Hidalgo!" he yells to give honor to the person who made our independence possible. The words "Viva Mexico, Viva Mexico, Viva Mexico!" give honor to our country.   *3*

On the morning of the 16th of September, people get together on the main street to see the parade. The parade includes children, business leaders, government leaders, clubs, police officers, and firefighters. Everyone under the sun. On this day, everyone feels the freedom that this day brought. Every town in Mexico has a street called "16 de Septiembre" where it begins and ends.   *4*

We give honor to the men who made us free. Mexicans believe in traditions. By giving honor to the men who made us free, we thank them our ancestors for the freedom that they have given us.   *5*

Revising

As you learned in the preceding chapters, when you revise a discovery draft, you concentrate on clarifying and supporting your ideas. You should resist the urge to correct errors when revising; that is your concern during the editing stage.

In this chapter, you will learn several revision techniques for organizing the ideas in your paragraphs most effectively. You will also learn how to achieve paragraph coherence, which refers to the smooth flow of ideas from one paragraph to the next that your readers need to follow your main points.

Organizing Ideas in Paragraphs

In Chapter Four, you learned how to organize paragraphs by using the directional order, chronological order, order-of-importance, and flashback techniques. In this chapter, you'll take another look at the order-of-importance, or progressive, pattern. You'll also experiment with several other ways of organizing paragraphs: topic-illustration-explanation (TIE), question and answer, general-to-specific order, and specific-to-general order.

Topic, Illustration, and Explanation. The *topic-illustration-explanation (TIE)* method is used to organize paragraphs that contain examples, facts, statistics, or expert testimony. You can organize the paragraph in this way:

- State the topic.
- Give an illustration (that is, an example, a fact, a statistic, or expert testimony).
- Explain the significance of the illustration.

The TIE method of organization is used in the following paragraph about an American cultural symbol—the T-shirt. Notice that the writer states the topic, gives an illustration, and then explains why the illustration is important.

> T-shirts with political or controversial statements can require the viewer to think about the message. A few years ago the slogan "A woman's place is in the House," was seen on many T-shirts. To understand this slogan, the viewer had to know the original saying of "a woman's place is in the home," and then understand that replacing "home" with "House" referred to the House of Representatives. The House of Representatives, a part of Congress, has always had fewer women than men elected as members. The wearer of the T-shirt, then, advocates electing more women to political office.

In this paragraph, the topic is stated in the first sentence: political statement T-shirts may require some thought. To illustrate, the writer uses a slogan—"A woman's place is in the House"—and then the writer explains the importance of the slogan.

Progressive Order. Another way of organizing the ideas in your paragraphs is to use progressive order, or order of importance. You might recall from Chapter Four that descriptive essays can be organized in this way. *Progressive order* involves arranging ideas in the order of their importance, usually from least to most important, or, less frequently, from most to least important. Since the final idea in a paragraph (or in an essay, for that matter) is the one that readers tend to remember most readily, ending with the most important idea is usually more effective.

Progressive order is often used by writers to organize examples, facts, and statistics. Thus, rather than presenting your illustrations randomly, you can arrange them progressively to give emphasis to the most important one.

Here's another paragraph from the essay about the American T-shirt. Notice that the writer uses progressive order to illustrate the various functions that the T-shirt serves in our culture.

> The common, ordinary T-shirt tells us much about the American culture. The T-shirt is a product of our casual lifestyle. People have been known to wear T-shirts under blazers at work and under cock-tail dresses at the Academy Awards. The T-shirt is also associated with sexuality—think of the Calvin Klein ads in magazines and on buses. Most importantly, the T-shirt gives people a way to express themselves. It tells others about our favorite schools, sports teams, or cartoon figures. It can also let others know our political views—whether or not they care to know.

In this paragraph, the most important function of T-shirts is stated at the end. The writer also emphasizes this fact with the introductory words, "most importantly."

Question and Answer. *Question and answer* is another method for organizing ideas in a paragraph. It involves asking a question at the beginning of the paragraph and then answering that question in the rest of the paragraph.

In the following paragraph from "Our Thanksgiving Tradition," the writer uses the question-and-answer method.

> But was it [Thanksgiving] a Yankee holiday? There are some who believe that the first Thanksgiving actually occurred on South-ern shores. The event took place December 4, 1619, on the banks of the St. James River shortly after the first landing of the English there. In affirmation, contemporary Virginians celebrate the gala Virginia First Thanksgiving Festival at the Berkeley Plantation on the first Sunday in November each year.
>
> WILLIAM C. BRISICK, "OUR THANKSGIVING TRADITION"

General-to-Specific Order. *General-to-specific order* may be used to organize ideas in a paragraph. Whereas general statements are broad, specific statements are more focused. For example, the statement "I love dogs" is general because it broadly refers to all dogs. But the statement "I love my dog Rupert because he's smart, funny, and af-fectionate" is specific because it cites a particular dog and several de-tails.

In general-to-specific order, the most general idea is given at the beginning of the paragraph, usually in the topic sentence. The more specific ideas that follow help to support and explain the general statement. Notice this pattern of general to specific in the following paragraph.

> The quinceañera, or coming-out party, is a tradition for many young Latinas. In this ritual, parents proudly present their fifteen-year-old daughter to their community. The ceremony consists of a Mass followed by a dinner and dance. Fourteen young couples serve as the girl's court. Long formal dresses, tuxedos, live music, and video cameras are all part of the spectacle.

Specific-to-General Order. In *specific-to-general order*, the most specific ideas are stated first and the general idea appears at the end of the paragraph. This pattern is most often used when you want to position a topic sentence at the end of a paragraph.

In the example that follows, the writer organizes ideas from the most specific to the most general.

> The audience gasps as colors explode in the night sky—red, blue, yellow, green. The explosions grow bigger and bigger until they cover the night sky, and then they slowly disintegrate like silvery rain. Although everyone enjoys a fireworks spectacle on the Fourth of July, few understand the origin of this ritual celebration. The Fourth of July commemorates America's fight for independence, and the fireworks are to remind us of the historic battles that ended the Revolutionary War.

GROUP
ACTIVITY
12

Identifying Patterns of Paragraph Organization. With your classmates, identify the pattern of organization in each of the following paragraphs as topic-illustration-explanation (TIE), progressive order, question and answer, general-to-specific order, or specific-to-general order.

1. With about a half-billion passengers a year boarding scheduled U.S. flights, air travel has become so routine that it's easy for people to forget what's outside their cabin cocoon. The atmosphere at 35,000 feet won't sustain human life. It's about 60 degrees below zero, and so thin that an inactive person breathing it would become confused and lethargic in less than a minute.

"BREATHING ON A JET PLANE," *CONSUMER REPORTS*

Pattern: _____

2. When you need a new car, do you go to the nearest auto dealer and buy the first car you see? Most of us don't. We shop and compare features, quality, and price. We look for the best value for our money.

O. M. NICELY, "USING TECHNOLOGY TO SERVE YOU BETTER"

Pattern: _____

3. When you go on a hike in the desert, the least of your worries is snakes and scorpions. If you stay away from them, they'll stay away from you. Instead of worrying about reptiles and bugs, worry about the sun. To avoid a serious burn, apply sunscreen to exposed skin and wear a hat. Most importantly, bring plenty of water—at least a gallon per person.

Pattern: _____

4. Many dogs, when they hear the words "Let's go on a hike!" can't contain their excitement. They wag their tails, jump up and down, and even bring their leashes to their owners. Most dogs love to hike, and their owners love to take them. Just as with humans, though, dogs need to be prepared for a rigorous day on the trail.

Pattern: _____

5. Almost everyone knows that smoking is bad for one's health, yet more and more young people are smoking every day. According to the National Cancer Institute, one million Americans begin to smoke each year, and most of them are teenagers. Experts believe so many young people are taking up smoking because they think smoking will make them look "cool."

Pattern: _____

Finding Patterns of Paragraph Organization. Working in a group, evaluate the organization of ideas in paragraphs in your textbooks for other courses. Find as many examples as you can of paragraphs that use the patterns discussed in this chapter: topic-illustration-explanation (TIE), progressive order, question and answer, general-to-specific order, and specific-to-general order. Make copies of your group's sample paragraphs to share with the rest of the class. ❏

GROUP
ACTIVITY
13

Developing Paragraph Coherence

To *cohere* means to fit smoothly together. Thus, just as building a table requires that all the parts fit together smoothly, without any rough edges or wobbly legs, in developing *paragraph coherence* you want the parts of your paragraphs to fit smoothly together. When your paragraphs cohere, your readers can easily follow your ideas.

There are two basic strategies for achieving paragraph coherence: repeating key words and using transitions.

Key Words. One way to connect your ideas in a paragraph is to repeat *key words*, words that pertain to the topic of the paragraph. By repeating a key word, you keep your reader focused on the topic. In the following paragraph from "Feather," for example, notice how the repetition of a key word (underlined) contributes to the coherent flow of ideas and keeps us focused on the topic.

> The down <u>feathers</u> of birds have a special value to Native Americans. Light and airy, fluffy and snowy, these <u>feathers</u> can be seen as a bridge between the spirit world and Mother Earth, or simply as messenger and prayer <u>feathers</u>. *Pahos*, as <u>they</u> are called among the Hopi, are used to mark sacred sites and to summon the deities as well as to ask their blessing.
>
> GERALD HAUSMAN, "FEATHER"

In addition to repetition of the same key word, you can use pronouns and synonyms as key words. A *pronoun* takes the place of the original word, as in the preceding paragraph from "Feather," where the pronoun *they* is used in place of the key word *feathers*. *Synonyms* are words that have the same meaning. In the following paragraph, notice how the use of synonyms and pronouns (italicized) for the key word *T-shirts* helps connect the writer's ideas.

> Another reason people like T-shirts is because they can purchase *them* at a variety of locations. *They're* sold at discount stores, flea markets, and garage sales. In fact, this is one *item of clothing* that many people don't mind getting second-hand. When people feel like going upscale, they can purchase T-shirts from a chic fashion designer. While *these shirts* might be made from the same fabric as the inexpensive *shirts*, people pay more money for *them* because of the designer's logo, strategically placed for all to see.

Transitions. Another way to connect your ideas is to use *transitions*, words that indicate the relationships between ideas. Here is a list of some common transitions and the relationships they express.

COMPUTER TIP

REORDERING SENTENCES WITHIN PARAGRAPHS

Use the "block" and "move" or "cut" and "paste" functions to experiment with different ways of organizing the sentences in a paragraph. You might, for example, try specific-to-general order and then general-to-specific order. Or you might try a question-and-answer format. Make printouts of the different versions so you can compare them. Or, if your word-processing program has the capability, you can put one version of a paragraph in a "window" at the top of the screen as you work on another version at the bottom of the screen.

to add further information: also, additionally, in addition, too, furthermore, as well, and

to show differences: in contrast, on the other hand, whereas, but

to show similarities: in the same way, similarly, in comparison

to show time: then, since, meanwhile, at that time, by then, during, when, while, soon, until then, after, before, now, sometimes

to show cause and effect: because, as a result, consequently, therefore, thus, hence, thereby

to contradict or contrast: although, however, in contrast, nevertheless, but, or

to add emphasis: indeed, in fact, in truth, actually, moreover, furthermore, most importantly

to give an example: for example, for instance, specifically, such as

to show sequence: first, last, next, finally

Whenever you use a transition, be sure it expresses the correct relationship between ideas. Using transitions inappropriately can confuse your readers.

Notice how transitions (italicized) are used in the following paragraph to connect ideas.

> *Another* way people use T-shirts to express themselves is by wearing one that bears the name of a particular college. *Sometimes* the college is prestigious, such as Harvard. Are we to think that the wearer of the T-shirt actually went to Harvard? *Or* perhaps the wearer just wants us to think that? *In contrast*, when we see a T-shirt from a lesser-known or less prestigious school, we are more likely to assume that the wearer is simply showing school pride. *In truth*, a T-shirt is a mode of expression—*but* it's not always clear what's being expressed.

COMPUTER TIP

IMPROVING PARAGRAPH COHERENCE

Try this method to improve the coherence of your paragraphs:

Use the "bold" function to highlight the key words in each paragraph. Check that your key words pertain directly to the topic of the paragraph. Add, delete, or revise key words as needed.

Then use the "italic" key to highlight the transitions in each paragraph. Add transitions where the flow of thought seems disconnected.

(Remember to delete the highlighting of key words and transitions before printing out your revised essay.)

Adding Key Words and Transitions. In the following paragraphs from *And the Beat Goes On: A Survey of Pop Music in America* by Charles Boeckman, key words and transitions have been deleted. Work with your classmates to make the paragraphs coherent by adding the necessary key words and transitions.

GROUP ACTIVITY

14

> In the 1950's, a revolution began in America. There was nothing quiet about it. It had happened before most people woke up to what was going on. It has been one of the most curious things in our history. The young people banded together, splintered off into a compartment totally their own. They formed their own culture, economy and morals. A generation of young people was totally immersed in its own music. It symbolized, reflected, dictated the very nature of its revolution.

The stage was set. Out of the wings stepped a young Memphis truck driver with a ducktail hair style and a sullen, brooding expression—Elvis Presley with his rock'n'roll guitar. In 1954, a Black group, the Chords, had played the rock'n'roll style. In 1955, Bill Haley and a white group, the Comets, recorded the hit "Rock around the Clock." They lacked Elvis's charisma. They lacked his sex appeal. Elvis did more than sing. He went through a whole series of gyrations filled with sexual implications. It was just the thing for the mood of the hour. His voice trembled and cried out. His guitar thundered. His torso did bumps and grinds and shimmies. A whole generation of young people blew its cool.

GROUP
ACTIVITY
15

Finding Key Words and Transitions. Working in a group, evaluate the coherence of paragraphs in your textbooks for other courses. Make copies of the paragraphs; then circle the key words, synonyms, and pronouns and underline the transitions that help to connect ideas. Share your group's findings with the rest of the class. ❑

Sandra's Revised Draft

Before you read Sandra's revised draft, reread her discovery draft (p. 205). Notice, in particular, how Sandra has improved the focus of her thesis and the organization of her paragraphs in her revision. Her ideas are better connected and flow more smoothly as a result. In addition, she has added information about the cultural ritual that her readers may be unfamiliar with. (You will also notice some errors in her revised draft; Sandra will correct these errors when she edits her revised essay.)

El Grito de Dolores

"Viva Mexico! Viva Mexico! Viva Mexico!" hundreds of people cry out   *1*
at the same time. Gathered in the town plaza at midnight on September

Key word (*holiday*) introduced and repeated

16, they are celebrating one of Mexicos most important holidays, "El Grito de Dolores." The holiday honors the men and women who fought for Mexico's independence. On this day, Mexicans feel united as they celebrate

Pronoun and synonym (*on this day*) used for *holiday*

their history.

What is "El Grito de Dolores"? This expression means "the cry from Do-   *2*
lores," and it refers to an important event that happened early in the morning

Transition (*At this time*)

on September 16, 1810. At this time, Mexico was ruled by the Spanish king.

But a priest named Miguel Hidalgo called together his parishioners at his church in Dolores, Guanajuato, Mexico. In a speech that was later called "El Grito de Dolores," Hidalgo urged his people to fight for freedom. This was the beginning of the Mexican revolution against Spain. Since then, the holiday is celebrated everywhere in Mexico. Even the smallest towns have their own celebrations.

Transition (Since then)

Another key word (celebration)

The celebration begins in the main plaza exactly at midnight the governor of each city goes on top of the municipal building. "Viva Don Miguel Hidalgo!" he yells to give honor to the person who began the movement for independence. ("Viva" means "long live.") The people shout "Viva Mexico! Viva Mexico! Viva Mexico!" Then fireworks light up the night sky, and everyone celebrates the countrys independence.

3   Repetition of key word

Transition (then); Repetition of key word

The next part of the celebration is a parade held on the morning of September 16th. Held on the street called "16 de Septiembre." Every town in Mexico has a street with this name. The parade includes children, business leaders, government leaders, members of clubs, police officers, and firefighters. Green, red, and white streamers float through the air. People waving little Mexican flags to show their pride in their country.

4   Transition (next); Repetition of key word

Sometimes Mexico is divided because of politics not on this day, though. "El Grito de Dolores" brings the Mexican people together in a celebration of their ancestors who fought for freedom.

5   Transition (though)

Repetition of key word

Analyzing Sandra's Revised Draft. Use the following questions to discuss with your classmates how Sandra improved her draft.

ACTIVITY
16

1. Is the purpose of Sandra's draft clear? What is that purpose?

_____

_____

_____

2. What is Sandra's thesis statement? Could it be improved?

_____

_____

_____

_____

3. Does Sandra tell her readers everything they need to know to understand the cultural ritual? Explain.

_____

_____

_____

4. How effective is Sandra's introduction? Conclusion? _____

_____

_____

_____

5. Are the paragraphs in Sandra's revision better organized and developed than those in her discovery draft? Are her paragraphs coherent? Explain, and give examples.

_____

_____

_____

6. How could Sandra's revised draft benefit from further revision?

_____

_____

_____

GROUP
ACTIVITY
17

Using Peer Review. Form a group with two or three other students and exchange copies of your drafts. Read your draft aloud while your classmates follow along. Take notes on your classmates' responses to the following questions about your draft.

1. Have I followed all of the instructions for this assignment?

_____

_____

_____

2. How interesting is my introduction? Do you want to continue reading the paper? Why or why not?

_____

_____

_____

3. What is my thesis statement? Do I need to make the thesis clearer?

_____

_____

_____

4. Where in the essay could I add detailed observations, sensory description, examples, or a comparison or contrast to help convey my message?

_____

_____

_____

5. How can I better organize the ideas in my paragraphs?

_____

_____

_____

_____

6. What parts of my essay, if any, do not support my thesis and could be omitted? Are there any sentences or words that seem unnecessary?

_____

_____

_____

7. Are my paragraphs coherent? How can I use key words and transitions more effectively?

_____

_____

_____

8. Where in the draft did my writing confuse you? How can I clarify my thoughts?

_____

_____

_____

9. How clear is the purpose of my essay? How well have I met the needs of my audience?

_____

_____

_____

10. How effective is my conclusion? Do I end in such a way that you know it's the end?

_____

_____

_____

Revising Your Draft. Taking your classmates' suggestions for revision into consideration, revise your essay. In particular, focus on organizing the ideas in your paragraphs effectively and on using key words and transitions to connect ideas. You might also consider adding supporting details and other information your readers will need to know about your topic. Finally, look for irrelevant or unnecessary material that can be omitted, and experiment with moving sections of your draft to achieve the best presentation. ❏

Editing

Now that you have revised your essay about a cultural symbol, ritual, or hero, you're ready to edit it for correctness. Remember, the fewer errors you make, the more your readers will focus on what you have to say.

Sandra's Edited Essay

You probably noticed that Sandra's revised draft contained errors in punctuation and sentence structure. Sandra corrected these errors in her edited essay. Her corrections are underlined here. Her editing log follows the essay.

El Grito de Dolores

"Viva Mexico! Viva Mexico! Viva Mexico!" hundreds of people cry out at   *1*
the same time. Gathered in the town plaza at midnight on September 16,
they are celebrating one of <u>Mexico's</u> most important holidays, "El Grito de
Dolores." The holiday honors the men and women who fought for Mexico's independence. On this day, Mexicans feel united as they celebrate their history.

What is "El Grito de Dolores"? This expression means "the cry from   *2*
Dolores," and it refers to an important event that happened early in the
morning on September 16, 1810. At this time, Mexico was ruled by the
Spanish king. But a priest named Miguel Hidalgo called together his parishioners at his church in Dolores, Guanajuato, Mexico. In a speech that was
later called "El Grito de Dolores," Hidalgo urged his people to fight for freedom. This was the beginning of the Mexican revolution against Spain. Since

then, the holiday is celebrated everywhere in Mexico. Even the smallest towns have their own celebrations.

The celebration begins in the main <u>plaza. Exactly</u> at midnight the gover- *3* nor of each city goes on top of the municipal building. "Viva Don Miguel Hidalgo!" he yells to give honor to the person who began the movement for independence. ("Viva" means "long live.") The people shout "Viva Mexico! Viva Mexico! Viva Mexico!" Then fireworks light up the night sky, and everyone celebrates the <u>country's</u> independence.

The next part of the celebration is a parade held on the morning of Sep- *4* tember 16th <u>on the</u> street called "16 de Septiembre." Every town in Mexico has a street with this name. The parade includes children, business leaders, government leaders, members of clubs, police officers, and firefighters. Green, red, and white streamers float through the air. People <u>wave</u> little Mexican flags to show their pride in their country.

Sometimes Mexico is divided because of <u>politics. Not</u> on this day, *5* though. "El Grito de Dolores" brings the Mexican people together in a celebration of their ancestors who fought for freedom.

Sandra's Editing Log

- • INCORRECT: Mexicos (1)
  - ERROR: possessive noun without apostrophe
  - CORRECT: Mexico's

- • INCORRECT: The celebration begins in the main plaza exactly at midnight the governor of each city goes on top of the municipal building. (3)
  - ERROR: run-on sentence
  - CORRECT: The celebration begins in the main plaza. Exactly at midnight the governor of each city goes on top of the municipal building.

- • INCORRECT: countrys (3)
  - ERROR: possessive noun without apostrophe
  - CORRECT: country's

- • INCORRECT: Held on the street called "16 de Septiembre." (4)
  - ERROR: sentence fragment
  - CORRECT: The next part of the celebration is a parade held on the morning of September 16th on the street called "16 de Septiembre."

- • INCORRECT: People waving little Mexican flags to show their pride in their country. (4)

ERROR:	sentence fragment
CORRECT:	People wave little Mexican flags to show their pride in their country.
• INCORRECT:	Sometimes Mexico is divided because of politics not on this day, though. (5)
ERROR:	run-on sentence
CORRECT:	Sometimes Mexico is divided because of politics. Not on this day, though.

Editing Your Essay. Read your essay word-for-word, looking for errors in grammar, spelling, and punctuation. Also ask a friend or classmate to help you spot errors you might have overlooked. Then use a dictionary and the Handbook in Part III of this book to help you correct the errors you find. Finally, record those errors in your editing log. ❑

ACTIVITY
19

Publishing

After you edit your essay you're ready to share it with your audience—your instructor, your classmates, and students who come from cultures other than your own (including, perhaps, students in your writing classroom and members of a campus club or organization for international students). You might also send your essay by e-mail to a friend who is also on the Internet. Finally, give some thought to the benefits of reading about and familiarizing yourself with other cultures.

Your Writing Portfolio

If you're proud of your essay about a cultural symbol, ritual, or hero, add it to your writing portfolio, which contains your best writing as well as your reflections on your writing. To help you reflect on the writing you did in this chapter, answer the following questions:

1. Did you enjoy writing about an aspect of your culture? Why or why not?
2. Which topic did you choose—a cultural symbol, ritual, or hero—and why?

3. What types of changes did you make when you revised?
4. If you had more time, what further revisions would you make to improve your essay? Why?

Using your answers to these questions, update the writing process report you began in Chapter Three.

Writing Process Report

Date:

Strengths:

Weaknesses:

Plans for improvement:

Once you complete this report, freewrite in your journal about what you learned about your writing process in this chapter and what you still hope to learn.

Chapter Summary

- Gather ideas by questioning, clustering, freewriting, and brainstorming.
- Organize the ideas in your paragraphs by using one or more of these patterns:
    - —topic-illustration-explanation (TIE)
    - —progressive order

    —question-and-answer format

    —general-to-specific order

    —specific-to-general order

- Make your paragraphs coherent by using key words, synonyms, pronouns, and transitions to connect ideas.

- Share your essay with readers from different cultures as well as with your instructor and classmates.

Knowledge is of two kinds. We know a subject ourselves, or we know where we can find information on it.
—Samuel Johnson

8

Explaining Concepts

In this chapter you will

- write about concepts relating to science, the social sciences, and business.

- learn how to do primary research: observations, surveys, and interviews.

- learn how to do secondary research: locate sources of information and take notes.

- learn how to avoid plagiarism.

- learn how to quote, paraphrase, and summarize sources of information.

- learn how to document sources.

- add to your writing portfolio.

It's the first day of the fall term. You take a seat in your Introduction to Business course. You're especially looking forward to this course because you think you might major in business. You take notes as the instructor starts her lecture. She discusses such concepts as "affective orientation toward others" and "organizational design." She refers to "mentors" and the importance of "corporate culture." You're unfamiliar with most of these concepts and not sure how to spell some of the terms. At home you learn more about them from reading the textbook assignment. The next lecture makes more sense. As the course progresses, you learn more business concepts. By the end of the semester, you can look back at the first day of class and laugh at your confusion.

Every academic subject is based on certain core concepts. In English composition, the writing process is a core concept. In business and law, the concept of a contract provides the basis for many transactions. Among the many key concepts in biology is evolution, and in computer science, key concepts include software and programming. You can probably quickly list some of the core concepts in your own college courses.

A *concept* is an idea, and all aspects of our lives involve ideas. The U.S. government is based on the concepts of freedom and democracy. In the workplace, the concepts of ambition and success apply. Our relationships with others are built on such concepts as love and trust, responsibility and fairness. In this chapter, our focus is on academic concepts.

ACTIVITY
1

Analyzing Your Purpose and Audience. Before you begin gathering ideas about your topic, think about your purpose and audience. For this chapter's assignment, you'll explain a concept to readers who may be unfamiliar with its meaning. Therefore, keep the needs of your audience in mind. Your responses to the following questions will help you decide how to approach your topic.

1. Does this assignment call for expressive, informative, or persuasive writing?

    _____

2. What previous courses in the subject area might your readers have taken in college or high school?

    _____

    _____

Writing Assignment

In this chapter you will explore concepts related to science, the social sciences, and business. You or your instructor may decide to do this assignment in one of several ways:

- You may gather ideas on one, two, *or* three topics.
- You may write a discovery draft on one, two, *or* three of these topics.
- You may choose one discovery draft to develop into a polished essay.
- You may combine your discovery draft ideas into a new topic for your essay.

After completing your essay, you'll want to share it with others—your instructor and classmates, for instance, as well as other students on campus who may be interested in your topic.

_____

_____

3. What other types of firsthand experience or knowledge might your readers have about the topic?

_____

_____

_____

4. What aspects of the subject are your readers most likely to be unfamiliar with?

_____

_____

_____

Given your responses to the preceding questions, ask yourself these questions:

5.   What do my readers already know about my topic? _____

_____

_____

_____

6.   What do my readers need to know about my topic?

_____

_____

_____

7.   How do my readers feel about my topic? Will they find it interesting, or will I have to work to get their attention?

_____

_____

_____

8.   How can I get my readers' attention and spark their interest in my topic?

_____

_____

_____

❑

Gathering Ideas

To gather ideas about concepts in academic fields, you can use the same techniques you worked with in earlier chapters: brainstorming, freewriting, clustering, questioning, interviewing, and relating aloud.

Concepts in Science

As a college student, you may take courses in the physical sciences, such as chemistry, geology, and physics, or in the life sciences, such as biology, microbiology, and botany.

One popular area in the life sciences is health and nutrition. Many people want to be well informed about these issues so they can live long and healthy lives. The reading that follows addresses one such issue: food additives, and the growing concern over these chemicals that are added to many foods to improve their taste and make them last longer. Jane Brody, a health writer for the *New York Times*, explains food additives in "Feasting on Food or Chemicals?"

JANE BRODY

From *Feasting on Food or Chemicals?*

It's Saturday. You're in the supermarket procuring the family food supply for the coming week. You pick up an item and read the label: *"Contents: water; triglycerides of stearic, palmitic, oleic, and linoleic acids; myosin and actin; glycogen; collagen; lecithin, cholesterol; dipotassium phosphate; myoglobin; and urea. (Warning: May also contain steroid hormones of natural origin.)"* *1*

Dropping this chemical concoction like a hot potato, you move down the aisle and reach for something else. This label reads: *"Water, starches, cellulose, pectin, fructose, sucrose, glucose, malic acid, citric acid, succinic acid, anisyl propionate, amyl acetate, ascorbic acid (vitamin C), beta carotene (vitamin A), riboflavin, thiamin, niacin, phosphorus, and potassium."* Again, with a shudder of disgust, you put the product back and move on. *2*

The next item has a shorter list but even stranger sounding ingredients: *"Caffeine, tannin, butanol, isoamyl alcohol, hexanol, phenyl ethyl alcohol, benzyl alcohol, geraniol, quercetin, 3-galloyl epicatechin, and 3-galloyl epigallocatechin."* Back on the shelf it goes. *3*

And so on down all eight aisles of the market. *Everything* was full of chemicals, and there was nothing you felt comfortable about buying. *4*

You're right. Everything *is* full of chemicals. But you're also wrong. Because the items you passed up were not concocted in a chemist's laboratory to undermine your family's health. Rather, they were *100-percent natural, unadulterated foods from farm and field.* The first was beefsteak, the second cantaloupe, and the third tea. Milk, as it comes from the cow, is a combination of 95 chemicals, including 12 fats, 6 proteins, lactose, 9 salts, 7 acids, 3 pigments, 7 enzymes, 18 vitamins, 6 miscellaneous compounds, and 3 gases. And the potato, just as it's dug up from untreated soil, contains 150 dif- *5* ferent chemical ingredients, including one—solanine—that's a poison.

All this is not meant to win converts for the food-chemical industry but to make a point crucial to understanding the nation's food supply: food *is* chemicals, and all creatures that eat are chemicals, too. If we refused to eat foods containing chemicals, we'd starve to death very quickly. Not all chemicals are bad, whether they're natural or added in a factory. Neither are all chemicals good, including many natural chemicals. In fact, some of the most poisonous chemicals known to humankind are perfectly natural. And some of the most beneficial chemicals in our foods are wholly synthetic. Your body can't tell the difference between a natural poison and an artificial one. Both can cause harm. Nor can your body distinguish between a natural beneficial chemical and one devised in a test tube. It's grateful for any chemical that helps it to function.

The American aversion to chemicals is hardly a new phenomenon. Many years ago, the food industry—knowing the public wariness of anything "chemical"—adopted the word "additives" to describe chemicals used in processing foods. The industry won the right to list several additives by their initials instead of their more forbidding chemical names. Thus, BHT on the label stands for butylated hydroxytoluene, and CMC is really sodium carboxymethylcellulose. And in some products covered by federal food standards (lists of mandatory and optional ingredients), certain food additives don't have to be listed on the label at all.

Following the Civil War, the American pattern of food production and consumption changed dramatically as industrial development brought rural residents to cities, which depended on food from distant sources. As American industry and cities grew, more and more people relied upon the foods produced and preserved by fewer and fewer people. Instead of growing it in their back yards, urban folk got their food from stores. Fewer women spent their days preparing meals "from scratch." Instead, they got jobs and became increasingly dependent on canned and packaged convenience foods from the local market. Today, 92 percent of Americans rely on foods grown and processed by others. Even the remaining 8 percent who are still "down on the farm" don't really feed themselves. They get most of their food from farms and factories hundreds or thousands of miles away. Instead of making a daily trip to the local general store and greengrocer, most Americans shop for food once a week. The food they buy may have left the factory weeks or months earlier, the farm even longer ago than that. Something has to keep it looking and tasting good and free from insects or disease-causing microorganisms. That something is food additives.

However, additives today serve a wide variety of purposes, not all laudatory. They make possible many nutritious convenience foods, such as packaged breads, canned fruits and vegetables, canned and packaged soups, margarine, and ready-to-eat cereals. But additives also permit the concoction of junk foods, trumped-up "imitations," nutritionally deficient replacements for nourishing natural foods, and entirely new "foods" for which there is no demand until one is artificially created by the manufacturer. The explosive growth of the food-processing industry in recent decades has led to more than a 50-percent increase in the use of additives since 1960.

The most serious problem with additives is less the safety of the *10* chemicals themselves (although for some this is certainly a legitimate concern) than the kinds of foods that are most heavily laden with them: foods processed to a fare-thee-well with lots of sodium, sugar, and/or fat, adding little of real nutritive value to the American diet. We don't need all those presweetened, heavily fortified cereals; fatty and salty processed meats, chips, and dips; sugary soft drinks; and the endless stream of heat-and-serve, mix-and-match, and eat-and-run products the American food industry foists on the public.

But to revert to a wholly unprocessed, additive-free food supply *11* just isn't practical for many reasons.

Many foods could only be purchased in small quantities because *12* they would spoil quickly without preservatives. And few of us have the time or inclination for the frequent shopping and lengthy food preparation that unprocessed foods require.

If everyone insisted on only fresh carrots, peas, green beans, *13* broccoli, tomatoes, and the like, during much of the year there wouldn't be enough of them to go around. Nor would it be possible to get fresh supplies to all parts of the country often enough.

The limited shelf life of most fresh foods would lead to a great *14* deal of waste, further diminishing the available food supply.

The food left might cost more. Distribution of conveniently *15* packaged and processed foods is already extremely expensive, and likely to get more so as energy supplies dwindle. Transporting fresh foods, which are less compact and far more perishable, could cost many times more.

So, like it or not, we are stuck with a food-processing industry *16* and the chemical additives it uses to keep food in good condition until it reaches the consumer's table. What's more, we have come to expect a quality product when we buy food, whether it comes from farm or factory. We want to be sure that every time we buy a loaf of . . . bread, it's going to be like the last loaf we had. We don't want ice crystals in our ice cream, bugs in our flour, rancid crackers, crumbly cakes, or mushy vegetables. High standards of uniformity and safety from food spoilage are the hallmarks of the modern American food industry. And when food processors occasionally fall down on the job, consumers complain loudly and clearly. . . .

ACTIVITY
2

Reading to Improve Writing. Discuss the following questions about "Feasting on Food or Chemicals?" with your classmates.

1. What are food additives and why are they used? _____

    _____

    _____

    _____

2. Why are food additives used much more today than they were a hundred years ago?

    _____

    _____

    _____

3. How does the author get your attention at the start of her essay?

    _____

    _____

    _____

4. Which of the following techniques does the writer use to support and clarify her ideas: examples, classification, cause and effect, comparison-contrast, definition, process analysis, facts, and statistics? Where in the essay are the techniques used?

    _____

    _____

    _____

ACTIVITY
3

Collecting New Words. Try to determine the meanings of the following words from the way they're used in "Feasting on Food or Chemicals?" Then verify their meanings by checking a dictionary.

procuring (1)   _____

concocted (5)   _____

synthetic (6)   _____

aversion (7)   _____

laudatory (9)   _____

laden (10)   _____

perishable (15)   _____

rancid (16)   _____

Gathering Ideas about a Concept in Science. First, select a concept related to science. You might choose a concept that you're especially interested in or one from this list:

ACTIVITY
4

Concepts in Science

Biology

environment	photosynthesis
evolution	pollution
ecosystem	equilibrium
ecology	food chain

Health Science

calorie	metabolism
nutrient	diet
anaerobic	aerobic
disability	bulimia

Earth Science

magnetism	erosion
dew point	humidity
weather front	geologic time
fossil	volcano

Chemistry

matter	compound
inorganic	organic
enzyme	chemical bonding
periodic table	kinetics

Then gather ideas in your journal about the concept. In addition to using one or more of the methods you learned in earlier chapters, such as brainstorming and freewriting, gather ideas by answering the following questions about the concept:

1. How does your dictionary or textbook define the concept?
2. What is your understanding of the concept?
3. Why is the concept important?
4. How does the concept relate to your own and your readers' lives?

❏

Here's how one student, Matthew, gathered ideas about a concept in science—vegetarianism. Working in his journal, Matthew freewrote his responses to the questions in Activity 4.

According to the dictionary, vegetarianism is "the practice or belief in eating a diet consisting primarily of vegetables, grains, fruits, nuts, seeds, and sometimes dairy products, such as milk or cheese." I think vegetarianism means not eating meat. There are different types of vegetarians—I need to find out what they're called. This concept is important because everyone needs to eat in a healthy way. Also, I'm concerned about the abuse of animals. This concept relates to everyone's life.

Put your writing about a science concept aside for now. You want to explore ideas about another possible topic for your essay—a concept related to the social sciences.

Concepts in the Social Sciences

The social sciences include the fields of history, political science, sociology, anthropology, economics, psychology, and others that involve the scientific study of the interactions between people and the societies in which they live. Psychology is the scientific study of human behavior—of what people do and why. Often, when we think of psychology, we associate it with mental illness, such as schizophrenia or multiple-personality disorder. But psychology also offers explanations for the behavior of mentally healthy people.

In the following reading, "Mind/Body Programming," psychologist Joan Borysenko explains the concept of conditioning. Conditioning is a part of all of our lives, and knowing how it affects us can benefit our mental health.

JOAN BORYSENKO

Mind/Body Programming

Every time you miss your exit on the highway because you are daydreaming, then "wake up" to discover yourself miles farther down the road, you are demonstrating the power of the unconscious mind. Once something is learned, we don't have to think about it consciously. The task simply repeats itself as soon as we initiate the program—in this case, by putting the key in the ignition. The rest of driving is second nature because our nervous system has been conditioned—or imprinted—with the driving pattern.

Because of our conditioning, we are all creatures of habit. Most people get anxious before taking an exam partly because they have become habituated to feeling anxious at exam time, whether or not the situation at hand is actually threatening. Once threatened by an exam, a neural connection is established. The next time an exam comes up, the probability is that we'll reactivate that same conditioned circuit.

Physiological conditioning is a kind of rapid learning that evolved to help us master cause-and-effect situations that might determine survival. We all are familiar with Pavlov's famous experiment. A dog is given meat powder, which naturally makes him salivate. A bell is then rung every time the meat powder is presented. After a time the dog salivates merely at the sound of the bell. We see the same mechanism operating in ourselves when we're working away contentedly, then glance up at the clock, notice it's lunch time, and suddenly become hungry.

The mind's power to affect the body through conditioning became crystal clear to me when I was six or seven years old. My Uncle Dick, a confirmed cheese hater, was eating Sunday dinner with us. For dessert there was a cheesecake camouflaged with ripe strawberries. It was so good that he ate two pieces. About an hour later my mother expressed her surprise at Uncle Dick's delight in the dessert, since she knew how much he hated cheese. At the sound of the word *cheese,* Uncle Dick turned pale, began to gag, and ran for the bathroom. Even as a child it was obvious to me that the problem was not the cheese itself, but some mental conditioning about cheese that produced such a violent reaction.

Many people who receive chemotherapy for cancer get sick to their stomachs from the medication. Soon, through conditioning similar to Uncle Dick's, they begin to get sick before they actually receive the drugs. Some people begin to get nauseous the night before treatment. Others may get nauseous coming to the hospital or even upon seeing their doctor or nurse. They have involuntarily learned to get sick as a conditioned response to the thoughts, sights, and smells of the chemotherapy situation.

What we've learned from Soviet studies following Pavlov's model is that the immune system itself can be conditioned. In this country Dr. Robert Ader and Dr. Nicholas Cohen at the University of Rochester injected rats with an immunosuppressant drug called cy-clophosphamide and at the same time added a new taste—saccha-rin—to the animals' drinking water. The saccharin acted like Pavlov's bell. After a while the rats were suppressing their immunity at the taste of saccharin alone.   *6*

Dr. G. Richard Smith and Sandra McDaniel did a fascinating study of the suppression of immune reactions in humans. Once a month for five months, volunteers who had reacted positively in a tuberculin skin test came into the same room with the same arrangement of furniture and the same nurse. Each time they saw a red and green vial on the desk, and each time the contents of the red vial—tuberculin—were injected into the same arm, and the contents of the green vial—a salt solution—were injected into the other.   *7*

Month after month the same procedure was followed, and month after month the volunteers had the same reaction to the tu-berculin—a red swollen patch on the same arm. There was never any reaction to the injection of the salt solution in the other arm.   *8*

On the sixth trial the contents of the vials were switched with-out the volunteers' knowledge. And this time the volunteers had al-most no reaction to the tuberculin. Their expectation that nothing ever happened after the injection from the green vial apparently was enough to inhibit the immune system's powerful inflammatory response to tuberculin.   *9*

Conditioning is a powerful bridge between mind and body. . . . *10* The reason is that the body cannot tell the difference between events that are actual threats to survival and events that are present in thought alone. The mind spins out endless fantasies of possible disasters past and future. This tendency to escalate a situation into its worst possible conclusion is what I call awfulizing, and it can be a key factor in tipping the balance toward illness or health. Perhaps you're hung up in traffic, sure to be late for an important 9 A.M. meeting. Or it's midnight and your child is still out, or the doctor tells you she wants to repeat a test, or so on in endless variation. The flood of "what ifs" and "if onlys" engages the various human emotions, which can influence virtually all bodily functions.

The way our minds work—the degree to which we awfulize—   *11* also depends on previous conditioning. The responses of our parents and other influential role models shape our own reactions to life. Awareness of our conditioning is the first step toward unlearning at-titudes that have outlived their usefulness. Such awareness opens

our ability to respond to what is happening *now* rather than reacting
out of a conditioned history that may be archaic. . . .

Reading to Improve Writing. Discuss the following questions
about "Mind/Body Programming" with your classmates.

ACTIVITY
5

1. What is conditioning? _____

    _____

    _____

    _____

2. How does conditioning come about? _____

    _____

    _____

    _____

3. How does the author relate conditioning to the lives of her readers?

    _____

    _____

    _____

4. In your view, what is the most effective example of conditioning
    given in the reading?

    _____

    _____

    _____

Collecting New Words. Try to determine the meanings of the
following words from the way they're used in "Mind/Body
Programming." Then verify their meanings by checking a dictionary.

ACTIVITY
6

initiate (1)   _____

neural (2)   _____

salivate (3)   _____

immune (6)   _____

vial (7)   _____

escalate (10)   _____

archaic (11)   _____

ACTIVITY
7   **Gathering Ideas about a Concept in the Social Sciences.** First, select a concept related to the social sciences. You can choose a concept you're especially interested in or one from this list:

Concepts in the Social Sciences

Political Science

pluralism	political party
electoral college	voting block
despot	monarchy
political action committee (PAC)	filibuster

Psychology

nonverbal communication	motivation
schizophrenia	psychoanalysis
altruism	perception
eating disorder	personality disorder

Anthropology/Archaeology

Homo sapiens	mummy
rite of passage	polygamy
clan	race
bilingualism	biculturalism

History

Black Panthers	Reconstruction
Sputnik	New Deal
Jim Crow laws	Woodstock
women's suffrage	baby boom

Then gather ideas in your journal about the concept. In addition to using one or more of the methods you learned in earlier chapters, such as clustering and relating aloud, gather ideas by answering these questions about the concept:

1.   How does your dictionary or textbook define the concept?
2.   What is your understanding of the concept?
3.   Why is the concept important?
4.   How does the concept relate to your own and your readers' lives?

❏

One student, Hortensia, gathered ideas about a concept in the social sciences—anorexia nervosa—by answering the questions in Activity 7. Here's how she responded:

1. The dictionary defines anorexia nervosa as "the pathological loss of appetite occurring chiefly in young women that is thought to be psychological in origin."

2. My understanding of anorexia nervosa is that it occurs when a woman is so afraid of becoming overweight that she starves herself.

3. The concept is important because many women have anorexia or another eating disorder, such as bulimia. I'd like my readers to know the symptoms so they could help someone with this disease.

4. One of my best friends in high school was anorexic, which made me interested in this disease.

Set aside your writing about a social science concept for now. You want to gather ideas about one more possible topic for your essay—a concept related to business.

Concepts in Business

Business is among the most popular majors in college, probably because it prepares the student for a specific job after graduation, without further study. Usually, a business student specializes in one area, such as general management, merchandising, marketing, finance, human resources, or information systems management. Each of these areas has its own set of key concepts, with some overlapping of concepts among the various areas of business.

The Internet applies to all areas of the business world. Accountants, sales representatives, and programmers use the Internet to communicate and receive information. In fact, just about everyone can find some use for the Net, as John R. Levine and Carol Baroudi point out in "What Is the Internet?"

JOHN R. LEVINE AND CAROL BAROUDI

From *What Is the Internet?*

The Internet—also known as the Net—is the world's largest computer network. "And what is a network?" you may ask. Even if you already know, you may want to read the next couple of paragraphs to make sure that we're speaking the same language. *1*

A computer network is basically a bunch of computers hooked together somehow. (Here in the world of computers, we like these crisp, precise definitions.) In concept, it's sort of like a radio or TV network that connects a bunch of radio or TV stations so that they can share the latest episode of *The Simpsons*. *2*

But don't take the analogy too far. TV networks send the same information to all the stations at the same time (what's called *broadcast* networking, for obvious reasons); in computer networks, though, each particular message is usually routed to a particular computer. Unlike TV networks, computer networks are invariably two-way, so that when computer A sends a message to computer B, B can send a reply back to A. *3*

Some computer networks consist of a central computer and a bunch of remote stations that report to it—a central airline-reservation computer, for example, with thousands of terminals at airports and travel agencies. Others, including the Internet, are more egalitarian and permit any computer on the network to communicate with any other. *4*

So, as we were saying, the Internet is the world's largest computer network. "So what?" you're probably saying. "I once saw the world's largest turnip on TV, and it didn't look very interesting—and I bet that it didn't taste so great either." Well, with networks, unlike vegetables, size counts for a lot because the larger a network is, the more stuff it has to offer. *5*

Actually, the Internet isn't really a network—it's a network of networks, all freely exchanging information. The networks range from the big and formal, like the corporate networks at AT&T, Digital Equipment Corporation, and Hewlett-Packard to the small and informal, like the one in John Levine's attic (with a couple of old PCs bought through the *Want Advertiser*), and everything in between. College and university networks have long been part of the Internet, and now high schools and elementary schools are joining up too. As of August 1994, more than 20,000 networks on every continent connecting more than 3 million computers were part of the Inter- *6* net, with 1,000 new networks and 100,000 computers per month being added. . . .

If you use a telephone, write letters, or do any kind of research, or if you are interested in what other people may have to say about darned near any topic in the whole wide world, the Internet can radically alter your whole world view. People of all ages, colors, creeds, and countries freely share ideas, stories, data, and opinions on the Net.

7

Seventh-grade students in San Diego use the Internet to exchange letters and stories with kids in Israel. Partly it's just for fun and to make friends in a foreign country, but a sober academic study reported that when kids have a real audience for their stuff, they write better. (Big surprise.)

8

In some parts of the world, the Internet is the fastest and most reliable way to move information. During the 1991 Soviet coup, for example, a tiny Internet provider called RELCOM, which had a link to Finland and through there to the rest of the Internet world, found itself as the only reliable path to get reports in and out of Moscow because telephones were shut off and newspapers weren't being published. RELCOM members sent out stories that would have been in newspapers, statements from Boris Yeltsin (hand-delivered by friends), and their personal observations from downtown Moscow. . . .

9

The Internet has more prosaic uses too. Here are some from our personal experience:

10

One day John's wife wanted to find patterns to make a 1960s-era military shirt. (A friend had an old shirt he loved from his days in the army, but it was running out of places on which to sew patches.) So John asked the Net to help. The Net has several running discussions on military topics and one on historical costuming, so he sent out a message asking for help. Within one day, five different people responded by giving the addresses of pattern makers. Most of them said that they would be happy to offer tips and advice if we ran into trouble.

11

The Internet is its own best source of software. Whenever we hear about a new service . . . , it usually takes only a few minutes to find software for one of our computers (a 386 laptop running Windows), download it, and start it up. Even better, nearly all the software available on the Internet is free.

12

The Internet has local and regional parts as well. When John wanted to sell a trusty but tired minivan, a note on the Internet in a local for-sale area found a buyer within two days.

13

We've established that the Internet is large and, for some people, useful. What does this mean for real people?

14

The Internet is probably the most open network in the world. Thousands of computers provide facilities that are available to any-

15

one who has Net access. This situation is unusual—*most* networks are very restrictive in what they allow users to do and require specific arrangements and passwords for each service. Although a few pay services exist (and undoubtedly more will be added), the vast majority of Internet services are free for the taking, once you are connected. If you don't already have access to the Internet through your company, your school, or John's attic, you'll probably have to pay for access to the Internet by using an Internet access provider. . . .

The final unusual thing about the Internet is that it is what 16 one might call *socially unstratified*. That is, one computer is no better than any other, and no person is any better than any other. Who you are on the Net depends solely on how you present yourself through your keyboard. If what you say makes you sound like an intelligent, interesting person, then that's who you are. It doesn't matter how old you are or what you look like or whether you're a student, a business executive, or a construction worker. Physical disabilities don't matter either—one of the authors of this [reading] corresponds with several people who are blind or deaf. If they hadn't felt like telling, we never would have known. Famous people are in the Net community too, some favorably and some unfavorably, but they got that way through their own efforts. . . .

ACTIVITY
8

Reading to Improve Writing. Discuss the following questions about "What Is the Internet?" with your classmates.

1. Without referring back to the reading, explain the Internet in your own words. Then look back at the reading to see how well you defined the concept.

   _____

   _____

   _____

2. Why has the Internet become so popular? _____

   _____

   _____

_____

_____

3. How do the authors catch their readers' attention and interest in the topic?

    _____

    _____

    _____

4. What are your experiences with the Internet?

    _____

    _____

    _____

Collecting New Words. Try to determine the meanings of the following words from the way they're used in "What Is the Internet?" Then verify their meanings by checking a dictionary.

ACTIVITY
9

analogy (3) _____

invariably (3) _____

egalitarian (4) _____

creeds (7) _____

data (7) _____

coup (9) _____

prosaic (10) _____

download (12) _____

unstratified (16) _____

ACTIVITY
10

Gathering Ideas about a Concept in Business. First, select a business concept. You might choose a concept you're especially interested in or one from this list:

Concepts in Business

General Management

group dynamics	contract
collective bargaining	mediation
grievance procedure	merit pay
negotiation	benefits

Merchandising

retail	wholesale
inventory	tax
customer service	outlet store
supply-and-demand theory	entrepreneur

Information Systems Management

World Wide Web	gopher
data bank	e-mail
information highway	software
local area network	listserv

Finance

capital	inflation
gross national product (GNP)	mutual fund
taxation	dividend
investment	credit

Then gather ideas in your journal about the concept. In addition to using one or more of the methods you learned in earlier chapters, such as questioning and interviewing, gather ideas by answering these questions about the concept:

1. How does your dictionary or textbook define the concept?
2. What is your understanding of the concept?
3. Why is the concept important?
4. How does the concept relate to your own and your readers' lives?

❏

One student, Arlene, decided to gather ideas about the concept of money. She conducted an e-mail interview of a friend, Nicole, a graduate student in finance. Here's a portion of the interview. Notice how Arlene used the questions in Activity 10 as her interview questions.

Arlene: What is the definition of money?

Nicole: Money is anything that people will accept as payment for services and goods. It can be a string of beads or a cow or the paper money that we use now.

Arlene: Why is it important to understand the concept of money?

Nicole: By understanding the concept of money you can also understand how the economy works. For instance, money is a unit of account, or the common measuring stick for services and goods. Without this measuring stick we'd have to negotiate a price for everything we buy.

Arlene: How does the concept of money relate to people's everyday lives?

Nicole: Well, every time you use a coin or a paper dollar to buy something, you show your faith in our government's ability to back that money. Without that faith in our government, our whole economic system wouldn't work and our money would be worthless.

Drafting

You have now gathered ideas about concepts in science, the social sciences, and business. You thus have a rich source of material for writing, but you need to decide how to proceed. Here are some of your options:

- You may select one of the three topics for your discovery draft.
- You may write drafts on two or three of the topics to see which one you prefer to continue working on.
- You may combine related topics in your discovery draft, or even choose a concept from some other academic area.

Above all, choose a topic that interests you, that you know something about, and that you want to learn more about through research. You'll have the chance to conduct some research on the topic later on, during revision. Before you begin drafting, write a preliminary thesis statement, although you may decide to revise it later on. Keep your audience and purpose in mind, but remember that your main goal at the drafting stage is to get your ideas down on paper.

Here's an example of a discovery draft written by a student, Matthew Ward, whose freewriting about vegetarianism you saw earlier in the chapter. As he drafted, Matthew put questions in parentheses to note where he needed to research more information about his topic. After you read his draft, discuss with your classmates what Matthew might do to revise it. (Note that the example contains the types of errors typically found in a discovery draft.)

COMPUTER TIP

HIGHLIGHT YOUR RESEARCH QUESTIONS AS YOU DRAFT

As you work on your discovery draft, highlight questions about your topic that you want to research later. First, enclose the questions in parentheses. Then, after you complete the draft, use the "block" and "move" functions to move your research questions to a separate file. Add to that file any other questions you have about your topic. Use this file to begin your research.

Vegetarianism

Vegetarians are sometimes stereotyped as hippies who eat bean   *1*
sprouts and live in communes. But there are many kinds of vegetarians under the sun. People become vegetarians for many reasons. There are also
different types of vegetarians. Who knows, after you learn more about these
vegetarians, you might want to become one yourself!

People become vegetarians for several reasons. One of them being   *2*
health. People who don't eat meat live longer, stay in better shape, and don't
have as many heart attacks. Another reason people become vegetarians is
because they think that eating animals is cruel and unnecessary. People also
become vegetarians because they don't like the way animals are treated before they're slaughtered. (Any other reasons?)

There are different types of vegetarians. Strict vegetarians don't eat any   *3*
animal products, including milk, eggs, and cheese. (What is the name of this
type?) Some vegetarians eat milk, eggs, and cheese but nothing else that
comes from an animal. (Name?) Another group of vegetarians doesn't eat
any meat except fish. (Name?) Some vegetarians eat meat on special occasions, like holidays where traditional food is served. (Name?)

(What are the benefits of becoming a vegetarian?)

(How do vegetarians make sure they're getting enough vitamins?)

If you're interested in becoming a vegetarian, decide which kind you   *4*
want to be. Start to eliminate meat from your diet gradually so you won't
crave it. Find some good vegetarian recipes to try out. After a month or so,
you'll wonder how you could have gone so long as a meat eater.

Revising

When you revise your discovery draft, remember to focus on the
strategies you learned in earlier chapters: writing an effective introduction and conclusion, organizing your paragraphs, and making
your ideas flow together.

For this chapter's assignment, you will also need to research your
topic in order to provide good supporting details. You'll learn how to
conduct the two basic types of research—primary research (such as
observing, surveying, and interviewing) and secondary research
(reading what others have written about the topic). For both kinds of
research you need to prepare specific research questions in advance.
After all, if you don't know what you're looking for, you won't know
whether you have found it.

Preparing Research Questions. To conduct your research efficiently, prepare a list of research questions beforehand. Include the questions that came to mind as you drafted. Also reread your discovery draft to see if other questions arise, and use brainstorming to come up with still more questions about your topic. You'll refer to these questions to keep your research on track. Don't hesitate to revise these questions if you change your approach to the topic. ❏

ACTIVITY
11

Primary Research

Research that you do on your own, rather than read about, is called *primary research.* Thus, when you do an experiment in science, you're doing primary research. When you ask friends to suggest a good movie, you're essentially taking a survey, another form of primary research.

Three common types of primary research involve making observations, surveying others, and conducting interviews. These types of primary research are used for different purposes:

- When you want to explain how something works or how something is done, consider making observations.

- When you want to explain your topic's importance in people's lives, consider conducting a survey.

- When you require specialized information or information known only to people involved in the field, consider conducting an interview.

Let's look at these three types of primary research more closely.

> **COMPUTER TIP**
> **CONDUCTING PRIMARY RESEARCH**
> Primary research can be conducted with relative ease when you have access to a computer. You can use the format options of your word-processing program to produce professional-looking surveys or questionnaires. Also, you can take notes on a laptop or notebook computer as you make observations or conduct an interview.

Making Observations. To *observe* something is to closely watch it. Observations enable you to explain your points clearly to your readers. If you're explaining the concept of mitosis, you can observe under a microscope the process of cell division. In your essay, you can describe what you saw to make the process come alive for your readers. Similarly, in an essay on the Internet, you might describe your observations of some on-line conversations and include a quotation that illustrates a key point.

Here are some tips for making observations:

- Obtain permission to observe an event relevant to your topic, if necessary.

- Take detailed notes as you observe the event.

- Ask questions about what you observe but may not understand.

Surveying Others. A *survey* contains information collected from many people about a certain topic. Newspapers often conduct surveys to find out how citizens plan to vote in an upcoming election. Market research companies are often hired by manufacturers to survey users of their products and thereby learn how to improve the products. In writing, a survey can help you point out the importance of a concept in people's lives. For example, to collect information for an essay on dieting, you might use a survey that asks people whether they've ever tried to lose weight. Your research findings would most likely support your main point that dieting is an important concern for many people.

Here are some tips for surveying others:

- Decide how you will conduct the survey—with an *oral survey* or a *written survey*. The advantage of the oral survey is that the respondents reply immediately. The disadvantage is that the respondents do not have much time to think about the questions. The written survey generates more detailed responses, but many people may not have the time to fill out a questionnaire. If you conduct an oral survey, take careful notes.

- Decide where you will conduct the survey. You want to find a place where many people come and go, such as the entrance of the college library or student union.

- Create a list of five to ten survey questions. Make them as brief as possible and easy to understand. Also use various types of questions, such as *yes/no* questions mixed with questions that require short answers.

- Decide who you will survey. For instance, do you want to survey both men and women from various age groups?

- Decide how many people you'll survey. The more people you include in a survey, the more reliable your results will be. But you need to consider your time limitations as well.

Conducting Interviews. As you learned in Chapter Three, interviewing others is a good way to gather ideas about a topic. The *interview* can also help you learn more about a research topic. By interviewing a knowledgeable person, you can collect information and gain an expert's perspective on your topic.

After writing his discovery draft, Matthew found that he needed more information on why people become vegetarians. He decided to interview an expert on his topic, Mary May, the president of a local organization called Vegetarians for Humanity. When Matthew called to arrange the interview, he gave his name, explained that he was a student involved in a research project, and requested an interview of approximately fifteen minutes. In preparation for the interview, Matthew wrote up a list of questions designed to elicit the informa-

---

COMPUTER TIP

CONDUCTING A SURVEY ON THE INTERNET

A written survey can be sent to users on the Internet. Be sure to include a deadline for responding. Consider posting the results of the survey for those who participated in it.

tion he needed about his research topic. During the interview, he took careful notes and used quotation marks to indicate Ms. May's exact words. However, Matthew wrote most of his interview notes in his own words.

Here are some tips for conducting interviews:

- Choose a knowledgeable person to interview. To determine whether someone is an expert on your topic, check his or her credentials, such as academic degrees, professional activities, and published works.
- Prepare a list of interview questions in advance.
- Dress appropriately and arrive on time if you conduct the interview in person.
- Keep the conversation focused on your questions. Be considerate of your interviewee's limited time.
- Take good notes. Put quotation marks around the person's actual words. You may tape-record the conversation only if you obtain the interviewee's permission beforehand.
- Ask the interviewee to clarify anything you do not understand.
- Send a thank-you note to the person soon after the interview.

Here's one more tip: if you're reluctant to contact a stranger for an interview, remember that most people enjoy talking about what they know and are especially eager to share their knowledge with interested students.

Conducting Primary Research. Working in a group of several students, discuss your topics for this chapter's writing assignment. Determine the type of primary research that will best suit each student's topic. Then use the appropriate set of questions to discuss how each group member can go about making observations, surveying others, or conducting an interview.

GROUP
ACTIVITY
12

Questions about Making Observations

1. What information do you need to obtain from your observations?

_____

_____

_____

2. Where will you make the observations? _____

_____

_____

_____

3. Do you need permission to observe? If so, from whom?

_____

_____

_____

4. What questions might you expect to have about the event you want to observe?

_____

_____

_____

Questions about Surveying Others

1. What information do you want the survey to provide?

_____

_____

_____

2. Do you want your respondents to answer orally or in writing? Why?

_____

_____

_____

3. Who will your respondents be, and how many people will you survey?

_____

_____

_____

_____

4. Where will you conduct the survey? _____

_____

_____

_____

5. What questions will you ask in the survey? _____

_____

_____

_____

Questions about Conducting an Interview

1. What information do you hope to obtain from the interview?

_____

_____

_____

2. Who could give you this information? _____

_____

_____

_____

3. What questions will you ask? _____

_____

_____

_____

❏

Secondary Research

Secondary research involves reading what others have written about your topic in books, articles, research reports, and other published works. To conduct secondary research, you need to know how to locate relevant sources of information; how to take notes and avoid plagiarism; how to quote, paraphrase, and summarize sources of information; and how to document the sources you cite in your research paper. Let's look at each of these steps in detail.

Locating Sources of Information. To begin your search for information, consult an encyclopedia. You're probably familiar with such general encyclopedias as *Encyclopedia Americana* and *Encyclopaedia Britannica,* but specialized encyclopedias are a better source of in-depth information because they cover specific fields of study. Some specialized encyclopedias are the *Encyclopedia of Computer Science and Technology, Encyclopedia of Psychology, Encyclopedia of Biological Sciences,* and *McGraw-Hill Encyclopedia of Science and Technology.* You can locate specialized encyclopedias by checking the library catalog or consulting a reference librarian.

Another way to locate sources of information is to consult an *index,* which usually lists articles by subject and author. Some indexes are computerized; *InfoTrac,* for example, lists articles from thousands of magazines and newspapers. After you find a source in an index, you'll need to locate it in your college's library. You can also find books on your topic by consulting your college library's subject catalog.

Secondary research need not be limited to library sources. The newspapers and magazines you subscribe to may also contain articles on your topic. Also check television listings for relevant documentaries or news shows. *All Things Considered,* broadcast daily on National Public Radio, is an excellent source of current news.

The credibility of the sources you consult is an important concern. A report isn't necessarily reliable simply because it appears in print or on television. Many magazines have a political bias. *The National Review,* for instance, has a conservative slant, whereas *The Nation* is considered liberal. Recent sources (that is, those published within the last five years) are almost always better than older ones because they contain more up-to-date information. If you gather information from television sources, be especially skeptical about what you watch. Some news-entertainment shows may exaggerate facts to make their stories more interesting to their audience. Avoid using material from a talk show unless you are certain it's not hearsay or gossip.

Conducting Library Research. Team up with a classmate to do some library research on your topic. First, explain to your partner the type of information you need to find. Then visit the campus library and, working together, locate specialized encyclopedias, magazine and newspaper articles, and books on your topics. Don't hesitate to ask a librarian for assistance if you cannot find the sources you need. Finally, record here the titles and authors of the various sources you find on your topic.

GROUP
ACTIVITY
13

1. Specialized encyclopedia (give the title) _____

   _____

2. Magazine article (give the titles of the article and the magazine and the author's name)

   _____

   _____

   _____

3. Newspaper article (give the titles of the article and the newspaper and the author's name)

   _____

   _____

   _____

4. Book (give the title and the author's name) _____

   _____

   _____

COMPUTER TIP

USING THE WORLD WIDE WEB

The World Wide Web, an information system on the Internet, is another excellent source for secondary research. Because topics are linked together, the Web allows you to jump from one topic to another quickly and easily. A computer program such as Netscape allows access to the Web.

❏

Avoiding Plagiarism. A very serious offense, *plagiarism* is the use of another writer's ideas or words without giving credit to that writer as the source. It is an obvious act of plagiarism to hand in someone else's work with your name on it. But it is also an act of plagiarism to use another writer's words or ideas in your paper without indicating where they came from, even if you do so unintentionally.

Therefore, you must be careful to avoid plagiarism. Always identify your sources when you borrow ideas, information, or quotations so that your readers can clearly distinguish between what has been borrowed and what is your own. Follow these guidelines:

- When you reproduce a writer's exact words, use quotation marks to enclose the quote and name your source.
- When you restate an author's words in your own words, you omit the quotation marks but you must still name your source.

The following sections on taking notes and on quoting, paraphrasing, summarizing, and documenting sources will also help you avoid plagiarism.

GROUP
ACTIVITY
14

Talking about Plagiarism. Plagiarism can come in many forms. Discuss the following situations with your classmates.

1. Because of her busy work schedule, Anne puts off writing a research paper until the night before the deadline and, as a result, doesn't take the time to identify the sources of borrowed words and ideas in her paper. A week later, her instructor calls her into his office and tells her that she has plagiarized.

   Why is this plagiarism? _____

   _____

   _____

   How should Anne respond? _____

   _____

   _____

   How should Anne be penalized? _____

   _____

   _____

2. Joanne belongs to a sorority that keeps a file of term papers written by its members. Looking in that file, she finds a paper on the same topic as an English paper she's writing. She copies several paragraphs from the paper, word-for-word, without indicating where they came from. Later, Joanne's instructor asks her why part of her paper sounds like someone else wrote it.

Why is this plagiarism? _____

_____

_____

Should Joanne offer to rewrite the paper? _____

_____

_____

How should Joanne be penalized? _____

_____

_____

3. Co-workers Sam and Eloise are asked by their supervisor to write a report on the company's recent sales figures. Eloise volunteers to draft the report, and Sam agrees to revise, edit, and submit it to the supervisor. The report that Sam submits, however, has only his name on it.

Why is this plagiarism? _____

_____

_____

What should Eloise do? _____

_____

_____

How should Sam be penalized? _____

_____

_____

4. Frank and Joe are roommates. Frank is enrolled in the same history course that Joe took last semester. Frank comes across one of Joe's old notebooks, and in it is the history paper that Joe wrote for last semester's course. Frank retypes the paper and submits it as his own.

Why is this plagiarism? _____

_____

_____

Do you think Frank's plagiarism of Joe's paper will be discovered?

_____

If so, how should Frank be penalized? Or, if not, how might Frank's experience influence his behavior in the future?

_____

_____

_____

What advice would you give Frank if you could? _____

_____

_____

❏

Taking Notes. Once you locate a book, an article, or another source on your topic, skim it to see if it answers any of your research questions. To skim a source, simply read the introduction, the headings and subheadings, and the conclusion. If it answers any of your research questions, take notes on the source or photocopy the relevant pages and highlight the important ideas. However, highlighting shouldn't replace taking careful notes. Note-taking forces you to select only what is useful from a source, to restate the information in your own words, and thereby to reflect on its meaning.

Consider using index cards for your notes. Because they're small, index cards help you focus on the information you need. Also, you can arrange the cards in various ways, which can be helpful in organizing your ideas during revision. Take notes for only one source on a notecard. Also record the author's name, the title, and the publication data on the notecard. This information varies somewhat depending on the type of source you consult. For magazine and newspaper articles, encyclopedia entries, and books, you must record the following information for each source you use:

Magazine article
 title
 author
 name of magazine
 date of publication (month and year)
 page numbers of the whole article
 page numbers for the information you used

Newspaper article
 title
 author
 name of the newspaper
 date of publication (month, day, and year)
 page numbers of the article
 page numbers for the information you used

Encyclopedia article or entry
 title
 author (if given, it usually appears at the end of the entry)
 name of the encyclopedia
 year and place of publication
 volume and page number (if the encyclopedia is not arranged alphabetically)

Book
 title
 author
 name of publisher
 year and place of publication
 page numbers

> **COMPUTER TIP**
> **INTERNET SOURCES**
> For sources accessed via the Internet, you should record the following information:
>
> title
> author (if given)
> publication medium
> name of computer
> service
> date of access
> source address

Here are some other tips for taking notes:

- Refer frequently to your research questions to keep you focused on your topic.

- Don't just copy information from sources. Add your own thoughts. You might note, for instance, where you could use the information in your essay.

- Use quotation marks to indicate where you record an author's exact words. Write the rest of your notes in your own words.

ACTIVITY

15

Practicing Taking Notes. Imagine that you're writing an essay on food additives and that one of your research questions is "What are food additives?" To answer this question, take notes on an index card on "Feasting on Food or Chemicals?" by Jane Brody, which appears earlier in this chapter. This piece was taken from *Jane Brody's Nutrition Book,* by Jane Brody, published in 1981 by Bantam Books, a publisher located in New York City. It appears on pages 463–466 of that book.

Compare your notecard with a classmate's. Did you answer the research question without giving unnecessary information? Did you put quotation marks around the author's exact words? Did you record the necessary publication information for the source?   ❑

COMPUTER TIP

TAKING NOTES

The computer screen can function like a set of notecards if your word-processing program has the capability to put your research questions in a small window that you can periodically refer to as you take notes. Label different types of information with icons. If you are using hypertext, create your own three-dimensional notecards. Organize your notes in different folders or files for easy reference.

Quoting Information. When an author uses an especially memorable phrase, you might want to quote it directly in your paper, or you might use quoted material to emphasize a point or sum up an idea. These should be brief quotations of one or two sentences. And, as a general rule, use quotations sparingly.

You should include an introductory phrase to tell your readers the source of each quotation. After the quoted information, put the page number of the source in parentheses. Here are some examples:

> According to nutrition expert Jane Brody, "If we refused to eat food containing chemicals, we'd starve to death very quickly" (464).

> Nutrition expert Jane Brody writes, "If we refused to eat food containing chemicals, we'd starve to death very quickly" (464).

> "If we refused to eat food containing chemicals, we'd starve to death very quickly," writes Jane Brody, a nutrition expert (464).

Also notice in the examples how the quotations are punctuated. (Refer to the Handbook in Part III of this book for help with punctuation.)

When you use a quotation, you can't just drop it into a paragraph. You need to explain its relevance to your topic or point. In the following paragraph from a student essay on food additives, for example, the writer quotes a memorable phrase from Jane Brody's essay—"food *is* chemicals, and all creatures that eat are chemicals, too"—then explains its relevance to his point:

> When you think of food additives, chemicals with such unpronounceable names as "calcium stearoly lactylate" probably come to mind. Not all chemicals in foods, though, have been added. According to science writer Jane Brody, "food *is* chemicals, and all creatures that eat are chemicals, too" (463). In other words, plants and animals—including human beings—are made up of chemicals. There's nothing wrong with chemicals in foods—it's the type of chemicals that matter.

Note, too, as this paragraph demonstrates, that the topic-illustration-explanation (TIE) pattern of organization is often used in paragraphs containing quotations (see Chapter Seven).

Quoting Sources. Working with several other students, write a paragraph about one of the main ideas in "What Is the Internet?" or "Mind/Body Programming." Use a quotation from the essay to help you develop the paragraph. Then create an introductory phrase for each quotation, and consider using the TIE pattern of paragraph organization. Compare your group's paragraph with those written by the other groups in the class. ❏

GROUP
ACTIVITY
16

Paraphrasing Information. To *paraphrase* is to restate a source in your own words. By paraphrasing information, you simplify complicated information and use your own writing style.

A paraphrase should be about the same length as the original passage and it should express the same ideas. Although when paraphrasing you might be tempted to simply substitute key words with synonyms (words that have the same meaning), this can lead to plagiarism. Use your own writing style instead. This might mean changing the sentence structure or word order. Here's an example:

ORIGINAL

"food *is* chemicals, and all creatures that eat are chemicals, too" (Brody 463).

POOR PARAPHRASE

Food is made up of chemicals, and all beings that eat are made up of chemicals, too (Brody 463).

GOOD PARAPHRASE

In fact, not only are foods made up of chemicals, so are we (Brody 463).

When you paraphrase, you don't use quotation marks because the words are your own. You must, however, indicate the source of the idea or information because it is not your own.

Here are some other tips for paraphrasing:

• First, read the material you want to paraphrase. Then put it away. Write down the thought, using your own words and writing style.

• After the paraphrase, put the name of the author whose ideas you have borrowed (if you haven't already given the author's name) and the page number of the source.

• Reread the original passage to make sure you have accurately captured the author's ideas without plagiarizing.

Here is the same student paragraph on food additives you saw earlier in the chapter, except here the Brody quotation is replaced with paraphrases:

> When you think of food additives, chemicals with such unpronounceable names as "calcium stearoly lactylate" probably come to mind. Not all chemicals in foods, though, have been added. Did you know that milk, straight from the cow, consists of ninety-five chemicals? Were you aware that an untreated potato consists of 150 chemicals? In fact, not only are foods made up of chemicals—so are we (Brody 463). There's nothing wrong with chemicals in foods—it's the type of chemicals that matter.

Notice, too, that the TIE (topic-illustration-explanation) method of paragraph organization is used with the paraphrased information.

GROUP ACTIVITY 17

Paraphrasing Sources. Working with a group of other students, paraphrase one or two paragraphs from "What Is the Internet?" or "Mind/Body Programming." Compare your group's paraphrases with those of the other groups in your class. ❑

Summarizing Information. A *summary* is a condensed version of a piece of text that contains that text's key ideas. A summary is always much shorter than the original because it omits details.

Summary writing is one of the most common types of writing used in college and the workplace. On the job, you might write a summary of sales over the past six months. In college courses, you might be asked to write summaries of lectures, lab experiments, or journal articles. In an essay, information summarized from primary or secondary research can provide good supporting examples, observations, definitions, facts, statistics, and expert testimony.

Here are some tips for summarizing sources:

• Reread the source and write down the main ideas. These ideas are usually expressed in the thesis statement, the topic sentences, and, at times, the conclusion. If the source has headings and subheadings, they may express main ideas as well.

• Focus on the main points only and omit the details.

• At the beginning of your summary, give the title and author of the source.

• Write the summary in your own words. Use a quotation only to emphasize an important point that cannot be conveyed as powerfully in your own words.

Depending on your purpose for writing, a summary may be as

short as a sentence or as long as a paragraph. Here's a one-sentence summary of Jane Brody's "Feasting on Food or Chemicals?"

> In "Feasting on Food or Chemicals?" Jane Brody explains that we can't exist without chemicals in our food, whether the chemicals occur naturally or are added during processing.

Here's a longer summary of the same article:

> In "Feasting on Food or Chemicals?" Jane Brody writes that Americans automatically react negatively to food additives. They don't like the idea that chemicals are added to their foods. But, as Brody says, "food *is* chemicals," and since we don't grow our own food, it is impossible to live without additives today. Without additives, many foods would spoil before they reached us, and food costs would skyrocket. Some additives actually improve the appearance and taste of food. It isn't additives we should avoid, but the junk foods created from chemicals with no nutritive value.

When you summarize information in your essay, remember that your ideas come first. Summarized information should only be used to support your own points.

Analyzing Summaries. Read the following two summaries of Jane Brody's "Feasting on Food or Chemicals?" How can they be improved?

ACTIVITY
18

1. In "Feasting on Food or Chemicals?" Jane Brody writes that milk is a combination of 95 chemicals. The potato contains 150 chemicals, one of which is poisonous. It's impossible for us to not eat chemicals when we eat food. Although some added chemicals aren't good for us, because of our dietary habits we can't completely get rid of them.

_____

_____

_____

_____

_____

_____

2. According to Jane Brody in "Feasting on Food or Chemicals?" if we refused to eat foods containing chemicals, we'd starve to death very quickly. Not all chemicals are bad, whether they're natural or added in a factory. Neither are all chemicals good, including many natural chemicals. The most serious problem with additives is less the safety of the chemicals themselves than the kinds of foods that they are most commonly added to. But to revert to a wholly unprocessed, additive-free food supply just isn't practical for many reasons.

_____

_____

_____

_____

_____

_____

GROUP
ACTIVITY
19

Writing a Summary. Working in a group, read the following short essay by Maya Angelou about the benefits of taking a day off. Then write a summary of the essay that includes one or two quotations. Compare your group's summary with those written by the other groups in your class.

MAYA ANGELOU

A Day Away

We often think that our affairs, great or small, must be tended continuously and in detail, or our world will disintegrate, and we will lose our places in the universe. That is not true, or if it is true, then our situations were so temporary that they would have collapsed anyway. *1*

Once a year or so I give myself a day away. On the eve of my day of absence, I begin to unwrap the bounds which hold me in harness. I inform housemates, my family, and close friends that I will not be reachable for twenty-four hours; then I disengage the telephone. I turn the radio dial to an all-music station, preferably one which plays the soothing golden oldies. I sit for at least an hour in a very hot tub; then I lay out my clothes in preparation for my morn- *2* ing escape, and knowing that nothing will disturb me, I sleep the sleep of the just.

On the morning I wake naturally, for I will have set no clock,   *3*
nor informed my body timepiece when it should alarm. I dress in comfortable shoes and casual clothes and leave my house going no place. If I am living in a city, I wander streets, window-shop, or gaze at buildings. I enter and leave public parks, libraries, the lobbies of skyscrapers, and movie houses. I stay in no place for very long.

On the getaway day I try for amnesia. I do not want to know   *4*
my name, where I live, or how many dire responsibilities rest on my shoulders. I detest encountering even the closest friend, for then I am reminded of who I am, and the circumstances of my life, which I want to forget for a while.

Every person needs to take one day away. A day in which one   *5*
consciously separates the past from the future. Jobs, lovers, family, employers, and friends can exist one day without any one of us, and if our egos permit us to confess, they could exist eternally in our absence.

Each person deserves a day away in which no problems are con-   *6*
fronted, no solutions searched for. Each of us needs to withdraw from the cares which will not withdraw from us. We need hours of aimless wandering or spates of time sitting on park benches, observing the mysterious world of ants and the canopy of treetops.

If we step away for a time, we are not, as many may think and   *7*
some will accuse, being irresponsible, but rather we are preparing ourselves to more ably perform our duties and discharge our obligations.

When I return home, I am always surprised to find some ques-   *8*
tions I sought to evade had been answered and some entanglements I had hoped to flee had become unraveled in my absence.

A day away acts as a spring tonic. It can dispel rancor, transform   *9*
indecision, and renew the spirit.

Summarizing Sources for Your Research Essay. Refer to the research questions you prepared at the start of your primary and secondary research. Answer these research questions by writing summaries of your sources. Use this summarized information when you revise your essay. ❏

ACTIVITY
20

Documenting Sources. Documentation of sources is a very important aspect of the research paper. To *document* is to refer your reader to your primary or secondary research sources. Proper documentation allows readers to locate and verify your sources for their own future research. It also keeps you from inadvertently plagiarizing others' words or ideas (see p. 252).

You document sources both in the essay itself—where you identify the author and page number for quotations, paraphrases, and summaries—and in a list of sources at the end of the paper. That list, called the *Works Cited* page, contains extensive information about the sources you cite, or use, in your essay. Every source you refer to in your essay should be included in the Works Cited list.

Different fields of study use different formats for the Works Cited list. The following discussion and sample entries are based on the format established by the Modern Language Association, or *MLA*, for short. Here are some guidelines for using the MLA format:

- Put the Works Cited list on a separate page at the end of your paper.
- Arrange the source entries alphabetically by the authors' last names, or by title if the author is not named.
- Double-space the entries.
- The first line of each entry should line up with the left-hand margin. The subsequent lines of each entry should be indented five spaces.
- Underline or italicize the titles of books, magazines, and newspapers.
- Put the titles of magazine and newspaper articles in quotation marks.

MLA format also requires that you present the information about your sources in a specific way. Books are different from magazines, which are different from newspapers. Encyclopedias are different still, and there is a particular way to list an interview. Also, the form varies slightly when a source has more than one author.

Here are some sample MLA-style entries:

Book with one author

Brody, Jane. *Jane Brody's Nutrition Book.* New York: Norton, 1981.

Book with more than one author

Riley, Richard, and Margaret Johnson. *Nutrition Facts and Myths.* Boston: Monolith, 1989.

Magazine article

Altman, Susan. "Nutrition in the '90s." *Newsweek* 15 June 1993: 34–35.

Newspaper article

Chin, Joseph. "Nutrition Fads on the Rise." *New York Times* 13 Apr. 1995: A8.

Article from a computer database

Jenson, Sara. "FDA Nears Approval of Fake Fat." *Los Angeles Times* 25 Nov.

1995: 3A. *InfoTrac: General Periodicals Index.* CD-ROM. Information Ac-

cess. Jan. 1996.

Encyclopedia article

"Nutrition." *Encyclopaedia Britannica.* 1974 ed.

Personal interview

Saber, Susan. Personal interview. 5 June 1997.

Telephone interview

Logan, Mark. Telephone interview. 10 May 1997.

For more information on how to document sources, consult the *MLA Handbook for Writers of Research Papers,* 4th edition (1995), available in the reference section of your library.

Creating a Works Cited Page. Write up a Works Cited page in the MLA format for the following five sources. All necessary information is given (as well as unnecessary information you need not use).

1. *Space Aliens* by Ernest Sider and Alice Morrow. Red Arrow Publishing House. Page 52. 1984. New York City.
2. Interview by telephone with Joan Johnson about her UFO experiences. Des Moines, Iowa. February 9, 1995.
3. "What Are the Marfa Lights?" *Time.* January 14, 1994, pp. 12–13.
4. *Los Angeles Times,* October 11, 1993. "Citizens Group Claims Cover-Up." Page B5.
5. "Where's the Proof?" by Janice Norton. *Newsweek.* New York, Newsweek, Inc. Page 18. August 3, 1994. ❏

ACTIVITY

21

COMPUTER TIP

FORMATTING THE WORKS CITED PAGE

Some software programs can arrange the source information into the correct format for your Works Cited page. All you need to do is type in the necessary instructions and information about your sources. Consult your software manual for more information.

Matthew's Revised Draft

Before you read Matthew's revised draft, reread his discovery draft (p. 244). Notice, in particular, how he has used primary and secondary research in the revision to support and clarify his points. (You will also notice some errors in the revised draft; these will be corrected when Matthew edits his essay later on.)

Vegetarianism: Beyond Stereotypes

Revised title is more interesting

What is a vegetarian? No, it's not someone who takes care of sick animals, or someone who eats only vegetables. A vegetarian is someone who doesn't eat meat. Despite this simple definition, no two vegetarians are alike. Vegetarians often have diverse reasons for not eating meat, and they can follow very different diets. Although being a vegetarian isn't easy, many people find it a worthwhile lifestyle.

Concept— vegetarianism—is defined

Thesis is clearer

You might imagine vegetarians as a group of old hippies eating rice while sitar music plays in the background. Actually, vegetarians can be young or old, rich or poor, liberal or conservative. Some people are vegetarians for health reasons. Vegetarians live longer, are less likely to develop heart disease and certain types of cancer, and are less likely to be overweight (Cerrato 74). Compared to meat eaters. Other people become vegetarians for ethical reasons. Mary May, the president of a local animal rights organization, says, "The more people who refuse to eat animals, the more animals who will be treated humanely." Another reason to become a vegetarian is because a vegetarian diet can be less expensive than a diet containing meat. Finally, some people just don't like the way meat tastes.

Secondary research supports point

Source and page number are given

Primary research supports point

A vegetarian diet differs from person to person. A "vegan" diet excludes all meat and meat by-products, such as eggs and milk, while a "lactovo" diet includes eggs and dairy products (Mukamal 14). A vegetarian can be very strict about their diet, even if it means inconveniencing themselves or others. Declining to eat the main course of a meal, the meat might be wasted. Some won't go to restaurants that only serve meat dishes. Others, however, permit themselves to eat meat on special occasions such as holidays.

Secondary research is used to classify vegetarian diets

This information comes from Matthew's own knowledge

Vegetarians must be careful that their diet contains enough nutrients. Lauren Mukamal, the former food and nutrition editor of *Veggie Life* magazine, writes that vegetarians must eat leafy vegetables and nuts to ensure that they consume sufficient iron, protein, and calcium. Whole grains and beans should round out the diet (15). As long as vegetarians are careful about what they eat, they'll be as healthy—if not healthier—than people who eat meat. As Mukamal writes, "Healthy vegetarian meals give you the energy and nutrients you need to keep going" (14).

Paraphrased source

Page number is given

Quote emphasizes the point of the paragraph

Just because you're a vegetarian doesn't mean you have to give up flavor. Most vegetarian dishes blend several different food groups for example, rice, beans, and vegetables will be mixed together. The combination results in a whole new taste. Vegetarians also experiment with different spices to

This information is from Matthew's own knowledge

1

2

3

4

5

make their food even more interesting. Many excellent vegetarian cookbooks, such as *The Greens Cookbook* by Deborah Madison and Edward Espe Brown, contain tasty, easy-to-prepare dishes.

Because our society is so meat-oriented, becoming a vegetarian requires discipline and committment. Vegetarians need to learn new recipes for cooking and have to turn down meat dishes that are offered to them. For many people, though, the advantages of a vegetarian diet, such as improved health or helping to alleviate cruelty to animals, far outweigh any difficulties they might encounter.

6

Matthew's readers might want to consult this book, so it's included in the Works Cited list

Conclusion summarizes the main ideas of the essay

Works Cited

Cerrato, Paul. "Becoming a Vegetarian: The Risks and the Benefits." *RN* Mar. 1991: 73–77.

Madison, Deborah, and Edward Espe Brown. *The Greens Cookbook.* Toronto: Bantam, 1987.

May, Mary. Telephone interview. 10 Apr. 1997.

Mukamal, Lauren. "Going Vegetarian." *Ms.* July–Aug. 1994: 14–18.

Remember to start your Works Cited list on a separate page

Analyzing Matthew's Revised Draft. Use the following questions to discuss with your classmates how Matthew improved his draft.

ACTIVITY
22

1. What is Matthew's thesis statement? Is it clear? Could it be improved?

_____

_____

_____

2. What kinds of primary and secondary research did Matthew conduct on his topic?

_____

_____

_____

3. What reasons, examples, facts, and expert testimony has he added? Are these revisions effective? Explain.

_____

_____

_____

4. How does Matthew organize the ideas and information in his paragraphs? How well does he use key words and transitions to create paragraph coherence?

_____

_____

_____

5. How does Matthew cite his sources in his essay? Are the entries in his Works Cited list formatted correctly?

_____

_____

_____

6. How could Matthew's revised draft benefit from further revision?

_____

_____

_____

_____

GROUP
ACTIVITY
23

Using Peer Review. Form a group with two or three other students and exchange copies of your drafts. Read your draft aloud while your classmates follow along. Take notes on your classmates' responses to the following questions about your draft.

1. Have I followed all of the instructions for this assignment?

    _____

    _____

    _____

2. How interesting is my introduction? Do you want to continue reading the paper? Why or why not?

    _____

    _____

    _____

3. What is my thesis statement? Do I need to make the thesis clearer?

    _____

    _____

    _____

4. How would primary and secondary research help clarify and support my points?

    _____

    _____

    _____

5. How might I use quotations, paraphrases, and summaries effectively in my paper?

    _____

    _____

    _____

    _____

6. What parts of my essay, if any, do not support my thesis and could be omitted? Are there any sentences or words that seem unnecessary?

_____

_____

_____

7. Where in the essay did my writing confuse you? How can I clarify my thoughts?

_____

_____

_____

8. How clear is the purpose of my essay? How well do I meet the needs of my audience?

_____

_____

_____

9. How effective is my ending? Do I end in such a way that you know it's the end?

_____

_____

_____

ACTIVITY
24

Revising Your Draft. Taking your classmates' suggestions for revision into consideration, revise your essay. In particular, focus on using the results of your primary and secondary research to clarify and support your main points. Correctly quote, paraphrase, and summarize information from your sources. Remember to document your sources properly, both in the text of your essay and in a Works Cited list at the end. Finally, as in other types of writing, the revision of a research paper may lead you to omit unnecessary material or to re-arrange parts of the essay more effectively.   ❏

Editing

At this point you have worked hard to explain a concept in science, the social sciences, or business. Now you're ready to edit your essay for correctness. Remember, the fewer errors you make, the more your readers will focus on what you have to say.

Matthew's Edited Essay

You probably noticed that Matthew's revised draft contained errors in grammar, spelling, and punctuation. Matthew corrected these errors in his edited essay. His corrections are underlined here. His editing log follows his essay.

Vegetarianism: Beyond Stereotypes

What is a vegetarian? No, it's not someone who takes care of sick animals, or someone who eats only vegetables. A vegetarian is someone who doesn't eat meat. Despite this simple definition, no two vegetarians are alike. Vegetarians often have diverse reasons for not eating meat, and they can follow very different diets. Although being a vegetarian isn't easy, many people find it a worthwhile lifestyle.   *1*

You might imagine vegetarians as a group of old hippies eating rice while sitar music plays in the background. Actually, vegetarians can be young or old, rich or poor, liberal or conservative. Some people are vegetarians for health reasons. <u>Compared to meat eaters, vegetarians live longer, are less likely to develop heart disease and certain types of cancer, and are less likely to be overweight (Cerrato 74).</u> Other people become vegetarians for ethical reasons. Mary May, the president of a local animal rights organization, says, "The more people who refuse to eat animals, the more animals who will be treated humanely." <u>Some people become vegetarians because</u> a vegetarian diet can be less expensive than a diet containing meat. Finally, some people just don't like the way meat tastes.   *2*

A vegetarian diet differs from person to person. A "vegan" diet excludes all meat and meat by-products, such as eggs and milk, while a "lactovo" diet includes eggs and dairy products (Mukamal 14). <u>Vegetarians can be very strict about their diet, even</u> if it means inconveniencing themselves or others.   *3*

They might decline to eat the main course of a meal or go to restaurants that serve only meat dishes. Others, however, permit themselves to eat meat on special occasions such as holidays.

Vegetarians must be careful that their diet contains enough nutrients. *4* Lauren Mukamal, the former food and nutrition editor of *Veggie Life* magazine, writes that vegetarians must eat leafy vegetables and nuts to ensure that they consume sufficient iron, protein, and calcium. Whole grains and beans should round out the diet (15). As long as vegetarians are careful about what they eat, they'll be as healthy—if not healthier—than people who eat meat. As Mukamal writes, "Healthy vegetarian meals give you the energy and nutrients you need to keep going" (14).

Just because you're a vegetarian doesn't mean you have to give up fla- *5* vor. Most vegetarian dishes blend several different food groups; for example, rice, beans, and vegetables will be mixed together. The combination results in a whole new taste. Vegetarians also experiment with different spices to make their food even more interesting. Many excellent vegetarian cookbooks, such as *The Greens Cookbook* by Deborah Madison and Edward Espe Brown, contain tasty, easy-to-prepare dishes.

Because our society is so meat-oriented, becoming a vegetarian requires *6* discipline and commitment. Vegetarians need to learn new recipes for cooking and have to turn down meat dishes that are offered to them. For many people, though, the advantages of a vegetarian diet, such as improved health or helping to alleviate cruelty to animals, far outweigh any difficulties they might encounter.

Works Cited

Cerrato, Paul. "Becoming a Vegetarian: The Risks and the Benefits." *RN* Mar. 1991: 73–77.

Madison, Deborah, and Edward Espe Brown. *The Greens Cookbook.* Toronto: Bantam, 1987.

May, Mary. Telephone interview. 10 Apr. 1997.

Mukamal, Lauren. "Going Vegetarian." *Ms.* July–Aug. 1994: 14–18.

Matthew's Editing Log

- INCORRECT: Compared to meat eaters. (2)
  - ERROR: sentence fragment
  - CORRECT: Compared to meat eaters, vegetarians live longer, are less

likely to develop heart disease and certain types of cancer, and are less likely to be overweight (Cerrato 74).

- INCORRECT: Another reason to become a vegetarian is because a vegetarian diet can be less expensive than a diet containing meat. (2)

  ERROR: wordiness

  CORRECT: Some people become vegetarians because a vegetarian diet can be less expensive than a diet containing meat.

- INCORRECT: A vegetarian can be very strict about their diet, even if it means inconveniencing themselves or others. (3)

  ERROR: incorrect pronoun reference

  CORRECT: Vegetarians can be very strict about their diet, even if it means inconveniencing themselves or others.

- INCORRECT: Declining to eat the main course of a meal, the meal might be wasted. (3)

  ERROR: dangling modifier

  CORRECT: They might decline to eat the main course of a meal or go to restaurants that serve only meat dishes.

- INCORRECT: Most vegetarian dishes blend several different food groups for example, rice, beans, and vegetables will be mixed together (5)

  ERROR: run-on sentence

  CORRECT: Most vegetarian dishes blend several different food groups; for example, rice, beans, and vegetables will be mixed together.

- INCORRECT: committment (6)

  ERROR: misspelled word

  CORRECT: commitment

Editing Your Essay. Read your essay word-for-word, looking for errors in grammar, spelling, and punctuation. Also ask a friend or classmate to help you spot errors you might have overlooked. Then use a dictionary and the Handbook in Part III of this book to help you correct the errors you find. Finally, record those errors on your editing log. ❑

ACTIVITY
25

Publishing

After you edit your essay, you're ready to share it with your audience — your instructor and classmates, as well as other students on campus who may be unfamiliar with the concept you explain. For example, you might share it with a student who plans to enroll in a course related to your topic. You might also send your essay by e-mail to a friend on the Internet. Finally, read several classmates' essays that explain concepts unfamiliar to you. How do people benefit from learning new concepts?

Your Writing Portfolio

If you're pleased with your essay about a concept in science, the social sciences, or business, add it to your writing portfolio, which contains your best writing as well as your reflections on your writing. To help you reflect on the writing you did in this chapter, answer the following questions:

1. What did you learn about the concept from writing about it?
2. What did you enjoy most about researching your topic? Which part of your research effort did you find most difficult?
3. How would you describe the process of writing a research paper to a student unfamiliar with the process?
4. If you had more time, what further revisions would you make to improve your essay? Why?

Using your answers to these questions, update the writing process report you began in Chapter Three.

Writing Process Report

Date:

Strengths:

Weaknesses:

Plans for improvement:

Once you complete this report, freewrite in your journal about what you learned about your writing process in this chapter and what you still hope to learn.

Chapter Summary

- A concept is an idea. All fields of study and areas of life are based on concepts.
- Primary research is research you conduct firsthand, such as observing, surveying, and interviewing.
- Secondary research involves reading what others have written about your topic in books, magazine and newspaper articles, research reports, encyclopedias, and other sources.
- Plagiarism—the stealing of another writer's words or ideas—is a serious offense. Avoid plagiarism by documenting your sources of borrowed material.
- Note-taking is an effective research tool.
- Use quotation marks to indicate where you use an author's exact words.
- Use a paraphrase to put an author's ideas into your own words.
- Use a summary to condense a lengthy passage from a source. A summary focuses on only the main ideas.
- Document sources properly by identifying them in the text of your essay and listing them on your Works Cited page at the end of your essay.
- Include a Works Cited entry with full publication information for every source you cite in your essay, and format the entries in your Works Cited list correctly.

The unexamined life is not worth living.
— SOCRATES

9

Evaluating Your World

In this chapter you will

- evaluate a product, performance, or place.

- write a thesis statement that expresses a judgment.

- base your judgment on criteria.

- support your judgment with evidence and comparisons.

- keep a balanced perspective.

- add to your writing portfolio.

Evaluating your world is something you do every day. In the morning you may decide that a new brand of breakfast cereal tastes better than your old standby brand. At school you may realize that this semester's chemistry instructor explains new terms more clearly than your previous instructor did. In the evening you may channel-surf to find a show you think is worth watching.

When you evaluate something, you decide on its value, worthiness, or merit. An evaluation is based on standards: a breakfast cereal should taste good and be good for you, a chemistry instructor should be an effective communicator, and a television show should divert you from your everyday worries. When you make an evaluation, you apply standards like these to your subject. You taste the cereal and examine the nutritional label on the box. You listen to see how well your chemistry instructor explains new terms. You examine television shows for amusing plots or interesting settings. After applying the appropriate standards to your subject, you can make a decision about its value, worthiness, or merit. Because you've followed this process, you can feel confident that your judgment is sound.

ACTIVITY

1

Analyzing Your Purpose and Audience. Before you begin gathering ideas about your topic, think about your purpose and audience. For this chapter's assignment, you'll evaluate a product, person, or place.

As you gather ideas, remember that your audience will include people directly affected by your topic. If you plan to evaluate a product, your readers will include consumers interested in purchasing that product. If you aim to evaluate a play, movie, or television show, your readers will be people interested in seeing the show. And if you plan to evaluate a shopping mall, museum, or tourist attraction, your audience will include people who would enjoy visiting that site. Keep in mind, also, that your classmates and instructor will be reading your essay as you write it. Your responses to the following questions will help you decide how to approach your topic.

1. Does this assignment call for expressive, informative, or persuasive writing?

   _____

2. What is your readers' average age? _____

3. What parts of the country or world are they from? _____

   _____

Writing Assignment

This chapter offers you the opportunity to evaluate a product, a performance, or a place. You or your instructor may decide to do this assignment in one of several ways:

- You may gather ideas on one, two, *or* three topics.
- You may write a discovery draft on one, two, *or* three of these topics.
- You may choose one discovery draft to develop into a polished essay.
- You may combine your discovery draft ideas into a new topic for your essay.

After completing your essay, you'll share it with your instructor, classmates, and perhaps others who are directly affected by your topic, such as fellow consumers, students, co-workers, friends, and family members.

4. What is your readers' experience with your topic? _____

_____

_____

5. What do you know about your readers' opinions and feelings about your topic?

_____

_____

_____

Given your responses to the preceding questions, ask yourself these questions:

6. What do my readers already know about my topic? _____

_____

_____

7. What information do I *not* have to give them? _____

_____

_____

8. What do my readers need to know about my topic? _____

_____

_____

9. How do my readers feel about my topic? Will they find it interesting, or will I have to work to get their attention?

_____

_____

_____

10. Are my readers likely to agree with my evaluation, or will I have to work to convince them of its validity? How can I do this?

_____

_____

_____

_____

❏

Gathering Ideas

To gather ideas about evaluating a product, performance, or place, select from among the various techniques you have practiced in the preceding chapters: brainstorming, freewriting, clustering, questioning, reading, interviewing, relating aloud, and reflecting.

Evaluating a Product

As a consumer, you evaluate products before purchasing them. If the product is inexpensive, such as a can of soup, your evaluation might be as simple as reading the label. If the product is a major purchase, such as a stereo system or a car, you might consult friends, read a magazine such as *Consumer Reports,* and comparison shop. Even after you purchase the product, you probably continue to evaluate it to see if you made a good choice.

In the following essay, Jeanne Twehous evaluates a type of camping tent. As you read, notice how the writer explains and supports her evaluation.

JEANNE TWEHOUS

Bibler Piñon Tent

I lay wide awake in the dark, listening to the wind scream off   *1*
Mt. Colden. In the middle of an otherwise mild November in New York's Adirondack Park, this storm had pounced out of nowhere, unleashing gale-force winds, rain, sleet, and snow.

Many tents would have collapsed in a tangle of nylon, but I was   *2*
safely ensconced in a burly, single-wall, three-season tent from Bibler—the new Piñon. When weather catches you off guard, it's nice to have gear that can stretch the limits. The Piñon, while not a true four-season tent, goes well into three and a half seasons.

I'd never used a single-wall tent before and held some initial   *3*
concerns about ease of setup, stability in extreme conditions, and waterproofness (one less layer between the rain and me). But after weathering that Adirondack howler, I became a firm believer that less is sometimes more.

The freestanding Piñon pops up quickly once you get the hang   *4*
of how the poles thread through the canopy. You just duck inside the tent out of the elements after the first pole is in place to erect your shelter. The tent also boasts two doors to boost flow-through ventilation.

The Piñon's stability proved to be exceptional, thanks to the   *5*
crisscrossing poles that fit snugly into the roof corners and tension the eaves into a sleek, skin-tight modified dome. The single-wall structure works well in high winds because the gusts can't sneak between fly and tent to cause the jerking, pulling, and flapping that so often plague double-wall designs.

Give this Bibler a gold star for waterproofing, too. Despite a   *6*
thorough pummeling by wind-driven snow, sleet, and rain, not a drop of water wormed its way into the tent, other than what we dribbled in—not even the typical drips and drops from condensation.

There was another pleasant surprise. I was suspicious when   *7*
reading about the tent's ability to wick away interior condensation. I thought that condensation on tent walls was just one of those facts of outdoor life that you put up with, like perpetual hat-hair or

crusted soup noodles in your coffee cup. Bibler uses a proprietary fabric called ToddTex (named after designer Todd Bibler) that minimizes condensation. The three-layer Todd-Tex laminate consists of a fuzzy polyester inner facing that helps dissipate condensation, a thin middle film of waterproof/breathable Teflon, and an outer layer of 30 denier ripstop nylon. Besides the two mesh walls, there's a ceiling vent protected by an adjustable awning that also helps airflow and prevents condensation.

My height of 5'10" makes me feel cramped in many backpacking tents, with my head and feet touching the end walls. In the Piñon, however, I could stretch out like a cat. And being a certified organization freak, the interior mesh pockets, 12 in all, and two gear hammocks in the vestibules were a blessing. I didn't have to cram headlamp, gloves, hat, book, watch, map, extra socks, and compass into one tiny pocket. I could stash my dripping-wet rain jacket and pants in one vestibule, and muddy boots in another.   8

The vestibules themselves could be bigger; they'll hold boots and various other small items, but not a big pack. The two combine for about 10 square feet of added shelter. The mesh doorways slope slightly, and tended to catch drips when I opened the vestibules, but it wasn't a big problem if I was conscientious about wiping or tapping away exterior water accumulation before opening the vestibule door.   9

Life on the trail rarely proves perfect, though, and the Piñon suffered a couple of battle scars. While disassembling the tent after the storm, I noticed two small tears at the corners of the wall that bore the brunt of the storm. The inch-long rips looked to be the result of too much stress on a lightweight nylon ribbon connecting the door zipper to the adjacent wall. Still, no water sneaked in, and the problem seems easily remedied with a heavier tape or ribbon. (Since this test, Bibler has upgraded the material, which allegedly solves the problem.)   10

Despite the Piñon's minor shortcomings, it turned me into a single-wall convert. I can only hope that next time Mother Nature surprises me, my shelter is as trusty as the test Piñon.   11

ACTIVITY

2

Reading to Improve Writing. Discuss the following questions about "Bibler Piñon Tent" with your classmates.

1. Why does Twehous believe the tent is a good product? _____

    _____

    _____

    _____

2. In addition to describing the tent's good qualities, why does Twehous describe the problems she encountered with the tent?

_____

_____

_____

3. What writing strategies (examples, comparison-contrast, process analysis, definition, classification, facts, statistics, and expert testimony) does the author use to support her evaluation?

_____

_____

_____

4. How does Twehous attempt to keep her audience interested in her topic?

_____

_____

_____

Collecting New Words. Try to determine the meanings of the following words from the way they're used in "Bibler Piñon Tent." Then verify their meanings by checking a dictionary.

ACTIVITY
3

ensconced (2) _____

burly (2) _____

plague (5) _____

pummeling (6) _____

condensation (6) _____

proprietary (7) _____

dissipate (7) _____

vestibule (8) _____

allegedly (10) _____

ACTIVITY
4

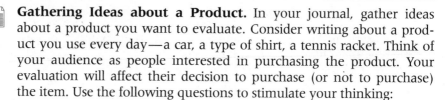

Gathering Ideas about a Product. In your journal, gather ideas about a product you want to evaluate. Consider writing about a product you use every day—a car, a type of shirt, a tennis racket. Think of your audience as people interested in purchasing the product. Your evaluation will affect their decision to purchase (or not to purchase) the item. Use the following questions to stimulate your thinking:

1. What is your overall opinion of the product? Why do you have this opinion?
2. What is good about the product? What is bad about it?
3. What experiences have you had with the product that formed your opinion of it?
4. Compare the product with other similar products. How is it better? How is it worse?
5. What research could you do to learn more about the product?
6. Who would be interested in reading about the product? Why would they be interested? ❏

One student, Janice, wrote in her journal about several possible products for her evaluation. Because she enjoys listening to music, she decided to write about the CD player she recently purchased, the Fitzhugh 6000. To gather ideas about her topic, Janice answered the questions in Activity 4:

1. My overall opinion is that the Fitzhugh 6000 is the best CD player on the market in its price range because of its excellent sound quality, convenience, and reliability.

2. What's good about it—how it sounds, that it's easy to use, that it never breaks down, and that it's a good value. What's bad about it—it doesn't have a remote volume. Also, some of my friends don't think it sounds as good as I think it does.

3. I've had this CD player for over a year, and I've listened to it nearly every day. I've never had any problems with it. It always sounds good. It even works well with some of my discs that are scratched.

4. I've listened to the same CDs on the Packer 250, which costs about the same but its sound quality isn't as good.

5. I could listen to some CDs on other CD players and compare how they sound. I could also read about CD players in music magazines.

6. A lot of people either own a CD player or are interested in purchasing one. I think these people would want to read my paper.

Put your writing about a consumer product aside for now, so you can gather ideas about another type of evaluation.

Evaluating a Performance

Before investing your hard-earned money in a movie ticket, you decide to read a review of the movie in a newspaper. If the review is positive, you're more likely to see the film. Newspapers and many magazines carry not only movie reviews but also reviews of music concerts, art shows, dance performances, museum exhibits, books, television shows, and sporting events.

In the following evaluation, movie critic Jack Garner evaluates the film *Waterworld*. As you read the essay, notice how the writer uses comparisons to other movies as a way of explaining his evaluation of *Waterworld*.

JACK GARNER

Expense Doesn't Make **Waterworld** *the Best*

Is the most expensive movie ever made also the best movie ever   *1*
made? Of course not; it's not even close. High budgets and high quality seldom have much to do with each other in Hollywood.

Is it the best movie of the summer? No, it's not even that. *Apollo*   *2*
13 flies circles around it.

When all the hoopla finally hits the screen we see Kevin Cost-   *3*
ner's *Waterworld* for what it is: A derivative summer action film of modest accomplishment.

The film confirms what the trailers originally led us to suspect: *Waterworld* is nothing more than *The Road Warrior* on jet skis. As such, it offers spectacular action sequences that are countered by dumb logic, and an action hero with little new to offer beyond webbed feet and mutated gills.   *4*

The debt owed to George Miller's stunning *Road Warrior* (1981) is inescapable; in fact, *Waterworld* originally was written more than a decade ago as a Roger Corman B movie rip-off. Notoriously low-budgeting Corman declined to make it, because it came with a $5 million price tag! (If he had to pay the eventual $172 million bill [estimated] he would probably go into cardiac arrest.)   *5*

Kevin Costner stars, co-produced and reportedly directed its last months of post production after a tiff with credited director Kevin Reynolds.   *6*

Costner plays the Mariner, a wandering loner of a hero in the long tradition of western and action films. Alan Ladd's Shane and Mel Gibson's Mad Max come immediately to mind.   *7*

On the horizon, the Mariner sees nothing but ocean. The story is set at a catastrophic time in the future, after the polar ice caps have melted, wiping out the world's land masses.   *8*

The Mariner is a hard-edged cynic, and he's admittedly given a wonderful entrance: When first viewed, he's relieving himself into a plastic pot. He then takes the urine and runs it through a Rube Goldberg device that turns it into drinking water. Then he has a drink.   *9*

The other survivors also have taken to the sea. Good folks struggle on floating, man-made atolls, created from junked boats and scrap metal. They're frequently harassed by marauding smokers, pirate like biker gangs of the future, led by a demonic bald ruler called the Deacon. He's played by today's king of psycho bad guys, Dennis Hopper.   *10*

Smokers are so named because they travel on oil-burning boats and jet skis, using a rare and diminishing stock of crude oil, taken from a salvaged tanker.   *11*

As the film opens, the Mariner comes upon an atoll settlement, where he docks to trade for hydro (drinking water, which is revered like 18-year-old single malt scotch). The settlers discover the Mariner has webbed feet and gills; he's a mutant, adapting to life on and in the water. Though those traits would seem desirable in a friend, the settlers vote to execute him. It's the first of several times that *Waterworld* defies logic.   *12*

However, just before the execution is completed, a howling tribe of smokers attacks the atoll. In the confusion, the Mariner escapes on his specially designed boat, reluctantly taking along a woman named Helen (Jeanne Tripplehorn) and her adopted daughter, Enola (Tina Majorino). The little girl has a tattoo that is believed to be a map to the mythical Dryland.   *13*

The rest of *Waterworld* details the struggle between the Mariner   *14*
and the nefarious smokers who want the little girl and her tattoo.
The battles take place on the flat, blue, ocean horizon, standing in
for the flat, dusty desert horizon of *The Road Warrior.*

Waterworld works best in the early portions, in part because of   *15*
Dennis Gassner's stunning design of the floating atoll.

But once the Mariner and his crew escape the atoll, *Waterworld*   *16*
slows. There are high energy moments to come, but also vast
stretches of calm seas. Fortunately, there are off-beat things to look
at, bits of flippantly sadistic humor from Dennis Hopper, and moments of exhilarating action. *Waterworld* may not have gotten everything it should have for its money, but, as the opening scene shows,
at least Kevin Costner has a pot to pee in.

Reading to Improve Writing. Discuss the following questions   ACTIVITY
about "Expense Doesn't Make *Waterworld* the Best" with your class-   **5**
mates.

1. What is Garner's opinion of *Waterworld*? Write a sentence from his
   evaluation that summarizes his opinion.

   _____

   _____

   _____

2. What reasons does Garner give to support his opinion of the film?

   _____

   _____

   _____

   _____

3. Why does Garner compare *Waterworld* to *The Road Warrior*?

   _____

   _____

   _____

4. How does the writer attempt to keep his audience interested in his evaluation?

_____

_____

_____

Collecting New Words. Try to determine the meanings of the following words from the way they're used in "Expense Doesn't Make *Waterworld* the Best." Then verify their meanings by checking a dictionary.

derivative (3) _____

trailers (4) _____

mutated (4) _____

tiff (6) _____

catastrophic (8) _____

marauding (10) _____

atoll (12) _____

nefarious (14) _____

sadistic (16) _____

exhilarating (16) _____

Gathering Ideas about a Performance. In your journal, gather ideas about a performance you want to evaluate. The performance may be a live one—such as a concert, comedy show, sporting event, dance recital, or play—or one that has been recorded—such as a movie or television show. Select a performance that you remember well and know something about. (If you select a movie or television show, you have the advantage of being able to watch it more than once on a VCR.) Think of your audience as people interested in attending or viewing the performance. Use the following questions to stimulate your ideas:

1. What is your overall opinion of the performance? Why do you have this opinion?
2. What is good about the performance? What is bad about it?
3. Compare the performance with other similar performances. How is it better? How is it worse?
4. What research could you do to learn more about the performance?
5. Who would be interested in reading about the performance? Why would they be interested? ❏

Here's how one student, Gus, used the questions in Activity 7 to brainstorm about the play *Steel Magnolias*. On his computer screen, he made a chart for his responses. Here's a sample:

Overall opinion: The play is excellent and shouldn't be missed, even if you've already seen the movie.

What was good: The acting made me feel for the characters. The humor was great.

What was bad: A little too long.

Comparison: The play was better than the movie because the actors were better.

Research: I could read the play so I could quote lines in my evaluation.

Audience: People interested in seeing the play, comparing it to the movie, or even acting in the play might want to read my review.

Put your ideas about a performance aside for now, so you can gather ideas for one more type of evaluation.

Evaluating a Place

A new shopping mall opens near your town and you spend an afternoon visiting the stores, examining the layout, and sampling products from the food court. Afterwards, you decide that you like the mall but wish it had a parking garage. You've just evaluated a place. Other places you might evaluate include a museum, park, college or office building, apartment, classroom, theater, store, library, and restaurant.

In "Cha Cha Cha Is Hot Hot Hot," David Nelson evaluates a restaurant in southern California. As you read the essay, notice how the writer supports his evaluation with descriptive details.

David Nelson

Cha Cha Cha Is Hot Hot Hot

When a hurricane whips through the Caribbean, as happened so often this year, it looks in satellite photographs like a maniacal blender bent on churning this bowl of islands and water into a tropical purée. And those of us who have viewed the Caribbean primarily through the daiquiri-tinted lenses of travel brochures might be excused for assuming that a homogeneity exists among the peoples—and the cuisines—of the many countries, colonies and territories that share palm trees and blue-water vistas as a common patrimony.

But while the Caribbean has some characteristics of a tropical melting pot, many of the elements decline to blend. Yes, the Spanish passed on a love of beans to their principal colonies, but Cuba prefers black beans while Puerto Rico claims fealty to red (and Spam, of course, is an American contribution to this Caribbean commonwealth). African cooks helped create a Creole style similar to that which developed in New Orleans.

And even though much of the area is known as the West Indies, it abounds in East Indians, whom the British brought in as laborers; hence the curries and spicy "jerk" dishes of Jamaica and other islands. Dutch culinary contributions have been less pronounced, French more so. Indigenous root vegetables and fruits, the plantain in particular, are elements that help homogenize the region's cooking.

It would seem that wrapping all this in a nutshell would be no easy task. Nonetheless, Toribio Prado, the chef-cum-decorator (a rare title, to be sure) who gave Los Angeles its trendy Cha Cha Cha Cafe and the Cava Restaurant, makes a go of it at his new Cha Cha Cha on La Jolla's preternaturally trendy Prospect Street.

And it happens to be a gorgeously wrapped nutshell. The unusual, semisubterranean layout of the place, which has accommodated numerous failed restaurants in the past, worked to Prado's advantage when he designed an environment that whacks you between the eyes with an explosion of sizzling Caribbean colors and artwork. No surface is left untouched—even the ceiling is painted with island scenes and characters—and the overall effect makes Disneyland's Pirates of the Caribbean seem a touch tame by comparison. No one returns from the restrooms without remarking on the eerily lifelike recordings of bird calls that play continuously over hidden speakers.

The menu, like everything in trendy cooking these days, is contemporary rather than traditional and pays disappointingly little attention to the cuisine of Prado's native Cuba. Nor was everything on a recent visit uniformly well cooked. But those dishes that succeeded rose right off the plate, and the recipes, which are primarily Prado's personal creations (they supposedly are kept locked in his Los Angeles safe), do take island themes in exciting directions.

7   One advantage of the lengthy menu is that it looks kindly on those of modest budgets. While entrée prices range up to $15.95, the specialty Cha Cha chicken sandwich, dressed with garlic mayonnaise, onion and avocado, goes for a moderate $6.25. And there are entrée-size salads, such as the barbecue salad of grilled vegetables tossed with mixed greens ($6.95), as well as thin-crust pizzas garnished variously with Jamaican jerk chicken ($8.25) or shrimp, vegetables and garlicky salsa Criolla ($9.95).

8   But it is a full-course dinner that makes the most of Prado's melding of styles and flavors. The appetizers rank among his best efforts, particularly the crispy jerk pork ($4.75), which seems an especially spicy and savory variant of Southern-style barbecue, and the banana boats ($4.25), hollowed plantains filled with a flavorful blend of ground beef and vegetables. Unusual salsas are a Prado trademark, and the banana boat gains interest from a salsa based on fresh pineapple (pineapples, rather than flowers, serve as table centerpieces at Cha Cha Cha).

9   One evening's special appetizer, pastellitos de plátano ($6), consisted of three cakes of mashed plantain topped with a delightful salsa of chopped papaya and fresh ginger; the spicy-sweet effect was wonderful. The soft texture of these cakes might not appeal to everyone, but plantains are a delicious addition to our national larder and a taste easily acquired.

10   Other good openers include the shrimp cakes with spicy tartar sauce ($6.25) and the tortilla soup ($3.95), which Prado personalizes by adding a touch of curry. And the chicken-based mambo gumbo ($4.25) might put a lift into the sagging arches of many an Arthur Murray graduate.

11   For serious eating, Prado has taken contemporary realities into account, and if you've guessed that the Cha Cha Cha menu includes pastas, waltz to the head of the class. There is nothing particularly Caribbean about these. The most interesting, the fettuccine con pollo ($10.50), tosses egg noodles with chicken breast, roasted peppers and Gorgonzola cheese—sure sounds Italian to me.

12   Chicken is a recurring theme, as are vegetarian dishes; star plates include a semitraditional arroz con pollo served with saffron rice ($10.50), a spice-marinated, twice-grilled Jamaican jerk chicken breast ($12) and the plato sin carne ($12.95), a meatless but lavish platter of steamed and grilled seasonal vegetables. An occasional special, grilled whole breast of chicken ($14) flavored with spices and fresh basil, topped with mango and arranged over a bed of grilled, pencil-size asparagus, is a most enjoyable presentation.

Prado's highest achievement may well be the camarones negros *13* ($15.50), or black shrimp, so called because they repose in a dark, grainy-looking sauce seasoned with black pepper and an additional 24 "secret" spices. Overspicing can result in torrid messes, but Prado's recipe has the right balance, and this is a sensational way to serve shrimp.

On the other hand, the "traditional Argentine steak sauce" that *14* tops a New York sirloin ($15.50) bears a strong, if unintentional, resemblance to ketchup. For meat with a spicy flavor, a better choice would be the curried lamb brochette ($14.95), topped with what the menu describes as "a pungent Barbados curry sauce" and turns out to be a lively salsa of pineapple, rosemary, onions and raisins. This plate, like most Cha Cha Cha entrées, is heaped with fried plantains, black beans and saffron rice.

A sweet seems almost de rigueur after a meal laden with Prado's *15* Caribbean flavors. In keeping with the restaurant's multinational influences, he offers the French tarte Tatin (excellent on one occasion, dismal on another), as well as a variety of baked-on-premises cheesecakes, peach flan and a "volcano" pie that layers ice cream with peanuts and fudge.

Cha Cha Cha serves lunch and dinner daily, as well as weekend *16* brunch. . . .

ACTIVITY
8

Reading to Improve Writing. Discuss the following questions about "Cha Cha Cha Is Hot Hot Hot" with your classmates.

1. Why does Nelson like this restaurant? _____

   _____

   _____

   _____

2. How does Nelson introduce his review? Why does he use this particular strategy?

   _____

   _____

   _____

   _____

3. Why does the writer describe many of the dishes served at the restaurant?

_____

_____

_____

4. How does Nelson keep his audience interested in his evaluation?

_____

_____

_____

Collecting New Words. Try to determine the meanings of the following words from the way they're used in "Cha Cha Cha Is Hot Hot Hot." Then verify their meanings by checking a dictionary.

ACTIVITY
9

homogeneity (1) _____

patrimony (1) _____

fealty (2) _____

jerk (3) _____

culinary (3) _____

indigenous (3) _____

plantain (3) _____

preternaturally (4) _____

semisubterranean (5) _____

entrée (7) _____

larder (9) _____

torrid (13) _____

de rigueur (15) _____

ACTIVITY
10

Gathering Ideas about a Place. In your journal, gather ideas about a place you want to evaluate. Choose a place that is important to you and that others might want to know about, such as a new restaurant close to campus or an overpriced entertainment park that recently opened for business. Use the following questions to stimulate your thinking:

1. What is your overall opinion about the place? Why do you have this opinion?
2. What is good about the place? What is bad about it?
3. Compare the place with other similar places. How is it better? How is it worse?
4. What research could you do to learn more about the place?
5. Who would be interested in reading about the place? Why would they be interested?   ❏

One student, Jody, decided to evaluate her dorm. Here is part of her freewriting:

> Dryden Hall is such a rip-off, I can't believe it. My room looks like a hospital room—no carpet, plain furniture, a small window that looks out at a brick wall. My roommate and I are squished together like rats. There aren't any social activities, and every time you turn on your computer or hair dryer you never know if there's going to be a blackout. If this place were cheap, it might be okay, but it's one of the most expensive dorms on campus! I wish I could live in Johnson Hall, which looks a lot nicer, has a lot of activities, and is cheaper.

Drafting

You have now gathered ideas for evaluating a product, performance, and place. You have a rich source of material to draw on. At this point, you must decide how to proceed.

- You may select just one of these topics for your discovery draft.
- You may write drafts on two or three of these topics to see which you would prefer to continue working on.
- You may combine your discovery draft ideas into a new topic for your essay.

Since you will do an evaluation, select a topic about which you can make a judgment.

Before you begin writing your discovery draft, narrow your topic and write a preliminary thesis statement. As you write, follow your train of thought, even if it means revising your thesis statement later on. Keep your audience and purpose in mind, but remember that your main goal at the drafting stage is to get your ideas down on paper. You'll have time later on to revise and edit your discovery draft.

Here's a discovery draft written by a student, Jody Albert, whose freewriting you read earlier. In this draft, Jody evaluates her college dorm. After reading the draft, discuss with your classmates what Jody might do to revise it. (Note that the example includes the types of errors that typically appear in a first draft.)

Avoid Dryden Hall

I was away from home for the first time, eager to move into my home away from home—Dryden Hall. I excitedly opened the door to my new dorm room. What I saw disappointed me. It was a little room with no carpeting and a window with a view of a brick wall. This was only the first of many disappointing things about this dorm. *1*

Dryden Hall is one of the most expensive dorms on campus, but you'd never know it by looking at it. Repainting is needed. The colors are drab and the walls are chipped. The furniture in the lobby looks like they got it at a flea market. The rooms look like hospital rooms, with plain cupboards and dirty white tile. *2*

Dryden Hall also needs to be renovated because so many students now use computers to get into the library's resources and to talk to each other on e-mail. Right now, the dorm isn't plugged into the campus computer system, so you can't do any of these things. The dorm also has an out-of-date intercom phone system, which can probably be eliminated because almost all residents have phones. Sometimes the electricity goes out because the electrical wiring can't take all of our microwaves, televisions, and VCRs. *3*

Socially, Dryden Hall is a disaster. When I came here, I didn't know anyone. I thought that living in a dorm would help me make friends. Not in Dry- *4* den Hall! Yes, I have gotten to know my roommate and a few of the other girls on my floor. But the social events that are planned are completely inadequate. The monthly pizza party only lasts about fifteen minutes because we run out of food and drinks so quickly. The other regular social activity is a Sunday morning breakfast from 8–10 a.m. Most of us sleep later than that.

One thing that is good about Dryden Hall is the number of study rooms,   5
several on each floor. These rooms have comfortable furniture. Also, tutors are available in most of the study rooms in the evenings. The dorm is usually quiet, so it's pretty easy to study even in your own room.

If I could do it all over again, I'd choose Johnson Hall, which is older   6
than Dryden Hall but which has recently been renovated. It has attractive rooms, many good social activities, and is less expensive compared to Dryden Hall. Choosing Dryden Hall was definitely a mistake.

Revising

When you review your draft, use the skills you acquired in the preceding chapters. Support and clarify your main ideas, organize your paragraphs, make your ideas flow smoothly, and write an effective introduction, conclusion, and title. Also, consider conducting primary or secondary research to gather more information about your topic.

In this chapter, you'll learn how to write an evaluative essay. First, you'll focus on writing a thesis statement that expresses a judgment. Then, you'll learn how to support your judgment with evidence and comparisons. Finally, you'll learn the importance of keeping a balanced perspective.

Express a Judgment

As you may recall from Chapter Three, the thesis states your topic and tells why the topic is important to you. In an evaluative essay, however, the thesis also expresses your judgment of the topic.

A good thesis statement for an evaluative essay has these characteristics:

- It expresses an opinion about the value or merit of something.
- It focuses on the subject.
- It is moderate, not extreme.
- It is clear and specific.

Let's look at each of these qualities in more detail.

Express an Opinion. A judgment is an opinion about the value or merit of something. It is *not* a fact. Notice the difference between fact and judgment in these statements:

FACT

The Ford Mustang was among the most popular cars of the 1960s.

JUDGMENT

The Ford Mustang was one of the best cars made in the 1960s.

The first statement is factual because it can be verified by statistics concerning best-selling cars in the 1960s. The second statement expresses an opinion about the worthiness of the car. Some but not all people will agree with this statement.

Focus on the Subject. A judgment focuses on the subject being evaluated, not on the writer.

FOCUS ON THE WRITER

I really like my new Hungarian sports car.

FOCUS ON THE SUBJECT

The new Hungarian sports car is surprisingly fast and economical.

In the first example, the first-person *I* shows that the focus is on the writer. In the second, the first-person *I* has been replaced by the third-person *it*—the car. This change reflects the shift in emphasis, from the writer to the subject being evaluated.

Be Moderate, Not Extreme. A good thesis statement for an evaluative essay gives a sensible opinion about the subject. A sensible opinion is moderate rather than extreme.

EXTREME

Central College's library is the best college library in the country.

MODERATE

Central College's library has one of the best library computer systems in the area.

The extreme statement cannot be proven without visiting every college library in the country, whereas the moderate version is much easier to support.

Be Clear and Specific. A good thesis statement for an evaluative essay also expresses a judgment that is immediately understandable. If your readers can't understand your thesis statement, they won't understand the rest of your essay either. To make your thesis statement clear, use standard written English.

UNCLEAR

The new Student Union building is gross.

CLEAR

The new Student Union building is a disappointment because of its plain facade and cold, gray cinderblock interior.

The nonstandard *gross* (in this context) has been replaced with *disappointment*, a more precise word, and details have been added to explain the judgment.

A good thesis statement also tells why you have reached your judgment so that your readers can better understand your opinion about the topic.

VAGUE

The Georgia O'Keefe show at the Art Institute was excellent.

SPECIFIC

The Georgia O'Keefe show at the Art Institute was excellent because it displayed some never-before-seen paintings.

The first statement leaves readers asking why the show was excellent. The second statement answers that question.

GROUP
ACTIVITY
11

Revising Judgments. Working in a group of several students, review the characteristics of a good thesis statement for an evaluative essay. Then determine what's at fault in each of the following thesis statements. Finally, revise each thesis statement accordingly.

1. The worst jeans ever made are manufactured by Salisbury, Inc.

    Fault(s): _____

    Revision: _____

    _____

    _____

2. *Apollo 13* is an OK action movie.

    Fault(s): _____

    Revision: _____

_____

_____

3. The Super Bowl is seen by millions of people around the world.

   Fault(s): _____

   Revision: _____

   _____

   _____

4. The Smithsonian is my favorite museum.

   Fault(s): _____

   Revision: _____

   _____

   _____

5. The Bradley running shoe is one of the newest shoes on the market.

   Fault(s): _____

   Revision: _____

   _____

   _____

Revising Your Judgment. Revise the thesis statement for your essay so that it meets the requirements for an evaluative essay: it expresses an opinion about the value or merit of your subject; focuses on the subject; is moderate, not extreme; and is clear and specific. ❑

ACTIVITY
12

Give Criteria

As in other types of essays, you must support your thesis statement in an evaluative essay as well. You do this by informing your readers of the criteria on which you base your judgment. *Criteria* are standards on which a judgment is based. In "Bibler Piñon Tent," for example, Jeanne Twehous informs us that the Bibler Piñon tent is good because of its ease of setup, stability, waterproof fabric, and spacious design. These are her criteria. Your criteria should be sufficient, appropriate, and either self-evident or explained.

COMPUTER TIP

HIGHLIGHT YOUR CRITERIA

To make it easier to determine whether you have sufficient criteria in your essay, highlight them using boldface type. The highlighting will show you the number of criteria you use to make your judgment and whether you need to include additional criteria.

Include Sufficient Criteria. An effective evaluation is based on sufficient criteria. In most cases, an effective evaluative essay has between three and five criteria. Judging a subject on the basis of only one or two criteria may not be enough to persuade your readers to accept your judgment. Imagine, for instance, if Jack Garner had evaluated *Waterworld* only on the basis of the film's setting. As readers, we would have been left with questions about the film's acting and plot, and we would have doubted the writer's judgment of the movie.

Use Appropriate Criteria. The criteria on which your judgment is based should be appropriate for your subject. In other words, the criteria must suit the subject. Jeanne Twehous, for example, does not base her claim that the Bibler Piñon tent is good because it comes in three easy-to-match colors; few campers would care whether the color of their tent matches that of their clothing or other gear. Rather, the criteria Twehous uses—ease of setup, stability, waterproof fabric, and spacious design—are appropriate because campers are concerned about such features in a tent.

How do you think of sufficient and appropriate criteria? Try these three steps:

1. "I think that _____ is good/bad because _____ ."

2. Imagine yourself reading about your subject. What other criteria would lead people to the same judgment that you have?

3. Keep in mind that you might think of more criteria than you can argue in your essay. After you collect as many criteria as you can think of, decide on the three to five criteria that seem most important.

ACTIVITY
13

Determining Whether Criteria Are Sufficient and Appropriate. Following is a list of subjects and criteria. For each subject, circle any criteria that are inappropriate for evaluating the subject. Then determine whether the number of criteria is sufficient for each subject. Add appropriate criteria where necessary.

1.   SUBJECT: sports car
     CRITERIA: handling, power, style, cleanliness

2.   SUBJECT: shopping mall
     CRITERIA: types of stores, number of pay phones, location, layout

3. SUBJECT: apartment
    CRITERIA: lighting, number of rooms, spaciousness

4. SUBJECT: symphony concert
    CRITERIA: clothes worn by musicians, type of music

5. SUBJECT: gym
    CRITERIA: number of weight machines, quality of weight machines

---

Generating Appropriate Criteria. Working in a group of several students, list appropriate criteria for evaluating each subject that follows. Here's an example:

GROUP
ACTIVITY
14

SUBJECT: action movie
CRITERIA: <u>plot, characters, setting, special effects</u>

1. SUBJECT: computer

    CRITERIA: _____

    _____

2. SUBJECT: college radio station

    CRITERIA: _____

    _____

3. SUBJECT: rock concert

    CRITERIA: _____

    _____

4. SUBJECT: fast-food restaurant

    CRITERIA: _____

    _____

5. SUBJECT: book bag

    CRITERIA: _____

    _____

ACTIVITY
15

Examining the Criteria in Your Essay. Examine the criteria in your own draft for this chapter. Are the criteria appropriate and sufficient? Make any necessary changes. ❑

Explain Your Criteria. When your readers won't immediately understand your criteria, you need to explain them. For example, in an evaluation of a computer, you would probably need to explain the importance of the computer's memory. Similarly, in evaluating a fashion show, you would explain why music is essential to the show's success.

But not all criteria require explanation. Some criteria are self-evident. In evaluating Cha Cha Cha, there's no need for David Nelson to explain why one of his criteria for a good restaurant is good food. Similarly, in evaluating a movie, you would not need to explain why good acting is a necessary criterion. Only when you think some readers will have questions about a particular criterion should you explain its appropriateness.

How do you explain your criteria?

- Ask yourself if your criteria are self-evident. Will your readers automatically see why your criteria are appropriate to your subject? If not, you need to explain the criteria.
- Tell why you include the criteria in your argument.
- For readers familiar with your subject, include a brief explanation of the criteria (such as "A pair of jeans needs to be comfortable because they're worn so frequently").
- For readers unfamiliar with your subject, include a detailed explanation of the criteria (such as "All the seats in a sports arena should give spectators good visibility. After all, why come if you can't see the action? Even if you only paid for a cheap seat, you shouldn't have to sit behind a post that partially obstructs your view").

GROUP
ACTIVITY
16

Explaining Your Criteria. Work with several other students to explain the criteria for each of the following subjects.

1.   SUBJECT: a VCR
    CRITERION: A VCR should last a long time.

    EXPLANATION: _____

    _____

CRITERION: A VCR should be easy to use.

EXPLANATION: _____

_____

CRITERION: A VCR should have good picture and sound quality.

EXPLANATION: _____

_____

2.   SUBJECT: the Student Union at your college
     CRITERION: The Student Union should offer a variety of food services.

EXPLANATION: _____

_____

CRITERION: The Student Union should offer different activities and programs.

EXPLANATION: _____

_____

CRITERION: The Student Union should offer comfortable places to relax.

EXPLANATION: _____

_____

3.   SUBJECT: a television documentary
     CRITERION: A television documentary should be truthful.

EXPLANATION: _____

_____

CRITERION: A television documentary should be entertaining.

EXPLANATION: _____

_____

CRITERION: A television documentary should be on a topic interesting to many viewers.

EXPLANATION: _____

_____

ACTIVITY

17

Explaining the Criteria in Your Essay. Examine the criteria in your essay. Which criteria are self-evident? Which criteria need to be explained? Add any necessary explanations. ❑

Provide Evidence

Most of an evaluative essay consists of providing evidence in support of a judgment. In other words, explain to your readers how well your subject measures up to the criteria you apply. Such explanation usually involves citing facts, examples, and expert testimony.

Facts. In "Bibler Piñon Tent," Jeanne Twehous uses facts to support her judgment that the tent is well waterproofed.

> Bibler uses a proprietary fabric called ToddTex (named after designer Todd Bibler) that minimizes condensation.

She supports her point about ease of setup with another fact:

> The freestanding Piñon pops up quickly once you get the hang of how the poles thread through the canopy. You just duck inside the tent out of the elements after the first pole is in place to erect your shelter.

Facts are a highly persuasive form of evidence, primarily because they can be verified by readers. They also demonstrate your knowledge of the topic.

Examples. In addition to facts, you can use examples to support a judgment. In "Cha Cha Cha Is Hot Hot Hot," David Nelson gives many examples to illustrate his points. For instance, he includes an example to show the range in meal prices:

> While entrée prices range up to $15.95, the specialty Cha Cha chicken sandwich, dressed with garlic mayonnaise, onion and avocado, goes for a moderate $6.25.

Nelson also gives examples of other dishes:

> [S]tar plates include a semitraditional arroz con pollo served with saffron rice ($10.50), a spice-marinated, twice-grilled Jamaican jerk chicken breast ($12) and the plato sin carne ($12.95), a meatless but lavish platter of steamed and grilled seasonal vegetables.

Examples make your essay more interesting to read as well as more convincing.

Expert Testimony. Expert testimony—the opinion of people knowledgeable about a subject—can be used to confirm a judgment. In evaluating a product, for instance, you might refer to *Consumer Reports'* rating of the product. In evaluating a performance or a place, you could check a magazine or newspaper to see if your subject has been evaluated by others. Awards can be considered a form of expert testimony because they're given by experts in a particular field. If a movie wins an Oscar for best director, it means that a team of successful movie directors thought highly of the film's director.

Identifying Types of Evidence. Work with a group of students to identify the types of evidence used in the following paragraphs.

GROUP
ACTIVITY
18

1.   The story of *sex, lies, and videotape* is by now part of movie folklore: how Soderbergh, at twenty-nine, wrote the screenplay in eight days during a trip to Los Angeles, how the film was made for $1.8 million, how it won the Palme d'Or at the 1989 Cannes Film Festival, as well as the best actor prize for Spader. I am not sure it is as good as the Cannes jury apparently found it; it has more intelligence than heart, and is more clever than enlightening.

ROGER EBERT, *ROGER EBERT'S VIDEO COMPANION*

Type(s) of evidence: _____

_____

2.   The most expensive hotels . . . pile on the extras and charge accordingly. Rooms at the *Four Seasons* in downtown Philadelphia visited by our reporter feature reproduction antique furniture, feather pillows, huge towels, lots of fancy soaps and shampoo, a telephone in the bathroom, and a minibar. The staff doted on our reporter and his family. The children got free cookies and milk (or soft drinks and popcorn), movies, and Nintendo games—all delivered to the room.

"THE BEST HOTELS," *CONSUMER REPORTS*

Type(s) of evidence: _____

_____

3.   The AMC Grand's parking lot, which AMC says it has expanded to include 2,200 spaces, can still be a headache for customers. The entrances and exits create irritating traffic tie-ups, and customers of-

ten have to walk several blocks to the box office. By that time, a cold drink seems more a necessity than an indulgence.

PHILIP WUNTCH, "DALLAS' TWO NEW 'MEGAPLEXES' SIZE UP NICELY"

Type(s) of evidence: _____

_____

4.   As cosmetics go, lipstick is the cheapest and most popular product on the market. That doesn't mean you can't spend a fortune on the stuff, however. Enter Princess Marcella Borghese's Superiore State-of-the-Art lipstick. Cost: $20 for 0.15 ounce. That comes to $133 an ounce. The same amount of Wet 'n' Wild or Artmatic lipstick, at less than $1 a tube, costs about $7. Of course, the Borghese lipstick has much prettier packaging. But you may want to save the $126 you'd spend for an ounce of this lipstick, and get yourself a whole line of beauty products instead.

"CHOOSING A LIPSTICK," CONSUMER REPORTS

Type(s) of evidence: _____

_____

ACTIVITY

19

Charting Your Criteria and Evidence. To help you visualize the connections between your criteria and evidence, list them in a two-column chart. In the left column, list the criteria that form the basis for your judgment. In the right column, list the evidence that supports your judgment. (You should include several pieces of evidence for each judgment.)

Here's an example of a chart based on Jeanne Twehous's "Bibler Piñon Tent."

Criteria	Evidence
1. ease of setup	poles easily thread through the canopy; you can get into the tent after only one pole is up
2. stability	crisscrossing poles fit snugly into roof corners; gusts can't sneak in between the fly and the tent
3. waterproof fabric	stays dry despite snow, sleet, and rain; fabric minimizes condensation
4. spacious design	room to stretch out; lots of storage space

COMPUTER TIP

CHART YOUR CRITERIA AND EVIDENCE

Use the graphics feature of your word-processing program to chart your criteria and evidence.

Examining Your Evidence. Examine the evidence you use in your draft. Is your judgment supported by facts, examples, or expert testimony? Where can you include additional evidence to make your points more convincing? Add that evidence where needed. ❏

Make Comparisons to Similar Subjects

Another way to support your judgment is to make comparisons between your subject and other similar subjects. In his movie review, for example, Jack Garner compares *Waterworld* to the movie *The Road Warrior:* both are action-adventure movies with many special effects. By comparing the two films, Garner makes his point that *Waterworld,* despite its high cost, is no better than other action-adventure movies. He also shows that he is familiar with action-adventure movies in general, which makes us more likely to accept his judgment.

When making comparisons, be sure you focus on similar subjects. In evaluating the new campus recreation center, for example, you would not compare it to the college library. Instead, you might compare the new center with the old center to point out the improvements that have been made. Keep in mind that you aren't writing a comparison-contrast paper; therefore, keep your comparisons brief and to the point.

> **COMPUTER TIP**
> **WRITE ON TWO SCREENS**
>   If your computer has the capability, use a separate window when gathering ideas for more evidence. Then use the cut-and-paste function to move your evidence to the main screen that contains your draft.

Comparing Similar Subjects. Work with your classmates on the following list of subjects and items for comparison. Underline any items that are not similar to the subject of the essay. Here's an example:

        SUBJECT: Ford Explorer
ITEMS FOR COMPARISON: Chevrolet Blazer, Nissan Pathfinder, <u>Chevrolet Cavalier</u>, Toyota Landcruiser

1.   SUBJECT: McDonald's
  ITEMS FOR COMPARISON: Denny's, Burger King, Jack-in-the-Box, What-a-burger

2.   SUBJECT: *Seinfeld* (the television show)
  ITEMS FOR COMPARISON: *Cheers, ER, Friends, Married with Children*

3.   SUBJECT: Häagen-Dazs Ice Cream
  ITEMS FOR COMPARISON: Ben & Jerry's, Breyers, Baskin Robbins, TCBY (The Country's Best Yogurt)

4.   SUBJECT: San Diego Zoo
  ITEMS FOR COMPARISON: Disneyland, Chicago Zoo, Philadelphia Zoo, Sea World

GROUP
ACTIVITY
22

Finding Similar Subjects for Comparison. Work with your class-mates on the following list of subjects. For each main subject, iden-tify two or three similar subjects that could be used to make a com-parison. Here's an example:

SUBJECT: Prodigy computer service
SIMILAR SUBJECTS: Compuserve, America Online

1. SUBJECT: L. L. Bean mail-order catalog

    SIMILAR SUBJECTS: _____

    _____

2. SUBJECT: Guess! jeans

    SIMILAR SUBJECTS: _____

    _____

3. SUBJECT: Smashing Pumpkins concert

    SIMILAR SUBJECTS: _____

    _____

4. SUBJECT: Wal-Mart department store

    SIMILAR SUBJECTS: _____

    _____

5. SUBJECT: Ford Escort

    SIMILAR SUBJECTS: _____

    _____

ACTIVITY
23

Using Comparisons in Your Essay. For the topic of your draft, list one or more similar subjects. Then consider how you might use a similar subject to make a comparison and thereby support your judg-ment. ❑

Keep a Balanced Perspective

Readers know that few subjects are all good or all bad. Informing readers of both the negative and positive aspects of your subject makes your evaluation more balanced. A balanced judgment is persuasive because it shows readers that your evaluation is fair, reasonable, and believable.

You may recall from the reading by Jeanne Twehous that she tells us about the tent's flaw: "Life on the trail rarely proves perfect, though, and the Piñon suffered a couple of battle scars" (par. 10). She then points out that the tent suffered two small tears during a storm. By telling readers about the tent's flaw, Twehous maintains a balanced perspective and thereby strengthens her believability.

Here are some tips for maintaining a balanced perspective in your evaluation:

- Identify what you think is good or worthwhile about your subject. Then consider what is not good or worthwhile.

- You don't have to give equal space in an evaluative essay to the strengths and weaknesses of your subject. If your judgment about the subject is positive, *briefly* describe the negative aspects, as Twehous does in her essay. If your judgment about the subject is negative, *briefly* describe the positive aspects.

> **COMPUTER TIP**
>
> **CHART THE POSITIVE AND NEGATIVE ASPECTS OF YOUR SUBJECT**
>
> Use the graphics feature of your word-processing program to chart the positive and negative aspects of your subject.

Analyzing for a Balanced Perspective. Work with a group of students to determine how Jack Garner maintains a balanced perspective in "Expense Doesn't Make *Waterworld* the Best" (pp. 283–285). First, create a two-column chart with the headings "Positive Aspects" and "Negative Aspects" at the top. Then, referring back to the reading as needed, list the positive and negative comments that Garner makes about *Waterworld*. Finally, analyze your findings by answering these two questions:

GROUP
ACTIVITY
24

1. How does Garner maintain a balanced perspective?
2. What effect does this balanced perspective have on you as the reader?

Charting the Positive and Negative Aspects of Your Subject. Gather ideas about the positive and negative aspects of your subject in a two-column chart. Label the columns "Positive Aspects" and "Negative Aspects." Then list the positive and negative features of your subject.

ACTIVITY
25

As you revise your draft, use this chart to maintain a balanced perspective. ❑

Jody's Revised Draft

Before you read Jody's revised draft, reread her discovery draft (pp. 293–294). Notice, in particular, how Jody has improved the evaluation of her subject in the revision. (You will also notice some errors in the revised draft; these will be corrected when Jody edits her essay later on.)

Avoid Dryden Hall

Introduction is more interesting

I walked down the long, gray hall, looking for room 315—my room for the school year. My arms ached from carrying my two heavy suitcases. I put the key in the lock, turned it, and opened the door. I couldn't believe my eyes. The room looked as if it belonged in a hospital. The vinyl floor was scuffed and dull, the window had a view of a brick wall, and the walls were painted a drab green. This was only the first of many disappointments I've had with my dorm. Dryden Hall is an overpriced dorm that lacks many of the amenities found in less expensive dorms. The inside of the building is unattractive, the wiring is outdated, and the social events are unsuccessful. 1

Judgment is more specific

Criteria are explained

Where a person lives is important to his well-being. Since so many students live in dorms, the college should try to make them attractive. The rooms should be clean, the walls painted an uplifting color, and the furniture fairly new. A dorm should also have updated facilities so that a student can plug into the college computer system in his own room. How else can students examine the library records or talk to their instructors on e-mail? A dorm should also offer opportunities for students to meet other people. Because many students are away from home for the first time. Finally, a dorm should be a good place to study. 2

Facts and examples support the judgment

Dryden Hall is unattractive from the first floor to the top floor. The lobby has shabby furniture and a stained carpet. One of the couches even has its stuffing hanging out. The halls are painted a dark gray that makes them seem like tunnels, many of the rooms have walls with chipped paint or that need cleaning. The walls in my room, for example, are filled with holes from where former occupants have hung pictures. The kitchen on the top floor has rusty cupboards and an ancient sink. 3

Dryden Hall also needs to be modernized. Part of our fees pays for an out-of-date telephone intercom system that is useless because most residents have their own telephones. Sometimes the electricity goes out because the wiring can't take all of our microwaves, televisions, and VCRs. 4

Most importantly, Dryden Hall isn't plugged into the campus computer system. Unlike students in other dorms, I can't use my computer to search the library records or communicate with instructors or students on e-mail. This is a major inconvenience when I'm working late at night on an assignment.

The most important evidence is saved for the end of the paragraph

Socially, Dryden Hall is a disaster. When I came here, I didn't know anyone. I thought that living in a dorm would help me make friends. Not in Dryden Hall! The main social event here is a monthly pizza party. Unfortunately, they run out of pizza after about fifteen minutes, so no one stays around to meet anyone else. The dorm also serves donuts and coffee in the lobby every Sunday from 8 to 10 a.m. Way too early for me and many others. Surely some of the money we pay to stay in Dryden Hall could be used for more, and better, social events.

5

Facts support the judgment

This statement emphasizes the writer's point

It is true that Dryden Hall is a good place to study. Each floor has several study rooms (all of them in need of repainting, of course). Tutors are available in most of these study rooms in the evenings. Because there's not much socializing, the dorm is usually quiet, so it's easy to study whenever necessary.

6

This positive aspect of the dorm helps create a balanced perspective

As I sit in my dorm room, staring at the cracked ceiling and the brick wall outside my window, I'm reminded again of the mistake I made when I moved into Dryden Hall. I wish I had chosen to live in Johnson Hall, which is less expensive than Dryden Hall. It has been renovated inside and out and has alot of parties. I only hope that the word gets out about Dryden Hall so that other students don't make the same mistake.

7

The comparison strengthens the judgment

The conclusion looks toward the future

Analyzing Jody's Revised Draft. Use the following questions to analyze how Jody has improved her draft.

ACTIVITY
26

1. How has Jody improved her introduction? _____

_____

_____

2. Why is her thesis statement more effective now? _____

_____

_____

3. What criteria does Jody use to evaluate Dryden Hall? How appropriate and sufficient are her criteria? Are they self-evident or in need of explanation?

_____

_____

_____

4. How well does Jody support her judgment with facts, examples, and expert testimony?

_____

_____

_____

5. Does the comparison with Johnson Hall further support Jody's judgment? Why or why not?

_____

_____

_____

6. Does Jody maintain a balanced perspective? Explain. _____

_____

_____

_____

7. How could Jody's revised draft benefit from further revision?

_____

_____

_____

Using Peer Review. Form a group with two or three other students and exchange copies of your drafts. Read your draft aloud while your classmates follow along. Take notes on your classmates' responses to the following questions about your draft.

1. Have I followed all of the instructions for this assignment?

_____

_____

_____

2. How interesting is my introduction? Do you want to continue reading the paper? Why or why not?

_____

_____

_____

3. What is my thesis statement? Is it effective? Does it express an opinion about the value or merit of my subject? Is it focused on the subject? Is it moderate rather than extreme? Is it clear and specific?

_____

_____

_____

_____

4. What are my criteria? Are they sufficient and appropriate? Are they self-evident, or do I need to explain them?

_____

_____

_____

5. How well do I support my judgment with facts, examples, and expert testimony?

_____

_____

_____

6. Do I maintain a balanced perspective? Why or why not?

_____

_____

_____

7. Do I make effective comparisons? Explain. _____

_____

_____

8. What parts of my essay, if any, don't support my judgment and could be omitted? Are there any sentences or words that seem unnecessary?

_____

_____

_____

9. Where in the draft does my writing confuse you? How can I clarify my thoughts?

_____

_____

_____

10. How clear is the purpose of my essay? How well do I meet the needs of my audience?

_____

_____

_____

_____

11. How effective is my ending? Do I conclude in such a way that you know it's the end?

_____

_____

_____

ACTIVITY
28

Revising Your Draft. Taking your classmates' suggestions for revision into consideration, revise your essay. In particular, focus on improving your thesis statement, criteria, evidence, and comparisons. Also work to maintain a balanced perspective. You may decide to omit unnecessary material or to rearrange parts of your essay more effectively as well. ❏

Editing

At this point you have worked hard to write an evaluation of a product, performance, or place. But before you can share your essay with your audience, you must edit it for correctness.

Jody's Edited Essay

You might have noticed that Jody's revised draft contained errors in grammar, spelling, and punctuation. Jody corrected these errors in her edited essay. Her corrections are underlined here. Her editing log follows her edited essay.

Avoid Dryden Hall

I walked down the long, gray hall, looking for room 315—my room for the school year. My arms ached from carrying my two heavy suitcases. I put the key in the lock, turned it, and opened the door. I couldn't believe my eyes. The room looked as if it belonged in a hospital. The vinyl floor was scuffed and dull, the window had a view of a brick wall, and the walls were painted a drab green. This was only the first of many disappointments I've had with my dorm. Dryden Hall is an overpriced dorm that lacks many of the amenities found in less expensive dorms. The inside of the building is unattractive, the wiring is outdated, and the social events are unsuccessful.

Where a person lives is important to his or her well-being. Since so many students live in dorms, the college should try to make them attractive. The rooms should be clean, the walls painted an uplifting color, and the furniture fairly new. A dorm should also have updated facilities so that students can plug into the college computer system in their own rooms. How else can students examine the library records or talk to their instructors on e-mail? Because many students are away from home for the first time, a dorm should also offer opportunities for students to meet other people. Finally, a dorm should be a good place to study.

Dryden Hall is unattractive from the first floor to the top floor. The lobby has shabby furniture and a stained carpet. One of the couches even has its stuffing hanging out. The halls are painted a dark gray that makes them seem like tunnels, and many of the rooms have walls with chipped paint or that need cleaning. The walls in my room, for example, are filled with holes from where former occupants have hung pictures. The kitchen on the top floor has rusty cupboards and an ancient sink.

Dryden Hall also needs to be modernized. Part of our fees pays for an out-of-date telephone intercom system that is useless because most residents have their own telephones. Sometimes the electricity goes out because the wiring can't take all of our microwaves, televisions, and VCRs. Most importantly, Dryden Hall isn't plugged into the campus computer system. Unlike students in other dorms, I can't use my computer to search the library records or communicate with instructors or students on e-mail. This is a major inconvenience when I'm working late at night on an assignment.

Socially, Dryden Hall is a disaster. When I came here, I didn't know anyone. I thought that living in a dorm would help me make friends. I was wrong. The main social event here is a monthly pizza party. Unfortunately, the organizers run out of pizza after about fifteen minutes, so no one stays around to meet anyone else. The dorm also serves donuts and coffee in the lobby every Sunday from 8 to 10 a.m., which is way too early for me and many others. Surely some of the money we pay to stay in Dryden Hall could be used for more, and better, social events.

It is true that Dryden Hall is a good place to study. Each floor has several study rooms (all of them in need of repainting, of course). Tutors are available in most of these study rooms in the evenings. Because there's not

2

3

4

5

6

much socializing, the dorm is usually quiet, so it's easy to study whenever necessary.

As I sit in my dorm room, staring at the cracked ceiling and the brick wall ₇ outside my window, I'm reminded again of the mistake I made when I moved into Dryden Hall. I wish I had chosen to live in Johnson Hall, which is less expensive than Dryden Hall. It has been renovated inside and out and has a lot of parties. I only hope that the word gets out about Dryden Hall so that other students don't make the same mistake.

Jody's Editing Log

- INCORRECT: Where a person lives is important to his well-being. (2)
    ERROR: sexist language
    CORRECT: Where a person lives is important to his or her well-being.

- INCORRECT: A dorm should also have updated facilities so that a student can plug into the college computer system in his own room. (2)
    ERROR: sexist language
    CORRECT: A dorm should also have updated facilities so that students can plug into the college computer system in their own rooms.

- INCORRECT: Because many students are away from home for the first time. (2)
    ERROR: sentence fragment
    CORRECT: Because many students are away from home for the first time, a dorm should also offer opportunities for students to meet other people.

- INCORRECT: The halls are painted a dark gray that makes them seem like tunnels, many of the rooms have walls with chipped paint or that need cleaning. (3)
    ERROR: comma splice
    CORRECT: The halls are painted a dark gray that makes them seem like tunnels, and many of the rooms have walls with chipped paint or that need cleaning.

- INCORRECT: Not in Dryden Hall! (5)
    ERROR: sentence fragment
    CORRECT: I was wrong.

- INCORRECT: Unfortunately, they run out of pizza after about fifteen minutes, so no one stays around to meet anyone else. (5)
    ERROR: vague pronoun reference
    CORRECT: Unfortunately, the organizers run out of pizza after about fifteen minutes, so no one stays around to meet anyone else.

- INCORRECT: Way too early for me and many others. (5)
    ERROR: sentence fragment
    CORRECT: The dorm also serves donuts and coffee in the lobby every Sunday from 8 to 10 a.m., which is way too early for me and many others.

•INCORRECT: alot (7)
    ERROR: misspelled word
    CORRECT: a lot

ACTIVITY
29

Editing Your Essay. Using the Handbook in Part III of this book as a guide, edit your revised essay for errors in grammar, spelling, and punctuation. Your classmates can help you locate and correct errors you may overlook. Add the errors you find and their corrections to your editing log. ❑

Publishing

You're ready to share your essay with your audience—your instructor and classmates, as well as others interested in your topic. For instance, if you evaluate a product, consider sharing your essay with someone interested in purchasing the product. If you evaluate a movie, share your essay with someone who has also seen the film and then discuss your different viewpoints. If you evaluate a place, share your essay with someone who is familiar with that place and ask the person for feedback. You might also send your essay to someone who can take action on the issues related to your topic. Jody, for example, sent a copy of her evaluation of Dryden Hall to the person in charge of maintaining the residence halls on campus. A few months later, Dryden Hall was repainted.

Your Writing Portfolio

Your writing portfolio consists of your best writing as well as your reflections on your writing. To help you reflect on the writing you did in this chapter, answer the following questions:

1. Compare your experience writing an evaluation with writing an expressive or informative essay. What did you find easiest and most difficult about these assignments?
2. What did you learn from writing this essay?
3. How will your audience benefit from reading your essay?
4. If you had more time, what more would you do to improve your essay before sharing it with readers?

Using your answers to these questions, update your writing process report.

Writing Process Report

Date:

Strengths:

Weaknesses:

Plans for improvement:

Once you complete this report, freewrite in your journal about what you learned about your writing process in this chapter and what you still hope to learn.

Chapter Summary

- To evaluate something, you decide on its value, worthiness, or merit.
- An effective thesis statement for an evaluative essay expresses an opinion or judgment about the value or merit of the subject; focuses on the subject, not the writer; is moderate, not extreme; and is clear and specific.
- Criteria are the standards on which your judgment is based.
- Criteria should be sufficient, appropriate, and self-evident or explained.
- Provide evidence—facts, examples, and expert testimony—to support your judgment.
- Make comparisons between your subject and other similar subjects to support your judgment.
- Give both the positive and negative aspects of your subject to maintain a balanced perspective. A balanced judgment is persuasive because it shows your reader that you're being fair.

Free speech is the whole thing, the whole ball game. Free speech is life itself.
—SALMAN RUSHDIE

10

Debating the Limits of Free Expression

In this chapter you will

- gather ideas about free expression in the schools, in the media, and on the Internet.

- make an argumentative claim.

- develop reasons to support your claim.

- argue against objections to your claim.

- order your argumentative points.

- learn to recognize faulty logic.

- add to your writing portfolio.

You have probably heard a lot about freedom of expression. A radio talk-show host who regularly offends listeners with his lewd and discriminatory comments may say he's just exercising his right to free expression. Parade organizers seeking to ban gay-rights demonstrators may refer to their right to free expression. Free expression is the defense used by protesters who block the entrance to an abortion clinic.

Freedom of expression is a part of the First Amendment to the Constitution:

> Congress shall make no law respecting an establishment of religion, or prohibiting the free exercise thereof; or abridging the freedom of speech, or of the press; or the right of the people peaceably to assemble, and to petition the Government for a redress of grievances.

The First Amendment gives the people of the United States the right to attend the church of their choice, to protest against the government's actions, and to express themselves freely.

But can freedom of expression be taken too far? Because of the First Amendment, Nazis demonstrate in the streets and the Ku Klux Klan publicly burns crosses. Some of the most popular music in the country advocates abusing women. Hard-core pornography, demeaning to women, is readily available. Children are exposed to an amazing number of acts of violence on television, which some experts believe promotes actual violence. Clearly, freedom of expression comes in many forms.

Rather than advocate total freedom or no freedom of expression, some people suggest a middle road: freedom of expression should be permitted unless the welfare of society is endangered. Yet who decides when society is endangered? And how will freedom of expression be restricted?

ACTIVITY

1

Analyzing Your Purpose and Audience. Before you begin gathering ideas about your topic, think about your purpose and audience. For this chapter's assignment, you'll give your opinion about an aspect of free expression. Remember that your audience includes your instructor and classmates as well as other people directly affected by your topic. For example, the audience for an essay about banning books from school libraries might include parents, teachers, and librarians, whereas the audience for an essay on regulating language use on the Internet might include Internet users and government officials. Your responses to the following questions will help you decide how to approach your topic.

Writing Assignment

This chapter offers you the opportunity to express your views on freedom of expression—in schools, in the media, or on the Internet. You or your instructor may decide to do this assignment in one of several ways:

- You may gather ideas on one, two, *or* three topics.
- You may write a discovery draft on one, two, *or* three of these topics.
- You may choose one discovery draft to develop into a polished essay.
- You may combine your discovery draft ideas into a new topic for your essay.

After completing your essay, you'll share it with your instructor and classmates, as well as with others directly affected by your topic, such as parents, friends, teachers, television producers, or government officials.

1. Does this assignment call for expressive, informative, or persuasive writing?

   _____

2. What is your readers' average age? _____

3. What parts of the country or world are they from? _____

   _____

   _____

4. What, if anything, do you know about your readers' political views? Would you expect most readers to have conservative, moderate, or liberal views, for example?

   _____

   _____

   _____

5. What is your readers' experience with your topic? _____

_____

_____

Given your responses to the preceding questions, ask yourself these questions:

6. What do my readers already know about my topic? _____

_____

_____

7. What information do I *not* have to give them? _____

_____

_____

8. What do my readers need to know about my topic? _____

_____

_____

9. How do my readers feel about my topic? Will they find it interesting, or will I have to work to get their attention?

_____

_____

_____

10. Are my readers likely to agree with my views on free expression, or will I have to work to convince them to accept my point of view? How can I do this?

_____

_____

_____

❏

Gathering Ideas

To gather ideas about free expression in schools, in the media, and on the Internet, select from among the various techniques you have practiced in the preceding chapters: brainstorming, freewriting, clustering, questioning, reading, interviewing, relating aloud, and reflecting.

Free Expression in Schools

In elementary and high school, free expression is an important issue. The subjects taught and the books students read are regulated by parents, teachers, school administrators, and school board members.

As you probably know, even such books as *Huckleberry Finn* and *Catcher in the Rye* have been banned in certain parts of the country. In recent years, certain books supposedly about satanism, or devil worship, have also been banned from school libraries. One school librarian, Kerry Leigh Ellison, addresses this issue in "Satan in the Library: Are Children in Danger?"

KERRY LEIGH ELLISON

From *Satan in the Library: Are Children in Danger?*

Last Halloween, in New Castle, Pennsylvania, school librarian   *1*
Nancy Prentice faced accusations of practicing satanism after she read the folk ballad "Tam Lin" to a group of fifth graders. A few months later, library aide Debbie Denzer of Kalispell, Montana, lost her job for lending her own books on the history of witchcraft to two seventh grade girls. The single largest category of book challenges last year consisted of religious objections, primarily the mention of witchcraft, satanism, and the occult.

Are our children in danger from books on satanism, Halloween,   *2*
magic, and New Age religions?

I have no doubt that satanism is practiced here in America and   *3*
that—in some groups at least—children who are born into it or attracted to it suffer horribly. I know this because I was raised in a family that practiced satanism. The horrors that survivors describe really do happen. I am a witness to these crimes, as are other members of my family who have made the long journey out of the cult.

As a survivor and a professional, I take an active interest in the   *4*
intellectual freedom of the children I serve. In my experience, indoctrination into satanic belief and practices involves a very rigid way of thinking: children must learn to see the world as inherently

chaotic, satan as more powerful than God, the cult as omnipresent, and love as a sign of weakness.

Cult activities take place behind a wall of secrecy and denial. In the "daytime" world, children must act as if nothing is wrong, all the while experiencing a "nighttime" reality of abuse and sexual exploitation. In our cult, we were taught that the leaders could see our every move, even when we were alone. We were taught that no outsider would believe us if we told and that any breach of secrecy was punishable with death.

Like the children of Jonestown, we were taught to never question authority. Like the children in the compound at Waco, Texas, we were not allowed to make choices for ourselves. Fear, ignorance and "magical thinking" kept us in line.

But in the daytime world—at school and in the public library— I *could* make choices. Once I discovered the world of books, I chose to read everything I could get my hands on.

One of my first chapter books was Johanna Spyri's *Heidi*, which I read over and over. The freedom of her life in the mountains was so delicious. Then there were those terrible months in Frankfurt with the ailing Klara. In a way I could not have described at the time, I felt understood and less alone when I was with Heidi. . . .

In fantasy novels such as Madeline L'Engle's *A Wrinkle in Time* (Farrar, 1962), I aligned myself with good in the fight against evil, and learned that love is more powerful than hate or fear. C. S. Lewis's *The Lion, the Witch and the Wardrobe* (Macmillan, 1988) gave me the vicarious experience of a benevolent deity, one who protects and heals children, rather than abuses them.

Reading Louise Fitzhugh's *Harriet the Spy* (HarperCollins, 1964), I saw a child like myself struggle with the confusing values of her parents and with classmates who could not understand her.

Early on, I crossed over into the adult section of the library where I found a mirror for many of my feelings in Anne Frank's *Diary of a Young Girl*. Here was the horror, the hiding, and the tenacious hope. Hope, too, is what I gleaned from *Fahrenheit 451* (Buccaneer, 1990). Ray Bradbury's hero questions accepted values and makes up his own mind about the burning of books. In the end, he helps keep learning alive, if only in his heart and mind.

George Orwell's *1984* (Dutton, 1950) gave me a basis for understanding the double-talk that permeates cult thinking. ("Do what thou wilt is the only law," really means complete sexual license for a few adults. A child who speaks the truth about what is happening is told she is "lying," "talking crazy," and "cruising for a bruising.") . . .

I may have felt unhampered in my reading as a child, but the truth is that children's libraries are not, and perhaps never should be, totally free of censorship. The distinction between "book selection" and "censorship" is primarily semantic. We all know of books that we would never put in a grade school library or read out loud to children. Wise choices must be made that take into account their interests and developmental needs. Most five-year-olds, for instance, are not ready to handle the scary stories that so delight middle graders.

The real question is: On what basis will we make our choices? *14* Will we limit children's access to information out of fear of angering one group or another? Should we try to keep controversy out of the library? Can reading about witches, magic, and demons really hurt children? . . .

Halloween is a time when small groups of perverts enact black *15* masses—where truly horrible things are done—but it is much more. It is the eve of All Saints' Day, an important Christian holiday, and Mexico's *los Días de los Muertos*, when loved ones who have died are honored with flowers and *ofrendas*. For most children, Halloween is a time of parties, laughter, and fun. And for getting scared and practicing being brave.

Satanists don't own Halloween any more than Hallmark owns *16* Mother's Day. How we choose to celebrate—or not—is what counts. . . .

If we kick out all the witches, we would lose Donna Jo Napoli's *17* *Magic Circle* (Dutton, 1993), and with it the most moving description of the state of grace I have yet to see in children's literature. We would lose, too, Monica Furlong's intelligent and moral portrayal of both good and evil practitioners of England's pre-Christian religion in *Wise Child* (Knopf, 1987).

If we ban the mention of satan from young adult collections, we *18* would lose Otfried Preussler's *The Satanic Mill* (Macmillan, 1991). This cautionary fantasy shows a young man's seduction into the "dark arts." It also shows how evil eventually enslaves him and how he breaks free, once again through the power of love.

If we fear even the depiction of controversy, we miss *Save Hal-* *19* *loween!* (Morrow, 1993) by Stephanie Tolan. In the story, a community is polarized when the daughter of an evangelical minister is asked by her teacher to write a class play on the history of Halloween. Tolan treats all of her characters with respect, and shows, in the end, that in our pluralistic society we can accommodate different viewpoints while preserving individual rights.

Certainly we must respect the very different backgrounds and *20* beliefs of the families we serve. In most cases, we can accomplish this by encouraging parents to be involved in their own child's reading choices and by discussing books with children as they read.

But if we let every parent remove any book that offends, our li- *21* braries will quickly be stripped of their worth. This was brought

home to me recently when a father complained about a book he
had been reading to his daughter.

"How can you recommend this for children?" he demanded. *22*
"Halfway through, the girl gets down on her knees and prays to
God. I don't want my children exposed to that garbage!"

The book this parent found so offensive was *Heidi*. *23*

Reading to Improve Writing. Discuss the following questions
about "Satan in the Library: Are Children in Danger?" with your
classmates.

1. How does Ellison feel about removing books related to satanism,
    Halloween, and magic from children's libraries?

    _____

    _____

    _____

2. What reasons does Ellison give to support her position?

    _____

    _____

    _____

3. Why does Ellison tell us about her own experiences with satanism
    as a child?

    _____

    _____

    _____

4. Do you think the writer's argument is effective? Explain.

    _____

    _____

    _____

Collecting New Words. Try to determine the meanings of the following words from the way they're used in "Satan in the Library: Are Children in Danger?" Then verify their meanings by checking a dictionary.

occult (1)   _____

indoctrination (4) _____

inherently (4)   _____

omnipresent (4)   _____

breach (5)   _____

benevolent (9)   _____

tenacious (11)   _____

semantic (13)   _____

pluralistic (19)   _____

Gathering Ideas about Free Expression in Schools. In your journal, gather ideas about free expression in schools. Use the following questions to stimulate your ideas:

1. Should students be taught sex education? If so, what type of sex education would be most appropriate?
2. Should certain books be banned from school libraries? If so, which books?
3. Should certain types of clothing be banned from school? If so, which types of clothing?
4. Should school newspapers be censored? If so, what type of coverage should be affected?
5. Should students be allowed to protest school policies they disagree with? Is there any type of protest that should be banned? ❏

One student, Regina, freewrote about wearing uniforms in public schools. Here's a sample of her freewriting:

A lot of people might disagree with me, but I think uniforms should be worn in high school. When I was in parochial school, we had to wear uniforms, and it really cut down on peer pressure and made you pay more attention to your grades. Plus we saved money because we didn't spend so much on clothes. I know some kids will say that they won't be able to express themselves with their clothing if they wear uniforms, but they can wear whatever they want outside of school. I think wearing uniforms would make schools more focused on academics.

Put your writing on free expression in schools aside for now. You want to gather ideas about another aspect of free expression.

Free Expression in the Media

One of the most controversial issues in the United States today is expression in the media. An increasing number of television shows and movies depict graphic violence, contain sexually oriented material, and use obscene language. To some viewers, violence, sex, and obscene language make the shows more realistic; other viewers argue that such portrayals are unnecessary and potentially harmful.

The music industry is also involved in the free expression controversy. Some popular song lyrics contain prejudiced language. Michael Jackson rewrote the words to one song because they were insulting to Jews. Other songs describe, and even advocate, violent acts against women and other groups of people. Should these songs be banned? Tipper Gore expresses her opinion on the issue in "Curbing the Sexploitation Industry."

TIPPER GORE

Curbing the Sexploitation Industry

I can't even count the times in the last three years, since I began   *1*
to express my concern about violence and sexuality in rock music, that I have been called a prude, a censor, a music hater, even a book burner. So let me be perfectly clear: I detest censorship. I'm not advocating censorship but rather a candid and vigorous debate about the dangers posed for our children by what I call the "sexploitation industry."

We don't need to put a childproof cap on the world, but we do   *2*
need to remind the nation that children live in it, too, and deserve respect and sensitive treatment.

When I launched this campaign in 1985 (long before my hus-   *3*
band dreamed of running for president), I went to the source of the

problem, sharing my concerns and proposals with the entertainment industry. Many producers were sympathetic. Some cooperated with my efforts. But others have been overtly hostile, accusing me of censorship and suggesting, unfairly, that my motives are political.

This resistance and hostility has convinced me of the need for a   4
two-pronged campaign, with equal effort from the entertainment industry and concerned parents. Entertainment producers must take the first step, by labeling sexually explicit material.

But the industry cannot be expected to solve the problem on its   5
own. Parents should encourage producers to cooperate and praise them when they do. Producers need to know that parents are aware of the issue and are reading their advisory labels. Above all, they need to know that somebody out there cares, that the community at large is not apathetic about the deep and lasting damage being done to our children.

What's at issue is not the occasional sexy rock lyric. What trou-   6
bles—indeed, outrages—me is far more vicious: a celebration of the most gruesome violence, coupled with the explicit message that sado-masochism is the essence of sex.

We're surrounded by examples—in rock lyrics, on television, at   7
the movies and in rental videos. One major TV network recently aired a preview of a soap opera rape scene during a morning game show.

The newest craze in horror movies is something called the "teen   8
slasher" film, and it typically depicts the killing, torture and sexual mutilation of women in sickening detail. Several rock groups now simulate sexual torture and murder during live performances. Others titillate youthful audiences with strippers confined in cages on stage and with half-naked dancers, who often act out sex with band members. Sexual brutality has become the common currency of America's youth culture and with it the pervasive degradation of women.

Why is this graphic violence dangerous? It's especially damaging   9
for young children because they lack the moral judgment of adults. Many children are only dimly aware of the consequences of their actions, and, as parents know, they are excellent mimics. They often imitate violence they see on TV, without necessarily understanding what they are doing or what the consequences might be.

One 5-year-old boy from Boston recently got up from watching   10
a teen slasher film and stabbed a 2-year-old girl with a butcher knife. He didn't mean to kill her (and luckily he did not). He was just imitating the man in the video.

Nor does the danger end as children grow older. National health   11
officials tell us that children younger than teen-agers are apt to react to excessive violence with suicide, satanism, drug and alcohol abuse. Even grown-ups are not immune. One series of studies by re-

searchers at the University of Wisconsin found that men exposed to films in which women are beaten, butchered, maimed and raped were significantly desensitized to the violence. Not only did they express less sympathy for the victims, they even approved of lesser penalties in hypothetical rape trials.

Sado-masochistic pornography is a kind of poison. Like most poisons, it probably cannot be totally eliminated, but it certainly could be labeled for what it is and be kept away from those who are most vulnerable.   *12*

The largest record companies have agreed to this—in principle at least. In November 1985, the Recording Industry Association of America adopted my proposal to alert parents by having producers either put warning labels on records with explicit sexual lyrics or display the lyrics on the outside of the record jackets. Since then, some companies have complied in good faith, although others have not complied at all.   *13*

This is where we parents must step in. We must let the industry know we're angry. We must press for uniform voluntary compliance with labeling guidelines. And we must take an active interest at home in what our children are watching and listening to. After all, we can hardly expect that the labels or printed lyrics alone will discourage young consumers.   *14*

Some parents may want to write to the record companies. Others can give their support to groups like the Parent Teacher Association, which have endorsed the labeling idea. All of us can use our purchasing power. We have more power than we think, and we must use it. For the sake of our children, we simply can't afford to slip back into apathy.   *15*

My concern for the health and welfare of children has nothing to do with politics: It is addressed to conservatives and liberals alike. Some civil libertarians believe it is wrong even to raise these questions—just as some conservatives believe that the government should police popular American culture. I reject both these views. I have no desire to restrain artists or cast a "chill" over popular culture. But I believe parents have First Amendment rights, too.   *16*

The fate of the family, the dignity of women, the mental health of children—these concerns belong to everyone. We must protect our children with choice, not censorship. Let's start working in our communities to forge a moral consensus for the 1990s. Children need our help, and we must summon the courage to examine the culture that shapes their lives.   *17*

ACTIVITY
5

Reading to Improve Writing. Discuss the following questions about "Curbing the Sexploitation Industry" with your classmates.

1. How does Gore suggest the "sexploitation industry" be curbed?

   _____

   _____

   _____

2. In Gore's view, why is curbing the "sexploitation industry" necessary?

   _____

   _____

   _____

3. How does Gore respond to people who disagree with her suggestions for curbing the "sexploitation industry"?

   _____

   _____

   _____

4. Do you find Gore's argument effective? Explain. _____

   _____

   _____

Collecting New Words. Try to determine the meanings of the following words from the way they're used in "Curbing the Sexploitation Industry." Then verify their meanings by checking a dictionary.

ACTIVITY

6

two-pronged (4)   _____

explicit (4)   _____

apathetic (5)   _____

sado-masochism (6) _____

simulate (8)   _____

degradation (8)   _____

complied (13)   _____

consensus (17)   _____

ACTIVITY

7

Gathering Ideas about Free Expression in the Media. In your journal, gather ideas about free expression in the media. Use the following questions to stimulate your ideas:

1. Should there be any attempt to regulate sex and violence in the media? Why or why not?
2. How effective is the rating system used for movies and videos? What changes in the system, if any, do you suggest?
3. How effective are warning labels on television shows and CDs? What changes in the labeling system, if any, do you suggest?
4. Should there be less violence and sexual content in shows aimed at young children? Explain your position.
5. Are magazines and newspapers containing sexual material too accessible to children? If so, what can be done to limit their accessibility?   ❏

Here's how one student, Toraino, brainstormed about violence in movies:

slit throats

assault rifles

blood

brains spilling

sometimes this is life

who takes it seriously

why take it seriously

kids in the movie theater

ratings not enforced

parents should be more responsible

Put your ideas about free expression in the media aside for now so you can gather ideas about one more aspect of freedom of expression.

Free Expression on the Internet

Computer technology has introduced a new player in the debate over the limits of free expression. Some popular video games, for example, contain violent material—bloody battles, sadistic villains, mutilated bodies—that some experts fear may encourage children to perform violent acts. Social scientists report that children who spend hours playing violent video games may be more prone to violence than children who do not play the games.

Most recently, the Internet has become part of the free expression controversy. The Internet consists of thousands of computer networks accessible to anyone—including children—with a computer and a modem. Some users have introduced sexually explicit material, including pornography, onto the Internet. While some people believe the government should regulate the Internet, others view government regulation as an infringement of free expression. The following editorial from *USA Today*, "Use Existing Laws to Rid the Internet of Obscenities," debates the issue.

USA TODAY

Use Existing Laws to Rid the Internet of Obscenities

There's some strange stuff on the Internet, that bit of cyberspace linking together tens of millions of computer users worldwide. *1*

Sick fantasy stories of rape, mutilation and murder using the names of real people. *2*

Pictures of toddlers having sex with adults. *3*

Adults sending sexually suggestive messages to teens, seeking to lure them on dates. *4*

Legislators, most recently Sen. James Exon, D-Neb., have pounced on these tales and are rushing to protect the young. Exon wants to impose fines of up to $100,000 and jail terms of up to two years for any obscene, indecent or harassing use of any telecommunications devices. *5*

The problem: The bill ignores the reality of cyberspace and applies to it laws meant for TV and telephones. It won't work. It would turn the core of the information superhighway into a pedestrian walkway, in the process trampling free speech and privacy rights in the dirt. *6*

The Internet is simply too different a means of communication. *7*

Like TV viewers, Internet users can surf through programs. There, they can find health information, political discussions, legal help and a host of other topics, including sex. *8*

But like telephone users, they also can directly interact with others. They can do so in groups or more privately by person-to-person messages. They can be readers. Or they can be publishers. It's up to them. *9*

With millions of users and private e-mail addresses and tens of thousands of discussion groups, enforcing stringent decency standards would be impossible. It would require on-line service *10* providers, through which users enter the Internet, to constantly snoop in their customers' business.

That's no good. And it's not needed. 11

Kiddie porn, adult solicitation of minors, stalking and harass- 12 ment already are as illegal in cyberspace as anyplace else. And police are cracking down hard.

Ask Jake Baker, a 20-year-old University of Michigan student. 13 He faces trial April 3. His crime: writing a gross tale of rape, using a fellow student's name as the victim, which he sent to an Internet queue. That, federal authorities say, amounts to a threat.

Or ask Lt. William Baker, a Jefferson County, Ky., police officer. 14 Last year he spent 2½ months tracking down a secretive kiddie porn purveyor to a university in England. He was arrested by British police.

A new law won't protect kids any better. It may only instill a 15 false sense of security. Parents can do better by themselves, without infringing on anyone's freedom.

On-line companies are giving parents the ability to block their 16 children's access to queues in which adult material might appear and to prevent youngsters from sending and receiving messages.

Parents can set rules, telling kids never to give out their name, 17 phone number or address over the computer and never to arrange a meeting with a computer friend.

On the sometimes accident-prone information highway, parents 18 can keep their kids safe far better than any law can.

ACTIVITY
8

Reading to Improve Writing. Discuss the following questions about "Use Existing Laws to Rid the Internet of Obscenities" with your classmates.

1. According to the editors of *USA Today*, who should regulate the Internet?

   _____

   _____

   _____

2. What is the strongest argument made in the editorial? _____

   _____

   _____

   _____

3. What is the weakest argument made in the editorial? _____

_____

_____

4. Were you persuaded by the editorial? Why or why not?

_____

_____

_____

Collecting New Words. Try to determine the meanings of the following words from the way they're used in "Use Existing Laws to Rid the Internet of Obscenities." Then verify their meanings by checking a dictionary.

ACTIVITY
9

cyberspace (1)   _____

harassing (5)   _____

surf (8)   _____

stringent (10)   _____

solicitation (12)   _____

queue (13)   _____

purveyor (14)   _____

infringing (15)   _____

Gathering Ideas about Free Expression on the Internet. In your journal, gather ideas about free expression on the Internet. Use the following questions to stimulate your thinking:

ACTIVITY
10

1. Should the government regulate the Internet? Explain your position.
2. Is it possible to regulate material on the Internet? If so, explain your ideas on regulation.

3. How can parents control what their children encounter on the Internet?

4. In addition to sexually explicit material, what other harmful material can appear on the Internet? What actions, if any, should be taken to prevent this material from appearing?   ❏

One student, Betty, decided to interview other students on the class electronic bulletin board about pornography on the Internet. She posted the following question: "Is there too much pornography on the Internet? If so, what should be done about it?" Here is how some of her classmates responded:

Sam: There's some really gross stuff out there. I'm sure some of it's illegal. I think there should be some censoring of the really bad stuff.

Angelica: I think too much emphasis is put on pornography. There's some, but the topic has been sensationalized way too much. People should pay more attention to what makes people say some of those things to each other. I mean, there's a lot of hate language, and people threatening violence against others or telling how to make bombs. Just telling people not to do something doesn't get to the root of the problem.

Beth: Really, only parents can police some of the bad stuff. No law is going to make a difference.

Drafting

You have now gathered ideas about free expression in the schools, in the media, and on the Internet. You have a rich source of material to draw on. At this point, you must decide how to proceed.

- You may select just one of these topics for your discovery draft.

- You may write drafts on two or three of these topics to see which you would prefer to continue working on.

- You may combine your discovery draft ideas into a new topic for your essay.

Because your essay will be persuasive, select a topic about which you have an opinion.

Before you begin writing your discovery draft, narrow your topic and write a preliminary thesis statement. As you write, follow your train of thought, even if it means revising your thesis statement later on. Keep your audience and purpose in mind, but remember that your main goal at the drafting stage is to get your ideas down on paper. You'll have time later on to revise and edit your discovery draft.

Here's a discovery draft written by a student, Regina Case, on uniforms in public schools. After reading the draft, discuss with your classmates what Regina might do to revise it. (Note that the example includes the types of errors that typically appear in a first draft.)

Uniforms in Public Schools:

The Time Is Right

The Constitution of the United States guarantees freedom of expression. *1* However, sometimes we have to sacrifice freedom of expression for the sake of the good of society. School uniforms are no exception.

Students who wear revealing clothing distract other students. Both boys *2* and girls like to wear tight clothes. Girls wear short skirts, and boys wear sleeveless shirts. Obviously they have something other than studying on their mind. Even studious students get distracted when someone wearing revealing clothing comes into the room.

All schools are having problems with gang violence. Because of gangs, *3* it's not safe anymore to wear certain colors or types of clothes in school. At my high school, a boy was stabbed for wearing the wrong kind of baseball cap. We have a choice: either we adopt school uniforms or we continue to have violence in our schools.

Everyone knows that in high school, peer pressure is intense. A big part *4* of peer pressure is the clothes you wear. Some of the most popular clothing is also the most expensive. If everyone wore uniforms, then everyone would be more equal.

For these reasons, school uniforms should be required. Sometimes sac- *5* rificing freedom of expression is necessary in order to improve an important part of our lives—education.

> **COMPUTER TIP**
> **ADD FIRST, THEN DELETE**
> During the drafting stage of your writing process, when you aim to produce as many ideas as you can, make use of the "add" or "insert" function of your word-processing program. Later on, during revision, use the "delete" function to omit irrelevant material.

Revising

When you revise your draft, use the skills you acquired in the preceding chapters. Support and clarify your main ideas, organize your paragraphs, make your ideas flow smoothly, and write an effective introduction, conclusion, and title. Also, consider conducting primary or secondary research to gather more information about your topic.

In this chapter, you'll focus on writing a persuasive argument. You'll learn how to make an argumentative claim, develop reasons to support that claim, respond to opposing arguments, organize your points, and avoid faulty logic.

Making a Claim

A *claim* is a statement asserting that something is true. In persuasive writing, a claim is a type of thesis statement. As you may recall from Chapter Three, the thesis announces your topic and tells why the topic is important to you. In an argument, however, your claim or thesis announces your topic and conveys your views or position on the topic.

An effective claim has these characteristics:

- It expresses an opinion.
- It relates to your readers' lives.
- It is focused.

Let's look at each of these qualities in more detail.

Express an Opinion. An effective claim expresses an opinion, not a fact. An opinion is an idea that some but not all people share. In contrast, a fact is something that can be verified as true by an objective observer.

FACT

There is a rating system for movies.

OPINION

Because it's not uniformly enforced, the rating system for movies should be changed.

The first statement can be verified by checking advertisements for movies. There's no need to prove that it's true. The second statement, however, is a claim because some people will disagree with it. Notice that the claim includes the word *should*. Similar words used in claims include *needs to, ought,* and *must*.

Be Persuasive. An effective claim also seeks to persuade readers by pointing out how the topic relates to their lives. A claim that conveys only your personal interests, tastes, or experiences is not likely to persuade or interest readers. Rather, connect the claim to some aspect of your readers' lives.

PERSONAL

Protesters should never burn the American flag because it means so much to me.

PERSUASIVE

Because the American flag symbolizes what this country stands for, it should be illegal to burn it in protest.

The first statement focuses on the writer. But the second statement relates the topic—burning the American flag—to a concept relevant to readers' lives.

Narrow the Focus. An effective claim focuses the topic so that it can be fully developed and supported. If your claim isn't sufficiently focused, you won't be able to discuss it in detail in your essay.

UNFOCUSED

There's too much violence on television.

FOCUSED

The excessive use of guns on *Cops and Gangs* glamorizes a deadly use of force.

To support the claim made in the first example, you would have to cover all types of violence on all types of television shows—a topic better suited for a book than an essay. The second claim requires only that you focus on one type of violence—the use of guns—on one television show—*Cops and Gangs*. Because it's better focused, this claim could be fully supported in an essay.

In addition, a focused claim does not leave readers with unanswered questions.

UNFOCUSED

Pornography should be banned.

FOCUSED

To stop the growth of child pornography, Congress should pass a law banning child pornography on the Internet.

In the first example, readers might ask: "What type of pornography? How should it be banned? Why should it be banned?" In the second, readers are told the type of pornography, how it could be banned (through federal legislation), and why it should be banned.

Revising Claims. Working in a group of several students, review the three parts of an effective claim. Then determine what's at fault in each of the following claims. Finally, revise each claim accordingly.

GROUP
ACTIVITY
11

1. On the Internet you can find information on how to build a bomb.

Fault(s): _____

Revision: _____

_____

_____

2. Because of the First Amendment, we shouldn't attempt to regulate violence on television.

Fault(s): _____

Revision: _____

_____

_____

3. Certain radio shows should be censored.

Fault(s): _____

Revision: _____

_____

_____

4. Some high school newspapers advertise events that minors are not allowed to attend.

Fault(s): _____

Revision: _____

_____

_____

5. I believe in total freedom of expression.

Fault(s): _____

Revision: _____

_____

_____

ACTIVITY
12

Revising Your Claim. Revise the claim for your essay so that it expresses an opinion, relates to your readers' lives, and is sufficiently focused. ❏

Generating Pro Points

Once you have an effective claim, you need to concentrate on developing support for that claim—your reasons or *pro points* (*pro* means "in favor of"). Pro points tell readers *why* you believe your claim is true or valid. You develop pro points from three sources: your experience, observation, and research.

From Experience. When trying to persuade others, we often look first to our own experience with the topic. This is what Kerry Leigh Ellison does in the reading, "Satan in the Library: Are Children in Danger?" when she describes her childhood experiences with satanism.

Suppose, for example, that you're writing about violent and obscene lyrics in rock music and that you believe the lyrics are harmless because listeners tend to focus on the music, not the words. This is true for you and for many of your friends. Thus, you have one pro point:

> Because most listeners focus on the music, not the lyrics, violent or obscene lyrics don't have a negative impact in rock music.

How would you support this pro point? You could detail your own experiences with music. For instance, you could point out that you can't remember the lyrics to your favorite song. However, keep in mind that what might be true for you may not be true for others. In addition to describing your own experiences, then, you might conduct a survey to obtain the opinions of others or do some other research on the topic.

From Observation. It may be that you have no personal experience with an issue that concerns you but that you've observed how it affects others. In this case, you may base your pro points on observation, as Tipper Gore does in "Curbing the Sexploitation Industry." Her argument is based on her observations of the music her children enjoy.

Imagine, for instance, that you're arguing against censoring literature in high schools. Books weren't censored in your high school, but your niece attends a school that has banned several classics, including Steinbeck's *Of Mice and Men* and Orwell's *1984*. Because she is unable to study these books in school, she will be less well prepared for her college entrance exams. From observing your niece's experiences, you generate this pro point:

> Censoring important works of literature can limit students' opportunities in higher education.

You can support this point by describing your niece's experience with censorship. However, what happened to your niece might not happen to everyone. Thus, to strengthen your case, you could interview other students about their experiences with censorship or conduct secondary research to collect facts and statistics that support your position.

From Research. To learn more about your topic, you can conduct primary or secondary research. The authors of "Use Existing Laws to Rid the Internet of Obscenities" researched how pornography on the Internet is being prosecuted to argue against regulation.

Say you're also arguing against government censorship of material on the Internet. You might research software programs that prevent a computer from accessing places on the Internet containing sexual material. From your research, you generate the following pro point:

> Rather than have the government censor the Internet, let computer owners censor whatever material they find obscene.

To support this pro point, you could describe the software program that individuals can purchase to prevent certain material from being loaded onto their computer.

GROUP
ACTIVITY
13

Generating Pro Points. Working in a group, generate pro points from experience, observation, and research for each claim that follows.

1. Claim: The excessive violence in cartoons and children's television shows can make children become overly aggressive.

Pro points from experience: _____

_____

_____

Pro points from observation: _____

_____

_____

Pro points from research: _____

_____

_____

2. Claim: Sex education courses should focus on teaching abstinence, not on teaching "safer sex."

    Pro points from experience: _____

    _____

    _____

    Pro points from observation: _____

    _____

    _____

    Pro points from research: _____

    _____

    _____

3. Claim: Dress codes in high school can do more harm than good.

    Pro points from experience: _____

    _____

    _____

    Pro points from observation: _____

    _____

    _____

    Pro points from research: _____

    _____

    _____

COMPUTER TIP

GENERATE PRO POINTS

If you have a classroom electronic messaging system, you can post your claim and ask fellow students to add pro points in support of it. Refer to your classmates' ideas when revising your essay.

Generating Pro Points for Your Claim. Develop several pro points in support of the claim you make about free expression in your draft. Draw on your experience, observation, and (if you wish) primary or secondary research. ❑

ACTIVITY
14

Supporting Pro Points

You support pro points with the same techniques used to support a thesis statement: examples, comparison-contrast, process analysis, definition, classification, facts, statistics, and expert testimony. Not all supporting material is equally effective, though. The best supporting information is recent, relevant, and easily understood by readers.

Use Recent Material. Since you're probably writing about a current topic related to free expression, be sure to use supporting material that is up-to-date. By using recent material, you show your readers you're knowledgeable about the topic.

Keep in mind that your own experiences might be dated. If you're arguing for dress codes in high schools, use your own experiences only if you're a recent high school graduate (within the last couple of years). If you're discussing the burning of the American flag, find out about the last Supreme Court ruling on the issue. If your topic concerns the Internet, make a point of obtaining current information about that rapidly changing technology.

Use Relevant Material. The material you use to support your pro points must be directly related to your topic. If your research isn't relevant, your readers will easily dismiss it. Thus, for example, if your topic is the banning of cigarette advertisements, don't use advertisements for cigars or chewing tobacco as supporting material. Similarly, in an essay about censoring music lyrics, you would not use information about censoring books.

Use Understandable Material. Remember that you probably know more about your topic than your readers do. You may need to explain the plot of a book, the meaning of a term, or the lyrics of a song to readers who lack your familiarity with the subject. Consider finding more understandable material to support your points if your explanation becomes too long and detailed.

GROUP
ACTIVITY
15

Evaluating Supporting Material. Working in a group, examine the claim and determine whether the supporting material given for it is up-to-date, relevant, and easily understandable.

Claim: The current rating system for movies needs to be improved.

1. More and more television shows are showing scenes of graphic violence.

2. Owners of movie theaters are reluctant to enforce the current rating system.
3. In 1988, half of all profitable movies contained sexually oriented material.
4. The profit margin for "R" rated movies is almost 2¼ of all movies when aggregated.
5. When I sold movie tickets, I almost never checked people's IDs.
6. Movie producers avoid the "R" rating by making two versions of the same movie: a milder version for movie theaters, and a more "hard-core" version for video stores.

Evaluating Your Supporting Material. Evaluate the supporting material in your draft. Is it recent, relevant, and easily understood? Make any necessary changes to improve it. ❑

ACTIVITY
16

Responding to Con Points

An argumentative essay is most persuasive when you anticipate readers' objections and argue against them. Therefore, in addition to presenting pro points, you need to argue against the *con points* (*con* means "against").

List Con Points. First, you need to identify the most important con points. To do this, imagine that you disagree with your claim, and then think of reasons why you disagree with it.

Suppose that this is your claim:

Sex education should focus primarily on abstinence, not on contraception or "safer sex."

Now, imagine that you *disagree* with this claim—that you think sex education should focus on contraception and sexually transmitted diseases. Here are two arguments against this claim:

1. Many teenagers will have sex, no matter how often they're told to be abstinent.
2. Information about contraception and sexually transmitted diseases can prevent the tragedies of unwanted pregnancy and death from AIDS.

These are your con points—the points against the claim you make. You don't have to list all con points, just the most important ones. Depending on your topic, you might end up with two or three con points.

ACTIVITY
17

Listing Con Points. For each of the following claims, list two con points.

1. English should be designated the official language of the United States.

    Con: _____

    _____

    _____

    Con: _____

    _____

    _____

2. Dress codes in high schools unfairly restrict students' right to express themselves through their choice of clothing.

    Con: _____

    _____

    _____

    Con: _____

    _____

    _____

3. An amendment to the Constitution should ban burning the American flag in protest.

    Con: _____

    _____

    _____

    Con: _____

    _____

    _____

Listing Con Points for Your Claim. Read your claim to the students in your group. Ask those who disagree (or who pretend to disagree) with your claim to explain their views on the topic. Use their responses to list several con points for your claim.

GROUP
ACTIVITY
18

Your claim: _____

_____

_____

Con: _____

_____

_____

Con: _____

_____

_____

Con: _____

_____

_____

❏

Refute Con Points. To *refute* means to argue against something. In your essay, you want to refute or argue against the con points in order to convince readers to accept your claim. To refute a con point, acknowledge what, if anything, is true about the con point, and then explain what you think is not true about it.

Let's return to the essay on sex education. This is your claim:

Sex education should focus primarily on abstinence, not on contraception or "safer sex."

Here's your first con point:

Many teenagers will have sex, no matter how often they're told to be abstinent.

Now, here's what you can say to refute, or argue against, this point:

It's true that we can't prevent *all* teenagers from having sex. But as

COMPUTER TIP

GENERATE CON POINTS

If you have a classroom electronic messaging system, you can post your claim and ask students to list con points. Refer to this list when revising your essay.

more and more teenagers understand the benefits of abstinence, more and more of them will be willing to wait to have sex.

Notice that you first point out what is right about the con point—"we can't prevent *all* teenagers from having sex." Then, you express what you think is wrong about the con point.

Here's your second con point:

Information about contraception and sexually transmitted diseases can prevent the tragedies of unwanted pregnancy and death from AIDS.

Here's one way to refute this con point:

Information about contraception and sexually transmitted diseases is appropriate for mature couples. However, teenagers are so impressionable that they interpret this information to mean that having sex is acceptable.

Again, notice that you point out what's right about the con point—that the information is appropriate for mature couples—before stating what's wrong with it.

GROUP
ACTIVITY
19

Debating. Working in a group, debate an issue related to freedom of expression. Follow these guidelines for organizing the debate and using pro and con points:

1. Choose a topic and make a claim. Here are some examples:

   • Rock lyrics should/should not be censored.

   • Advertisements for smoking should/should not be banned.

   • Sex education should/should not teach contraception and "safer sex."

   • Burning the American flag should/should not be illegal.

2. Elect a moderator.
3. Divide the group into two sides—a pro side (students in favor of the claim) and a con side (students against the claim).
4. Allow each side ten minutes to brainstorm reasons to support its position.
5. The moderator chooses a student on the pro side to state a pro point in support of the claim.
6. A volunteer on the con side refutes this pro point.
7. Another student on the pro side states a pro point in support of the claim.
8. Another student on the con side refutes this pro point.
9. This interchange continues until everyone on both sides of the debate has had the opportunity to participate.

Refuting Your Con Points. Return to the list of con points for your essay generated in Activity 18. Refute each con point in the space provided here.

ACTIVITY
20

1. Con point: _____

   _____

   Argument against the con: _____

   _____

   _____

2. Con point: _____

   _____

   Argument against the con: _____

   _____

   _____

3. Con point: _____

   _____

   Argument against the con: _____

   _____

   _____

COMPUTER TIP

DEBATE ON A COMPUTER

If your class has access to a computer terminal that is available to all students, hold a debate. Identify your claim and one pro point. Leave the screen on. When it's convenient, other students can read what you have posted and add a pro point, add a con point, or refute a con point.

If you're in a class where students are on-line simultaneously, carry on a debate similar to the one outlined in Activity 19. An on-line debate can give you the opportunity to think about your pro and con points before you debate them with others.

Organizing Pro and Con Points

Imagine how your readers will likely react to your pro and con points as they read your essay from beginning to end. Will they become less convinced as they read along, and if so, how can you better persuade them to accept your claim? The order of your pro and con points is crucial.

Order Pro Points. It will happen that some of your pro points will be more persuasive than others. Decide which one is the most convincing, the next most convincing, and so on.

How do you make this decision? Here are some suggestions:

- A pro point is convincing when it applies to a large number of people or situations.

- A pro point is convincing when you can support it thoroughly and logically.

- Your most convincing pro point is usually your longest one. For example, you might write two paragraphs about it, whereas each of your other pro points may be discussed in a single paragraph.

Save your most convincing pro point for last so that you leave readers thinking about it. You might begin a paper with the least convincing pro point and slowly build up to the most convincing one. Or, you might begin with the second most convincing point, save the less convincing points for the middle, and end with the most convincing one.

GROUP
ACTIVITY
21

Examining the Order of Pro Points. Working in a group, examine the order of the pro points in "Satan in the Library," "Curbing the Sexploitation Industry," or "Use Existing Laws to Rid the Internet of Obscenities." List the pro points in the order in which they're given. How effective is that order?

GROUP
ACTIVITY
22

Ranking Your Pro Points. Read your pro points to the students in your group. Also explain how you plan to support each pro point. Ask the group to rank your pro points from least to most persuasive. Keep the rankings in mind when you order the points of your essay during revision.   ❑

Arrange Con Points. Where should you put the con points in your essay? You have several options.

You can put con points at different spots in an essay, particularly when certain con points are closely connected to certain pro points. This pattern can help make the pro and con points flow smoothly in an essay. Here's an example of this pattern:

CLAIM

Sex education should discuss "safer sex."

Some people believe that talking about "safer sex" encourages teenagers to have sex [*con point*]. In fact, talking about "safer sex" can make teenagers less likely to have sex [*argument against the con point*]. If they pause to take precautions, they might think about the consequences of their actions. Thus, it's possible that "safer sex" can result in "less sex" [*pro point*].

You can also begin an essay with the con points. After refuting them, you give your pro points. Kerry Leigh Ellison uses this strategy in "Satan in the Library." She begins by describing the dangers of satanism (the con points), and then goes on to say that censorship won't stop these dangers (the pro points).

Finally, you can save your con points until the end of the essay, but only when you can refute those points well. You don't want readers to finish your essay agreeing with the opposition. In "Curbing the Sexploitation Industry," Tipper Gore saves her con points until the second to the last paragraph (16), where she writes: "I have no desire to restrain artists or cast a 'chill' over popular culture. But I believe parents have First Amendment rights, too." In other words, to those who claim that labeling rock music violates their freedom, Gore says concerned parents have rights as well. Because the idea of parental rights comes at the end of the essay, Gore's readers are sure to take it with them.

Ordering Pro and Con Points. Working in a group, review the following list of pro and con points from Regina's essay, "Uniforms in Public Schools: The Time Is Right." Then order the pro and con points in the most effective way, combining any points as needed. Finally, compare your group's ordering of the pro and con points with the order that Regina uses in her revised draft (pp. 355–357).

GROUP
ACTIVITY
23

CLAIM

• Uniforms should be worn in public high schools.

PRO POINTS

• Uniforms promote an academic environment.

• Uniforms can decrease gang violence because students are not permitted to wear gang-related clothing.

• Because all students wear the same outfit, poor students are not stereotyped by other students.

• Uniforms keep students from feeling pressured to wear the most trendy clothing.

• Uniforms are attractive, easy to take care of, and less expensive than regular clothes.

CON POINTS

• At least in the beginning, enforcement might be a problem if uniforms are not popular.

• Making students wear uniforms prevents them from expressing themselves through their clothing.

COMPUTER TIP
MOVE YOUR PRO AND CON POINTS
Use the "move" function of your word processor to create several different lists of your pro and con points. Compare the various lists to determine the most effective ordering of the points for your revised draft.

ACTIVITY
24

Ordering Your Pro and Con Points. Think about the pro and con points for your essay about freedom of expression. List your pro points in the order in which they should appear in your revised draft. Then decide where you can include your con points, and add them to your list.   ❑

Avoiding Faulty Logic

A persuasive essay makes sense to readers. An essay that is not persuasive usually is based on *faulty logic,* or flawed reasoning. Let's look at the five most common forms of faulty logic.

Hasty Generalization. A *hasty generalization* is a conclusion drawn from too little evidence. Suppose, for example, that you once had a bad experience dealing with a salesperson at a particular store. Based on that single experience, you conclude that all salespeople in that store are rude. Your conclusion, based on insufficient evidence (your one experience), would be a hasty generalization. Just because one salesperson was rude doesn't mean that all others are rude. One instance cannot prove a point.

Here's another example: you argue that violence in children's programming has no harmful effects because it didn't harm you as a child. Your conclusion is based on insufficient evidence (only one example). More convincing evidence would include studies conducted to determine the effects of television violence on children or surveys of children and their parents.

Slippery Slope. The term *slippery slope* is used to refer to an argument that claims one event inevitably led to (or will lead to) another event, without any evidence to support that claim. Suppose you argue that (1) if handguns are banned, (2) all guns will end up being banned and (3) the military could eventually take over the government. To support these claims, you would need to give evidence that (1) would lead to (2), and that (2) would lead to (3). Similarly, you could not argue that censorship of music lyrics will lead to censorship of movies, art, and television without providing logical evidence to support your claim.

Faulty Either-Or Reasoning. *Either-or reasoning* is faulty when it proposes only two possible alternatives even though more than two options actually exist. For instance, you would use faulty *either-or* reasoning if you said to yourself, "Either I lose ten pounds or I won't get a date." The reasoning is faulty because more than these two alternatives exist. You might get a date without losing any weight. Or you might lose ten pounds and still not get a date. Or you could lose five pounds and get several dates.

A writer who argues, "Either we regulate cigarette advertisements or more and more people will die from lung cancer," is using faulty logic because other alternatives also exist, such as efforts to decrease smoking through public service announcements and educational programs. Because of these efforts, fewer people might get lung cancer, whether or not cigarette advertising is regulated.

Faulty Cause-and-Effect Reasoning. *Faulty cause-and-effect reasoning* involves attributing an event to an unrelated cause. Superstitions are based on faulty cause-and-effect reasoning, such as when we blame the black cat that crossed our path, the salt we spilled, or the broken mirror we gazed into for a bad day. Logically, these events couldn't have caused the bad day because they were unrelated to what we experienced. Thus, we cannot assume that one event was caused by another event simply because one took place before the other.

Political candidates often use faulty cause-and-effect reasoning: "Since my opponent has been in the Senate, your taxes have increased." However, just because taxes went up after the senator was elected doesn't mean that the senator raised the taxes. Perhaps they were increased by the previous Congress. Similarly, an essay writer who argues, "Ever since certain types of music have become popular, violence against women has risen," fails to acknowledge other possible causes for the rise in violence against women. Unless the writer provides evidence to support this point, the argument is based on faulty cause-and-effect reasoning.

Biased, Unreliable, or Inexpert Sources. Suppose you want to argue that marijuana should be legalized. As part of your argument, you refer to your Uncle Jack, who has used marijuana for over twenty years and claims that it poses no health threats. Your Uncle Jack, however, is not an objective source because he's related to you. Also, he might not be a reliable source because he's used marijuana for too long. Finally, he's not an expert. An objective, reliable, and expert source on this topic would be a research scientist who has studied the effects of marijuana on people's health.

When you conduct research on a topic, be skeptical of studies that may be biased because of who funded them. Cigarette companies, for instance, have funded studies in which cigarettes were not found to cause cancer, in contrast to the numerous objective studies that conclude otherwise.

Labeling Faulty Logic. Identify the type of faulty logic in each of the following arguments.

ACTIVITY
25

1. My sister hates *The Simpsons*. Therefore, it's a bad show.

   Type of faulty logic: _____

2. If we let Jill get away with sloppy work, soon everyone will be doing sloppy work.

   Type of faulty logic: _____

3. Last semester I worked more than twenty hours a week and my grades were poor. Working more than twenty hours a week leads to poor grades.

   Type of faulty logic: _____

4. Either attend college or get a low-paying job.

   Type of faulty logic: _____

5. My cousin Jim, who plays fullback for State, says athletes make great students.

   Type of faulty logic: _____

6. If you don't buy Squishy peanut butter, your children will end up throwing their sandwiches away.

   Type of faulty logic: _____

7. Women can't be firefighters. I don't know any woman who has enough upper-body strength.

   Type of faulty logic: _____

ACTIVITY
26

Analyzing Faulty Logic. The following letter contains various types of faulty logic. First, determine the types of faulty logic it contains. Then revise the letter to eliminate the errors in reasoning.

Dear Mom and Dad,

   Hope you are doing well. I'm doing well, too, except that I'm tired of studying. In fact, I just heard someone at the union say that you can fail a test because you've studied too hard. I'll have to lay off for a while.

   I could really use a break! A couple of my friends are planning a rafting trip in Placido next weekend. But right now I'm broke. Last time I heard from you, you said I should get a job. I don't think that getting a job would be good for me. Everyone I know who has a job gets poor grades. After all, a few poor grades can lead to a low grade point average, which can keep me from getting a good job after graduation. I don't want that to happen to me.

Anyway, can you send some money so I can go on the rafting trip? A friend of Joe's who has a cousin who's a rafter who works at Placido says that Placido is one of the best places for rafting. It's a little expensive, though. What do you say?

I'm studying hard, but not too hard because I don't want to flunk any tests.

Love, Bart ❏

Regina's Revised Draft

Before you read Regina's revised draft, reread her discovery draft (p. 337). Notice, in particular, how her argument is stronger in the revision. (You will also notice some errors in the revised draft; these will be corrected when Regina edits her essay later on.)

Uniforms in Public Schools:

The Time Is Right

How can we improve public high schools? Many people have suggested hiring more teachers or changing course requirements. These changes might be helpful, but they also cost money. We need to consider another way to improve education, a way that many parochial schools have used for years. By requiring students to wear affordable, attractive uniforms to school, we can reduce gang violence, promote equality, decrease peer pressure, have a more academic environment, and save money.

Claim is more specific

The words "uniform" and "teenager" might not seem to go together. After all teenagers love to experiment with clothes as a part of expressing their identity. Freedom of expression is guaranteed in the Constitution. However, students who wear uniforms in school can still wear whatever they want after school. Teenagers also love to rebel, so it might be hard to make them wear uniforms at first. Enforcement would be less difficult if it's done consistently and firmly. Once students understand the benefits of uniforms, they'll be less likely to resist wearing them.

The con points are refuted

One of the benefits of having students wear uniforms is that it would reduce gang violence in schools. Unfortunately in many high schools students aren't safe from gangs. A big part of gang life is wearing a certain color or type of clothing to identify whos in the gang and whos not. Some students have been shot for accidently wearing the wrong color or type of clothing. If uniforms were mandatory, these deaths would be reduced. Gangs would be less likely to occupy high schools because members would be unable to identify themselves through their clothing.

A strong pro point comes first

Second pro point, supported by observations

Uniforms would also encourage equality among students. Right now, students who wear expensive clothing are viewed as rich, whereas students who wear cheap or secondhand clothing are considered poor. These perceptions can hurt student's self-esteem. Some students might work an after-school job to buy expensive clothing and, as a result, have less time to study.   *4*

Third pro point, supported by observations

Uniforms can also keep students from being to concerned with the latest fashions. Peer pressure in high school is tremendous. Students feel that if they don't wear the latest brand of shoe or the most fashionable type of pants, they'll be ostracized. Requiring uniforms can reduce this type of peer pressure, helping students focus on their studies.   *5*

Fourth pro point

In addition, uniforms would promote a more academic atmosphere. Because teenagers can be preoccupied with sex, some of them wear provocative clothing, such as revealing shirts, sleeveless T-shirts, or short skirts. This clothing can be very distracting. Sending the message that what counts is your body, not your brain. This doesn't happen in parochial schools, which have always required students to wear uniforms. According to one major study, parochial schools are more successful than public schools because they "maintain an environment that is more orderly, secure, and academically focused" (Traub 77). I believe that wearing uniforms contributes to this beneficial environment. The environment of public schools would change for the better if students were required to wear uniforms.   *6*

Secondary research is used as support

The fifth and strongest pro point is saved for last

Although the school uniform may be more modest than some of the clothing now worn by students, it need not be unattractive. Some of today's school uniforms are attractive and comfortable; they include knee-length skirts, button-down shirts, and chino slacks. Students could be provided with several different uniforms to choose from. These outfits would be easier to care for and less expensive than most of the clothing teenagers wear. In an interview, the chairman of the Ridgeford School District, Ms. Allison Keene, said that the district could contract out with private companies to make sure the cost of the uniforms was as inexpensive as possible. Students and their parents would save money, an important fact in these economic times.   *7*

Primary research is used as support

Conclusion restates the claim

Given the problems in public high schools, school uniforms are an idea whose time has come. Though the uniforms would not be popular at first, once students became accustomed to wearing them, they would see the quality of their education improve.   *8*

Works Cited

Keene, Allison. Personal interview. 6 May 1996.

Traub, James. "It's Elementary." *New Yorker* 17 July 1995: 74–79.

Analyzing Regina's Revised Draft. Use the following questions to analyze how Regina has improved her draft.

GROUP
ACTIVITY
27

1. Is Regina's claim more effective now? Why or why not?

_____

_____

_____

2. How has Regina improved her pro points? _____

_____

_____

_____

3. How effective are her con points? _____

_____

_____

_____

4. In your view, how well does she organize her pro and con points?

_____

_____

_____

5. What types of faulty logic has Regina eliminated in her revision?

_____

_____

_____

_____

6. How could Regina's revised draft benefit from further revision?

_____

_____

_____

GROUP
ACTIVITY
28

Using Peer Review. Form a group with two or three other students and exchange copies of your drafts. Read your draft aloud while your classmates follow along. Take notes on your classmates' responses to the following questions about your draft.

1. Have I followed all of the instructions for this assignment?

_____

_____

_____

2. How interesting is my introduction? Do you want to continue reading the paper? Why or why not?

_____

_____

_____

3. How effective is my claim? Suggest an improvement. _____

_____

_____

_____

4. What are my pro points? Are there any pro points I should add or delete?

_____

_____

_____

5. How well do I support my pro points? Is that supporting material recent, relevant, and easily understood?

_____

_____

_____

6. What are my con points? Are these the most important arguments against my claim?

_____

_____

_____

7. How well do I refute the con points? _____

_____

_____

_____

8. Are my pro and con points effectively organized? Can you suggest a better way to order them?

_____

_____

_____

9. Where in my draft should faulty logic be eliminated? _____

_____

_____

_____

10. What parts of my draft, if any, don't support my thesis and could be omitted? Are there any sentences or words that seem unnecessary?

_____

_____

_____

11. Where in the draft does my writing confuse you? How can I clarify my thoughts?

_____

_____

_____

12. How clear is the purpose of my essay? How well do I meet the needs of my audience?

_____

_____

_____

13. How effective is my ending? Do I conclude in such a way that you know it's the end?

_____

_____

_____

Revising Your Draft. Taking your classmates' suggestions for revision into consideration, revise your essay. In particular, focus on making your claim more specific, supporting your pro points, refuting your con points, and eliminating faulty logic. You might also decide to omit unnecessary material or to rearrange parts of your essay more effectively. ❑

Editing

At this point you have worked hard to persuade readers to accept your views on an issue related to freedom of expression. But before you can share your essay with your audience, you must edit it for correctness.

Regina's Edited Essay

You might have noticed that Regina's revised draft contained errors in grammar, spelling, and punctuation. Regina corrected these errors in her edited essay. Her corrections are underlined here. Her editing log follows her edited essay.

Uniforms in Public Schools:

The Time Is Right

How can we improve public high schools? Many people have suggested   *1*
hiring more teachers or changing course requirements. These changes might
be helpful, but they also cost money. We need to consider another way to improve education, a way that many parochial schools have used for years. By
requiring students to wear affordable, attractive uniforms to school, we can
reduce gang violence, promote equality, decrease peer pressure, have a
more academic environment, and save money.

The words "uniform" and "teenager" might not seem to go together.   *2*
After all, teenagers love to experiment with clothes as a part of expressing
their identity. Freedom of expression is guaranteed in the Constitution. However, students who wear uniforms in school can still wear whatever they want
after school. Teenagers also love to rebel, so it might be hard to make them
wear uniforms at first. Enforcement would be less difficult if it's done consistently and firmly. Once students understand the benefits of uniforms, they'll
be less likely to resist wearing them.

Uniforms would reduce gang violence in schools. Unfortunately, in many   *3*
high schools students aren't safe from gangs. A big part of gang life is wear-

ing a certain color or type of clothing to identify who's in the gang and who's not. Some students have been shot for accidently wearing the wrong color or type of clothing. If school uniforms were mandatory, these deaths would be reduced. Gangs would be less likely to occupy high schools because members would be unable to identify themselves through their clothing.

Uniforms would also encourage equality among students. Right now, students who wear expensive clothing are viewed as rich, whereas students who wear cheap or secondhand clothing are considered poor. These perceptions can hurt students' self-esteem. Some students might work an after-school job to buy expensive clothing and, as a result, have less time to study. 4

Uniforms can also keep students from being too concerned with the latest fashions. Peer pressure in high school is tremendous. Students feel that if they don't wear the latest brand of shoe or the most fashionable type of pants, they'll be ostracized. Requiring uniforms can reduce this type of peer pressure, helping students focus on their studies. 5

In addition, uniforms would promote a more academic atmosphere. Because teenagers can be preoccupied with sex, some of them wear provocative clothing, such as revealing shirts, sleeveless T-shirts, or short skirts. This clothing can be very distracting, sending the message that what counts is your body, not your brain. This doesn't happen in parochial schools, which have always required students to wear uniforms. According to one major study, parochial schools are more successful than public schools because they "maintain an environment that is more orderly, secure, and academically focused" (Traub 77). I believe that wearing uniforms contributes to this beneficial environment. The environment of public schools would change for the better if students were required to wear uniforms. 6

Although the school uniform may be more modest than some of the clothing now worn by students, it need not be unattractive. Some of today's school uniforms are attractive and comfortable; they include knee-length skirts, button-down shirts, and chino slacks. Students could be provided with several different uniforms to choose from. These outfits would be easier to care for and less expensive than most of the clothing teenagers wear. In an interview, the chairperson of the Ridgeford School District, Ms. Allison Keene, said that the district could contract out with private companies to make sure the cost of the uniforms was as inexpensive as possible. Students and their parents would save money, an important fact in these economic times. 7

Given the problems in public high schools, school uniforms are an idea   *8*
whose time has come. Though the uniforms would not be popular at first,
once students became accustomed to wearing them, they would see the
quality of their education improve.

Works Cited

Keene, Allison. Personal interview. 6 May 1996.

Traub, James. "It's Elementary." *New Yorker* 17 July 1995: 74–79.

Regina's Editing Log

• INCORRECT:	After all teenagers love to experiment with clothes as a part of expressing their identity. (2)
ERROR:	comma fault
CORRECT:	After all, teenagers love to experiment with clothes as a part of expressing their identity.
• INCORRECT:	One of the benefits of having students wear uniforms is that it would reduce gang violence in schools. (3)
ERROR:	vague pronoun reference
CORRECT:	Uniforms would reduce gang violence in schools.
• INCORRECT:	Unfortunately in many high schools students aren't safe from gangs. (3)
ERROR:	comma fault
CORRECT:	Unfortunately, in many high schools students aren't safe from gangs.
• INCORRECT:	whos (3)
ERROR:	contraction without an apostrophe
CORRECT:	who's
• INCORRECT:	student's (4)
ERROR:	misplaced apostrophe
CORRECT:	students'
• INCORRECT:	to (5)
ERROR:	wrong word
CORRECT:	too
• INCORRECT:	Sending the message that what counts is your body, not your brain. (6)
ERROR:	sentence fragment
CORRECT:	This clothing can be very distracting, sending the message that what counts is your body, not your brain.
• INCORRECT:	chairman (7)
ERROR:	sexist language
CORRECT:	chairperson

ACTIVITY
30

Editing Your Essay. Using the handbook in Part III of this book as a guide, edit your revised draft for errors in grammar, spelling, and punctuation. Your classmates can help you locate and correct errors you may overlook. Add the errors you find and their corrections to your editing log. ❑

Publishing

You're ready to share your essay with your audience—your instructor and classmates, as well as others affected by your topic. If, for instance, you argue that a certain law should be enacted or repealed, you might send your essay to the appropriate government official, such as your senator or congressional representative. If you advocate a change in a television show, you could share your essay with the network on which the show appears. An essay on censorship in schools could be shared with local school superintendents, school board members, and others in charge of matters related to censorship.

Your Writing Portfolio

Your writing portfolio consists of your best writing as well as your reflections on your writing. To help you reflect on the writing you did in this chapter, answer the following questions:

COMPUTER TIP

SWITCH TERMINALS TO EDIT

Ask several classmates to read your essay on the computer terminal and to highlight in boldface the errors they find. The more student readers you enlist to help you spot errors in your essay, the more error-free it will be. If necessary, consult your instructor, a tutor, or the Handbook in Part III of this book to verify the errors and help you correct them.

1. Compare your experience writing a persuasive essay with writing an expressive or informative essay. What did you enjoy most and least about these assignments?
2. What did you learn from writing this essay?
3. How persuasive do you think your essay would be to someone who strongly disagrees with your claim?
4. If you had more time, what more would you do to improve your essay before sharing it with readers?

Using your answers to these questions, update your writing process report.

Writing Process Report

Date:

Strengths:

Weaknesses:

Plans for improvement:

Once you complete this report, freewrite in your journal about what you learned about your writing process in this chapter and what you still hope to learn.

Chapter Summary

- Freedom of expression is guaranteed in the First Amendment to the Constitution.
- A claim, which asserts that something is true, is most effective when it expresses an opinion, relates to your readers' lives, and is focused.
- Pro points, which can come from experience, observations, and research, are used to support a claim.
- Pro points should be supported by material that is recent, relevant, and easily understood.
- Con points, or objections to a claim, should be refuted, or argued against.
- Pro points are usually discussed in the order of their importance, with the most important pro point coming last. However, other arrangements are possible.
- Con points may be refuted at the beginning, middle, or end of an essay depending on how they best fit into your flow of thought.
- Faulty logic, or flawed reasoning, comes in five common forms:
  - A hasty generalization draws a conclusion from too little evidence.
  - A slippery slope argues that one event led to (or will lead to) another event without providing evidence to support that claim.
  - Faulty either-or reasoning occurs when only two of many other alternatives are claimed to exist.
  - Faulty cause-and-effect reasoning involves attributing an event to an unrelated cause.
  - Biased, unreliable, or inexpert sources can result in arguments that are based on faulty reasoning.

Injustice anywhere is a threat to justice everywhere.
—MARTIN LUTHER KING, JR.

11

Identifying Issues, Proposing Solutions

In this chapter you will

- write about a campus, regional, or national issue.
- provide evidence that the problem exists.
- propose a solution to the problem.
- learn to persuade readers by using logical, emotional, and ethical appeals.
- learn to maintain a reasonable tone.
- add to your writing portfolio.

Think about some of the arguments you have been involved in. Did you ever become so angry that you couldn't discuss the issue at hand? Did you yell, stomp your feet, and leave the room, slamming the door behind you? Sometimes when we're angry, we don't think clearly, and afterwards we realize that we forgot to say something important, or that we said something we wish we could take back. Seldom is anything accomplished as a result of a heated argument.

At the center of any argument is an *issue*, something on which people disagree. Almost anything can be an issue—the clothes you wear, the books you choose to read, even your choice of friends. There are also larger issues that affect many people, such as campus, regional, and national issues.

Campus issues affect students, staff, and faculty on a college campus. Can you think of some issues on your campus? Do students need better advising? Is computer access adequate? Is residence hall food edible? Are there enough parking spaces? Regional issues affect the people of a town, city, state, or region of the country. Does Mason Township need a new animal shelter? Should more money be allocated to protect the Everglades? Is the New Mexico state income tax too high? National issues affect nearly everyone within a particular country. Does the United States need better gun-control laws? Does the welfare system need to be revamped? Should illegal immigrants receive social services?

As you think about these larger issues, consider your responsibility to your college, your region, and your country. What problems can you identify, and what solutions can you propose? By writing about a problem and possible solutions to it, you may help resolve an issue for yourself and others.

ACTIVITY

1

Analyzing Your Purpose and Audience. Before you begin gathering ideas about your topic, think about your purpose and audience. For this chapter's assignment you will describe your views on an issue, propose a solution, and attempt to convince your audience to accept and take action on your proposal.

Keep in mind that in addition to your instructor and classmates, your audience will include someone with the authority to act on your proposal. For example, if you choose a campus issue, such as inadequate advising or unsafe parking lots at your college, your audience would include, respectively, the dean or the campus police chief. Similarly, for a local or regional issue, such as the need for a new local animal shelter or for adequate state prison facilities, your audience would include local government officials or the state governor. Finally, for a national issue, such as the federal government's proposed cuts in financial aid benefits to students, your audience

Writing Assignment

This chapter offers you the opportunity to write about a campus, regional, or national issue that concerns you. You will state a problem and give your position on it, provide evidence that it exists, and propose a solution. You or your instructor may decide to do this assignment in one of several ways:

- You may gather ideas on one, two, *or* three topics.
- You may write a discovery draft on one, two, *or* three of these topics.
- You may choose one discovery draft to develop into a polished essay.
- You may combine your discovery draft ideas into a new topic for your essay.

After completing your essay, you'll share it with your instructor and classmates, as well as with someone who can take action on the issue.

would include your congressional representative and the U.S. president.

Once you identify your audience and purpose, use the following questions to help you decide how to approach your topic.

1. Does this assignment call for expressive, informative, or persuasive writing?

   _____

2. What is your readers' average age? _____

3. What is your readers' average educational level? _____

   Ethnic background? _____

   Economic level? _____

   Political orientation—conservative, moderate, or liberal (for a regional or national issue)?

   _____

Given your responses to the preceding questions, ask yourself these questions:

4. Is my audience most likely to be opposed to, neutral to, or in agreement with my views on the issue?

_____

_____

5. What do my readers already know about my topic?

_____

_____

_____

6. What do my readers need to know about my topic?

_____

_____

_____

7. Will my readers find my topic interesting, or will I have to work to get their attention?

_____

_____

_____

8. How can I convince my readers to accept my views on the issue?

_____

_____

_____

9. How can I persuade my readers that my proposed solution is worth-while?

_____

_____

_____ ❏

Gathering Ideas

To gather ideas about a campus, regional, or national issue, select from among the various techniques you have practiced in the preceding chapters: brainstorming, freewriting, clustering, questioning, reading, interviewing, relating aloud, and reflecting.

A Campus Issue

Think about some of the issues affecting students on your campus. What could be done to improve education or campus life? Perhaps you would like to see more courses offered in photography or more school spirit among students. Maybe you want the registration process streamlined or the campus parking situation improved in some way. Which issue do you complain about most often? Now is your chance to do something about it.

You might ask, "But who will listen to me?" Despite many college students' assumption that they can't change "the system," most college administrators are eager to listen to students. After all, you're their customers. However, they must be aware of problems and, more important, they must find solutions. As a student writer, you can play an important role in helping campus administrators perform these functions.

In the following essay, Patricia Shahabi-Azad identifies a problem: the poor condition of desks in a campus classroom. She then goes on to propose a solution: replace the desks.

Patricia Shahabi-Azad

212 Quinn Hall: Where to Sit?

I realize that the employees of Facilities Services work very hard *1* to keep things in good working order, and I compliment them on the many fine improvements that they have made on our campus. I must, however, bring to their attention the deplorable condition of the desks in room 212 of Quinn Hall.

I am one of the hundreds of students attending classes in this particular room. It has always been my priority to sit in the first row, but due to the poor condition of the desks, I have been forced to try different seats around the room. Unfortunately, they are all in the same poor condition. The seat cushions are worn out, leaving only the metal frames and springs. The metal is extremely hard, and the springs gouge anyone who sits on them.

These poor seating conditions not only affect the comfort of the students who attend classes in this room; they affect the instructors as well. While teaching, instructors are aware of uncomfortable students moving from one side of the seat to the other. In one instance, a student sat on the floor, no longer able to tolerate her desk. This incident led to a discussion with the instructor about the condition of the desks and the need to change them. Consequently, a great part of class time was spent discussing the seating arrangements rather than the course content. Even the instructor commented, "Something has to be done about these seats."

As a result of this discussion, I spoke to the director of Facilities Services about this problem. He stated, "We are in the process of installing a computerized inventory system that will help us effectively organize the work to be performed on campus." Undoubtedly, the new computerized inventory system will help in the future, but I would like to suggest that Facilities Services not wait for the new computer system to be put into place. Reupholstering or replacing the desks in room 212 in Quinn Hall should be placed at the top of the priority list.

I am hopeful that in the near future, students will not experience the pain of sitting at these desks and will instead be able to focus their attention solely on the class discussion rather than on the comfort of their seats.

ACTIVITY
2

Reading to Improve Writing. Discuss the following questions about "212 Quinn Hall: Where to Sit?" with your classmates.

1. What evidence does Shahabi-Azad use to convince her readers that the desks in 212 Quinn Hall should be replaced?

_____

_____

_____

2. What are the results of the poor seating conditions, according to the writer?

    _____

    _____

    _____

3. Do you agree with Shahabi-Azad's assertion that poor seating can affect students' learning?

    _____

    _____

    _____

4. What does Shahabi-Azad propose to be done about the deplorable seating conditions?

    _____

    _____

    _____

5. List several problems that need attention on your campus.

    _____

    _____

    _____

Collecting New Words. Try to determine the meanings of the following words from the way they're used in "212 Quinn Hall: Where to Sit?" Then verify their meanings by checking a dictionary.

ACTIVITY
3

deplorable (1) _____

priority (2) _____

gouge (2) _____

incident (3)   _____

solely (5)   _____

ACTIVITY
4

Freewriting about a Campus Issue. In your journal, gather ideas about the campus issue that most concerns and interests you. Use the following questions to stimulate your thinking:

1. What is your position on the issue?
2. What do you already know about it?
3. What more do you need to know about the issue?
4. What do you think should be done?
5. Who has the power to act on your proposed solution?   ❏

Li Chaing, a student writer concerned about the computer lab on his campus, did some freewriting in response to the questions in Activity 4. Here's a sample:

> *I am concerned about the computer lab on campus. My position is that the computer lab does not serve the needs of students. Even though we pay a $50 user fee each semester, we don't get good service. I know quite a bit about the lab because I spend most of my spare time there. I don't own a computer and must use the lab to complete assignments. From my own observations, I know that the hardware is outdated, the software selection is inadequate, and the students who work there are not very helpful. However, I need to find out whether other students on campus agree with my position, as well as why the college administration has not made any attempt to improve the computer lab. I think part of the user fee students pay each semester should be used to update the computer lab on a regular basis. The Vice President for Academic Affairs is the person in charge of this matter.*

Put your material about a campus issue aside for now. You want to think about a regional issue that concerns you.

A Regional Issue

Your college campus is only one of the environments in which you live. When you leave the campus, you interact with family, friends, and other members of your local and regional community. As you interact, you cannot help but notice problems. Perhaps your neighbors don't show an interest in recycling. Maybe a local factory pollutes the air, or nearby cities are taking water needed to irrigate farms in your county.

Regional issues can be solved only by showing people that a problem exists and then persuading them to correct it. Sometimes a solution requires people to forgo comfort or personal gain for the good of the entire community, in which case it becomes more difficult to persuade people to accept change. But if you succeed, you'll have benefited not only yourself but others who live in your region as well.

In the following essay, "A Cry for My City," Senator Daniel Patrick Moynihan identifies a problem—the deteriorating quality of life in New York City—and proposes a solution—a renewed spirit.

DANIEL PATRICK MOYNIHAN

A Cry for My City

It has been 50 years since I graduated from Benjamin Franklin High School in East Harlem. As World War II raged, my mother worked to support our single-parent household. And I helped make ends meet by shining shoes and hustling newspapers after school. *1*

My world might have been a place of impossibilities and despair. But in New York I received the family support and public education I needed to become a Naval officer, university professor and U.S. Senator. *2*

Now, at this half-century mark, I wonder where so much went wrong in the city I love. Like so many other cities, New York is wealthier than it was 50 years ago, yet it is immeasurably worse in nearly every aspect of urban life: violent streets, disintegrating families and crumbling infrastructure. *3*

In 1943, out of a population about the same as today's, only about 90,000 people were on relief. Now, over one million people are trapped in a hopeless welfare system. *4*

New York in 1943 had the most admired urban school system in the world, the finest housing, the best subways and in many ways the best-behaved citizens. When a patrolman told Mayor Fiorello La Guardia that young people were hanging around "cider stubes" and downing soft drinks, the mayor was scandalized and closed them down. *5*

The city was much poorer then, but it prepared us better for   6
prosperity when it came. I heard the news about Pearl Harbor from
a man whose shoes I was shining near the planetarium across the
street from Central Park. Five years later, I was an officer in the
United States Navy. Our schools prepared me to succeed—that was
routine. Is this behind us?

New York once had a vital infrastructure that could respond   7
quickly to growing needs. The George Washington Bridge was built
in four years and a month, and planners thought far enough ahead
to allow for a second deck. When the mayor's airplane was routed to
Newark once because New York's small airfield was fogged in, he
decided that was enough of that. Construction began, and La
Guardia Airport opened 25 months later. Today, it takes weeks just
to fill a pothole in the streets.

Even worse is the decline in our social institutions—especially   8
families, the small platoons without which a society this large cannot function. In 1943 the illegitimacy rate in New York City was no
more than three percent of births. The *New York Times* reported then
with shock that the number of abandoned children was increasing—"74 Brought into Foundling Hospital This Year."

Today, almost 50,000 children are in the limbo of the New York   9
City foster-care system. The city's illegitimacy rate is 43 percent. In
some districts, four out of five children are born to single mothers.

The dramatic increase in fatherless families has contributed to a   10
steep rise in crime—the inevitable outcome when young men never
acquire any stable relationship to male authority and have no hope
for the future.

"The slaughter of the innocent marches unabated," says New   11
York State Supreme Court Justice Edwin Torres. He's right; it grows
worse by the year. There were 44 homicides by gunshot in 1943. In
1992 there were 1,537.

Judge Torres was raised in the New York barrio, not far from my   12
old high school. Like other New Yorkers who remember a different
era, the judge is horrified by the passive acceptance of violence, the
victims in his courtroom who say, "Well, I suppose I shouldn't have
been out at that hour of the night."

New York City Police Commissioner Raymond Kelly recently re-   13
flected on those "No Radio" signs posted in the windows of parked
cars. "The translation of 'No Radio' is *Please break into someone else's
car, there's nothing in mine,*" Kelly observed. "These signs are flags of
urban surrender."

People do not seem to expect or insist on change. In 1929 the   14
infamous Valentine's Day Massacre of seven Chicago gangsters
shocked and outraged the whole country. This past Valentine's Day
in New York City there was an eerie re-enactment: six people were
forced to lie on the floor and then shot in the head. Later, a witness

was murdered in a courthouse. But this ghastly slaughter hardly stirred public interest; there are gang and drug-related executions every night.

Social scientists tell us that all societies have a certain amount of   *15* aberrant behavior. But when you get too much—too much crime, too many broken families—you can start to convince yourself it's not really all that bad. Pretty soon you're accepting behavior that a healthy community needs to condemn.

In Judge Torres's words, "A society that loses its sense of outrage   *16* is doomed to extinction." We dare not lose memory of what we have lost. We need to be intolerant about today's violence, intolerant about the destruction of America's families and urban communities.

"Instead of 'No Radio,'" says Commissioner Kelly, "we need new   *17* signs that say 'No Surrender.'"

If more of us shared that spirit, we might surprise ourselves just   *18* how great New York, and all our cities, could once again become.

Reading to Improve Writing. Discuss the following questions about "A Cry for My City" with your classmates.

ACTIVITY
5

1. What urban problems does Moynihan identify in the reading?

_____

_____

_____

2. What is his position on those problems?

_____

_____

_____

3. What supporting details does the writer use to convince his readers that the problems exist?

_____

_____

_____

4. What is his proposed solution?

_____

_____

_____

5. Does Moynihan persuade you that these problems exist? Why or why not?

_____

_____

_____

6. Do you think Moynihan's solution is a practical one? Why or why not?

_____

_____

_____

ACTIVITY
6

Collecting New Words. Try to determine the meanings of the following words from the way they're used in "A Cry for My City." Then verify their meanings by checking a dictionary.

infrastructure (3) _____

cider stubes (5) _____

platoons (8) _____

limbo (9) _____

inevitable (10) _____

unabated (11) _____

barrio (12) _____

passive (12) _____

ghastly (14) _____

aberrant (15) _____

extinction (16) _____

Reading to Gather Information. In the reference section of your library, consult several magazine and newspaper articles on the regional issue you want to explore. Use these questions to evaluate the articles:

ACTIVITY
7

1. Do most of the articles support or oppose your position on the issue?
2. What supporting details do the authors use to convince readers of their views?
3. Can you add additional details to these arguments?
4. Do the authors propose any worthwhile solutions? ❏

COMPUTER TIP

**GATHERING INFORMATION
ON THE INTERNET**

With access to the Internet, you can interact with local newsgroups, bulletin boards, or listservs on community issues. Contact your campus computer center for help with locating local newsgroups.

After reading Moynihan's "A Cry for My City," one student, Joy, decided to write about the death penalty in an attempt to persuade her governor that, in her view, capital punishment is a deterrent to violent crime. To learn more about the issue, Joy read several articles about crime. Here is how she answered the questions in Activity 7:

1. As a resident of this state, I am concerned about the increasing violence in our cities and what can be done about it. Newspaper accounts of violence appear regularly. According to some articles I've read, capital punishment is one means to deter violent crime.

2. Most authors use crime statistics to support the view that crime is out of control. Since 1973, violence has more than doubled. According to statistics provided by the Justice Department, 48,445 acts of violence were reported in the United States in 1992. During that same time in our city, 44 murders, 272 reported forcible rapes, 1,610 robberies, and 3,900 aggravated assaults occurred. The Department of Justice estimates that one out of every six people will be a victim of some form of crime.

3. In support of those statistics, I can cite several recent examples of violent crime in my area. On April 27, 1996, at

12:30 a.m., a local university student was shot to death for blowing his car horn in front of his girlfriend's apartment. A week later, a thirteen-year-old boy was set on fire for standing too close to a car.

4. The authors propose various solutions, including capital punishment. It would allow us to express indignation for certain heinous acts, such as capital murder. It would also send the message that violent crime will not be tolerated.

Set your writing on a regional issue aside for now, so you can explore one more possible topic for your essay—a national issue.

A National Issue

National issues affect all of us in one way or another. Drugs, crime, welfare, educational reform, and taxation are all national issues. Usually more complex than local or regional issues, national issues are also more difficult to resolve. Americans' diversity is one of this country's greatest strengths, but it also contributes to the complexity of many national issues. People living in different parts of the country and who are ethnically, religiously, and socioeconomically diverse tend also to hold diverse opinions about national issues.

Solutions to national problems often require imaginative solutions. In "Perils of Prohibition," Elizabeth M. Whelan identifies a problem: the legal drinking age of twenty-one encourages irresponsible drinking. She then proposes a surprising solution: lower the drinking age to eighteen and educate teens about alcohol abuse.

ELIZABETH M. WHELAN

Perils of Prohibition

My colleagues at the Harvard School of Public Health, where I   1
studied preventive medicine, deserve high praise for their recent study on teenage drinking. What they found in their survey of college students was that they drink "early and . . . often," frequently to the point of getting ill.

As a public-health scientist with a daughter, Christine, heading   2
to college this fall, I have professional and personal concerns about teen binge drinking. It is imperative that we explore *why* so many young people abuse alcohol. From my own study of the effects of alcohol restrictions and my observations of Christine and her friends' predicament about drinking, I believe that today's laws are unrealis-

tic. Prohibiting the sale of liquor to responsible young adults creates an atmosphere where binge drinking and alcohol abuse have become a problem. American teens, unlike their European peers, don't learn how to drink gradually, safely and in moderation.

Alcohol is widely accepted and enjoyed in our culture. Studies show that moderate drinking can be good for you. But we legally proscribe alcohol until the age of 21 (why not 30 or 45?). Christine and her classmates can drive cars, fly planes, marry, vote, pay taxes, take out loans and risk their lives as members of the U.S. armed forces. But laws in all 50 states say that no alcoholic beverages may be sold to anyone until that magic 21st birthday. We didn't always have a national "21" rule. When I was in college, in the mid-'60s, the drinking age varied from state to state. This posed its own risks, with underage students crossing state lines to get a legal drink.

In parts of the Western world, moderate drinking by teenagers and even children under their parents' supervision is a given. Though the per capita consumption of alcohol in France, Spain and Portugal is higher than in the United States, the rate of alcoholism and alcohol abuse is lower. A glass of wine at dinner is normal practice. Kids learn to regard moderate drinking as an enjoyable family activity rather than as something they have to sneak away to do. Banning drinking by young people makes it a badge of adulthood—a tantalizing forbidden fruit.

Christine and her teenage friends like to go out with a group to a club, comedy show or sports bar to watch the game. But teens today have to go on the sly with fake IDs and the fear of getting caught. Otherwise, they're denied admittance to most places and left to hang out on the street. That's hardly a safer alternative. Christine and her classmates now find themselves in a legal no man's land. At 18, they're considered adults. Yet when they want to enjoy a drink like other adults, they are, as they put it, "disenfranchised."

Comparing my daughter's dilemma with my own as an "underage" college student, I see a difference—and one that I think has exacerbated the current dilemma. Today's teens are far more sophisticated than we were. They're treated less like children and have more responsibilities than we did. This makes the 21 restriction seem anachronistic.

For the past few years, my husband and I have been preparing Christine for college life and the inevitable partying—read keg of beer—that goes with it. Last year, a young friend with no drinking experience was violently ill for days after he was introduced to "clear liquids in small glasses" during freshman orientation. We want our daughter to learn how to drink sensibly and avoid this pitfall. Starting at the age of 14, we invited her to join us for a glass of champagne with dinner. She'd tried it once before, thought it was "yucky" and declined. A year later, she enjoyed sampling wine at family meals.

When, at 16, she asked for a Mudslide (a bottled chocolate-milk-and-rum concoction), we used the opportunity to discuss it with her. We explained the alcohol content, told her the alcohol level is lower when the drink is blended with ice and compared it with a glass of wine. Since the drink of choice on campus is beer, we contrasted its potency with wine and hard liquor and stressed the importance of not drinking on an empty stomach.   8

Our purpose was to encourage her to know the alcohol content of what she is served. We want her to experience the effects of liquor in her own home, not on the highway and not for the first time during a college orientation week with free-flowing suds. Although Christine doesn't drive yet, we regularly reinforce the concept of choosing a designated driver. Happily, that already seems a widely accepted practice among our daughter's friends who drink.   9

We recently visited the Ivy League school Christine will attend in the fall. While we were there, we read a story in the college paper about a student who was nearly electrocuted when, in a drunken state, he climbed on top of a moving train at a railroad station near the campus. The student survived, but three of his limbs were later amputated. This incident reminded me of a tragic death on another campus. An intoxicated student maneuvered himself into a chimney. He was found three days later when frat brothers tried to light a fire in the fireplace. By then he was dead.   10

These tragedies are just two examples of our failure to teach young people how to use alcohol prudently. If 18-year-olds don't have legal access to even a beer at a public place, they have no experience handling liquor on their own. They feel "liberated" when they arrive on campus. With no parents to stop them, they have a "let's make up for lost time" attitude. The result: binge drinking.   11

We should make access to alcohol legal at 18. At the same time, we should come down much harder on alcohol abusers and drunk drivers of all ages. We should intensify our efforts at alcohol education for adolescents. We want them to understand that it is perfectly OK not to drink. But if they do, alcohol should be consumed in moderation.   12

After all, we choose to teach our children about safe sex, including the benefits of teen abstinence. Why, then, can't we—schools and parents alike—teach them about safe drinking?   13

Reading to Improve Writing. Discuss the following questions about "Perils of Prohibition" with your classmates.

1. Why does Whelan believe the current legal drinking age is a problem?

    _____

    _____

    _____

2. What is her position on the issue? _____

    _____

    _____

    _____

3. What supporting details does she use to convince her readers that the problem exists?

    _____

    _____

    _____

4. What is her proposed solution to the problem? _____

    _____

    _____

    _____

5. Does Whelan persuade you that the problem exists? Why or why not?

    _____

    _____

_____

_____

6. Do you think Whelan's solution is practical? Why or why not?

_____

_____

_____

Collecting New Words. Try to determine the meanings of the following words from the way they're used in "Perils of Prohibition." Then verify their meanings by checking a dictionary.

imperative (2)   _____

predicament (2)   _____

binge (2)   _____

proscribe (3)   _____

per capita (4)   _____

tantalizing (4)   _____

disenfranchised (5)   _____

dilemma (6)   _____

exacerbated (6)   _____

anachronistic (6)   _____

prudently (11)   _____

Relating Aloud to Gather Ideas. Read your material about a national issue aloud to the members of your peer response group. One member should take notes on (or tape-record) your description of the problem and proposed solution. Respond to the group's questions about your topic. Then use the group's suggestions to gather additional ideas about your topic. ❑

━━━━━━━━━━━━━
COMPUTER TIP
**GATHERING IDEAS ON THE
WORLD WIDE WEB**
With access to the
World Wide Web on the
Internet, you can search
for Web pages on your
topic. Some programs
permit you to search
simply by entering your
topic as a search term.
The program then
provides the Internet
addresses for the
relevant pages. Web
pages are just like book
pages, but they appear
on your computer and
have links to other
similar pages on the
same topic. They also
provide a vast amount of
information on any given
topic. Contact your
campus computer center
for more information
about accessing the
World Wide Web.
━━━━━━━━━━━━━

Here's how one student, Bruce, related his ideas about a national issue to his peer response group.

> My biggest concern is how the welfare system seems to break up families. Did you know that if a teenage girl becomes pregnant, she can't receive welfare for her baby unless she moves out of her parents' home? Because of this law, teenage girls from poor families are forced to leave home and try to make it on their own. They not only have a rough time making it alone, but they also lose the emotional support of their family at a time they need it most. I would like to see this law changed. I don't think we want to encourage unwed mothers to have babies, but if they do and if their families are eligible, I think they should be able to remain with their families and still receive public assistance benefits.

In response to his group members' questions about his topic, Bruce admitted that he needed to do some additional research:

> I'll need to find more about why the welfare system is set up this way and how it could be changed without costing taxpayers more money. I'm sure the idea is to save money, but I'm not sure how this works. I think I'll call my congressional representative and see if she has any information.

Drafting

You have now gathered ideas on campus, regional, and national issues. You have a rich source of material for writing, but you need to decide how to proceed. Here are some of your options:

- You may select one of the three topics for your discovery draft.
- You may write drafts on two or three of the topics to see which one you prefer to continue working on.
- You may combine your discovery draft ideas into a new topic for your essay.

Above all, choose a topic that concerns and interests you and that you know something about. In addition, make sure you narrow the topic if it is too broad to handle within the space of an essay. For example, you would not be able to address world peace, pollution, or homelessness in one essay, but you could focus on one specific aspect of the problem.

Before you begin writing your discovery draft, write a tentative thesis statement. Keep your audience and purpose in mind as you draft, but remember that your main goal at this stage is to get your ideas down on paper. You'll have time later on to revise and edit your discovery draft.

Here's a discovery draft written by Li Chaing, the student whose freewriting about the campus computer lab you read earlier. After reading the draft, discuss with your classmates what Li might do to revise it. (Note that the example includes the types of errors that typically appear in a first draft.)

Tollroad on the Information Superhighway

I am one of thousands of students who doesn't yet own a personal computer and must use the campus computer lab. Due to the poor condition of this facility, I have been forced to go elsewhere to use a computer. The equipment is outdated, it breaks down often, and the lab staff doesn't seem very helpful. What really makes me angry is that students pay a $50 user fee as part of their tuition each semester. You would think that this fee would entitle students to first-rate computer facilities.   *1*

Instead, we have to use old IBM 286 computers or Macintosh Plus computers. These computers aren't even powerful enough to run the software that provides students access to the Internet. There is one IBM 486 computer connected to the Internet, but this is hardly sufficient for thousands of students. What's more, on any given day, one-third of the two hundred computers have "Out of Order" signs on them. What gives? With thousands of students needing these computers, they should all be kept in working order. Also, the staff isn't very helpful. Who trains these clowns anyway? They often sit around doing their homework instead of offering to help students learn how to use the computers and the software programs. We need more software, too.   *2*

The college needs to upgrade the campus computer lab or quit charging students to use campus computing facilities. We're being ripped off! The way it is now, we pay a toll, but can't even get on the information superhighway.   *3*

Revising

As you review your discovery draft, use the skills you acquired in the preceding chapters. Support and clarify your main ideas, organize your paragraphs, make your ideas flow smoothly, and write an effective introduction, conclusion, and title. Also refer back to the audience analysis you completed in Activity 1. What does your audience need to know to understand the problem? How can you propose your solution so that your readers will act upon it?

In this chapter, you'll learn how to write a problem-solution essay. You will state the problem, provide evidence that the problem exists, propose a solution, attempt to persuade your readers, and maintain a reasonable tone.

State the Problem

As you may recall from Chapter Three, the thesis announces your topic and tells why it is important to you. An effective thesis for a problem-solution essay, however, has two additional characteristics:

- It describes a specific problem or issue.
- It conveys your position on the issue.

Here are some examples of vague and specific thesis statements:

VAGUE

Something should be done about students who cheat.

SPECIFIC

Students caught cheating on their final exams should be expelled from this college.

VAGUE

City roads need improvement.

SPECIFIC

Montana Road between the airport and the freeway should be resurfaced because of the many potholes.

VAGUE

Financial aid to students should not be cut.

SPECIFIC

If Congress passes a bill to cut the Stafford Loan program, thousands of college students will not be able to continue their education.

Analyzing Thesis Statements. Rewrite each thesis statement that follows so that it defines the specific problem or issue at hand and clearly states your position on the issue.

ACTIVITY

11

1. Students shouldn't have to pay to attend games. _____

    _____

    _____

    _____

2. The community sports arena doesn't offer a wide range of sports ac-
    tivities.

    _____

    _____

    _____

3. Cigarette taxes should be raised. _____

    _____

    _____

    _____

4. The welfare system must be abolished. _____

    _____

    _____

    _____

ACTIVITY
12

Revising Your Thesis Statement. Evaluate the preliminary thesis
statement you wrote for your essay about a campus, regional, or national issue. Does it identify a specific problem and clearly state your
position? Revise your thesis accordingly. ❑

Provide Evidence

    When writing a persuasive essay, it isn't enough to simply state
the problem. You need to convince readers that the problem is serious enough to require a solution. Evidence can help you do this. You
may include a brief history of the problem, its causes, and the conse-

quences of leaving it unsolved. You can support your ideas by using definition, classification, process analysis, facts, and expert testimony (see Chapter Six).

Suppose, for instance, that in her essay Elizabeth M. Whelan had stated her thesis without providing any evidence:

> Prohibiting the sale of liquor to responsible young adults creates an atmosphere where binge drinking and alcohol abuse have become a problem.

You might ask: "Wouldn't fewer sales result in less binge drinking and fewer problems?" and "How does Whelan define 'young adults' and 'binge drinking'?" If you hadn't already read her essay, you probably wouldn't agree with her thesis. You would want evidence that prohibiting the sale of liquor to young adults encourages alcohol problems.

Recognizing Evidence of a Problem. Reread Whelan's essay on pages 380–382. List the types of evidence she uses to convince readers that the problem requires attention. For example, look for detailed observation, sensory description, dialogue, examples, comparison-contrast, cause and effect, definition, classification, facts, expert testimony, questions, and anecdotes.

ACTIVITY
13

Examining Your Evidence. Examine the types of evidence you use in your draft to support your problem statement. Do you include sufficient supporting details to convince readers that the problem is serious and in need of a solution? Consider how you can revise to make your evidence more persuasive. ❑

ACTIVITY
14

Propose a Solution

After you state the problem and provide evidence of it, you are ready to propose a solution. A good solution offers a specific and practical course of action for correcting the problem or addressing the issue at hand.

Let's look again at the solutions proposed in this chapter's readings. Notice that in each case, the writer identifies a specific and practical resolution to the problem:

SHAHABI-AZAD'S ISSUE: Poor seating conditions in a campus classroom

SHAHABI-AZAD'S SOLUTION: Reupholster or replace the desks

MOYNIHAN'S ISSUE:	The deteriorating quality of life in New York City
MOYNIHAN'S SOLUTION:	A renewed spirit
WHELAN'S ISSUE:	The legal drinking age of twenty-one encourages irresponsible drinking
WHELAN'S SOLUTION:	Lower the legal drinking age to eighteen and educate teens about alcohol abuse

These solutions are relevant and practical. Shahabi-Azad suggests that student comfort should take priority over a new computer inventory system. Moynihan claims that his solution is practical because it is a prerequisite to solving urban problems generally. Whelan makes her solution practical by telling us about its success in other countries. Your solution should be specific and practical too, one that your readers will consider worthy of their attention.

ACTIVITY
15

Writing Practical Solutions. Return to the four thesis statements you prepared in Activity 11. For each thesis, propose a specific solution to the problem. Then state why you believe the solution is practical.

1. _____

_____

_____

_____

2. _____

_____

_____

_____

3. _____

_____

_____

4. _____

_____

_____

_____

Revising Your Solution. Working with your peer response group, discuss the solution you propose in your draft about a campus, regional, or national issue:

GROUP ACTIVITY 16

1. Is the proposed solution to the problem specific? Why or why not?
2. Is the proposed solution practical? Why or why not?

Use your classmates' feedback to revise your solution accordingly. ❏

Persuade Your Readers

In identifying a problem or issue and proposing a solution, you also aim to be persuasive. That is, you want your readers to understand the problem, accept your proposed solution, and perhaps take action on the issue. Three types of appeals—logical, emotional, and ethical—can help you be persuasive.

Logical Appeals. In a *logical appeal,* you provide objective, verifiable evidence for your position on the issue. Such evidence may include the following:

detailed observation	definitions
sensory description	classifications
dialogue	facts
examples	expert testimony
comparisons and contrasts	questions
causes and effects	anecdotes

By providing logically sound evidence, you convince your readers that you know your topic well and that your solution has merit. For example, let's look at an overview of Whelan's essay to see how she uses appeals to logic:

PROBLEM (par. 1–2):

• College students drink " 'early and . . . often.' "

• Observations and research support the writer's claim that the current laws are unrealistic.

- Prohibiting sales of alcohol encourages binge drinking.
- American teens don't learn how to drink safely.

EVIDENCE OF THE PROBLEM (par. 3):

- Studies show moderate drinking can be beneficial.
- Teens accept other adult responsibilities.
- In the 1960s, the drinking age varied by state.

ADDITIONAL EVIDENCE (par. 4–6):

- Teens in other countries learn to drink responsibly.
- American teens are forced to use false IDs to get into clubs or must hang out in the streets.
- Teens are more sophisticated today than in the 1960s and should be treated as adults.

RESULTS OF THE PROBLEM (par. 7–10):

- Teens with no prior drinking experience tend to abuse alcohol.
- Teens introduced to alcohol in a responsible way don't abuse it.
- Incidents of teenage alcohol abuse are evident on many college campuses.
- Such binge drinking results from lack of education about and exposure to alcohol.

SOLUTION (par. 11–12):

- Make alcohol legal at age eighteen.
- Crack down on alcohol abusers.
- Educate young people about alcohol.

GROUP ACTIVITY 17

Identifying Logical Appeals. Working in a group, reread Moynihan's essay on pages 375–377 and make a list of the writer's logical appeals. Then discuss how each appeal to logic contributes to Moynihan's persuasiveness.

ACTIVITY 18

Improving Your Logical Appeals. Under the headings *Problem, Evidence,* and *Solution,* list the points you make in your draft. Review each point to ensure that it is presented logically. Then consider adding details to strengthen your logical appeals. ❑

Emotional Appeals. Sometimes a logical appeal is not enough to spur readers to action. In this case, an *emotional appeal* may be more effective; it aims to make readers feel strongly about a problem or is-sue—compassionate, proud, sad, angry, or intolerant, for example. But be careful when using an appeal to emotion: readers dismiss such appeals when they are overly emotional, assuming that the writer is too close to the problem to propose an objective solution. Remember, too, that emotional appeals only supplement a logical ar-gument. You must always include logical evidence to support your thesis statement.

Moynihan uses several emotional appeals in "A Cry for My City." Even the title of his essay suggests Moynihan's strong feelings about his topic. In addition, by relating his childhood experiences and his long-standing love and respect for New York City, Moynihan encour-ages his readers to do the same. He then introduces evidence of the current problems—poor road conditions, illegitimacy rates, and crime—and uses, as an emotional appeal, a Supreme Court judge's interpretation of the problems: "The slaughter of the innocent marches unabated." With such appeals to emotion, Moynihan hopes to foster a renewed sense of spirit that will spur New Yorkers to ac-tion.

Recognizing Emotional Appeals. Working in a group, collect ar-ticles, editorials, and advertisements from newspapers and magazines and analyze their use of emotional appeals. Which emotions do the appeals aim to make readers feel? Do the emotional appeals effec-tively strengthen the logical argument? Which appeals seem overly emotional and, therefore, less effective? What conclusions can you draw about the emotional appeals used in articles and editorials ver-sus those employed in advertisements?

GROUP
ACTIVITY
19

Improving Your Emotional Appeals. Evaluate your draft to de-termine whether an appeal to emotion would make your logical ap-peals more persuasive. Where in your essay might you appeal to your readers' compassion, pride, anger, or some other emotion to spur them to action? Revise your draft accordingly. ❑

ACTIVITY
20

Ethical Appeals. With an *ethical appeal*, you aim to demonstrate your genuine concern about the problem or issue, your commitment to the truth, and your respect of others' differing opinions. You sup-port your position with verifiable evidence—facts, statistics, exam-ples, and expert testimony—and you ask readers to make a fair judgment based on that evidence.

Earlier in the chapter, you saw how several writers use ethical appeals in this way. Each demonstrates a genuine concern for the problem identified: Shahabi-Azad with the effects of poor seating conditions on students' education, Moynihan with the problems and future of New York City, and Whelan with the effects of the current legal drinking age. These writers also provide verifiable evidence to demonstrate their commitment to the truth and show respect for their readers' opinions. In return, they ask us, as open-minded readers, to evaluate their arguments fairly.

ACTIVITY
21

Recognizing Ethical Appeals. Reread the essay by Shahabi-Azad, Moynihan, or Whelan earlier in the chapter for additional ethical appeals. How does the author persuade you that he or she is a fair-minded person? How does the writer ask you, in return, to evaluate the argument fairly?

ACTIVITY
22

Improving Your Ethical Appeal. Evaluate the ethical appeal in your draft. Does it demonstrate your genuine concern about the issue, your commitment to the truth, and your respect for others' opinions? Revise your ethical appeal accordingly, and eliminate any details that are exaggerated or not factual. ❑

Use a Reasonable Tone

Tone is affected by a writer's choice of words and their placement in sentences. You should always strive to convey a reasonable tone. Earlier you saw several examples of an angry tone and a snide tone in Li Chaing's discovery draft, "Tollroad on the Information Superhighway":

ANGRY TONE

"What really makes me angry. . . ."

"What gives?"

SNIDE TONE

"Who trains these clowns anyway?"

"We're being ripped off!"

It is important to adopt a reasonable tone because venting your anger in writing has the same effect as raising your voice, stomping your feet, or slamming the door in an argument. Instead of bridging the gap between you and your readers, you widen it. If you're too quarrelsome, your readers may even refuse to read your essay.

Remember, your goal is to persuade your readers to acknowledge the problem and to accept your solution. A harsh, negative tone won't accomplish this nearly as well as a reasonable tone will. In order to be persuasive, you must show respect for your readers' opinions by maintaining a reasonable tone.

Creating a Reasonable Tone. Revise the following snide or angry statements so that they convey a reasonable tone.

ACTIVITY
23

1. The mayor of our city is a real jerk. _____

    _____

2. Who came up with this stupid plan anyway? _____

    _____

3. I demand that something be done about this problem! _____

    _____

4. This is the worst senator in the history of our state. _____

    _____

5. Advising at our college is for the birds. _____

    _____

Improving Your Tone. Reread your draft, looking for snide remarks or angry statements that show a lack of respect for others' opinions. Revise as needed to create a reasonable tone. ❑

ACTIVITY
24

Li's Revised Draft

Before you read Li's revised draft, reread his discovery draft (p. 386). Notice, in particular, how Li has improved his tone and added evidence in the revision. (You will also notice some errors in the revised draft; these will be corrected when Li edits his essay later on.)

Tollroad on the Information Superhighway

Fact (logical appeal)

Fact (logical appeal)

Adjusted tone (ethical appeal)

Stating the problem: thesis statement

Thousands of students on our campus who don't yet own a personal   *1*
computer must rely on the campus computer lab for their computing needs.
Every student pays a $50 user fee each semester for access to this lab. The
college administration should be congratulated for providing these computing
services and for keeping the fee reasonable. However, the computer hardware, software, and student assistance provided in the campus computer lab
are inadequate to meet students' needs.

Example (logical appeal)

Example (logical appeal)

Expert testimony (logical appeal)

The computer hardware is outdated and is often not working, my room-   *2*
mate, for instance, has been forced to go off campus to find a computer powerful enough to run the statistical program required in his Introduction to Statistics class. Only one computer, a Macintosh Power PC, is fast enough and
powerful enough for students to access the World Wide Web on the Internet.
The reason is because as the director of the computer lab states, "This lab
was founded in 1990, and we are still using the same computers we did on
the day we opened. I would love to be able to serve our students better, but
there just isn't money to upgrade the equipment."

Example (emotional appeal)

Statistics (logical appeal)

Adjusted tone (ethical appeal)

As if outdated equipment weren't bad enough, some of the existing hard-   *3*
ware doesn't even work. A quick survey of the equipment one day this week
revealed that of the 150 machines available in the computer lab, 48 of them
had "Out of Order" or "Off the Network" signs on them. Meanwhile, hundreds
of fee-paying students must either wait in line for the remaining machines or
make other arrangements to use a computer.

Example (logical appeal)

Question (emotional appeal)

Fact (logical appeal)

Expert testimony (logical appeal)

The software offered in this lab is also inadequate. Yes, you can do word   *4*
processing, if a machine is available, but what if you want to add graphics,
charts, or diagrams? You're out of luck, because there are no desktop publishing, database, or spreadsheet programs available. What's more, with only
one computer connected to the Internet, access to the information superhighway is severely limited. One student claims, "I have waited in line up to
three hours to get on the Internet. On the day before Thanksgiving, the computer lab director actually had to call in campus security to maintain order because several students started fighting over this one computer."

Example (emotional appeal)

Observation (logical appeal)

Statistics (logical appeal)

In addition, the students hired to work in this lab are not friendly or help-   *5*
ful. On three separate occasions, I observed lab tutors doing homework even
though they were waiting for help with the software program ClarisWorks. According to a survey reported in last Friday's campus newspaper, 60 percent
of the students who use the computer lab are dissatisfied with the service of-

fered. Most would prefer more assistance with computer hardware and software and would like to see this assistance offered twenty-four hours a day.

When questioned about campus computing services, the vice-president for instructional technology responded that the majority of the funds collected through the computer use fee were being used to create a computerized telephone registration system. Once this system is in place, the computer lab will be upgraded and services improved. When asked, she acknowledged that students had no input into the decision on how these computer use fees are spent. Meanwhile, students on campus make do with woefuly inadequate computing facilities.

This situation is obviously unfair. Students are paying a fee for computing services that they are not receiving. This college needs to upgrade the campus computer lab or quit charging students for inadequate campus computing facilities. If students are going to pay the toll, at least give them access to the information superhighway.

6   **Expert testimony (logical appeal)**

Expert testimony (logical appeal)

7   **Expert testimony (emotional appeal)**

Proposing a solution: adjusted tone (ethical appeal)

Analyzing Li's Revised Draft. Use the following questions to discuss with your classmates how Li improved his draft.

GROUP
ACTIVITY
25

1.   What is Li's thesis statement? Is it effective? _____

_____

_____

_____

2.   What kinds of evidence does Li provide to show a problem exists?

_____

_____

_____

3.   Does his solution seem practical? _____

_____

_____

_____

4. How does Li appeal to his readers logically, emotionally, and ethically?

_____

_____

_____

_____

5. How has Li adjusted his tone to make it more reasonable than in his discovery draft?

_____

_____

_____

6. How could Li's revised draft benefit from further revision?

_____

_____

_____

GROUP
ACTIVITY
26

Using Peer Review. Read your draft aloud to the members of your peer response group. Take notes on your classmates' responses to the following questions about your draft.

1. Have I followed all of the instructions for this assignment?

_____

_____

_____

2. How effective is my thesis statement? Do I clearly state the problem?

_____

_____

_____

_____

3. Do I provide adequate evidence of the problem? _____

_____

_____

_____

4. Do I propose a practical solution to the problem? _____

_____

_____

_____

5. How could I improve my logical, emotional, and ethical appeals?

_____

_____

_____

6. Where in my essay do I need to adjust my tone? _____

_____

_____

_____

7. How clear is the purpose of my essay? How well do I meet the needs of my audience?

_____

_____

_____

COMPUTER TIP

USING THE INTERNET FOR REVISIONS

Post your draft essay on a newsgroup, listserv, or bulletin board, asking readers to respond with suggestions for revision. As you revise, use any suggestions you think will improve your draft.

Revising Your Draft. Taking your classmates' suggestions for revision into consideration, revise your essay. In particular, focus on improving your thesis, evidence, and solution. Also evaluate your use of logical, emotional, and ethical appeals, and adjust your tone as needed. ❑

Editing

At this point you have worked hard to communicate your position on a campus, regional, or national issue. Now that you're satisfied with the content of your revised draft, you're ready to edit it for correctness. Editing is important; an essay that contains errors distracts readers from focusing on the writer's ideas. It also creates the impression among readers that a careless writer is responsible. A clean, error-free essay, in contrast, implies that a careful writer probably is genuinely concerned about the topic and worthy of readers' attention. Therefore, edit your essay carefully before sharing it with your readers.

Li's Edited Essay

You probably noticed that Li's revised draft contained errors in grammar, spelling, and punctuation. Li corrected these errors in his edited essay. His corrections are underlined here. His editing log follows his essay.

Tollroad on the Information Superhighway

Thousands of students on our campus who don't yet own a personal   *1*
computer must rely on the campus computer lab for their computing needs.
Every student pays a $50 user fee each semester for access to this lab. The
college administration should be congratulated for providing these computing
services and for keeping the fee reasonable. However, the computer hardware, software, and student assistance provided in the campus computer lab
are inadequate to meet students' needs. They should be improved or the fee
should be abolished.

The computer hardware is outdated and is often not <u>working. My room-</u>   *2*
<u>mate,</u> for instance, has been forced to go off campus to find a computer powerful enough to run the statistical program required in his Introduction to Sta-

tistics course. Only one computer, a Macintosh Power PC, is fast enough and powerful enough for students to access the World Wide Web on the Internet. As the director of the computer lab states, "This lab was founded in 1990, and we are still using the same computers we did on the day we opened. I would love to be able to serve our students better, but there just isn't money to upgrade the equipment."

As if outdated equipment weren't bad enough, some of the existing hardware doesn't even work. A quick survey of the equipment one day this week revealed that of the 150 machines available in the computer lab, 48 of them had "Out of Order" or "Off the Network" signs on them. Meanwhile, hundreds of fee-paying students must either wait in line for the remaining machines or make other arrangements to use a computer.

The software offered in this lab is also inadequate. Yes, students can do word processing, if a machine is available, but what if they want to add graphics, charts, or diagrams? They're out of luck, because there are no desktop publishing, database, or spreadsheet programs available. What's more, with only one computer connected to the Internet, access to the information superhighway is severely limited. One student claims, "I have waited in line up to three hours to get on the Internet. On the day before Thanksgiving, the computer lab director actually had to call in campus security to maintain order because several students started fighting over this one computer."

In addition, the students hired to work in this lab are not friendly or helpful. On three separate occasions, I observed lab tutors doing homework even though students were waiting for help with the software program, *Claris Works.* According to a survey reported in last Friday's campus newspaper, 60 percent of the students who use the computer lab are dissatisfied with the service offered. Most would prefer more assistance with computer hardware and software and would like to see this assistance offered twenty-four hours a day.

When questioned about campus computing services, the vice president for instructional technology responded that the majority of the funds collected through the computer use fee were being used to create a computerized telephone registration system. Once this system is in place, the computer lab will be upgraded and services improved. When asked, she acknowledged that students had no input into the decision on how these computer use fees are spent. Meanwhile, students on campus make do with <u>woefully</u> inadequate computing facilities.

This situation is obviously unfair. Students are paying a fee for comput-   7
ing services that they are not receiving. This college needs to upgrade the campus computer lab or quit charging students for inadequate campus com-puting facilities. If students are going to pay the toll, at least give them ac-cess to the information superhighway.

Li's Editing Log

• INCORRECT:	The computer hardware is outdated and is often not working, my roommate, for instance, has been forced to go off campus to find a computer powerful enough to run the statistical pro-gram required in his Introduction to Statistics course. (2)
ERROR:	comma splice
CORRECT:	The computer hardware is outdated and is often not working. My roommate, for instance, has been forced to go off campus to find a computer powerful enough to run the statistical pro-gram required in his Introduction to Statistics course.
• AWKWARD:	The reason is because as the director of the computer lab states, "This lab was founded in 1990, and we are still using the same computers we did on the day we opened." (2)
IMPROVED:	As the director of the computer lab states, "This lab was founded in 1990, and we are still using the same computers we did on the day we opened."
• INCORRECT:	Yes, you can do word processing, if a machine is available, but what if you want to add graphics, charts, or diagrams? You're out of luck, because there are no desktop publishing, data-base, or spreadsheet programs available. (4)
ERROR:	inappropriate shift from third to second person
CORRECT:	Yes, students can do word processing, if a machine is avail-able, but what if they want to add graphics, charts, or dia-grams? They're out of luck, because there are no desktop pub-lishing, database, or spreadsheet programs available.
• INCORRECT:	On three separate occasions, I observed lab tutors doing home-work even though they were waiting for help with the software program ClarisWorks. (5)
ERRORS:	unclear pronoun reference; software title not underlined or itali-cized
CORRECT:	On three separate occasions, I observed lab tutors doing home-work even though students were waiting for help with the soft-ware program *ClarisWorks*.
• INCORRECT:	Meanwhile, students on campus make do with woefuly inade-quate computing facilities. (6)
ERROR:	misspelled word

CORRECT: Meanwhile, students on campus make do with woefully inadequate computing facilities.

Editing Your Essay. Edit your revised draft. Read it word-for-word, looking for errors in grammar, spelling, and punctuation. If you know you often make a particular type of error, read the essay one time for only that error. Also ask a friend, family member, or classmate to help you spot errors you may have overlooked. Then use a dictionary and the Handbook in Part III of this book to help you correct the errors you find. Finally, record those errors on your editing log. ❏

ACTIVITY
28

Publishing

You're ready to share your essay about a campus, regional, or national issue with your audience—your instructor and classmates, as well as with someone with the authority to act on your proposal.

According to an ancient Chinese proverb, "A journey of a thousand miles begins with one step." Perhaps your essay will be the first step in bringing about a needed change on your campus, in your region, or in our nation. You may be surprised by the power of your writing. If you receive a reply, share it with your instructor and classmates.

Your Writing Portfolio

Your writing portfolio consists of your best writing as well as your reflections on your writing. To help you reflect on the writing you did in this chapter, answer the following questions:

1. Why did you choose the issue you did?
2. How did you determine the audience for your essay?
3. Which supporting details in your essay do you think provide the strongest evidence for your position? Why?
4. Which type of appeal—logical, emotional, or ethical—do you think you use most effectively in your essay? Why?
5. If you had more time, what more would you do to improve your essay before sharing it with readers?

Using your answers to these questions, update your writing process report.

Writing Process Report

Date:

Strengths:

Weaknesses:

Plans for improvement:

Once you complete this report, freewrite in your journal on what you learned about your writing process in this chapter and what you still hope to learn.

Chapter Summary

- Gather ideas for a problem-solution essay by reviewing journal entries, brainstorming, freewriting, clustering, questioning, reading, interviewing, relating aloud, and reflecting.
- State in your thesis statement the specific problem and your position on it.
- Give evidence to persuade your readers that the problem exists and merits their attention.
- Include as evidence detailed observations, sensory description, dialogue, examples, comparisons and contrasts, causes and effects, defi-

nition, classification, facts, expert testimony, questions, or anecdotes.

- Propose a practical solution to the problem.
- Use logical, emotional, and ethical appeals to persuade your readers to accept your position on the issue.
- Convince readers that you are a fair-minded person by using a reasonable tone.

Good writing excites me, and makes life worth living.
—HAROLD PINTER

12

Your Writing Portfolio

In this chapter you will

- complete your writing portfolio.
- edit and bind your portfolio.
- reflect on what you have learned about writing.
- consider other audiences for your portfolio.

Your writing portfolio is a collection of your best writing. Writers, artists, photographers, models, and others use portfolios to showcase their talents and accomplishments. They choose from among all their works only the very best ones for their portfolio. By organizing a portfolio, professionals not only demonstrate their abilities but reveal their character as well. A well-designed portfolio can reveal a person's creativity, organizational skills, thoroughness, neatness, and competence.

Throughout this book you have collected your best work in a portfolio and reflected on your writing strengths and weaknesses in writing process reports. Now you're ready to complete your writing portfolio and to reflect on what it reveals about you.

ACTIVITY

1

Analyzing Your Purpose and Audience. Just as you have done for each essay within your portfolio, think about your purpose and audience for the entire portfolio itself. Answer the following questions:

1. Is your portfolio primarily designed to express, inform, or persuade?

    _____

2. Who is the primary audience for your writing portfolio?

    _____

Given your responses to the preceding questions, ask yourself these questions:

3. What writing qualities would I like to demonstrate through my portfolio?

    _____

    _____

    _____

4. How can I best demonstrate these qualities in my portfolio?

    _____

    _____

    _____

Writing Assignment

Your Portfolio

This chapter offers you the opportunity to complete your writing portfolio and reflect on what you have learned about writing and your own writing process.

After completing your portfolio, you'll share it with your instructor and classmates. You'll also consider how you might revise the contents of your portfolio to suit other, future audiences.

5. What character traits would I like to demonstrate through my portfolio?

_____

_____

_____

6. How can I best demonstrate these traits in my portfolio?

_____

_____

_____❏

Showcasing Your Writing

The Contents

The contents of your portfolio will vary depending on your audience. You'll begin by sharing your portfolio with your instructor and classmates; therefore, you should include pieces that will interest them. But remember that your purpose is to persuade your audience that you have become a skilled writer as a result of your work throughout this book. You may demonstrate your growth as a writer by including a broad range of topics and formats in your portfolio. In addition, you want to demonstrate your character traits through your portfolio.

Your writing portfolio should include the following:

1. Your best essays
2. Selected journal entries
3. Other types of writing you have done
4. A cover letter
5. A table of contents

Selected Essays. Although you might be tempted to include all of the essays you have written for this book, your portfolio should include only your best writing. Most likely, you'll choose three or four essays as examples of your best work.

How do you choose which essays to include? You want to demonstrate your skill as a writer as well as your creativity. Your most creative essays are probably those you most enjoyed working on and were eager to share with readers. To demonstrate your writing skills, select essays that include

- a lively title.
- an effective introduction.
- unified and coherent paragraphs.
- good supporting details.
- smooth transitions.
- a powerful conclusion.

ACTIVITY
2

Selecting Your Best Essays. Using the criteria for essay selection just discussed, choose from among the many essays you have written for this book the three or four essays that best demonstrate your skill as a writer for inclusion in your writing portfolio. ❑

Selected Journal Entries. In addition to demonstrating your writing skills, you want your portfolio to show your growth as a writer. Your journal contains your reflections on your writing process and indicates how you have grown as a writer. Perhaps you recorded an interesting discovery about your writing process or reflected on your commitment to writing. By including selected journal entries in your writing portfolio, you can demonstrate this growth to your readers.

Begin by reviewing your writing process reports and the freewriting you did in your journal at the end of Chapters Three through Eleven. How did your strengths, weaknesses, and plans for improvement change? How did your writing improve? Look for journal entries that reflect those improvements, reveal your growth as a writer, or indicate a new understanding about your writing process. Retype and edit the journal entries you plan to include in your portfolio, correcting any errors in grammar, spelling, and punctuation.

One student, Patrick, selected the following two journal entries for his portfolio. The entries demonstrate his growth as a writer, his ability to handle a difficult writing task, his work with other students, and his approach to the writing process.

Journal Entry, dated 9/18/97

I have always had trouble writing about my personal feelings. When I was asked to write an essay about an incident that changed my life, I decided to write about my grandfather's death. I wrote the essay "An Idea Whose Time Has Gone," which is about my grandfather's willingness to face death. At first, I was afraid I wouldn't be able to write on this topic because it would bring back many painful memories.

Many thoughts crossed my mind, but I finally put all my feelings into this essay. Not only did I want to show myself that I could write about my feelings, but I also wanted to understand why I was feeling the way I did. Never have I opened up to anybody as I did when I wrote this essay.

When I read it aloud to some friends, they told me they had never heard anything so moving. My peer response group also thought it was a good essay because it expressed my thoughts and feelings well. My group asked questions that helped me see the need for more specific details about my grandfather's death. This essay helped me open up and express my feelings in writing.

I think the essay is well written. When I read it to my dad, he felt like he was experiencing my grandfather's death all over again. Others reacted strongly, too: some cried and others just stayed silent. I remembered from class that a good expressive essay should move the reader. I knew I had done this because I had written the essay from my heart.

Journal Entry, dated 12/7/97

I signed up for this writing class thinking it would be just another class in which the professor lectures and gives assignments to take home, write about, and then turn in for a grade. Was I wrong! Taking this course has made me enjoy writing for the first time. Of the essays I've written so far, I think the one about rap music is my favorite. Not only did I look forward to writing this essay, but I also acquired a greater appreciation for this form of music as a result.

Writing this essay didn't seem like an assignment for me when I realized I wanted to share my excitement for rap with my classmates. The writing process I used for this essay was easy and simple. On the day the essay was assigned, I began reading and interviewing people about rap music, and I continued working on it every day until the deadline. First, I concentrated on what I wanted to say; then I revised, adding more description and dialogue to make the essay more interesting. Near the end of the process, I concentrated on deleting unnecessary paragraphs and sentences and editing to eliminate errors. This essay is a good piece of writing because of the effort and dedication I put into it.

ACTIVITY
3

Selecting Journal Entries. Select several entries from your journal in which you reflect on your growth as a writer or on your writing process. Revise and edit the entries to improve their readability and appearance. Then add the journal entries to your writing portfolio. ❏

Other Writing. In addition to the essays and journal entries you have selected to demonstrate your skills and growth as a writer, your portfolio may include other types of writing that show a broader range of your work. For example, you might include a term paper or summary you wrote for another course, or a short story or poem you wrote for your own pleasure. By including other types of writing in your portfolio, you can demonstrate your ability to write well on a wide range of topics and in various different formats.

Patrick included the following poem in his portfolio to showcase his ability to write descriptively and concisely:

Composure

Her head leaned

against the creamy plaster wall;

her arms hung at her sides,

tense.

Her shoulders rigid,

taut with anticipation.

Her eyes, full of love

and sweet expectation,

watched her baby sleep.

ACTIVITY
4

Selecting Other Types of Writing. Review the other writing you have done on your own or for other courses. Select several examples for your portfolio that demonstrate your ability to write well in a range of formats. ❏

Cover Letter. After you assemble your best essays, journal entries, and other writing for your portfolio, consider whether including a cover letter is appropriate given your purpose and audience. A cover letter might briefly explain the contents of your portfolio and how it represents your growing skills in various writing formats. (If you include a cover letter, list it on your Contents page.)

Patrick included the accompanying cover letter to his writing instructor in his portfolio. Notice that his letter uses a business letter format with single-spaced copy.

COMPUTER TIP

ASSEMBLING A PORTFOLIO FROM COMPUTER FILES

If you have saved your files on disk, you can now choose those you want to put in your portfolio. Use your printer to make neatly printed final copies of your work for your portfolio.

Patrick Callahan
1203 Devonshire
Salt Lake City, Utah 17032
December 15, 1997

Ms. Deborah Smith
Department of English
Salt Lake City College
Salt Lake City, Utah 17036

Dear Ms. Smith:

As you requested, I have compiled the following portfolio of my best writing. Included in this portfolio are three essays, two journal entries, and one poem.

The three essays demonstrate my skill and range as a writer. I chose one expressive, one informative, and one persuasive essay to demonstrate that I can write for a variety of purposes and to several different audiences. In each one, I develop my ideas well and present them in an interesting, informative way.

I have also included two journal entries to show how I have grown as a writer and how I have come to enjoy writing as a result of this course. I used to dread having to communicate in writing, but I now feel more confident in my ability to handle writing assignments in all of my courses.

Finally, I have included one of my favorite poems to demonstrate that I can write descriptive poetry as well. I have always enjoyed writing poetry and welcome this opportunity to share my poem with you and my classmates.

If you have any questions or comments about my portfolio, please contact me.

Sincerely,

Patrick Callahan

Patrick Callahan

Writing a Cover Letter. Write a cover letter to introduce your portfolio. In it describe the contents of your portfolio and explain how the selections reflect on you as a writer—your skills, growth, and ability to handle diverse writing situations. ❑

Table of Contents. You should include a table of contents in your portfolio. It tells readers what they can expect to find in the portfolio. It also demonstrates your ability to organize your work.

The table of contents should appear on a separate page, headed *Contents*, at the start of your portfolio and should include your name. Organize the table of contents in three columns for easy reference (see the accompanying example). In the first column, give headings for the types of writing and the titles of the essays in your portfolio. In the second column, give the date you wrote each selection. In the third column, give the appropriate page numbers for the selections in the portfolio. (The pages of your portfolio should be numbered sequentially.) Notice, in the accompanying example, how Patrick prepared a table of contents in this way for his portfolio.

Patrick Callahan's Writing Portfolio Contents		
	Date Written	Page
COVER LETTER	12/15/97	1
ESSAYS		
• "An Idea Whose Time Has Gone" (expressive writing)	9/30/97	2
• "Local Rap Group Makes Headlines" (informative writing)	10/24/97	5
• "Capital Punishment: Your State Tax Dollars at Work" (persuasive writing)	11/29/97	10
JOURNAL ENTRIES		
• Journal entry	9/18/97	14
• Journal entry	12/7/97	15
OTHER WRITING		
• "Composure" (poem)	6/2/97	16

Creating a Table of Contents. Create a table of contents for your portfolio by following these directions:

ACTIVITY

6

- Create a portfolio title that includes your name.
- Divide the page into three columns.
- Label the types of writing you included in your portfolio.
- List the title of each selection under the appropriate heading.
- List the date you wrote each selection.
- Give the appropriate page number for each selection. ❑

Polishing Your Portfolio

Think again about the impression you want to make with your portfolio. You want to persuade your readers that you're a skilled writer. You do this in part by including selections that demonstrate your writing skills and character traits. But you also need to present your work neatly.

First, you want to ensure that your work communicates well. Reread the summary that appears at the end of each chapter of this book. Then reread each selection in your portfolio and make any final revisions that may be needed. For instance, you might reword an ineffective introduction or conclusion, add supporting details, or revise an unclear sentence.

Turn next to your editing log. Reread the entries, and then check your portfolio selections for errors you may have overlooked. If you're unsure about a grammar or punctuation rule, refer to the Handbook in Part III of this book for help.

Finally, look at the manuscript format for each selection in the portfolio. Use a consistent format, and retype or reprint selections as needed to produce clean, error-free copies.

Revising and Editing Your Portfolio. Reread each portfolio selection and make any final revisions now. Then edit your work to eliminate errors in grammar, spelling, and punctuation, and retype or reprint any selections that are not clean and neat.

ACTIVITY

7

Finally, revise your Contents page so that it accurately lists the selections within your portfolio. Check that the columns are aligned, that all dates are included, and that the page numbers are correct. ❑

Binding Your Portfolio

Once you assemble your portfolio, you'll need to bind it in some way. The size of your portfolio will determine whether you should use a folded piece of construction paper or a sturdy three-ring note-book. When choosing a binding, select one that is attractive and holds the pages in a way that makes them easy to read.

It's a good idea to use divider pages to mark each section of your portfolio. Add tabs to the divider pages to match the headings given in your table of contents.

Some students choose to decorate the cover of their portfolios with photographs of themselves or of their classmates, family, or friends. Others use markers and other art supplies to design a cre-ative cover.

ACTIVITY

8

Binding Your Portfolio. Assemble and bind your portfolio. Divide the sections of the portfolio and, if you wish, decorate the cover. ❑

Uses for Your Portfolio

You're now ready to share your portfolio with your instructor and classmates. But before you do, let's consider several other uses for your portfolio.

Reflection

By now, you should have a fairly good idea of what works best for you when gathering ideas, drafting, revising, and editing. Know-ing this will help you complete writing assignments in other courses as well as in the workplace. Now that you have assembled your port-folio, you can use it to reflect on how you have grown as a writer during your work in this course.

ACTIVITY

9

Reflecting on Your Writing. In your journal, reflect on what you have learned about your writing process. Use the following questions as a starting point:

1. What are your writing strengths? Your writing weaknesses?
2. How can you continue to improve your weak areas?
3. Which selections in your portfolio were the easiest for you to write? Which were the most difficult?
4. How did you accomplish these difficult assignments?
5. Are there any types of writing that you haven't done, but that you would like to add to your portfolio? Explain.
6. Do you now consider yourself an effective writer? Why or why not?

❑

Presentation

Your writing portfolio is a permanent record of the writing that you have done in this course. In sharing it with your instructor and classmates, you can demonstrate your writing skills. Save your portfolio for use with future audiences, including employers and colleges.

Employers. When you apply for a job, particularly one requiring writing skills, you may want to present your portfolio to your prospective employer. Before presenting your portfolio, though, consider your audience and revise your portfolio accordingly. If Patrick, for instance, were applying for a summer job in an insurance office, he would replace the poem in his portfolio with business letters he had written. He might also include a resumé listing his job skills, work history, and education.

Colleges and Universities. Some colleges and universities ask applicants to submit samples of their writing with their application for admission. If you transfer to another school, you may wish to use your portfolio. Again, you'll want to consider the specific requirements of the university. If Patrick were applying to another school, he would probably replace the poem in his portfolio with a term paper that he wrote for one of his courses.

When you complete your portfolio, congratulate yourself—there isn't anyone who knows as much about your writing as you do. In Chapter One, we asked, "What comes into your mind when you think of a writer?" Your answer should now be "I do."

Chapter Summary

- Showcase your skill and growth as a writer and your ability to write in a range of formats in a writing portfolio.
- Demonstrate your organizational skills, creativity, thoroughness, neatness, and other character traits in your portfolio.
- Include in your portfolio only your very best writing—essays, journal entries, and other writing—as well as a table of contents and a cover letter.
- Revise and edit your portfolio to ensure that your work communicates well, is free of errors, and is clean and neat.
- Bind your portfolio in a way that is attractive and easy to read.
- Use your portfolio to reflect on how you have improved as a writer.
- Vary the contents of your portfolio for different purposes and audiences, such as when applying for employment or for admission to other colleges.

III
Handbook with Exercises

Parts of Sentences
Correct Sentences
Choosing Words
Punctuation
Spelling
Mechanics

When we write, we want to communicate our ideas as clearly as possible. Using correct grammar, spelling, and punctuation helps our readers understand what we mean. Error-free writing also demonstrates our interest in our readers and our desire to do the best possible job of communicating our message.

You'll probably find yourself using this Handbook in various ways. You may consult it during the editing stage as well as when you compile your editing log. Your instructor may assign certain sections of the Handbook on grammar, spelling, or punctuation to target specific problem areas. You may be asked to work in a group on some of the activities. Above all, you should use this Handbook to recognize and eliminate errors from your writing.

Parts of Sentences

It's helpful to understand the basic structure of the sentence when you're working on your writing. You may have been drilled in grammar before, but if you didn't apply what you learned about sentence grammar to your own writing, chances are you didn't see much improvement in your papers even if you always earned A's on grammar tests. The activities in Part III will help you learn how to write correctly. But the most important activity for you will be to apply what you learn to your own writing.

What Is a Sentence?

A *complete sentence* consists of a subject and a verb and expresses a complete thought. Usually the subject is a *noun*—a person, place, or thing. But a subject can also be a *pronoun*—a word that takes the place of a noun. The subject tells who or what is doing the action.

Mary works.

She is a hard worker.

The *verb* in a sentence conveys the action or links the subject to the rest of the sentence.

Flowers *bloom* in the spring.

Roses *are* my favorite flower.

Sometimes there may be more than one subject or more than one verb in a sentence.

Marty and Susan work at K-Mart.

They *stock* shelves and *help* customers.

421

ACTIVITY

1

Identifying Subjects and Verbs. Circle the subjects and underline the verbs in the following sentences.

1. I walk five miles a day.

2. My dog walks with me.

3. We walk along an abandoned railway trestle.

4. Great Western built the railroad here in 1856.

5. The trains stopped in 1982.

6. Mountain bikers and hikers travel the railroad tracks now.

7. I found a rusted railroad spike on the trail.

8. We worked with Rails to Trails.

9. It organizes groups of hikers.

10. The hikers build wilderness paths on the old railroad easements. ❑

Subjects

In order to understand the basic structure of a sentence, you need to be able to identify its subject. Often the subject is easy to spot because it consists of one word. Other times, though, the subject can be hard to detect.

Subject Pretenders

Sometimes it's difficult to identify the subject of a sentence because there is a word in a prepositional phrase that is pretending to be the subject. But the subject of a sentence is *never* found in a prepositional phrase. Therefore, if you block out the prepositional phrases in a sentence, you know that one of the remaining words is the subject.

Many (of the students) forgot their books. [The subject is *many*.]

John (from Portland) attended the meeting. [The subject is *John*.]

The *cat* (next to the tree) frightened the child. [The subject is *cat*.]

COMMON PREPOSITIONS

about	beside	inside	since
above	between	into	throughout
against	by	like	to
among	despite	near	toward
as	down	next to	under
at	during	of	until
before	except	off	up
behind	for	on	upon
below	from	out	within
beneath	in	past	without

Identifying Prepositions. Underline the prepositions in the following paragraph.

ACTIVITY

2

Leticia went into her bedroom and took her journal from her bedside table. She sat in her favorite chair while recording her thoughts. Throughout the day she had felt tense. During breakfast she had studied for her chemistry test. At school she couldn't find a parking spot. Despite all of her studying, she felt unprepared for the test. After the test, she had gone to the Student Union where she had spilled ketchup on her white blouse. Now she was happy to put the day behind her and just write in her journal. ❏

A *prepositional phrase* consists of the preposition and its object. Here are some examples:

PREPOSITION	OBJECT	PREPOSITIONAL PHRASE
into	her bedroom	into her bedroom
after	the test	after the test
in	her journal	in her journal

ACTIVITY
3

Writing Prepositional Phrases. Complete each sentence that follows by adding a prepositional phrase.

EXAMPLE

He ironed his shirt <u>before leaving for work</u>.

1. She put her books _____.

2. He made dinner _____.

3. The dog ran _____.

4. Jane watched television _____.

5. Harry felt sick _____.

6. _____ May parked the car.

7. _____ he knocked on the door.

8. Li hid the gift _____.

9. Yvette walked _____.

10. I received an A _____.

❏

Since you know that the subject of a sentence is never in a prepositional phrase, you can find the subject of the sentence easily. First cross out all of the prepositional phrases; then decide which of the remaining words is performing the action.

She applied (for a job) (as a short-order cook) (at Gino's). [The subject is *she*.]

One (of my favorite comic strips) (in the Sunday paper) is *Doonesbury*. [The subject is *one*.]

ACTIVITY
4

Identifying Prepositional Phrases and Subjects. In each of the following sentences, cross out the prepositional phrases and circle the subject.

1. A student in his class published her story in the paper.

2. An essay on Eileen's travels in Mexico won the award.

3. One of her poems was in our textbook.

4. Donna often writes about her childhood in Alaska.

5. Her letters from college describe her friends and her teachers.

6. Bob's seat in the top row made it easy for him to see the band.

7. The hour before a test is always difficult for Chuck.

8. Luther's trip to Asia took him through Australia.

9. Their house by the river has been flooded five times.

10. His stories about the floods appeared in national news magazines. ❑

 ESL Writers

Prepositions showing time, such as *for*, *during*, and *since*, have subtle differences in meaning.

For refers to an exact period of time, one that has a beginning and an end.

I went to college *for* six years.
It has been raining *for* two hours.
I've been cooking *for* a long time.

During refers to an indefinite period of time.

Several times *during* the semester I was very busy.
I plan to visit my parents sometime *during* the summer.
It snowed *during* the night, but I don't know exactly when.

Since refers to time that has elapsed.

I've gained weight *since* moving into the dorm.
Since Joe graduated, he's been looking for a job.
Pete's been so happy *since* his daughter was born.

ESL Writers

Do not omit the subject of a sentence.

INCORRECT
I love math. Is my favorite subject.

CORRECT
I love math. *It* is my favorite subject.

INCORRECT
Walks to the store.

CORRECT
My mother walks to the store.

 ESL Writers

A noun and its pronoun cannot *both* be the subject of a sentence.

INCORRECT
Henry he stayed up late.

CORRECT
Henry stayed up late.

INCORRECT
Barbara Jordan she was a great orator.

CORRECT
Barbara Jordan was a great orator.

Ask Yourself

What is the easiest way to find the subject of a sentence? Since you know that the subject of a sentence never appears in a prepositional phrase, you can cross out all of the prepositional phrases in the sentence and decide which of the remaining words is the subject.

Verbs

Action and Linking Verbs

An *action verb* conveys the action of the subject.

Veronica *races* her bike.

The train *left* for Chicago.

Our family *met* Dave in Dallas.

A *linking verb* connects the subject to a word that renames or describes it. The most common linking verbs include the forms of *to be: am, are, is, was, were, be, been, being.*

Amanda *is* seventeen.

We *are* lost.

I *am* happy.

Certain other words can also act as linking verbs. Most of these other words have to do with our senses:

appear	grow	smell
feel	look	sound
get	seem	taste

Notice how such words act as linking verbs in the following sentences:

The coffee *tastes* bitter.

She *grows* taller every year.

My feet *feel* tired.

However, these same words can act as action verbs, as in the following sentences:

She *tastes* the chef's special.

My sister *grows* tomatoes in her garden.

He *feels* the rough edges of the desk.

How can you tell whether one of these words is acting as a linking verb or an action verb in a sentence? Try replacing the verb with one of the forms of *to be* to see if the sentence still makes sense. If you can substitute a *to be* verb (as in "The coffee *is* bitter"), then the word is acting as a linking verb. If you cannot exchange a *to be* verb (as in "She *is* the chef's special"), then the word is acting as an action verb.

Identifying Action and Linking Verbs. In each of the following sentences, underline the verb and identify it as an action verb or a linking verb.

ACTIVITY

5

1. My parents went home on Sunday. _____

2. In this part of the country the sun shines nearly every day.

   _____

3. She is with her best friend. _____

4. Sam and Louise were already at the park. _____

5. The store appears to be out of business. _____

6. Harry felt the cold rain on his face. _____

7. The lasagna smells delicious. _____

8. The children danced shyly in front of their parents. _____

9. I was late for the third time this month. _____

10. Anna felt the sting of the cold air. _____

   ❏

Helping Verbs

In addition to action verbs and linking verbs, sentences may contain helping verbs. A *helping verb* indicates the time of other verbs in the sentence.

- *to be* verbs: *am, are, is, was, were, be, been, being*
- *to have* verbs: *have, has, had*
- *to do* verbs: *do, does, did*
- *may, might, must*
- *can, could, shall, should, will, would*

I *should* wash my car. [The helping verb *should* indicates that the action, *wash,* needs to be completed in the future.]

Jorge *had* finished the job. [Here the helping verb *had* indicates that the action, *finish,* was completed in the past.]

Tron *will* drive the car. [Here the helping verb *will* indicates that the action, *drive,* will be completed in the future.]

 ESL Writers

Helping verbs always come before action and linking verbs in sentences.

Identifying Helping Verbs. Circle the helping verbs in the following sentences. (Note that some sentences may not contain helping
verbs.)

ACTIVITY
6

1. I must finish studying for this test before I go to the party.

2. This customer can pay with a credit card.

3. The dog chased its tail.

4. May I close the door?

5. You might not want to go shopping today.

6. Jane could take a nap after lunch.

7. April smoothed out the wrinkles in her skirt.

8. The snow is not going to stop soon.

9. My computer needs more memory.

10. Before his shift is over, Deion should return all the phone calls. ❏

 ESL Writers

When you write questions and negative statements in the past
tense using the helping verb *do,* put only *do* in the past tense. Do
not change the main verb to the past tense.

INCORRECT
When *did* she *left* the movie?

CORRECT
When *did* she *leave* the movie?

INCORRECT
I *did* not *washed* my clothes.

CORRECT
I *did* not *wash* my clothes.

ACTIVITY
7

Identifying Action, Linking, and Helping Verbs. Underline the verbs in the following sentences. Then, in the space provided, identify each verb as an action, linking, or helping verb.

1. I should have registered for my classes earlier. _____

   _____

2. I registered during late registration. _____

   _____

3. Most of the classes were full. _____

   _____

4. The only English class I could take is at 6:30 in the morning.

   _____

5. My math class will meet on Saturdays. _____

   _____

6. I did ask for an overload in algebra. _____

   _____

7. Biology classes were completely full. _____

   _____

8. I could have signed up for my classes earlier. _____

   _____

9. I will remember my early registration date next semester.

   _____

10. I have a difficult schedule for the next four months. _____

   _____

Regular and Irregular Verbs

Regular verbs form the past tense and past participle by adding *-ed*.

REGULAR VERBS

Verb	*Past Tense*	*Past Participle*
cook	cooked	cooked
measure	measured	measured
study	studied	studied
walk	walked	walked

Irregular verbs form the past tense and past participle in different ways.

IRREGULAR VERBS

Verb	*Past Tense*	*Past Participle*
to be	was, were	been
begin	began	begun
catch	caught	caught
choose	chose	chosen
come	came	come
do	did	done
drink	drank	drunk
eat	ate	eaten
feel	felt	felt
fly	flew	flown
get	got	gotten
go	went	gone
leave	left	left
ride	rode	ridden
see	saw	seen
sleep	slept	slept
take	took	taken
write	wrote	written

Past participles are used with *has* or *have*, as in the following examples:

I *have eaten* a big dinner.

Joan *has caught* two fish.

The children *have done* their chores.

ESL Writers

Always use the appropriate verb tense, even when phrases such as *now*, *yesterday*, or *a week ago* already indicate when the action took place.

INCORRECT

Yesterday I *catch* two fish.

CORRECT

Yesterday I *caught* two fish.

INCORRECT

Tomorrow my sister *leave* for China.

CORRECT

Tomorrow my sister *will leave* for China.

 ESL Writers

Do not omit the verb from a sentence, even when the meaning is evident without it.

INCORRECT

Bernard a hard worker.

CORRECT

Bernard *is* a hard worker.

INCORRECT

The Rocky Mountains steep and rugged.

CORRECT

The Rocky Mountains *are* steep and rugged.

ACTIVITY
8

Using Regular and Irregular Verbs. Write the correct form of the verb in the space provided. If necessary, consult your dictionary for the correct form.

1. Janice _____ more than ten hours last night. *(sleep)*

2. The doorbell has _____ three times in the last hour. *(ring)*

3. I only _____ thirty minutes for the test. *(study)*

4. The turkey _____ all afternoon. *(cook)*

5. My brother and I have _____ three fish today. *(catch)*

6. Last night Sam _____ so much he woke with a hangover. *(drink)*

7. My favorite book is *One* _____ *over the Cuckoo's Nest.* *(fly)*

8. Someone has _____ my purse. *(steal)*

9. Yesterday I _____ my favorite pair of pants in the wash. *(place)*

10. My best friend and I have _____ each other for ten years. *(know)* ❏

 ESL Writers

Many verbs in English consist of two words. Here are some of the most common ones:

ask out	keep up
break down	leave out
call up	make up
clean up	pick up
drop in	play around
get along	put together
give up	shut up
help out	wake up

INCORRECT

Susan *picked* her room.

CORRECT

Susan *picked up* her room.

INCORRECT

When buying gifts, James *left* his cousin.

CORRECT

When buying gifts, James *left out* his cousin.

ESL Writers

Do not omit verb endings.

INCORRECT
The student *need* more money.

CORRECT
The student *needs* more money.

INCORRECT
Yesterday she *ask* for a raise.

CORRECT
Yesterday she *asked* for a raise.

ACTIVITY
9

Identifying Subjects and Verbs. Circle the subjects and underline the verbs in the following paragraph.

Every night at my grandmother's house, I would go to sleep to the whirring sound of the sewing machine. My grandmother was a seamstress. She didn't work during the day. During the day, she slept. But she worked all night. Sometimes my mother and my aunt would help her. Then they would stay awake all night. After those nights, my brother and I would fix ourselves breakfast. Then we would quietly watch cartoons. In the afternoons, the customers would come for their dresses. They would hand my sleepy grandmother checks and cash and step out of the door full of life into the beautiful sunlit days. ❑

Verb Pretenders

Like subject pretenders, there are verb pretenders—words that look like verbs but that do not act as verbs in sentences. The most common verb pretenders are the *verb + -ing* and *to + verb* combinations.

singing	to climb
talking	to go
rowing	to rest

When an *-ing* verb appears in a sentence *without a helping verb,* it modifies, or describes, other words in the sentence.

We could hear Dad *singing* in the shower. [The *-ing* verb modifies *Dad.*]
He *was singing* "She Loves Me." [The complete verb is *was singing.*]

Yelling loudly, Peter hailed the cab. [The *-ing* verb modifies *Peter.*]
Peter *yelled* loudly at the cab. [The complete verb is *yelled.*]

We can spot the crew *rowing* toward shore. [The *-ing* verb modifies *crew.*]
The crew *is rowing* toward shore. [The complete verb is *is rowing.*]

Identifying *-ing* Verbs. In the space provided, indicate whether the *-ing* verb in each sentence functions as a modifier or as a verb.

ACTIVITY
10

1. Alice was studying with me. ⎯⎯⎯⎯⎯⎯⎯⎯⎯⎯

2. Studying together, Alice and I learned most of the equations.

   ⎯⎯⎯⎯⎯⎯⎯⎯⎯⎯⎯⎯⎯⎯⎯⎯⎯⎯⎯⎯⎯⎯

3. The swimming pool is green from algae. ⎯⎯⎯⎯⎯⎯⎯⎯

4. I was swimming when the phone rang. ⎯⎯⎯⎯⎯⎯⎯⎯

5. Nicole loves the cartoon with the dancing bears. ⎯⎯⎯⎯⎯⎯

6. Working as a team, we finished the project in an hour. ⎯⎯⎯⎯

7. She was mowing the lawn when Fred came home. ⎯⎯⎯⎯⎯

8. The changing room at the gym is filthy. ⎯⎯⎯⎯⎯⎯⎯

9. My mother was shocked to see me lighting a cigarette. _____

10. That barking dog is driving me crazy. _____

ACTIVITY
11

Using Verbs and Verb Pretenders. For each of the following *-ing* verbs, write two sentences. In the first sentence, use the word as a verb. In the second sentence, use the word as a modifier.

EXAMPLE

listening

Verb: <u>I was listening to the beautiful music.</u>

Pretender verb: <u>Listening to the music, I forgot about the time.</u>

1. boiling

Verb: _____

_____

Verb pretender: _____

_____

2. growing

Verb: _____

_____

Verb pretender: _____

_____

3. dripping

Verb: _____

_____

Verb pretender: _____

_____

4. sleeping

    Verb: _____

    _____

    Verb pretender: _____

    _____

5. trembling

    Verb: _____

    _____

    Verb pretender: _____

    _____

The *to* + *verb* combination also looks like a verb but does not act as a verb in a sentence; rather, it can act as either a noun or a modifier.

> I can't wait *to open* my gifts. [Because *to* appears in front of the verb *open*, *to open* does not act as a verb. Rather, it acts as a modifier.]
>
> I *opened* my gifts. [Here *opened* acts as a verb.]

> Susan went to the store *to buy* apples. [Because *to* appears in front of the verb *buy*, *to buy* does not act as a verb. Rather, it acts as a modifier.]
>
> Susan *bought* apples at the store. [Here *bought* acts as a verb.]

> *To study* would be the sensible thing to do. [Because *to* appears in front of the verb *study*, *to study* does not act as a verb. Rather, it acts as a noun.]
>
> I *studied*, which was the sensible thing to do. [Here *studied* acts as a verb.]

Using *to* + *Verb* Combinations. Complete each sentence with a *to* + *verb* combination.

ACTIVITY
12

EXAMPLE
Joe waited until June <u>to buy a car</u>.

1. Erin didn't want _____.

Sentences

2. _____ was boring, according to Ned.

3. Joss decided _____.

4. My friends desired _____.

5. After being on my feet all day, I couldn't wait _____.

6. "_____," said Hamlet.

7. I love _____.

8. After two days on the road, we need _____.

9. My favorite hobby is _____.

10. _____ is Matilda's greatest wish.

ACTIVITY
13

Identifying Subjects and Verbs. Circle the subjects and underline the verbs in the following paragraph.

Amanda waited to study until the night before the test. After studying all night, she slept late the next morning. Waking late, she had ten minutes to drive to school. She arrived at class just as the bell started to ring. The teacher was handing out the tests. Amanda took a deep breath before picking up the questions. She hoped to make at least a C+ on the test. During the test, her mind kept wandering. Running late for school, she hadn't had time to eat breakfast. Leaving the classroom after the test, Amanda promised to improve her study habits. ❑

Ask Yourself

What is the easiest way to find the verb in a sentence? Find out whether it's a verb or a verb pretender. When a verb + *ing* combination appears in a sentence without a helping verb, it's a verb pretender. When a *to* + verb combination appears directly in front of a verb, it's a verb pretender.

Adjectives and Adverbs

Adjectives modify nouns by describing or adding information about them.

He prepared her *favorite* meal.

The *yellow* pansy stood out in the *beautiful* flower bed.

My *new* car really impresses my *classy* friends.

He looked at the *dilapidated* bus and wondered if he dared get on it.

Adjectives may also be used to show comparison. When comparing two things, add *-er* or *more*. When comparing three or more things, add *-est* or *most*.

Mary is *shorter* than Joan.

He was *more* fearful of the lion than she was.

Mary is the *shortest* of her three friends.

He was the *most* fearful of the lion of all his friends.

 ESL Writers

Some adjectives are forms of verbs that end with *-ing* or *-ed*. A verb form that ends with *-ing* modifies a person or thing *causing* an experience. A verb form that ends with *-ed* modifies a person or thing *undergoing* an experience.

An example:

INCORRECT

The movie is *interested*.

(continued)

(continued)

CORRECT

The movie is *interesting*.

The first sentence is incorrect because the movie isn't experiencing interest. The second sentence is correct because the movie is causing interest.

Another example:

INCORRECT

After the tournament, the tennis player was *exhausting*.

CORRECT

After the tournament, the tennis player was *exhausted*.

In these examples, the first sentence is incorrect because the tennis player isn't causing exhaustion. Instead, the tennis player is experiencing exhaustion. Thus, the second sentence is correct.

ACTIVITY

14

Identifying Adjectives. Underline the adjectives in the following sentences.

1. My Aunt Jamie is a lovely person.

2. My flighty niece, however, is a chatterbox.

3. They usually sell honey-roasted peanuts on overseas flights.

4. He gave her the biggest piece of cake.

5. The old dog jumped onto the plaid sofa and slept away the sunny afternoon.

6. The cold weather forces me to wear my warm overcoat.

7. His was the smaller of the two suitcases.

8. Susan decided to buy the red dress.

9. This was the most expensive item on the menu.

10. The wrecked car was parked next to the curb. ❑

ESL Writers

Do not make adjectives plural even when the nouns they modify are plural.

INCORRECT

The *browns* shoes need to be polished.

CORRECT

The *brown* shoes need to be polished.

INCORRECT

I found three *larges* boxes.

CORRECT

I found three *large* boxes.

Adverbs modify verbs, adjectives, or other adverbs by describing or adding information about them. Adverbs usually answer the questions how, when, where, why, or how often.

The coach ran *toward* the swimmers. [modifies the verb]

The swimmers returned to the pool *very* slowly. [modifies the adverb]

The swimmers were *frequently* late getting to practice. [modifies the adjective]

Adverbs may also be used for comparison. When comparing two things, add *more*. When comparing three or more things, add *most*.

Jan spends her money *more wisely* than Betty.

Among Jan, Betty, Lisa, and Helena, Jan spends her money *most wisely* of all.

Identifying Adverbs. Underline the adverbs in the following sentences.

ACTIVITY

15

1. The birds chirped noisily at my bedroom window.

2. The hike was very worthwhile.

3. The cat was more likely to lie in the sun than the dog.

4. The gasping, perspiring runner quickly dropped out of the race.

5. He ran swiftly toward his mother.

6. Tammy stepped to the door and listened silently.

7. He was the most respected professor on campus.

8. He seldom cared for horror movies.

9. I was surprised that I had done well on the exam.

10. We carefully opened the door. ❑

 ESL Writers

Most adjectives come *before* the words they modify. Adverbs, however, can come at any point in the sentence.

 ESL Writers

When comparing two things, put the word *than* between the adverb or adjective and the second thing.

INCORRECT

Mike is smaller Roberto.

CORRECT

Mike is smaller *than* Roberto.

INCORRECT

My cat Freckles runs faster my dog Murphy.

CORRECT

My cat Freckles runs faster *than* my dog Murphy.

Clauses

Clauses are the building blocks of sentences. There are two kinds of clauses: independent and dependent.

Independent Clauses

An *independent clause* is a group of words with a subject and a verb that expresses a complete thought. In other words, it can stand alone as a complete sentence. All sentences contain at least one independent clause. Some sentences contain two or more independent clauses.

> Marty enjoyed his first year of college. [This sentence is an independent clause because it contains a subject and a verb and expresses a complete thought.]
>
> He learned how to study, and he learned to manage his time. [This sentence consists of two independent clauses.]
>
> He had time to complete his schoolwork properly and time for his friends. [This sentence consists of one independent clause.]

ACTIVITY
16

Identifying Independent Clauses. Underline the independent clauses in the following groups of words. Then add punctuation and capitalization to make the independent clause a complete sentence. If the group of words is not an independent clause, mark an X after it.

1. my high school English teacher taught me a lot about writing

2. writing every day in her class

3. who made us write at the beginning of each class for fifteen minutes

4. in the beginning I didn't think all that writing helped

5. when we finally started our research papers two months before the end of school

6. my writing had improved

7. I also felt more confident as a writer

8. because she encouraged us to write about our interests

9. my final research paper earned an A

10. it was also fun to write ❑

Dependent Clauses

A *dependent clause*, as its name implies, depends on other information to make a sentence complete. Although a dependent clause contains a subject and a verb, it does not express a complete thought and cannot stand alone as a sentence. Many dependent clauses begin with one of these words:

after	if	until
although	since	when
as	that	where
because	though	while
before	unless	

Because the electricity went out, I couldn't study for my chemistry test. [This dependent clause contains a subject and a verb, but it does not complete the thought and cannot stand alone.]

Before the week was over, I'd received two job offers. [This sentence also starts with a dependent clause.]

I'd never known extreme heat *until I visited Phoenix in the summer.* [This dependent clause comes at the end of the sentence.]

ACTIVITY
17

Identifying Dependent Clauses. Underline the dependent clauses in the following paragraph.

This year's football team has been a huge disappointment. We've struggled with our passing game after our quarterback was injured. Until he comes back, we have to rely on our running game. Our running backs are experienced, although they fumble the ball too much. Because the kicker is a freshman, our kicking game has been poor. Unless the team gets better, we might end up with our worst record since we finished last in our division in 1990. ❑

A dependent clause may also begin with one of these words:

that	who
what	whoever
whatever	whom
where	whomever
which	whose

Don't forget *where you hid the Easter eggs.* [The dependent clause can't stand alone.]

Whoever left crumbs on the table should wipe them up. [This dependent clause is the subject of the sentence.]

The student *who studies hard* will do well. [Here the dependent clause modifies the subject of the sentence.]

Identifying Dependent Clauses. Underline the dependent clauses in the following paragraphs.

ACTIVITY
18

1. When I first enrolled in college, I expected it to be like high school. I've learned that college teachers expect you to work harder. They also expect you to think critically. If you don't want to work hard and try new things, I wouldn't suggest college.

2. My college composition class is filled with students who did well in high school English. We were surprised when our teacher asked us to revise our papers. Whenever I wrote a paper for English, I just wrote it quickly the night before the paper was due. After we got our first papers back, I realized that I couldn't write that way in college. After I began to revise, my grades improved. I feel my writing has also improved since I started this class. ❏

Ask Yourself

How do you tell the difference between an independent and a dependent clause? An independent clause can stand on its own as a complete sentence because it contains a subject and a verb and expresses a complete thought. Although a dependent clause also contains a subject and a verb, it doesn't express a complete thought and can't stand alone as a complete sentence.

Correct Sentences

Sentence Fragments

A *sentence fragment* is a group of words that looks like a sentence—the first letter is capitalized and it ends with a period—but is *not* a sentence. At times, writers use them intentionally for emphasis or in dialogue. The science fiction writer Ray Bradbury, for instance, uses sentence fragments to describe the destruction of a house in his short story "August 2026: There Will Come Soft Rains." In the same way that the house is in pieces, the writing is in pieces—or fragments.

> The crash. The attic smashing into kitchen and parlor. The parlor into cellar, cellar into sub-cellar. Deep freeze, armchair, film tapes, circuits, bed, and all like skeletons thrown in a cluttered mound. Smoke and silence.

Sentence fragments may be used by writers in dialogue to reflect people's tendency to speak in fragments. Here's an example from Richard Selzer's autobiography, *Down from Troy:*

> In the lower grades of Public School No. 5 the first half hour of each day was spent taking attendance. As each name was called, we were required to leap to our feet and recite a proverb.
> "Kathleen McGuire!"
> "A rolling stone gathers no moss."
> "Patrick Logan!"
> "Empty barrels make the most noise."
> "Richard Selzer!"
> "A stitch in time saves nine."

In most other writing situations, however, and especially in the writing you do in college or at work, sentence fragments are considered errors. To avoid unintentional sentence fragments, you first have to understand the components of a *complete* sentence. A complete sentence has a subject and a verb and expresses a complete thought. Usually, the *subject* tells who or what is doing the action. The *verb* conveys the action or links the subject to the rest of the sentence.

The *ball is* red.

I danced at the party.

Douglas gave his speech.

I moved back home.

(For more information on complete sentences, see p. 421.)

Identifying Sentence Fragments. In the space provided, indicate whether each group of words is a sentence fragment or a complete sentence.

ACTIVITY
1

1. My dog loves to hike. ＿＿＿＿＿＿＿＿＿＿＿＿＿＿

2. On Caroline's birthday. ＿＿＿＿＿＿＿＿＿＿＿＿＿＿

3. The oldest dinosaur known to exist. ＿＿＿＿＿＿＿＿＿

4. When will you come home tonight? ＿＿＿＿＿＿＿＿＿＿

5. That cupcake is loaded with empty calories. ＿＿＿＿＿＿

6. My daughter, the smartest student in the class.＿＿＿＿＿＿

7. Running as fast as she could. ＿＿＿＿＿＿＿＿＿＿＿＿

8. Today of all days. ＿＿＿＿＿＿＿＿＿＿＿＿＿＿＿＿

9. The restaurant smelled of cigarette smoke and barbecued meat.

＿＿＿＿＿＿＿＿＿＿＿＿＿＿＿＿＿＿＿＿＿＿＿＿＿

10. Splashed water all over the bathroom floor. ＿＿＿＿＿＿
❏

Phrases

If a group of words lacks a subject or a verb or both, it's a *phrase*. A phrase is not a complete sentence. Notice the difference between phrases and sentences in these examples:

PHRASE

To make my house safe from burglars.

SENTENCE

I need to make my house safe from burglars.

PHRASE

Making a quilt.

SENTENCE

Elaine spent weeks making a quilt.

PHRASE

Including a new computer.

SENTENCE

My goal is to buy new equipment, including a computer.

PHRASE

Walking through the mall.

SENTENCE

We spent the day walking through the mall.

ACTIVITY
2

Turning Phrases into Sentences. Rewrite each of the following phrases to make it a complete sentence.

1. Running after the ball _____

_____

_____

_____

2. After the delicious Thanksgiving dinner _____

_____

_____

_____

3. Divided up my time equally _____

_____

_____

_____

4. Because of the traffic jam _____

_____

_____

_____

5. To avoid the freezing temperatures up north _____

_____

_____

_____

6. Having to go out of town _____

_____

_____

_____

7. Jane's smiling face _____

_____

_____

_____

8. The Olympic games held in Atlanta, Georgia _____

_____

_____

_____

9. This expensive but beautiful coat _____

_____

_____

_____

10. Drinking the coffee as fast as I could _____

_____

_____

_____

❑

 ESL Writers

Don't confuse a verb with a verbal. A *verbal* acts as a modifer or a noun.

In the following phrase, *barking* is a verbal because it describes the dog:

SENTENCE FRAGMENT

The barking dog.

But in this sentence, the word *barks* shows what the subject —*The dog*—is doing:

COMPLETE SENTENCE

The dog barks every morning.

In this phrase, *cooking* acts as a noun:

SENTENCE FRAGMENT

The cooking that Henry did.

But here *cooks* shows what the subject is doing:

COMPLETE SENTENCE

Henry cooks every evening.

A verbal acting as a noun can be the subject of a sentence:

COMPLETE SENTENCE

The cooking that Henry did will never be forgotten.

Here *The cooking that Henry did* serves as the subject.

Many phrases begin with the word *who, whom, whose, which, who-ever,* or *whomever.*

PHRASE

Whose purse was stolen.

SENTENCE
Janet, not Beverly, is the student *whose purse was stolen.*

PHRASE
Which was very spicy.

SENTENCE
Steve eagerly ate the chile, *which was very spicy.*

PHRASE
Who was always there for me.

SENTENCE
I miss my best friend, *who was always there for me.*

Turning Phrases into Sentences. Rewrite each of the following phrases to make it a complete sentence.

1. Who knew my cousin Jim _____

_____

_____

_____

2. Who ate my homework _____

_____

_____

_____

_____

3. Whose clothes are on the floor _____

_____

_____

_____

_____

4. Whoever left the phone off the hook _____

_____

_____

_____

5. Which was her last meal _____

_____

_____

_____

6. Whose bookbag was stolen from the library _____

_____

_____

_____

7. Whoever last did the dishes _____

_____

_____

_____

8. Who left the front door open _____

_____

_____

_____

9. Who sang "The Star-Spangled Banner" at the baseball game

_____

_____

_____

10. Whose car ran out of gas on the freeway _____

_____

_____

_____

❏

Incomplete Thoughts

Sometimes a group of words contains a subject and a verb but doesn't express a complete thought. This group of words, called a *dependent clause,* can't stand alone as a sentence. Therefore, it is a sentence fragment. (For more information on dependent clauses, see pp. 443–445.)

FRAGMENT

Because my family is very close.

SENTENCE

Because my family is very close, we always get together on holidays.

The fragment doesn't express a complete thought, so it can't stand alone as a sentence. The sentence can stand alone. It contains a subject (*we*), a verb (*get together*), and expresses a complete thought. Here's another example:

FRAGMENT

When we ate our Sunday dinner.

SENTENCE

Darkness had fallen when we ate our Sunday dinner.

The fragment doesn't express a complete thought, so it isn't a sentence. The sentence contains a subject (*darkness*), a verb (*had fallen*), and expresses a complete thought, so it can stand alone.

Turning Incomplete Thoughts into Sentences. In the space provided, rewrite each of the following incomplete thoughts to make it a sentence.

ACTIVITY
4

1. Before I went home for the last time _____

_____

_____

_____

2. Although my family had to struggle to pay for my tuition

_____

_____

_____

3. When you drive down rutted mountain roads_____

_____

_____

_____

4. Where each of her children had been born _____

_____

_____

_____

5. That I finished high school at the top of my class _____

_____

_____

_____

6. Unless you get home before midnight _____

_____

_____

_____

7. While Eunice waited for the bus _____

_____

_____

_____

8. Where you put your dirty laundry _____

_____

_____

_____

9. Because I was so hungry _____

_____

_____

_____

10. Although the election was still a month away _____

_____

_____

_____

❑

Correcting Sentence Fragments

How do you correct a sentence fragment? One way is to connect it to the sentence that comes before or after it.

FRAGMENT

After eating the last piece of chicken. Matt smiled guiltily.

SENTENCE

After eating the last piece of chicken, Matt smiled guiltily.

FRAGMENT

My family consists of my brother, two sisters, and grandmother. *And, of course, my mother.*

SENTENCE

My family consists of my brother, two sisters, grandmother, *and, of course, my mother.*

Another way to correct a sentence fragment is to revise it into a complete sentence.

FRAGMENT

To leave my sister at home alone.

COMPUTER TIP

TEST FOR SENTENCE FRAGMENTS

Press the "return" key after each period in your essay to create a list of your sentences. Read the list to check for fragments that need to be corrected.

Grammar

SENTENCE

It was a crime *to leave my sister at home alone.*

FRAGMENT

So I didn't vote.

SENTENCE

I didn't vote because I didn't like either of the candidates.

Ask Yourself

How can you spot a sentence fragment? Ask these questions:

- Does it have a verb? (Keep in mind the difference between a verb and a verb pretender.) If the answer is no, it's a fragment. If the answer is yes, go to the next question.
- Does it have a subject? (Usually the subject comes before the verb.) If the answer is no, it's a fragment. If the answer is yes, go to the final question.
- Is it an incomplete thought? If the answer is yes, it's a fragment.

ACTIVITY
5

Correcting Sentence Fragments. Identify each of the following items as a complete sentence or a sentence fragment. Then correct each sentence fragment by connecting it to the sentence that comes before or after it or by rewriting it as a complete sentence.

1. Both of my father's parents lived past their ninetieth year. His mother to a hundred and four and his father to ninety-five.

_____

_____

_____

2. Driving through the deserted town. I remember the stories my grandfather told me.

_____

_____

_____

Correct Sentences **457**

3. In order to spend time with my grandmother. I decided to move to my father's hometown.

_____

_____

_____

4. Before I'd heard about my grandmother's trip to Mexico in the 1920s. I was afraid to travel alone.

_____

_____

_____

5. It is very important. Remembering where you came from.

_____

_____

_____

6. Watching the flowers bloom each spring takes me back to my childhood. My mother planted our yard with bulbs and flowers that bloomed from April to July.

_____

_____

_____

7. I walk for an hour each evening. Because we spent so much time walking the fields of our parents' farm. I need my evening walks to clear my head.

_____

_____

_____

8. That change is both good and bad. I understand that. _____

_____

_____

_____

9. After I returned to my hometown and found most of the Main Street stores closed. I realized that my parents' dream of a country life for their children had disappeared.

_____

_____

_____

10. Seeing my sisters for the first time in two years and laughing with them about how much we had changed.

_____

_____

_____

ACTIVITY
6

Correcting Sentence Fragments. Rewrite the following paragraph to eliminate the sentence fragments.

My father floats three feet above the ground. His eyes look directly out at me. From this photograph taken of him his first year on the college football team. His hair, what there is left of it, sticks up less than a half-inch from his head. A cut that he would keep all his life. No grass stains spoil his white jersey. His shoes are polished. If I could see the spikes that fly out behind him. I feel certain I wouldn't find any old mud or grass clinging to the steel. His arms are spread wide and his mouth is set in a determined grimace. In a darker gray than either the grass or sky in this black and white photograph. The number on his jersey says 49. My favorite picture of my father. He is young and strong, and he is flying. If only for a moment.   ❏

Run-on Sentences

A *run-on sentence* contains two or more independent clauses that run together without a connecting word or punctuation. A run-on sentence is difficult to read because it is unclear where one idea ends and another begins. Unlike a complete sentence, which consists of a subject and a verb and expresses a complete thought, a run-on sentence expresses more than one thought without the correct punctuation or connecting word.

Here is an example:

RUN-ON SENTENCE

I gave my dog Ralph the bone he liked it so much that it was gone in a minute.

This sentence is confusing because its two independent clauses are not separated. To correct this run-on sentence, separate the independent clauses with a period, a semicolon, or a comma and a connecting word (such as *and, but, or, nor, for, yet,* or *so*).

CORRECTED WITH A PERIOD

I gave my dog Ralph the bone. *He* liked it so much that it was gone in a minute.

CORRECTED WITH A SEMICOLON

I gave my dog Ralph the bone; he liked it so much that it was gone in a minute.

CORRECTED WITH A COMMA AND CONNECTING WORD

I gave my dog Ralph the bone, *and* he liked it so much that it was gone in a minute.

Grammar

Correcting Run-on Sentences. Correct the following run-on sentences by separating the independent clauses with a period, a semicolon, or a comma and connecting word.

1. It was a dark and stormy night isn't it always dark and stormy when something bad happens?

_____

_____

_____

2. Mary stood close to the doorway, her hand resting on her hip a child peered out from behind her.

_____

_____

_____

3. My teacher tried to get me to make more friends she would give me assignments that required group work.

_____

_____

_____

_____

4. Once I realized I could no longer live in a city, I searched for communities less than a hundred miles away I couldn't live in a city but I did want to visit now and then.

_____

_____

_____

_____

5. His blond hair, cut at awkward angles and sticking straight up from his skull, formed an eerie halo around his head whether that halo told of good or evil, I couldn't tell.

_____

_____

_____

6. Keith's upper arms are covered in intricate purple and yellow floral designs his left eyebrow is accentuated with a small gold hoop a small black chain is etched into the skin of his right ankle.

_____

_____

_____

7. Although no music pounded out of the huge speaker on either side of the raised platform, the noise from the crowd was deafening then the stadium lights went out.

_____

_____

_____

8. Maria may be the 1990s version of June Cleaver her brown hair is layered and cut just below the chin she teaches aerobics classes three times a week and attends the community college three days a week.

_____

_____

_____

9. In 1974, I was content to sit in front of the television for hours watching *The Brady Bunch* or whatever mindless programing the networks presented to kids home from school long before their parents arrived from work I'm not content to let my daughter

waste her time watching reruns of *Roseanne* or *Beverly Hills 90210,* though.

_____

_____

_____

10. The coach's eyes narrow and his jaw tightens he looks ready to bolt as he watches his student prepare for her dismount on the uneven bars.

_____

_____

_____

ACTIVITY
8

Eliminating Run-on Sentences. Eliminate the run-on sentences from the following paragraph by using a period, a semicolon, or a comma and connecting word as needed.

Up north we had a saying for girls like Jessica whose hair was teased impossibly high. Makeup was plastered in layer after layer her eyelashes matted in thick clumps. Her fingernails were long and hard and a bright red. Her lipstick matched her fingernails. She wore pantyhose even in the heat of summer she wore high heels even if she had to stand all day. In Boston, we looked at girls like that and said, "Hey, Revere." We didn't mean Paul Revere we were referring to a small suburb east of Boston known for its beautiful girls. Of course, we assumed some lack of intelligence with those girls from Revere who in their right mind would wear hose when it's 106 degrees outside? I never really knew any girls from Revere when I was growing up, so I never corrected the assumption that Revere girls weren't the brightest bulbs on the tree Jessica corrected that assumption for me. She constantly scored higher on zoology tests than I did. Unlike me, she could focus the microscopes in zoology lab her fingernails were even useful during some of our more difficult dissections. ❏

Comma Splices

A *comma splice* contains two independent clauses separated by a comma. But the comma, which indicates only a slight pause, is not a strong enough punctuation mark to separate the two independent clauses. A comma splice is similar to a run-on sentence in that it expresses more than one thought without the correct punctuation.

Here is an example:

COMMA SPLICE

My sister is still in law school, she expects to finish in June.

To correct this comma splice, separate the two independent clauses with a period, a semicolon, or a comma and a connecting word.

CORRECTED WITH A PERIOD

My sister is still in law school. *She* expects to finish in June.

CORRECTED WITH A SEMICOLON

My sister is still in law school; she expects to finish in June.

CORRECTED WITH A COMMA AND CONNECTING WORD

My sister is still in law school, *but* she expects to finish in June.

Correcting Comma Splices. Correct the following comma splices by separating the two independent clauses with a period, a semicolon, or a comma and connecting word as needed.

ACTIVITY
9

1. I first met Angie in high school, we were in the same class.

_____

_____

_____

2. He asked the instructor to repeat herself, then he pushed his hair back from his forehead.

_____

_____

_____

3. Someone once told me that I couldn't say bad things about myself, he said there were enough people around to do that for me.

_____

_____

_____

4. When I first got married, I cooked dinner every night, now, more often than not, we heat microwave dinners and eat them in front of the television.

_____

_____

_____

5. Brian pulls his English notebook from his backpack, I catch a glimpse of black ballet slippers next to his biology book.

_____

_____

_____

_____

Grammar

6. Meredith's auburn hair always looks a bit unkempt, she dresses in clothes that look several sizes too large for her lanky body.

_____

_____

_____

7. She took an egg out of the refrigerator and cracked it into a bowl, it still looked fresh.

_____

_____

_____

8. When I was twelve, a boy named Derrick shot me in the forehead with a BB gun, the next year he asked me to the junior high homecoming.

_____

_____

_____

9. Once Dan had decided to decline the football scholarship, he was relieved that he'd finally made up his mind, however, he was afraid his father wouldn't help him with his college expenses.

_____

_____

_____

10. I became active in the homeless shelter four blocks away from my house, what I've learned since going to work there has helped me understand the homeless.

_____

_____

_____

ACTIVITY
10

Eliminating Comma Splices. Eliminate the comma splices from the following paragraph by using a period, a semicolon, or a comma and connecting word as needed.

When I went from a small community college to a large university, I actually forgot to go to my classes. I remembered to go to Philosophy: Humans and the Universe for the first six weeks because the first book we read was *Alice's Adventures through the Looking Glass,* I remembered to go to my other philosophy class because the professor was cute. Somehow, though, I only made it to art history three or four times during the semester, I even liked art history, but the class was on Friday at one o'clock, by then I was usually on my way back to my hometown to spend the weekend with my boyfriend. About halfway through the semester, I stopped attending all of my classes. My boyfriend and I were breaking up, I felt out of place at such a big school. I hadn't made any friends. I had a job at the library, I stopped going to work, too. After I realized I couldn't keep a decent grade point average if I didn't go to class, I called the registrar and dropped all my classes. I went home for the summer, applied to a smaller state college, and, in the fall, I went to a smaller pond, I wasn't so afraid the big fish would swallow me there. I guess I'm lucky I was able to withdraw before a line of failures appeared on my permanent records, on the other hand, my tuition didn't get refunded.   ❑

Subject–Verb Agreement

In a complete sentence, the subject tells who or what is doing the action, and the verb conveys the action or links the subject to the rest of the sentence. To maintain *subject–verb agreement* in a sentence, a *singular subject* must have a *singular verb* and a *plural subject* must have a *plural verb*.

INCORRECT

John don't like anchovies. [singular subject; plural verb]

CORRECT

John doesn't like anchovies. [singular subject; singular verb]

INCORRECT

The *boat skim* the top of the lake. [singular subject; plural verb]

CORRECT

The *boat skims* the top of the lake. [singular subject; singular verb]

INCORRECT

We was going to order a sausage pizza. [plural subject; singular verb]

CORRECT

We were going to order a sausage pizza. [plural subject; plural verb]

INCORRECT

The *cars swerves* to avoid hitting the fence. [plural subject; singular verb]

CORRECT

The *cars swerve* to avoid hitting the fence. [plural subject; plural verb]

Maintaining Subject–Verb Agreement. Add a singular or plural verb to the following sentences as needed to maintain subject–verb agreement.

ACTIVITY
11

1. The sun _____ in the evening.

2. My sisters _____ their violins every day.

3. The table _____ a good cleaning.

4. The newspapers _____ interesting stories to read.

5. Jerome _____ a mean fiddle.

6. Tacos _____ my favorite food.

7. Mr. Meyers _____ next door.

8. Tessie _____ her bike to the beach.

9. Caroline and Carley _____ their bikes too.

10. Camping _____ fun in the summer.   ❏

To check for subject–verb agreement, you must first identify the subject of the sentence. As noted earlier, you do this by crossing out the prepositional phrases and dependent clauses. Once you identify the subject, you can add the correct verb form.

INCORRECT

The *book* above the desks *need* to be put away. [singular subject; plural verb]

CORRECT

The *book* above the desks *needs* to be put away. [singular subject; singular verb]

INCORRECT

The *girl* from my hometown *run* every day. [singular subject; plural verb]

CORRECT

The *girl* from my hometown *runs* every day. [singular subject; singular verb]

INCORRECT

Men who don't know me very well *thinks* that I'm unfriendly. [plural subject; singular verb]

CORRECT

Men who don't know me very well *think* that I'm unfriendly. [plural subject; plural verb]

INCORRECT

Movie *theaters* located in the center of town *is* not for me. [plural subject; singular verb]

CORRECT

Movie *theaters* located in the center of town *are* not for me. [plural subject; plural verb]

Identifying Subject–Verb Agreement. Underline the correct verb form in each sentence that follows.

1. The books found in the parking lot *(was, were)* mine.

2. This book of jokes *(is, are)* very funny.

3. The man who lives next to the Parkers *(goes, go)* for a walk each day.

4. The flowers among the baskets *(is, are)* beautiful.

5. The swimming pool, crammed with swimmers, *(was, were)* dangerous.

6. Mr. Smith, along with his sons, *(hikes, hike)* in the summer.

7. Those dogs on the side of the yard *(looks, look)* friendly.

8. My best friend *(swims, swim)* every day.

9. Don't *(sits, sit)* on that chair.

10. We *(plays, play)* the saxophone.   ❑

When using the following singular pronouns as subjects, use singular verbs.

anybody, anyone, anything
everybody, everyone, everything
nobody, no one, nothing, none
somebody, someone, something

INCORRECT
Anybody carry books more easily than I do.

CORRECT
Anybody carries books more easily than I do.

INCORRECT
Someone like me!

CORRECT
Someone likes me!

INCORRECT
No one study as hard as I do.

CORRECT

No one studies as hard as I do.

INCORRECT

Something always *happen* when I'm least expecting it.

CORRECT

Something always *happens* when I'm least expecting it.

ACTIVITY

13

Identifying Subject–Verb Agreement with Singular Pronouns. Underline the correct verb form in each sentence that follows.

1. Everybody *(wants, want)* to go to the park.

2. No one *(cares, care)* whether I finish my soda.

3. Everything about my life *(is, are)* wonderful!

4. Nothing *(bothers, bother)* me anymore.

5. Something in the boxes *(is, are)* missing.

6. Nobody who knows me well *(believes, believe)* that.

7. Somebody *(like, likes)* me.

8. Anything they do *(helps, help)* us learn.

9. Someone we know *(is, are)* coming over.

10. Everyone we meet *(shakes, shake)* our hand.

ACTIVITY

14

Identifying Subject–Verb Agreement. Underline the correct verb form in each sentence that follows.

1. The players *(is, are)* on the varsity basketball team.

2. The book *(doesn't, don't)* tell us much about life at the end of the nineteenth century.

3. Everyone in that class *(like, likes)* to write.

4. I *(listen, listens)* to Irish folk music.

5. We *(was, were)* happy to receive our varsity letters.

6. None of the band members *(listen, listens)* to other popular music.

7. The woman who wore that red dress on Monday *(doesn't, don't)* have good taste.

8. The coach of the losing team *(sit, sits)* with his head in his hands.

9. The coaches from both teams *(study, studies)* the plays of the top college teams.

10. Nobody *(appreciate, appreciates)* big band jazz anymore.

Correcting Subject–Verb Agreement. Revise the following paragraph as needed to correct errors in subject–verb agreement.

ACTIVITY

15

Steve play on a local roller hockey league. On Sunday nights, just as other families are sitting down to their last weekend meal, Steve opens his trunk and load in about fifty pounds of hockey equipment. The equipment that he takes with him protect him from injuries and help him play a better game. Kevin, the enthusiast who started the league, drive fifty miles to get to the local rink. Anyone, even people who doesn't play hockey, are welcome, but most of the players grew up, like Steve, playing ice hockey. "Roller hockey is a kinder, gentler sport than ice hockey," Steve say. "In high school, we wasn't trying to hurt each other, but players got hurt anyway. Here we're just happy to play. No one ever get hurt." Anyone who watches ice hockey know the aggressiveness of the sport, but is

roller hockey really less aggressive? Kevin's broad scar indicate

just how rough roller hockey can be.   ❑

Pronoun Usage

A *pronoun* takes the place of a noun. Here are some of the most common English pronouns:

I, me, mine, we, us, our, ours
you, your, yours
he, him, his, she, her, hers
it, its
they, them, their, theirs
this, these, that, those
who, whom, whose, which, that, what
all, any, another, both, each, either, everyone
few, many, most, nobody, several, some, such
myself, yourself, himself, herself, itself
ourselves, themselves, yourselves

Pronoun Reference

When you use a pronoun to refer to a noun, make sure the reference is clear, not vague.

VAGUE

In the article "Jobs for the Twenty-first Century" *it* said that computer skills will be important. [What does *it* refer to?]

CLEAR

I read in the article "Jobs for the Twenty-first Century" that computer skills will be important.

VAGUE

Regina told Nicole *she* was going to the store. [Does *she* refer to Regina or Nicole?]

CLEAR

Regina said, "Nicole, I'm going to the store."

VAGUE

In New York *they're* used to crowds. [Who does *they* refer to?]

CLEAR

New Yorkers are used to crowds.

VAGUE

Last summer Joe loved being a camp counselor and working out-doors. *It* made him change his major to elementary education. [Does *it* refer to being a camp counselor, working outdoors, or both?]

CLEAR

Because Joe loved working with children last summer, he's changed his major to elementary education.

To correct vague pronoun references, follow these guidelines:

• Substitute the pronoun for the noun it refers to.

• Or, rewrite the sentence so the pronoun is no longer needed.

Grammar

Correcting Vague Pronoun Reference. Correct vague pronoun reference as needed in the following sentences. Note that some of the sentences may be correct as written; mark these "Correct."

ACTIVITY
16

1. Whenever Frank tries to speak German with George, he makes many mistakes.

   _____

   _____

   _____

2. In France, they're very proud of their language. _____

   _____

   _____

   _____

3. My father made the tuna casserole and the salad. It was delicious.

   _____

   _____

   _____

4. In the morning paper, it said that today was going to be hot.

_____

_____

_____

5. The brakes are wearing out, but it has never been in a wreck.

_____

_____

_____

6. Mark told Pablo that he needed to spend more time studying and less time partying.

_____

_____

_____

7. In my nutrition textbook, they say that Americans eat too much fat.

_____

_____

_____

8. Grandmother told Lisa that she needed to spend more time reading.

_____

_____

_____

9. Yesterday I cleaned out the closets and washed all the windows. It left me exhausted.

_____

_____

_____

_____

10. In Seattle they aren't used to snow, so yesterday's storm took every-
    one by surprise.

_____

_____

_____

❏

Pronoun Agreement

A pronoun should agree in number with the noun it takes the place of. To maintain *pronoun agreement,* use a *singular pronoun* to refer to a *singular noun,* and a *plural pronoun* to refer to a *plural noun.*

NO PRONOUN AGREEMENT

A *student* should bring *their* books to class. [*A student* is singular, but *their* is plural.]

PRONOUN AGREEMENT

A *student* should bring *his or her* books to class.
OR
Students should bring *their* books to class.

NO PRONOUN AGREEMENT

Mrs. Rowley asked *everyone* to raise *their* hands. [*Everyone* is singular, but *their* is plural.]

PRONOUN AGREEMENT

Mrs. Rowley asked *everyone* to raise *his or her* hands.
OR
Mrs. Rowley asked *the students* to raise *their* hands.

NO PRONOUN AGREEMENT

No one wanted to hand over *their* wallets. [*No one* is singular, but *their* is plural.]

PRONOUN AGREEMENT

No one wanted to hand over *his or her* wallet.
OR
The spectators didn't want to hand over *their* wallets.

To correct errors in pronoun agreement, follow these guidelines:

• Make the pronoun and noun agree in number.

• Or, rewrite the sentence to eliminate the problem.

ACTIVITY
17

Correcting Errors in Pronoun Agreement. Correct the errors in pronoun agreement as needed in the following sentences (or write "Correct" if the sentence contains no error). Remember to avoid sexist language when using pronouns (see pp. 490–494 for more information on sexist language).

1. A veterinarian studies for many years to earn their degree.

_____

_____

_____

2. The coach asked her players, "Has everyone finished their warm-ups?"

_____

_____

_____

3. Somebody in the back office keeps forgetting to turn their lights off at night.

_____

_____

_____

4. No one was willing to volunteer his or her time to pick up litter.

_____

_____

_____

5. An older student usually makes school their top priority.

_____

_____

_____

6. A politician should keep their word. _____

_____

_____

_____

7. Did anyone leave the lights on in their car? _____

_____

_____

_____

_____

8. A college graduate will earn much more money in their lifetime than someone without a college education.

_____

_____

_____

_____

9. A person is trusted if he or she never breaks a promise.

_____

_____

_____

_____

Grammar

Grammar

10. The instructor asks that everyone bring their homework to the main office.

_____

_____

_____

❑

Ask Yourself

How do you know if you have used correct pronoun reference and agreement?

• Read what you have written, sentence by sentence.
• Identify the pronouns in each sentence.
• Identify the noun that each pronoun takes the place of. Is the noun easy to identify? Is it close to the pronoun?
• Do the noun and the pronoun agree in number?
• Revise by changing the pronouns or rewriting the sentence accordingly.

Shifts in Person

When you write, you have a choice of *first-person* (*I, we*), *second-person* (*you*), or *third-person* (*he, she, they*) *pronouns* in the singular and plural. In an expressive essay in which you share your personal history, you would probably choose to write in the first person. However, in an informative essay in which you give "how-to" directions, you would probably use the second person. But in other types of informative essays, the third person might be more appropriate. And in a persuasive essay, you might combine the third person (such as in quoting others) with the first person (such as when you state your position).

Here is a complete list of singular and plural pronouns in the first, second, and third person.

SINGULAR

First Person	*Second Person*	*Third Person*
I	you	he, she, it, one
me	you	him, her, it
my, mine	your, yours	his, her, hers, its

PLURAL

First Person	*Second Person*	*Third Person*
we	you	they
us	you	them
our	your, yours	their, theirs

As a general rule, stay with the pronoun you begin with at the start of a paragraph. Avoid shifting from one pronoun to another unnecessarily, as these shifts may confuse your reader.

CONFUSING

She loves to go to the mountains in the spring. *You* never know what wildlife *one* can see when hiking those trails. *She* finds that *one* never gets tired of seeing deer, elk, and bobcats. *You* just can't help but love the outdoors.

REVISED

She loves to go to the mountains in the spring. *She* never knows what wildlife *she'll* see when hiking those trails. *She* finds that *she* never gets tired of seeing deer, elk, and bobcats. *She* just can't help but love the outdoors.

CONFUSING

You begin by mixing the dough by hand. Then *one* rolls the dough out on a wooden board. *You* allow it to dry a bit, and then *one* places it into the pasta machine. *You'll* find the results very satisfactory.

REVISED

You begin by mixing the dough by hand. Then *you* roll the dough out on a wooden board. *You* allow it to dry a bit, and then *you* place it into the pasta machine. *You'll* find the results very satisfactory.

Correcting Unnecessary Shifts in Person. Revise the following paragraphs as needed to correct unnecessary shifts in person.

ACTIVITY
18

1. Although the sport is dangerous, bull riding has taught me to overcome my fear and learn from my mistakes. You have to do what you think is best and not what others think you should do. Bull riding has brought my family back to-

gether. They support me by watching me ride sometimes and telling me what I'm doing wrong. I feel bull riding is a hobby, yet I will use the experience with everything I do. It gives you the determination to succeed.

2. They wanted to go to law school, but one has to have a high grade point average to be accepted. You just never know whether you'll be able to cut it or not until you send in that application. Then they wait and wait for the word on whether they've been accepted. You are so disappointed if you are turned down, but what's one to do? They can't just give up. ❏

Shifts in Verb Tense

The *tense* of a verb tells the time of the verb's action. If you're writing about something that is taking place now, use the *present tense*. If you're writing about something that has already happened, use the *past tense*. To show that something will happen in the future, use the *future tense*.

As a general rule, stay with the tense you begin with at the start of a paragraph. Avoid shifting from one verb tense to another unnecessarily, as these shifts may confuse your reader.

CONFUSING

He *went* to Massachusetts every fall and this year *is* no exception. He and his friend always *enjoyed* jumping in the piles of leaves that the neighbors *are* raking up. Those leaves *will make* a wonderful playground. He *couldn't wait* to get at them.

REVISED

He *went* to Massachusetts every fall and this year *was* no exception. He and his friend always *enjoyed* jumping in the piles of leaves that the neighbors *were* raking up. Those leaves *made* a wonderful playground. He *couldn't wait* to get at them.

Correcting Awkward Shifts in Verb Tense. Rewrite the following passage in the past tense.

ACTIVITY
19

A lot of people have a special person who influences their life, such as a parent, sibling, or friend. In my case, the person who influences me the most is my ex-boyfriend. He is special because of the times we spend together and the things we do. For example, we go to the movies, dinner, and graduation parties. I have stuffed animals, letters, and pictures that remind me of him. All of these warm and wonderful memories remind me of how we used to be. ❏

Dangling and Misplaced Modifiers

A *dangling modifier* is a phrase or clause that is not clearly linked to the word or words it modifies. The result is often an unclear or comical sentence.

DANGLING MODIFIER

Walking to class, snow was everywhere. [The snow seems to be walking.]

REVISED

Walking to class, we noticed snow was everywhere.

DANGLING MODIFIER

Having fleas, my sister said I couldn't keep the dog. [The sister seems to have the fleas.]

REVISED

Because the dog had fleas, my sister said I couldn't keep him.

DANGLING MODIFIER

Waiting for the bus, my handbag fell open. [The handbag seems to be waiting for the bus.]

REVISED

As I was waiting for the bus, my handbag fell open.

A *misplaced modifier* is a phrase or clause that is separated from the words it modifies, resulting in an unclear or comical sentence.

MISPLACED MODIFIER

There is a swimming pool in the backyard full of water. [The backyard seems to be full of water.]

REVISED

There is a swimming pool full of water in the backyard.

MISPLACED MODIFIER

He borrowed the suit from his friend with pinstripes. [The friend seems to have pinstripes.]

REVISED

He borrowed the suit with pinstripes from his friend.

MISPLACED MODIFIER

Maria took her dress to the seamstress that needed to be altered. [The seamstress seems to need to be altered.]

REVISED

Maria took her dress that needed to be altered to the seamstress.

ACTIVITY
20

Correcting Dangling and Misplaced Modifiers. Underline the dangling and misplaced modifiers in the following sentences. Then rewrite each sentence, moving the modifier to its correct position in the sentence.

1. Having left his apartment fifteen minutes late, getting to school on time was difficult for Brad.

   _____

   _____

   _____

2. Painted by her brother, Sue treasured the small portrait.

   _____

   _____

   _____

3. His book was finally found by looking under every bed in the house.

_____

_____

_____

4. She drove the car over the bridge with the windows open.

_____

_____

_____

5. Reading the e-mail notice, a grin appeared on Frank's face.

_____

_____

_____

6. After flooring the brakes, the bottles in the back of my car crashed into the front seat.

_____

_____

_____

7. Embarrassed but determined to overcome his shyness, Marcel asked the girl to have dinner with him in a red dress.

_____

_____

_____

_____

8. Fresh from the oven, he enjoyed the biscuits his mother had made.

_____

_____

_____

9. My brother has read every book written by Stephen King, who has always enjoyed horror fiction.

_____

_____

_____

10. My English paper was done after staring into the computer until three this morning.

_____

_____

_____

❏

Active versus Passive Voice

A sentence in the *active voice* has the subject of the sentence at the beginning. A sentence in the *passive voice* places the subject at the end. Readers prefer the active voice because they expect to find the subject at the beginning of the sentence. The passive voice forces them to read more slowly because the subject is at the end.

PASSIVE

A home run was hit over the stadium wall by Jerry.

ACTIVE

Jerry hit a home run over the stadium wall.

PASSIVE

The textbook was read by everyone in the class.

ACTIVE

Everyone in the class read the textbook.

Using the Active Voice. Rewrite the following passive voice sentences in the active voice.

1. The new movie was enjoyed by us all. _____

_____

_____

_____

2. Her hours had been posted by the manager. _____

_____

_____

_____

3. First place in the tournament was won by the home team.

_____

_____

_____

4. The candlelight vigil was held by the students on May 2.

_____

_____

_____

5. The dog was walked around the block by their daughter.

_____

_____

_____

6. The dinner was made by Tony, but the dessert was prepared by his son.

_____

_____

_____

7. The appointment had been made a month earlier by her husband.

_____

_____

_____

8. The university was designed by an architect from Atlanta.

_____

_____

_____

9. The soundtrack was written by Sting, and the songs were performed by other artists.

_____

_____

_____

10. The child was rocked to sleep by his mother. _____

_____

_____

_____

❑

Choosing Words

Clichés

Clichés are overused expressions. You often hear them spoken in everyday conversation:

"I'm as tired as a dog."

"That sales pitch knocked his socks off."

"All weekend she was as happy as a lark."

When most clichés originally appeared years ago, they probably communicated ideas forcefully. The cliché "kick the bucket," for example, came from a way of committing suicide: with a noose tied around the neck, a suicide victim would kick away the bucket he or she was standing on. But with overuse, clichés lose their meaning. Here are some other clichés to avoid in your writing:

beat around the bush	crystal clear
playing with fire	blind as a bat
in a nutshell	silver lining
bite the dust	light as a feather
cool as a cucumber	crack of dawn
rat race	luck of the Irish

Although clichés are acceptable in informal speech and writing, they're inappropriate in formal writing situations, including the writing you do in college and the workplace. If you find a cliché in a draft of your own writing, delete it and express the idea in your own words.

CLICHÉ

My grandmother lived to a *ripe old age*.

487

Words (sidebar)

REVISED

My grandmother lived to *be ninety-three.*

CLICHÉ

You'll succeed if you *keep your nose to the grindstone.*

REVISED

You'll succeed if you *work hard.*

CLICHÉ

Even though Amanda is young, she's *no shrinking violet.*

REVISED

Even though Amanda is young, she's *not shy.*

ACTIVITY

1

Eliminating Clichés. Underline the clichés in the following sentences. Then rewrite each one, expressing the idea in your own words.

1. Sue was never one to beat around the bush. If she thought you were playing with fire, she'd let you know.

   _____

   _____

   _____

2. Throughout his life, Peter seemed to have the luck of the Irish.

   _____

   _____

   _____

3. Fred was on the couch, looking like he'd seen a ghost. _____

   _____

   _____

   _____

4. The best thing about working with Darren was that he was always as cool as a cucumber.

5. After I handed in my final exam, I felt light as a feather.

6. Yolanda's batting average is so bad! She must be as blind as a bat.

7. Bob is as proud as a peacock about his A in calculus. _____

8. I'm quitting the rat race and moving to Alaska. _____

9. My boss always has to have things done her way. She's as stubborn as a mule.

Words

_____

_____

10. Michael Bolton's new album is selling like hot cakes. _____

_____

_____

_____

❏

Sexist Language

Sexist language is language that unfairly excludes or denigrates women or men. *Nonsexist language*, in contrast, either makes no mention of sex or includes both sexes.

One kind of sexist language involves using the masculine pronouns *he, his,* and *him* to refer to both men and women. Today, this usage is recognized as sexist because it excludes women. To avoid this form of sexist language, use both masculine and feminine pronouns, such as *his or her,* or recast the sentence in the plural and use the plural pronoun *they, theirs,* or *them.*

SEXIST

A student deserves *his* vacation.

NONSEXIST

A student deserves *his or her* vacation.

NONSEXIST

Students deserve *their* vacations.

SEXIST

Because *her* work is important, a nurse should be well paid.

NONSEXIST

Because *his or her* work is important, a nurse should be well paid.

NONSEXIST

Because *their* work is important, nurses should be well paid.

SEXIST

Every voter needs to make up *his* own mind.

NONSEXIST

Every voter needs to make up *his or her* own mind.

NONSEXIST

Voters need to make up *their* own minds.

Another kind of sexist language occurs when we refer to occupations that traditionally excluded women or men. Because of changes in the workplace, these terms are no longer accurate. Use terms that include both women and men. Here are some examples:

SEXIST LANGUAGE	NONSEXIST LANGUAGE
stewardess	flight attendant
actress	actor
fireman	firefighter
policeman	police officer
chairman	chairperson
congressman	member of Congress; congressional representative
salesman	salesperson
weatherman	weather forecaster

Similarly, *man* and *mankind* should be substituted by a nonsexist term when they are used to refer to both sexes.

SEXIST

the average *man* in the street

NONSEXIST

the average *person*

SEXIST

what's good for all of *mankind*

NONSEXIST

what's good for all of *humanity*

SEXIST

manmade fabric

NONSEXIST

synthetic fabric

Eliminating Sexist Language. Revise the following sentences as needed to eliminate sexist language.

ACTIVITY
2

1. Airline stewardesses are responsible for passengers' safety.

_____

_____

Words

_____

_____

2. Every student should bring his book to class. _____

_____

_____

_____

3. The weatherman reported an 80 percent chance of rain.

_____

_____

_____

4. Because a salesman spends so much time traveling, he should have a good car.

_____

_____

_____

5. Mankind has a long history of warfare. _____

_____

_____

_____

6. Each graduate was happy he was finally getting a job. _____

_____

_____

_____

_____

7. Every little boy wants to become a policeman. _____

_____

_____

_____

8. For many years Patricia Schroeder was a congressman from Colorado.

_____

_____

_____

9. Has everyone done his homework? _____

_____

_____

_____

10. The new secretary will get her own desk and computer.

_____

_____

_____

Avoiding Sexist Language. Rewrite the following paragraph as needed to eliminate sexist language.

ACTIVITY
3

Sarah wrote the councilmen in her district to argue that

the city needed to hire more firemen. "In addition," she said in

her letter, "a full review needs to be done of the policemen

who are employed to protect our town's streets." She never

saw a policeman patrolling her street. Moreover, a burglar had broken into her home once, and he had robbed other homes in her neighborhood ten times in the past month. What were the police doing to catch this criminal? She worked as a stewardess and her husband worked as a salesman, so they were often both out of town at the same time. They had replaced the electronic equipment the burglar had stolen on his last visit, but she was sure the insurance company would raise her rates. She said that everyone in town had a right to feel safe in his own home and that each of the councilmen should do his best to motivate the police to spend more time patrolling the neighborhoods of the upstanding men of the community. "Mankind has fallen into the depths of depravity," she wrote, "when a safe suburb like ours becomes the playground of troubled young boys." ❏

Wordiness

Writing that is wordy confuses readers or causes readers to lose interest. *Wordiness* is often caused by either unnecessary repetition or empty phrases.

Unnecessary Repetition

Unnecessary repetition occurs when you say the same thing twice. Sometimes the repetition is in the form of synonyms.

WORDY

Many students *in school* hold jobs *while going to school.*

REVISED

Many students hold jobs while going to school.

WORDY

The letter *showed and demonstrated* how angry I was.

REVISED

The letter showed how angry I was.

WORDY

The movie seat *moaned and creaked* every time I sat *up and down* in it.

REVISED

The movie seat creaked every time I sat in it.

WORDY

The *little, small* house sat back from the road.

REVISED

The little house sat back from the road.

REVISED

The small house sat back from the road.

The following phrases are repetitious. There is no need, for example, to say "past history" because history is necessarily about past events.

past history	new beginning
at this point in time	connect together
end result	end product
true fact	blue in color
each and every	7 A.M. in the morning
personal opinion	serious tragedy
invited guest	preplan

Eliminating Unnecessary Repetition. Revise the following wordy sentences as needed to eliminate unnecessary repetition.

ACTIVITY
4

1. Joe died as a result of being shot to death. _____

_____

_____

_____

2. Lunch will be served at twelve noon. _____

_____

_____

_____

3. I sent the letter in the mail. _____

_____

_____

_____

4. Susan was so tired and exhausted that she couldn't wait to go to bed and get some sleep.

_____

_____

_____

5. At this point in time I can't remember exactly or precisely what happened at 9 P.M. in the evening.

_____

_____

_____

6. The sweater was yellow in color. _____

_____

_____

_____

7. We need to have more advance planning in the future.

_____

_____

_____

Words

8. "In my personal opinion," said Ms. Connally, "we require and need more hard work and labor from everyone involved."

    _____

    _____

    _____

9. It was my father's usual, habitual custom to get up every morning at 5 A.M., rain or shine.

    _____

    _____

    _____

10. The public official urged her fellow colleagues to cooperate together to eliminate altogether unnecessary wasteful spending.

    _____

    _____

    _____

    ❏

Empty Phrases

Empty phrases cause wordiness because they take up space without adding meaning to the sentence.

WORDY

Due to the fact that it was snowing, school was canceled.

REVISED

Because it was snowing, school was canceled.

WORDY

Nancy was *very* pleased that the party was *really* successful.

REVISED

Nancy was pleased that the party was successful.

WORDY

In the event that it rains, the dinner will be held indoors.

REVISED

If it rains, the dinner will be held indoors.

Here is a list of some other empty phrases to avoid and their more precise substitutes:

WORDY	PRECISE
owing to the fact that	because
through the use of	with
in the neighborhood of	about
for the purpose of	for
in order to	to
until such time as	until
at the present time	now
by means of	by
as of that date	then

In addition, note that the phrases *in my opinion, I believe, I feel,* and *I think* are empty because they state the obvious. The fact that *you* are writing the statement means it is *your* thought or opinion or belief. You are not adding new information for your reader.

WORDY

In my opinion, the drinking age should be lowered to eighteen.

REVISED

The drinking age should be lowered to eighteen.

WORDY

I think all my hard work has finally paid off.

REVISED

All my hard work has finally paid off.

WORDY

I feel the food in the Student Union is getting better.

REVISED

The food in the Student Union is getting better.

ACTIVITY
5

Eliminating Empty Phrases. Revise the following sentences as needed to eliminate empty phrases.

1. As of this date, we haven't received the letter. _____

_____

_____

_____

2. I received an A on the test due to the fact that I studied up until the time the test began.

_____

_____

_____

3. I refused to pay the bill for the reason that the service was so poor.

_____

_____

_____

4. The fact that it was so cold didn't stop me from jogging every morning.

_____

_____

_____

5. Jill will continue to drive her car until such time as her license is revoked.

_____

_____

_____

6. In my opinion, you should save money in the event that you lose your job.

_____

_____

_____

Words

7. I went to college for the purpose of getting a good job. _____

_____

_____

_____

8. I think, in the final analysis, the person who works hard will be well rewarded.

_____

_____

_____

9. I was late paying my rent owing to the fact that my paycheck was late.

_____

_____

_____

10. I believe we should leave early so as to arrive at the movie on time.

_____

_____

_____

❏

COMPUTER TIP

ELIMINATE WORDINESS

Press the "return" key at the end of each of your sentences to create a list of sentences. Read each sentence, looking only for wordy areas. Then revise wordy sentences as necessary.

Ask Yourself

How can you detect unnecessary repetition and empty phrases in your sentences?

- Read your writing aloud—slowly and loudly. Sometimes you can hear wordiness you didn't detect by reading silently.
- Whether reading silently or aloud, read each sentence individually, checking only for wordiness.
- Consider reading the last sentence of the paper first, then the second to the last sentence, and so on, until you reach the beginning of the paper.

Jargon

Jargon is the specialized language used by members of professions, organizations, trades, and other groups. Jargon is an acceptable way to communicate when you're writing to a specialized audience familiar with the terminology. However, you should avoid using jargon when your readers aren't familiar with the specialized language. Jargon also tends to be unnecessarily wordy or technical.

JARGON

Officer Miller *made the collar.*

REVISED

Officer Miller made the arrest.

JARGON

At midnight we *put the newspaper to bed.*

REVISED

At midnight the newspaper was ready to be printed.

JARGON

Jackie is a poor shooter *at the line.*

REVISED

Jackie doesn't make many of her free-point shots.

Eliminating Jargon. Underline the jargon in the following paragraph. Then rewrite the paragraph as needed to eliminate the jargon. (You may need to ask a weight lifter for help.)

ACTIVITY
6

He'd always thought that pumping iron would be fun, so when he finally had enough money to join the muscle mart, he jumped at the chance. He'd read muscle mags for years, so he thought he knew how to train. On his first day at the gym, he walked out of the locker room in awe of all the buff guys pushing their max loads for eight to ten reps. He tightened his body belt and went straight to the gauntlet. He knew better than to push his weight before he'd loosened his muscles. After twelve minutes climbing the stairs, he joined the 'roid rats by the free weights. A guy next to him with quads as big as trees offered to spot him on the bench, but Joe shook his head. He pushed his reps, cooled, then pushed again. On the third push, he felt something in his pecs rip, and he dropped the weights onto his chest. Mr. Tree Legs came over and lifted his bar with one arm. When Joe finally caught his breath, he thanked the trunk and went to the locker room. On his way out, he stopped by the front desk to get the name of a trainer. ❑

Words

Punctuation

If you have ever taken a cross-country road trip, you know that you depended on road signs to help you get from one place to another. Without them, you would have become hopelessly lost and unable to continue without asking directions. In writing, punctuation marks act as road signs, guiding readers through the text. If the writing is incorrectly punctuated, readers may become confused or lost and unable to understand the writer's meaning. Writers use punctuation, then, to communicate more effectively, and readers depend on punctuation to guide them toward an understanding of the writer's meaning.

Commas

The *comma (,)* is used in many writing situations:

- To set off an introductory word or words (p. 504)

- To separate three or more words, phrases, or clauses used in a series (pp. 504–505)

- To separate two independent clauses separated by a connecting word (pp. 506–507)

- To separate a descriptive phrase that interrupts the flow of the sentence (p. 507)

- To separate transitional words and phrases from the rest of the sentence (pp. 507–508)

- To separate the day of the month from the year (p. 508)

• To separate a street address from the name of a city and to separate the name of a city from the name of a state (pp. 508–509)
• To set off dialogue or a direct quotation (p. 509)

Use a comma to separate an introductory word, phrase, or clause from the main sentence.

> Ella, please go pick up some milk at the store.
> According to Ella, there was enough milk in the refrigerator.
> Although she didn't really want to go, Ella went to the store for more milk.

ACTIVITY

1

Using Commas with Introductory Words. Add commas as needed to the following sentences.

1. Listening to the hum of the subway beneath my apartment I wondered if I would be able to sleep without its familiar rumble.

2. When Jason turned the corner he fell over a window washer's bucket and into a flower cart.

3. For example the neighbors in small towns take more interest in your successes and failures.

4. In the barn at the back of his property my grandfather stores his collection of rusted steel and tin.

5. After we'd sat for twenty minutes without being waited on David said that we should leave. ❑

Use a comma to separate three or more words, phrases, or clauses used in a series.

> Ella decided she would buy gum, bread, and hot dogs as well as milk.
> Ella stopped to water the flowers, talk to a neighbor, and admire the sunset on her way to the store.
> Ella went to the store, John went to the movie, and Chi decided to stay home.

Using Commas in a Series. For each of the following lists of items, write a complete sentence using the series comma.

1. a loaf of bread, a book of poems, a bottle of grape juice

_____

_____

_____

2. lettuce, tomatoes, carrots, cucumbers, green onions _____

_____

_____

_____

3. behind the gas station, under a tree, in an old tire _____

_____

_____

_____

4. you lose your car keys, you forget to turn off the coffee pot, you spill coffee on your white shirt, you snag your pantyhose

_____

_____

_____

5. listening for crickets, smelling the jasmine, swatting mosquitoes

_____

_____

_____

❑

Use a comma to separate two independent clauses that are separated by a connecting word (*and, but, or, nor, for, yet, so*). (For information on independent clauses, see pp. 442–443)

> Ella didn't really want to go to the store, *and* she didn't want her sister to have to go either.

> Ella didn't really want to go to the store, *but* her sister had asked her to get some milk.

ACTIVITY

3

Using Commas with Connecting Words. Use a comma and a connecting word to join the two independent clauses into a single sentence.

1. I could hear the rain outside. I was too tired to look out the window for damage.

_____

_____

_____

2. The room buzzed with the voices and laughter of children five years old. It was time to graduate from kindergarten.

_____

_____

_____

3. She waited on the corner. She kept a wary eye on the speeding traffic.

_____

_____

_____

4. Mark kept his eyes closed. He wouldn't see how high he was when he reached the top of the roller coaster.

_____

_____

Punctuation

_____

_____

5. The sand stung my cheeks. The wind pushed me back toward the water.

_____

_____

_____

❏

Use a comma before and after a descriptive phrase that would otherwise interrupt the flow of the sentence.

Ella, who loved her sister dearly, decided to go to the store.
Ella's sister, a health nut, insisted on having her milk right away.

Using Commas with Descriptive Phrases. Add commas as needed to the following sentences.

ACTIVITY
4

1. Martha who had always been quick to comfort me wasn't home when I called her.

2. The students in her English class hoping for an extension of the due date left the classroom disappointed.

3. The green floral dress which I had purchased for the party lay in a heap on the bottom of the closet floor.

4. The man who had asked if he could photograph their house stood in the driveway.

5. Her hair as a result was frizzy. ❏

Use a comma to separate transitional words and phrases from the rest of the sentence.

In addition, Ella stopped to mail some letters that she had in her purse.

> When she arrived at the mailbox, however, she realized that she had forgotten the stamps.

Using Commas to Set Off Transitional Words and Phrases. Add commas as needed to the following sentences.

1. It wasn't until I'd walked into the bright light of day however that I felt I'd accomplished something important.

2. The restaurant on the corner on the other hand serves breakfast all day.

3. Moreover the coat smelled musty and stale.

4. Amanda meanwhile stared at her reflection in the storefront glass.

5. Consequently Jake refused to finish the run. ❑

Use a comma to separate the day of the month from the year.

Ella went to the store on June 1, 1997.
The store had opened on December 15, 1986.

Using Commas in Dates. Add commas as needed to the following sentences.

1. I hope to graduate on May 31 1999.

2. He headed back to Little Rock on June 2 1997.

3. September 15 1972 was the day my brother left the service.

4. January 25 1986 is a day I'll always remember.

5. I was born on August 8 1975. ❑

Use a comma to separate a street address from the name of a city. Also use a comma to separate the name of a city from the name of a county or state.

Ella lived at 713 Washington Street, Chicago, Illinois.

My boyfriend sent the letter to 234 East Main, Los Angeles, California.

Using Commas in Street Addresses. Add commas as needed to the following sentences.

ACTIVITY
7

1. We mailed the letter to 1610 Main Street Los Angeles California.

2. We spent our vacation in Tijuana Mexico.

3. He lives in Hudspeth County Texas.

4. My favorite city is New York New York.

5. My uncle lives at 500 Elm Street Chicago Illinois. ❏

Use a comma to set off dialogue or a direct quotation in a sentence.

"I'm headed to the store," Ella said to her neighbor.

The author of this article says, "Don't forget to read to your children."

"He just won't do it," she exclaimed to her boss, "even though I've asked him several times."

Using Commas with Dialogue and Direct Quotations. Add commas as needed to the following sentences.

ACTIVITY
8

1. "I'll meet you at ten o'clock" Jose said to his friend.

2. According to John Lantham "The trees are always their most beautiful in October."

3. "Who cares if we don't get to go" she yelled at her father.

4. "I'll take you to the library" Leonore said "as soon as I finish my lunch."

5. My mother always said "You can do whatever you set your mind to."

ACTIVITY
9

Using Commas Correctly. Add commas as needed to the following paragraph.

My mother told me about an incident that happened to our family in Savannah Georgia on August 8 1923. She and my father were sharecroppers and food including staples were impossible to buy on their salaries. One day my father said to her "Naomi let's take these kids into town for a good time." My mother however was worried that they didn't have the money for a good time. She had just discovered much to her dismay that they were not only out of flour but rice beans and milk as well. How could they spend money on entertainment when they didn't even have food? My father surprised her though with a small amount of money that he had stashed under the mattress and so we went into town to buy food and have a good time. ❏

Semicolons

Use a *semicolon (;)* to link two independent clauses that are closely related in meaning.

> We went to the Little League playoffs; the Blasters won the game.
> The Blasters have always been a good team; their coach is one of the best in the league.

Use a semicolon to separate items in a series when those items already include commas.

> We had followed that team to Gainesville, Florida; Biloxi, Mississippi; and Shreveport, Louisiana.

Using Semicolons Correctly. Use the semicolon to correctly punctuate each of the following sentences.

1. We were aware of the many dangers we might face nevertheless, we decided to hike the canyon.

2. I could hear the ocean throwing pebbles onto the sand the seagulls swirled above me.

3. I have been to all the major U.S. cities except for New York, New York, Chicago, Illinois, and Miami, Florida.

4. We had forgotten to pack the Coleman stove as a result, we only spent one night at the campsite.

5. For the most part, the summer had been dry we were surprised, therefore, when it began to rain as soon as we'd set up our tent. ❑

Colons

Use a *colon (:)* to introduce a list, clause, or phrase that explains the independent clause. (Remember that the independent clause must be able to stand alone as a sentence.) Don't use a colon following a verb or with *such as*.

INCORRECT

The supplies we bought for class include: books, pens, and a calculator.

CORRECT

The supplies we bought for class include books, pens, and a calculator.

CORRECT

We bought the following supplies for class: books, pens, and a calculator.

INCORRECT

There are many ways to stay out of debt, such as: make a budget and stick to it, buy only what you need, and cut up those charge cards.

CORRECT

There are many ways to stay out of debt: make a budget and stick to it, buy only what you need, and cut up those charge cards.

CORRECT

There are many ways to stay out of debt, such as making a budget and sticking to it, buying only what you need, and cutting up those charge cards.

ACTIVITY

11

Using Colons Correctly. Use a colon as needed in the following sentences to introduce a list, clause, or phrase that explains the independent clause. If the sentence is correct as written, write "Correct."

1. For school, I need paper, pens, books, and a calculator.

2. Please do the following mop the floor, vacuum the carpet, and dust the furniture.

3. I've seen two good movies this year *Forrest Gump* and *Pulp Fiction*.

4. When I get home, I will study, cook dinner, and feed the cats.

5. He tried swimming strokes such as the butterfly, the crawl, and the backstroke.   ❑

End Punctuation

End punctuation signals the reader that you have completed a thought and ended a sentence. End punctuation includes the period, exclamation mark, and question mark.

Use a *period (.)* to end a sentence, an indirect question, and a command.

He waited for her to come home.
He asked her where she had been.
Call me if you plan to be late again.

Use an *exclamation mark (!)* to give emphasis or to show emotion.

She was shocked that he would question her!
Don't ever talk to me like that again!

Use a *question mark (?)* to end a direct question.

Why didn't she understand that he was just worried about her?
How many times did she have to tell him?

Using End Punctuation Correctly. Insert the correct end punctuation mark at the end of each group of words.

1. It took a long time for me to realize that my mother and I were very much alike

2. When I returned to my hometown, I tried to find the house I lived in as a child

3. I realized then that Thomas had been telling the truth

4. When did your family stop spending Saturdays at the beach

5. Get a grip on yourself

Correcting Errors in End Punctuation. Revise the following paragraph to correct errors in end punctuation.

The porch swing groaned as my grandfather pushed gently forward and back in time to the music of the story he was telling. We'd sit and watch the garden grow, as he called it! What we were really doing, though, was story-telling? At twenty, I hadn't been around long enough to have interesting stories of my own. What will he talk about tonight. Every afternoon while I did my homework and he watched his soap opera, I'd ask myself that question. We had this talk after dinner each night during the two years I lived with him. We'd sit out back, and he'd tell me the stories of his seventy-eight years. He talked about growing up on a farm, and he often complained about how lazy his brothers had been. They left him to do all the work! He talked about his year playing semi-pro baseball? He told me stories about my father and about my aunts and their many children! One night, by the time he finished telling his story, Grandma was in bed, and the bright moon of east Texas was high overhead. This story, more than any other, revealed my grandfather's gentle spirit as well as the harshness of his life! More than that, it told me more about east Texas and the oil business than any of my Texas history books had revealed. Who wouldn't have felt fortunate to have a living history book sitting across from them on the swing. ❑

Apostrophes

Use the *apostrophe (')* to show possession. A possessive word is followed by something that belongs to it. If the possessive word refers to just one person, use *'s*.

The *student's* notes were clearly written. [one person]
Jessie's golf swing was the best in the state. [one person]

If the possessive word refers to more than one person, use *s'*.

All of the *students'* notes were clearly written. [more than one person]
The *golfers'* scores were the best in the state. [more than one person]

Possessive pronouns, such as *his, hers, yours, theirs,* and *ours,* do not require apostrophes.

His book was more interesting than *theirs.*
Hers was a better cup of coffee than *yours.*

Using Apostrophes to Show Possession. In the following sentences, underline the words in which apostrophes are missing or misused. Then write the correct form of the word in the space provided.

1. Mary Smiths house is on the corner of Dodge and Elm.

   _____

2. Is this book your's? _____

   _____

3. Michael tried to return the mans umbrella, but the man rushed out the door.

   _____

4. The girls sweatsuits lay crumpled on the floor. _____

   _____

5. Jerrys pets were always running around the yard. _____

   _____

   ❏

Use the apostrophe to form a contraction. A *contraction* is formed by combining two words with an apostrophe taking the place of the omitted letters. Here are some common contractions:

I'm	I am	can't	cannot
you're	you are	aren't	are not
he's	he is	wasn't	was not
she's	she is	weren't	were not
it's	it is	don't	do not
they're	they are	doesn't	does not
we're	we are	won't	will not
he'll	he will	wouldn't	would not
she'll	she will	hasn't	has not
we'll	we will	haven't	have not
they'll	they will	there's	there is
I've	I have	here's	here is
they've	they have	who's	who is

It's [it is] always a good idea to take notes.

I *don't* [do not] care if you *can't* [cannot] remember to carry your backpack.

Caution: Student writers often confuse the contraction *it's* (for *it is*) for the possessive pronoun *its*.

INCORRECT

The restaurant was known for *it's* wonderful entertainment.

CORRECT

The restaurant was known for *its* wonderful entertainment.

ACTIVITY

15

Using Apostrophes in Contractions. In the following sentences, underline where apostrophes are missing from contractions. Then write the correct form of the contractions in the space provided.

1. Because its sunny outside, Ive decided to take the dog for a walk.

    _____

2. We arent planning a vacation this year because we cant afford one.

    _____

3. Well put all the toys in the red basket. _____

    _____

4. If youre going to the store, please get hot dog buns.

    _____

5. Its better to ask a question when you dont understand something than to leave this class confused.

    _____

ACTIVITY

16

Using Apostrophes Correctly. The following paragraph contains several apostrophe errors. First underline where apostrophes are missing or misused. Then revise the paragraph to correct those errors.

(sidebar) **Punctuation**

We wanted to stop by Daves house on the way to see Oliver Stones new movie, but we didnt have time. Dave had borrowed Amys English textbook, and Amys instructor had assigned reading over the weekend. I couldnt let Amy borrow my book because I hadnt finished my reading yet. Dave had Amys textbook for a week, so Amy hadnt been prepared for her last English class. Shed been embarrassed when her instructor called on her to discuss the days reading assignment. When we arrived at the theater, Amy called Dave from the pay phone. Hed gone out of town for the weekend. "Isnt that just my luck," Amy said. I told her that she didn't need to worry. We could study together over the weekend and Id let her borrow my book for Tuesdays class. ❏

Quotation Marks

Use *quotation marks (" ")* to show a speaker's or a writer's exact words.

Homer declared, "The Beatles are back!"

According to the *Washington Post,* "The Beatles have reunited for another world tour."

Use quotation marks to enclose the titles of articles, essays, book chapters, speeches, poems, short stories, and songs.

John Deaver's newspaper column, "Close-Up," is the first one I read in the morning.

I especially liked the chapter entitled "What It Means to Be Free" in my sociology text.

Martin Luther King's "I Have a Dream" is a well-known speech.

Robert Frost's poem "Stopping by Woods on a Snowy Evening" is Alma's favorite.

My class read Katherine Anne Porter's short stories "María Concepción" and "Flowering Judas."

We sing "Amazing Grace" at least once a month at my church.

Using Quotation Marks Correctly. Revise the following sentences as needed to correct missing quotation marks.

1. During that time, I read the short story The Fly by Katherine Mansfield.

2. We decided that Pink Floyd's song Comfortably Numb would be our song.

3. You didn't think I was stupid, did you? asked Jessica.

4. Well, my grandfather said, I guess it's about time for us to go.

5. Marta said, I feel better about myself when I dress up. ❑

Dashes

Use *dashes* to signal an abrupt change in thought. A dash (—) is typed as two unspaced hyphens (--) with no space before or after it.

John came to my house—much later than I expected—to return the books he'd borrowed.

Maria wanted to buy gifts for everyone—although money was tight—because she loved her friends so dearly.

It came to her in a daydream—she was going to move to New York City.

Use dashes sparingly. Too many dashes can make writing sound choppy.

Using Dashes Correctly. Revise the following sentences as needed by supplying missing dashes.

1. Everything I did running, jumping rope, bicycling was exhilarating.

2. Where I come from Las Vegas, Nevada we don't worry about buying overcoats.

3. Our campus bookstore next to the Food Court has everything you need for your classes.

4. All of our needs food, lodging, and transportation were covered by the scholarship.

5. He does it just the way I would splendidly! ❑

Italics or Underlining

COMPUTER TIP
USING ITALICS
Most word-processing programs allow you to italicize instead of underline.

Use underlining to indicate *italics* in handwritten or typewritten copy. Italicize (underline) the titles of books, magazines, films, television shows, newspapers, journals, computer software, music albums, or anything else that is not part of a larger collection.

I read *Moby Dick* in my literature course.
The *Los Angeles Times* is my favorite newspaper.
I have *Windows '95* on my office computer.

Using Italics Correctly. In the following paragraph, underline to indicate where italics should be used.

ACTIVITY
19

One of my favorite authors is Gary Larson, the author of

The Far Side calendars. His cartoons are just as funny as the

ones I read in the San Francisco Examiner. The only thing I

find funnier is the movie Blazing Saddles. Larson is hilarious. I

would recommend that you purchase one of his calendars. ❑

Punctuation

Spelling

English spelling is difficult, partly because many English words come from other languages. However, several spelling rules can help you master some of the most commonly misspelled words. These rules tell you when to use *ie* versus *ei*, when to double the final consonant, when to drop a final silent *e*, and when to change *y* to *i*.

i *before* e, *except after* c

Write *i* before *e*
Except after *c*
Or when sounded like *ay*
As in *neighbor* and *weigh*

This rhyme can help you remember the rules for using *ie* and *ei*.

Write *i* before *e*

believe	piece
fierce	priest
grieve	reprieve
niece	thief

Except after *c*

ceiling	deceit
conceited	receipt
conceive	receive

Or when sounded like *ay*

eight	neighbor
freight	weight

Here are some exceptions to this rule:

counterfeit	leisure
foreign	neither
height	seize
heir	weird

Because there are exceptions, check your dictionary or use your computer's spell-check feature to verify your spelling.

Using *i* before *e* except after *c*. In the space provided, correct the misspelled words or write "Correct" if the word is spelled correctly.

ACTIVITY

1

1. recieve _____

2. decieve _____

3. beige _____

4. sleigh _____

5. conciet _____

6. decieve _____

7. leisure _____

8. releive _____

9. wieght _____

10. peice _____

❑

Doubling the Final Consonant

When adding an ending that begins with a vowel (such as *-ed* or *-ing*) to a word that ends with a consonant, double the consonant when it is preceded by a single vowel and ends a one-syllable word or a stressed syllable. (A *stressed syllable* is one that is accented. In the word *believe,* for example, the stress is on the second syllable. Say the word to hear the stressed syllable.)

Double the consonant when it's preceded by a vowel and ends a one-syllable word:

hop	hopping
bet	betting
sad	sadder
win	winner
quit	quitting

Double the consonant when it's preceded by a vowel and ends a stressed syllable:

commit	committed
prefer	preferred
control	controller
omit	omitted
refer	referring

However, this rule does not apply when the ending doesn't begin with a vowel, such as *-ment* or *-ness*.

commit	commitment
wet	wetness
sad	sadness
disappoint	disappointment

ACTIVITY
2

Doubling the Final Consonant. Add the specified ending to each word in the space provided.

1. stop + *ed* _____

2. rid + *ance* _____

3. dry + *ness* _____

4. tip + *ing* _____

5. plan + *ed* _____

6. refer + *ence* _____

7. repeat + *ed* _____

8. occur + *ence* _____

9. bet + *ing* _____

10. labor + *ed* _____

❑

Dropping the Final Silent e

When adding an ending that begins with a vowel, drop the final *e*.

age	aging
care	caring
desire	desiring
fame	famous
remove	removable
use	usable

When adding an ending that begins with a consonant, keep the final *e*.

care	careful
dense	denseness
lone	lonely
safe	safety
state	statement

Some exceptions to this rule include *acknowledgment, argument, judgment, ninth,* and *truly.*

Dropping the Final Silent *e*. Add the specified ending to each word in the space provided.

ACTIVITY
3

1. achieve + *ment* _____

2. remove + *able* _____

3. desire + *ing* _____

4. argue + *ment* _____

5. hope + *ing* _____

6. hate + *ful* _____

7. judge + *ment* _____

8. sure + *est* _____

9. manage + *ment* _____

10. write + *ing* _____

❑

Spelling

Changing y to i

When adding an ending to a word that ends in *y,* change the *y* to *i.*

apply	applied
carry	carries
ceremony	ceremonies
easy	easiest
family	families
happy	happiness
study	studies

However, this rule does not apply to words ending with *-ing.*

apply	applying
carry	carrying
dry	drying
study	studying

Also do not omit the final *y* when it is preceded by a vowel (*a, e, i, o,* or *u*).

buy	buys
play	playful
monkey	monkeys
stay	stayed

ACTIVITY
4

Changing *y* to *i*. Add the specified ending to each word in the space provided.

1. employ + *ment* _____

2. busy + *ness* _____

3. try + *ing* _____

4. apology + *s* _____

5. easy + *ly* _____

6. beauty + *ful* _____

7. dry + *ed* _____

8. play + *ing* _____

9. attorney + *s* _____

10. stay + *ing* _____

❏

 ESL Writers

Spelling varies somewhat among English-speaking countries. Note, for example, how the following words are spelled differently in American and British English.

AMERICAN	BRITISH
canceled	cancelled
center	centre
check	cheque
civilization	civilisation
color	colour
defense	defence
humor	humour
judgment	judgement
realize	realise
traveled	travelled

Correcting Misspelled Words. Correct the misspelled words in the following paragraph.

ACTIVITY
5

Every Sunday my stepfather went to the garage, grabed a fourty pound bag of charcol, and dumped it into the larg kettle grill on the patio. Mom scrubbed the potatos, and my brother and I set the table. We rarly ate dinner at the antiqe dinning room table, so Sunday diners were an ocassion. I was responsible for chosing the placemats and napkins; my brother polished the silverware and the glases. Earlier that morning, my mother had preparred her special secret marinate. I'm still

COMPUTER TIP

USE YOUR SPELL-CHECK

Your spell-check can help you catch many misspelled words. Keep in mind, though, that it cannot distinguish between words that sound alike but that have different meanings and spellings, such as *it's* versus *its* and *accept* versus *except*. Only careful proofreading will help you spot these misspellings.

not sure what ingredience she used, but the smel of her herbs and spices and the thik T-bone steaks always got our mouths watering. When my stepfather came in to get the plate for the steaks, we knew it was time to sit down. The table would be crowded with fresh rolls, real buter, sour cream, and a huge green salad. We'd end our Sunday ritual siting arond the stereo listening to Jerry Clower albums and eating big peices of fresh fruit pie with ice cream. ❑

Ask Yourself

How do you learn to be a good speller?

- Learn when to use *ie* versus *ei,* when to double the final consonant, when to drop the final silent *e,* and when to change *y* to *i.*
- Use your spell-check, keeping in mind that it won't catch all misspelled words.
- Pay attention to how words are spelled when you read.
- Keep a log of words you tend to misspell.
- Consult a dictionary frequently.

Spelling

Mechanics

Capitalization

Capitalize *proper nouns*—nouns that refer to a specific person, place, event, or thing. Do *not* capitalize *common nouns*, which refer to a general category of persons, places, events, or things.

COMMON NOUNS	PROPER NOUNS
a holiday	Thanksgiving
a war	the Civil War
a president	President Kennedy
a day of the week	Tuesday
a college	Smith College
a house	the White House
a country	Venezuela
a mother	Mom
a professor	Professor Snow

Capitalize the names of organizations, institutions, and trademarks.

My uncle is a *Shriner.*

I'm neither a *Republican* nor a *Democrat.*

My next car will be a *Honda.*

Correcting Errors in Capitalization. Correct the errors in capitalization in the following sentences.

1. I always thought Miami university was in Florida, so I was surprised to find out it was in Ohio.

2. My favorite museum is the smithsonian.

3. My Father retired last year.

4. All I have to drink is seven-up.

5. One of our most important holidays is veteran's day.

6. My Great-Grandmother lived to be 101.

7. One of my favorite professors is professor smith.

8. I wish we had more holidays like thanksgiving.

9. After work Mike went to the chevrolet dealership.

10. When she was a girl Leticia had been a girl scout.   ❏

In titles, capitalize all words *except* articles (*a, an, the*), connecting words (*and, but, or, for, nor, so*), and prepositions (*of, on, in, at, with, for*), unless they are the first or last word of the title.

Pulp Fiction	the *New York Times*
Gone with the Wind	*The Sound of Music*
A Night to Remember	*Married with Children*
Pride and Prejudice	*Nick of Time*

ACTIVITY
2

Capitalizing Titles Correctly. Correct the errors in capitalization in the following sentences.

1. When *The house on Mango Street* was published, it was received well by the *San Francisco Examiner*.

2. One of my favorite magazines is *Sports illustrated*.

3. My grandfather's favorite show is *seinfeld*.

4. One of my favorite songs is Bonnie Raitt's "the road's my middle name."

5. The orchestra practiced Franz Schubert's "Scenes From Childhood."

6. We had a test on *the Scarlet Letter*.

7. In my psychology class we read *the man who mistook his wife for a hat.*

8. For financial news, read The *wall street journal.*

9. I loved reading *For Whom The Bell Tolls* by Ernest Hemingway.

10. *Dances With Wolves* won Kevin Costner an Academy Award. ❑

Abbreviations

An *abbreviation* is a shortened version of a word or phrase.

Mr. Daniel Adams
Dr. Lin Chao
Linda Larson, *M.D.*
Oscar Olivarez, *M.B.A.*
GM (General Motors)
ABC (American Broadcasting Company)
CIA (Central Intelligence Agency)
FBI (Federal Bureau of Investigation)
MADD (Mothers against Drunk Driving)
NAACP (National Association for the Advancement of Colored
    People)
AIDS (acquired immune deficiency syndrome)
RAM (random access memory)
ESP (extrasensory perception)

The first time you use the name of a company, organization, society, or special term, spell out the name and identify the abbreviation in parentheses. You may then use the abbreviation in subsequent references. For example:

> The computer teacher introduced us to the computer term *random access memory* (RAM). We were then instructed to check the RAM needed for the software we planned to run. I discovered that I didn't have enough RAM to use the software.

Using Abbreviations Correctly. Rewrite the following sentences, spelling out the name or using abbreviations as needed.

ACTIVITY
3

1. I had always hoped to go to work for the Central Intelligence Agency. My grandfather worked for the CIA.

_____

_____

Mechanics

_____

_____

2. Every time I hear someone from MADD talk about drunk drivers, I'm so glad that I don't drink. MADD has greatly influenced my life.

_____

_____

_____

3. Don't even tell me that you have ESP; I don't believe in ESP.

_____

_____

_____

4. The American Broadcasting Company (ABC) is my favorite network. I watch more shows on ABC than any other network.

_____

_____

_____

5. I've always wanted to join the National Association for the Advancement of Colored People because the goals of the NAACP appeal to me.

_____

_____

_____

❏

Numbers

Spell out whole numbers from one through ninety-nine and use numerals for all remaining numbers.

He wanted to purchase *eighteen* hot dog buns for his cookout.

We collected *204* cans of food for the homeless shelter.

Spell out numbers that begin a sentence.

Eighty-six students protested the new curfew laws.
Two hundred and fifty horses roamed the field.
One thousand of us crowded into the stadium.

Use numerals to indicate decimals, percentages, page numbers, and time of day.

The rod is *3.45 inches* in length.

My car has appreciated *8 percent* since I purchased it.

Please turn to *page 283* in your textbook.

The plane leaves Boise, Idaho, at *8:50 A.M.* and reaches Chicago, Illinois, at *2:30 P.M.*

Using Numbers. Using the preceding guidelines on formatting numbers, underline the correct form in each of the following sentences.

ACTIVITY
4

1. He counted *45/forty-five* freckles on her face.

2. She claimed to have only *5/five* freckles.

3. *101/One hundred and one* people came to see my father play the violin.

4. Taxes have risen an average of *8 percent/eight percent* in the last year.

5. *One by one/1 by 1,* they filed into the classroom. ❑

Acknowledgments

Scott Weckerly, excerpt from "Free Falling," in *The Great American Bologna Festival*. Copyright © 1991 by St. Martin's Press, Inc. Reprinted by permission of St. Martin's Press, Inc.

Jeffrey Trachtenberg, excerpt from "New Artists and Older Buyers Inspire a Record Year in Music." *The Wall Street Journal* (February 16, 1995). Copyright © 1995 by Dow Jones & Company, Inc. Reprinted by permission of *The Wall Street Journal*. All Rights Reserved Worldwide.

Martin Luther King, Jr., excerpt from "I Have a Dream." Copyright © 1963 by Martin Luther King, Jr.; renewed 1991 by Coretta Scott King. Reprinted by arrangement with the heirs of the estate of Martin Luther King, Jr., care of the Joan Davies Agency as agents of the proprietor.

Janet Singleton, "Whose lungs are they, anyway?" *USA Weekend* (October 1994). Copyright © 1994 by Janet Singleton. Reprinted by permission of the author. Janet Singleton is a Denver-based journalist who has won the Society of Professional Journalists (Colorado Chapter) Award for commentary and the National Writers Association Award for short fiction.

Comtrad Industries Catalog Excerpt from *Tech Update* catalog. © January 1995 Comtrad Industries, Midlothian, Virginia 23112. Reprinted by permission.

Elizabeth Hansen, excerpt from p. 11 in *Frommer's Australia*. Copyright © 1989 by Simon & Schuster, Inc. Reprinted with permission of Macmillan Reference USA, a Division of Simon & Schuster.

Rachel Carson, excerpt from *The Silent Spring* by Rachel Carson. Copyright © 1962 by Rachel L. Carson; renewed 1990 by Roger Christie. Reprinted by permission of Houghton Mifflin Company, Inc. All rights reserved.

Horace Deets, excerpt from "It's Time to Smash Stereotypes about Aging." *AARP Bulletin*, Vol. 36, No. 2 (February 1995). Copyright © 1995 *AARP Bulletin*. Reprinted with permission.

Eudora Welty, excerpt from "Of course, it's easy to see why . . . when I ran" in *One Writer's Beginnings* by Eudora Welty. Copyright © 1983, 1984 by Eudora Welty. Reprinted by permission of Harvard University Press.

Rosie Fisher Rowlett, excerpt from *The Quilters: Women and Domestic Art*, Cooper and Allen, eds. Copyright © 1977 by Rosie Fisher Rowlett. Reprinted by permission of Doubleday, a division of Bantam Doubleday Dell Publishing Group, Inc.

Roy Hoffman, excerpt from "On Keeping a Journal." *Newsweek* magazine (October 1983). Copyright © 1983 by Roy Hoffman. Reprinted by permission.

Pat Mora, excerpt from "Clever Twist" in *Borders* by Pat Mora. Copyright © 1986 by Pat Mora. Reprinted with permission of the publisher Arte Publico Press—University of Houston: Houston, Texas.

Nancy Friday, excerpt from *My Mother, My Self*. Copyright © 1977, 1987 by Nancy Friday. Used by permission of Dell Books, a division of Bantam Doubleday Dell Publishing Group, Inc.

Sarah and A. Elizabeth Delany with Amy Hill Hearth, excerpt from pp. 41–45 in *Having Our Say: The Delany Sisters' First 100 Years*. Copyright © 1993 by Amy Hill Hearth, Sarah Louise Delany and Annie Elizabeth Delany, published by Kodansha America, Inc. Reprinted with permission.

Amy Tan, "Double Face" reprinted with permission of G.P. Putnam's Sons from an excerpt from "Double Face" from *The Joy Luck Club* by Amy Tan. Copyright © 1989 by Amy Tan.

Leo Buscaglia, "Papa's Ritual." From *Papa, My Father* by Leo F. Buscaglia. Copyright © 1989 by Leo F. Buscaglia. Published by Slack, Inc. 6900 Grove Road, Thorofare, New Jersey 08086. Reprinted by permission of the author.

Benjamin Alire Saenz, excerpt from "Ceballeros" in *Flowers for the Broken*. Copyright © 1992 by Benjamin Alire Saenz. Reprinted by permission of Broken Moon Press.

Dawn Sanders, excerpt from "Free Falling" in *The Great American Bologna Festival*. Copyright © 1991 by St. Martin's Press, Inc. Reprinted with permission of St. Martin's Press, Inc.

Harvey Daniels and Steven Zemelman, excerpt from "Questions" in *A Writing Project: Training Teachers of Composition from Kindergarten to College*. © 1985 (Portsmouth, N.H.: Heinemann). Reprinted by permission of the publisher.

Beverly P. Dipo, excerpt from "No Rainbows, No Roses" in *Student Writers at Work and in the Company of Other Writers: The Bedford Prizes*, edited by Nancy Sommers and Donald McQuade. Copyright © 1989 by St. Martin's Press, Inc. Reprinted with permission of St. Martin's Press, Inc.

Malcolm X, "Prison Studies" from *The Autobiography of Malcolm X* by Malcolm X with the assistance of Alex Haley. © 1964 by Alex Haley and Malcolm X. Copyright © 1965 by Alex Haley and Betty Shabazz. Reprinted by permission of Random House, Inc.

William K. Zinsser, excerpt from "Simplicity" in *On Writing Well*, Fifth edition. © 1995 by William K. Zinsser. Published by HarperCollins Publishers, Inc. Reprinted by permission of the author.

Joyce Carol Oates, excerpt from "Shopping." Published in 1987 by *Ms.* Magazine. Copyright © 1987 by The Ontario Review, Inc. Reprinted by permission of John Hawkins & Associates, Inc.

Patricia Raybon, excerpt from "A Case of 'Severe Bias'" from *Newsweek* (October 2, 1989), p. 11. Copyright © 1989 by Patricia Raybon. Reprinted with permission of the author.

Ethan Smith, "Travelin' Band" (pp. 60–61), and Jeff Gordinier, excerpt from "Live Through This" (p. 48); in *Entertainment Weekly* #266 (March 17, 1995). Copyright © 1995 Entertainment Weekly, Inc. a wholly owned subsidiary of Time, Inc. Reprinted by permission. All rights reserved.

Jacqueline Berke, excerpt from *Twenty Questions for the Writer: A Rhetoric with Readings*, Second Edition, by Jacqueline Berke. Copyright © 1976 by Harcourt Brace & Company. Reprinted by permission of the publisher.

Mark Mardon, "City Kids Go Wild," from *Sierra* (January/February 1995), pp. 136–137. Copyright © 1995 by Mark Mardon. Reprinted by permission of the author.

"Gone Fishin'" reprinted from *Family PC* (July/August 1995). Copyright © 1995 *Family PC*. Reprinted by permission of Ziff-Davis Publishing Company.

Excerpt from "Camera Collector Cheng Jiangou" in *Beijing Review* (April 20–26, 1992), p. 42. Reprinted by permission.

Laurence Parent, excerpt from pp. 37–38 of "Hike 18, Wheeler Peak" in *The Hiker's Guide to New Mexico*. Copyright © 1991 by Laurence Parent. Reprinted by permission of Falcon Press Publishers.

Bryan Strong and Christine DeVault, excerpt from p. 51 of *The Marriage and*

Now by Maya Angelou. Copyright © 1993 by Maya Angelou. Reprinted by permission of Random House, Inc.

Jeanne Twehous, "Bibler Pinon Tent" from *Backpacker* magazine (August 1995): 80. Copyright © 1995 by Jeanne Twehous. Published by Rodale Press, Emmaus, Pennsylvania 18098-0099. Reprinted by permission.

Jack Garner, "Expense Doesn't Make Waterworld the Best." The *El Paso Times* (July 29, 1995). Copyright © 1995 by Jack Garner. Reprinted by permission.

David Nelson, "Cha Cha Cha Is Hot Hot Hot." *San Diego* magazine (December 1995): 180–182. Copyright © 1995 by *San Diego* magazine. Reprinted by permission of *San Diego* magazine.

Roger Ebert, "sex, lies, and videotape." Excerpt from p. 643 in *Roger Ebert's Video Companion*, 1995 edition. Copyright © 1995 by Roger Ebert. Reprinted by permission of Universal Press Syndicate, Inc.

"The Best Hotels" excerpt from *Consumer Reports* (July 1994): 434, by Consumers Union of U.S., Inc., Yonkers, NY 10703-1057. Reprinted by permission from *Consumer Reports*.

Philip Wuntch, excerpt from "Dallas' Two New Megaplexes Size Up Nicely." *Dallas Morning News* (July 30, 1995): 6C. Reprinted by permission.

"Choosing a Lipstick" excerpt from *Consumer Reports* (July 1995): 455, by Consumers Union of U.S., Inc., Yonkers, NY 10703-1057. Reprinted by permission from *Consumer Reports*.

Kerry Leigh Ellison, "Satan in the Library: Are Children in Danger?" *School Library Journal* (October 1994): 46–47. Reprinted by permission of Cahners Reprint Services, Division of Reed Publishing (USA) Inc.

Tipper Gore, "Curbing the Sexploitation Industry." *The New York Times* Op-Ed page (March 14, 1988). Copyright © 1988 by The New York Times Company. Reprinted by permission of *The New York Times*.

USA Today, "Use Existing Laws to Rid Internet of Obscenities." (March 13, 1994): 14A. Copyright © 1995 *USA Today*. Reprinted by permission.

Patricia Shahabi-Azad, "212 Quinn Hall: Where to Sit?" Originally titled "Dear Mr. Ontivros," excerpted from pp. 181–182 in *A Guide to Freshman Composition* Third edition by Burgess International Group, Inc. © 1993 Burgess International Group, Inc. Reprinted by permission.

Senator Daniel Patrick Moynihan, "A Cry for My City." Originally titled "The Class of '43" by Senator Daniel Patrick Moynihan. From a speech delivered by Senator Daniel Patrick Moynihan to the Association for a Better New York, April 15, 1993. Reprinted with permission from Senator Daniel Patrick Moynihan.

Elizabeth Whelan, "Perils of Prohibition." *Newsweek* (May 29, 1995). © 1995 Newsweek, Inc. All rights reserved. Reprinted by permission.

Index